Spin Cycle

Howard Kurtz, longtime media reporter for *The Washington Post* is the author of several award-winning books. Named best media reporter by the *American Journalism Review*, Kurtz has also written for *The New Republic*, *TV Guide*, *New York*, and numerous other magazines. He lives in America.

Howard Kurtz

Spin Cycle

INSIDE THE CLINTON PROPAGANDA MACHINE

PAN BOOKS

First published 1998 by the Free Press,
a division of Simon & Schuster Inc., New York

This edition with a new epilogue published 1998 by Pan
an imprint of Macmillan Publishers Ltd
25 Eccleston Place, London SW1W 9NF
and Basingstoke

Associated companies throughout the world

ISBN 0 330 37381 1

Copyright © Howard Kurtz 1998

The right of Howard Kurtz to be identified as the
author of this work has been asserted by him in accordance
with the Copyright, Designs and Patents Act 1998.

All rights reserved. No part of this publication may be
reproduced, stored in or introduced into a retrieval system, or
transmitted, in any form, or by any means (electronic, mechanical,
photocopying, recording or otherwise) without the prior written
permission of the publisher. Any person who does any unauthorized
act in relation to this publication may be liable to criminal
prosecution and civil claims for damages.

9 8 7 6 5 4 3 2

A CIP catalogue record for this book is available from
the British Library

Printed and bound in Great Britain by
Mackays of Chatham plc, Chatham, Kent

This book is sold subject to the condition that it shall not,
by way of trade or otherwise, be lent, re-sold, hired out,
or otherwise circulated without the publisher's prior consent
in any form of binding or cover other than that in which
it is published and without a similar condition including this
condition being imposed on the subsequent purchaser.

To Mary, Judy, and Bonnie,

who don't always buy my spin

Contents

Acknowledgments

A BOOK IS, AT BOTTOM, A COLLABORATIVE ENTERPRISE. MY DEEPEST thanks to my editor, Paul Golob, for helping to mold and shape the material and even for depositing some of my prose on the cutting-room floor. My thanks as well to Rafe Sagalyn, my agent, for instantly grasping the promise of this project and for all sorts of invaluable assistance. I am indebted to the dozens of people who gave generously of their time, despite crushing schedules, to help me understand the daily interplay between the White House and the press. And I'm grateful to my family for their patience and support along the way.

Introduction

On the afternoon of January 21, 1998, a year and a day after Bill Clinton's second inauguration, a grim-faced Mike McCurry walked into the White House Briefing Room to face the music.

The news, McCurry knew, was bad, so undeniably awful that any attempt at spin would be ludicrous. The canny press secretary had bobbed and weaved and jabbed and scolded his way through all manner of Clinton scandals, from the arcane Whitewater land dealings to the crass campaign fundraising excesses to the tawdry tale of Paula Jones. But this one was different. The banner headline in that morning's *Washington Post* made clear that this was a crisis that could spell the end of the Clinton presidency. The Big Guy, as the staffers called him, had been accused of having sex with a former White House intern, Monica Lewinsky, in the executive mansion for more than a year, from the time that she was twenty-one years old. Even worse, Clinton was being accused of lying under oath about the affair—committing perjury—and urging the young woman to lie as well.

The reporters, McCurry believed, would be poised to pummel him. That was his job, of course, to stand at the podium and take whatever abuse the fourth estate wanted to dish out, hoping to score a few points in the process and convey what he could of the president's agenda. But the White House correspondents had been supremely frustrated for the past year as Clinton kept slip-sliding his way through the scandalous muck. The president had maintained his extraordinary popularity despite their dogged efforts to hold him accountable for what they saw as the misconduct and the evasions that marked his administration. He had connected with the American public, and they had largely failed. Clinton, in their view, had gotten away with it. Until now.

That morning, the president and three of his lawyers—his outside attorneys, Robert Bennett and David Kendall, and Charles Ruff, the White House counsel—had hammered out a carefully worded statement in which Clinton denied any "improper relationship" with Monica Lewinsky. McCurry had checked the final version with the boss—"Fine," Clinton said—and then read the statement to the press. McCurry had not asked the president himself if he had been banging the intern. That was not his role; he was not a reporter or an investigator. His job was to repeat whatever facts or assertions the lawyers had approved for public consumption. He may have been a nationally known spokesman, the chief interpreter of administration policy, but in the end he was a flack protecting his client, no matter how distasteful the task.

As McCurry walked in front of the familiar blue curtain toward the podium and faced the assembled correspondents, the bank of cameras behind the wooden seats made clear that this was no ordinary briefing. Many of these sessions were replayed at a later hour for C-SPAN junkies, and if McCurry delivered any newsworthy phrases, a few seconds might show up on the network news. But this briefing was being carried live by CNN, by MSNBC, by Fox News Channel. The reporters, he knew, would be trying to bait him, to knock him off stride, to trick him into departing from the safety of his script. And he was equally determined to stand his ground.

The shouting began with the network correspondents taking the lead, demanding that McCurry explain what Clinton meant by an "improper" relationship.

"I'm not going to parse the statement," McCurry said.

"Does that mean no sexual relationship?" asked NBC's Claire Shipman.

"Claire, I'm just not going to parse the statement for you, it speaks for itself."

What kind of relationship did Clinton have with Lewinsky?

"I'm not characterizing it beyond what the statement that I've already issued says," McCurry replied.

Shipman's NBC colleague, David Bloom, uncorked a broader question: "Mike, would it be improper for the president of the United States to have had a sexual relationship with this woman?"

"You can stand here and ask a lot of questions over and over again and will elicit the exact same answer."

"So Mike, you're willing to—"

"I'm not leaving any impression, David, and don't twist my words," McCurry shot back, jabbing his finger.

John Harris of *The Washington Post* tried a different tack, invoking McCurry's own reputation for honesty, which the reporters knew he dearly prized. "Would you be up here today if you weren't absolutely confident these are not true?"

"Look, my personal views don't count," McCurry said. "I'm here to represent the thinking, the actions, the decisions of the president. That's what I get paid to do."

McCurry bit his lower lip as Deborah Orin of the *New York Post* tried next. "What is puzzling to many of us is that we've invited you probably two dozen times today to say there was no sexual relationship with this woman and you have not done so."

"But the president has said he never had any improper relationship with this woman. I think that speaks for itself."

"Why not put the word 'sexual' in?" asked ABC's Sam Donaldson.

"I didn't write the statement," McCurry said.

They went round and round, the reporters demanding answers and McCurry repeating the same unsatisfactory phrases that seemed only to stoke their anger. As the tension level escalated, McCurry tried a bit of humor.

What was the administration's next move?

"My next move is to get off this podium as quick as possible," McCurry said.

Thirty-six minutes and one hundred forty-eight questions later, it was finally over.

Just a week earlier, the start of Clinton's sixth year in office had seemed so promising. The White House spin team had enjoyed extraordinary success in what they called the "rollout" for the following week's State of the Union address, leaking proposals and policy tidbits to selected news organizations to create a sense of momentum for Clinton's lackluster second term. The president's approval rating was hovering at around 60 percent in the polls, and for all the scandalous headlines and political bumps in the road, the country finally seemed to have grown comfortable with him. McCurry and his colleagues had mastered the art of manipulating the press and were reaping the dividends.

And now, just when they thought they had survived the worst of the investigations and the harshest media scrutiny, the latest sex scandal had hit them like a punch in the stomach. They were reeling, depressed, uncertain of the facts but all too certain that Clinton's days might be numbered. The irony was inescapable: The president who worried so openly about his historical legacy, who staunchly insisted that Whitewater was nothing next to Watergate, might make history by following Richard Nixon into oblivion because he could not resist a lowly intern. For now, at least, McCurry and his colleagues could not spin their way out of this one. They did not know whether Bill Clinton was telling the truth about Monica Lewinsky, and some of them suspected he was not.

．　　　．　　　．

THE WHITE HOUSE SPIN OPERATION HAD PLENTY OF EXPERIENCE in crisis management. A yearlong investigation into campaign fundraising abuses and influence-peddling charges had built to a dramatic crescendo in the fall of 1997. On the morning of October 3, the Clintonites were once again on the defensive. The Justice Department had just decided to expand its investigation into questionable fundraising calls by Vice President Al Gore and was moving toward a stepped-up probe as well of Bill Clinton's frenetic efforts to raise campaign cash in the 1996 election. The relentless charges that the administration had improperly vacuumed up millions of dollars by crassly selling access to the president was now reaching critical mass. *The New York Times*, not surprisingly, trumpeted the new developments as its lead story.

But there was another article vying for attention that day at the top of the *Times*'s venerable front page, one that probably resonated with many more readers than were following the twists and turns of the latest Washington scandal. Four days earlier, one of the administration's least favorite investigative reporters, Jeff Gerth, who had long been tormenting Clinton and his wife, Hillary, over the Whitewater affair, had weighed in with a lengthy *Times* report on how federal inspections of imported food had plummeted just as scientists were finding more outbreaks of food-borne diseases. In fact, Gerth had learned that David Kessler, the former head of the Food and Drug Administration, had failed to persuade Clinton to give his agency the power to bar imported food that did not meet American standards. The story was a major embarrassment, but Clinton had a genius for stealing good ideas from his enemies, even those he most despised in the press. And so the White House promptly staged a ceremony in the picturesque Rose Garden as Clinton proposed giving the FDA new power to ban imported fruit and vegetables, the very power he had refused to grant years earlier. Mike McCurry even credited the *Times* for its role in spotlighting the problem.

"I've never seen anything like it," Kessler told Gerth. "They're terrified of you." Still, the White House had managed to neutralize the dogged Jeff Gerth, who called McCurry to thank him for the acknowledgment.

The day's dueling headlines revealed a larger truth about the Clinton White House and its turn-on-a-dime ability to reposition its battered leader. The central mystery of Bill Clinton's fifth year in office was how a president so aggressively investigated on so many fronts could remain so popular with the American people. Indeed, his approval rating was nearly as lofty as that of Ronald Reagan at the peak of his powers, and with the economy humming along at an impressive clip, bad news was failing to make much of a dent in those numbers.

To be sure, Clinton's performance had helped create the sense that the country was doing just fine on his watch. But it was a carefully honed media strategy—alternately seducing, misleading, and sometimes intimidating the press—that maintained this aura of success. No day went by without the president and his coterie laboring mightily to generate favorable headlines and deflect damaging ones, to project their preferred image on the vast screen of the media establishment.

For much of Clinton's first term, these efforts to control the message were clumsy at best. The core of the original Clinton team—chief of staff Thomas "Mack" McLarty, longtime confidant Bruce Lindsey, senior adviser George Stephanopoulos, counselor David Gergen, press secretary Dee Dee Myers—had trouble fashioning a consistent media message, and Clinton himself was unfocused and error-prone. His casual response, at his first postelection news conference in 1992, about his plans to change the Pentagon's policy toward gays in the military plunged his administration into a long and bruising battle that pushed other issues off the radar screen. Clinton would often stop to talk to reporters after his morning jog, the sweat dripping down his face in decidedly unpresidential fashion. He seemed unable to leave any question unanswered, even one on MTV about his underwear.

In the second half of the term, the president's new chief of staff, Leon Panetta, imposed some much-needed order on the operation; McCurry smoothed relations with the press; communications director Don Baer brought some coherence to long-range planning; deputy chief of staff Harold Ickes rode herd on the political operation; special counsel Mark Fabiani deflected the endless scandal stories; secretive consultant Dick Morris steered Clinton toward the political center, and the president himself was more disciplined in his dealings with reporters. He carefully measured his words about the Oklahoma City bombing and the two government shutdowns. Whatever the question, he would stick to the script, repeat his campaign priorities about protecting Medicare, Medicaid, education, and the environment, brush off scandal questions with the briefest of replies, and hold his famous temper in check.

The second-term lineup was more seasoned but less adventurous. Senior adviser Rahm Emanuel assumed Stephanopoulos's role of behind-the-scenes press handler. Special counsel Lanny Davis became the chief spinmeister on the burgeoning fundraising scandal, an effort crisply supervised by deputy chief of staff John Podesta. Communications director Ann Lewis handled the substantive planning. Chief of staff Erskine Bowles presided over the entire operation like the corporate executive he was. Counselor Doug Sosnik served up political advice, joined over the summer by colorful strategist Paul Begala and former journalist Sidney Blumenthal. McCurry stayed on for a final mission, determined to broker a cease-fire between the president and a hostile press corps. He and his colleagues were engaged in a daily struggle to control the agenda, to seize the public's attention, however fleetingly, for Clinton's wide-ranging initiatives. They had to manage the news, to package the presidency in a way that people would buy the product.

The small group of journalists who shouted questions at the press secretary each day in the White House Briefing Room had a very different agenda. They were focused, almost fixated, on scandal, on the malfeasance and misfeasance and plain old embarrassments that had seemed to envelop this administration from the very start. They were interested in conflict, in drama, in behind-the-scenes maneuvering, in pulling back the curtain and exposing the Oz-like manipulations of the Clinton crowd. It was their job to report what the president said, but increasingly they saw it as their mission to explain why he said it and what seedy political purpose he was trying to accomplish along the way.

When the reporters had the upper hand, the headlines were filled with scandal news, a cascade of Watergate-style charges that drowned out nearly everything else. Indeed, they had plenty of material to work with. The Whitewater investigation, which had dragged on throughout the first term, involved the Clintons' role in a complicated Arkansas land deal, their partnership with a crooked couple, and allegations of a subsequent cover-up. The Travelgate probe involved charges that the first lady had orchestrated the ouster of seven employees of the White House travel office so the work could be given to friends of the Clintons. The Filegate inquiry involved charges that White House aides had deliberately obtained the sensitive FBI files of prominent Republicans. The Paula Jones lawsuit turned on allegations by a former Arkansas state employee that Clinton, while governor, had asked for sex in a Little Rock hotel room. And the campaign finance scandal, in its broadest form, involved an alleged conspiracy by Clinton and Gore to use the perks of high office to solicit cash from foreign operatives, Asian American donors, and garden-variety fat cats, perhaps in exchange for political favors.

Against this dark backdrop, what the White House press operatives did was to launder the news—to scrub it of dark scandal stains, remove unsightly splotches of controversy, erase greasy dabs of contradictions, and present it to the country crisp and sparkling white. The underlying garment was the same, but it was often unrecognizable.

A larger challenge loomed as well—simply put, to change the subject, and to do so without the benefit of dramatic presidential action like fighting a war or battling a recession or tackling some grave national crisis. When the White House team broke through, they secured precious column inches and airtime for Clinton's proposals on national education standards or seat-belt enforcement or funding for mammograms, efforts that the president's people felt resonated far more broadly than the inside-the-Beltway obsessions of the media. At stake in this competing cacophony, they felt, was nothing less than the success of the second term, since history had demonstrated that a reelected president was at the peak of his power in the first year after his victory, when the echoes of his mandate were loudest and his impending lame-duck status least apparent.

History held other lessons for the Clintonites when it came to co-opting the press. Franklin D. Roosevelt told reporters at his first news conference in 1933 that he did not want to be quoted directly but would provide "background" and "off-the-record" information. It was a remarkable innovation: the president as chief source, setting strict ground rules that enabled him to shape the news agenda. The assembled reporters gave Roosevelt a standing ovation, and for the twelve and a half years of his presidency he was treated with deference and affection by the correspondents, none of whom dreamt of telling the public that Roosevelt was confined to a wheelchair.

John Kennedy was the first president to hold live televised press conferences, an innovation that permanently altered the nature of White House communications by staging a regular drama, with the reporters as extras, that reached every American living room. He also personally befriended reporters (notably *Newsweek*'s Ben Bradlee), marketed his wife, Jacqueline, as a cultural phenomenon, and drew stunningly positive coverage by today's standards. But even JFK could be stung by journalistic criticism, and he once canceled his subscription to the New York *Herald Tribune* for its "biased" coverage.

Lyndon Johnson made prodigious efforts to wheedle and cajole the press, dispatching military aircraft to pick up the likes of anchor David Brinkley and *Washington Post* publisher Katharine Graham and fly them to his Texas ranch for private meetings and intimate dinners.

But Johnson's mounting deceptions over Vietnam produced disillusionment among the press corps and the public, saddling the White House with the dreaded phrase "credibility gap."

Richard Nixon conducted a virtual war against the press. He ordered wiretaps and tax audits of selected journalists, had CBS's Daniel Schorr investigated by the FBI, demanded an immigration probe of household help employed by *Los Angeles Times* publisher Otis Chandler, and moved to revoke television licenses held by the Washington Post Company, even as he railed about "outrageous, vicious, distorted reporting" during Watergate. It fell to Nixon's press secretary, Ron Ziegler, to dismiss the Watergate break-in as a "third-rate burglary," to feed the press corps the administration's lies about the scandal, and to attack reporters for unfairly maligning all the president's men. Ziegler used a kind of corporate-speak in his briefings, offering "operative" statements that appeared to be true "at this point in time" but were later declared "inoperative" as more evidence of wrongdoing emerged.

Ziegler was hardly the first White House spokesman to engage in deception. When Woodrow Wilson suffered a massive stroke in 1919 that paralyzed the left side of his body, reporters were told that he had had a nervous breakdown and would be back at work soon, and the truth did not emerge for four months. When Dwight Eisenhower had a serious heart attack in 1955, the press was initially told that he had suffered a digestive upset. Jimmy Carter's press secretary, Jody Powell, told the *Los Angeles Times* in 1980 that a rescue mission to free the American hostages in Iran would make no sense, two days before the mission that ended in disaster. Reagan's spokesman, Larry Speakes, declared in 1983 that an American invasion of Grenada would be "preposterous"; the marines landed the next day.

Some presidents have deliberately kept their spokesmen in the dark as a way of concealing the truth. Kennedy's press secretary, Pierre Salinger, complained that he had not been told about the 1961 invasion of Cuba and thereby misled the press about the impending Bay of Pigs disaster. Gerald Ford's first spokesman, Jerald terHorst, resigned in protest after Ford's staff lied to him by denying that the president was considering a pardon for Nixon.

In recent years the modern practice of spin has come to occupy a sort of gray zone between candor and outright falsehood. Larry

Speakes kept a sign on his desk: "You don't tell us how to stage the news and we don't tell you how to cover it." It was a revealing motto, for the Reagan administration revolutionized the staging of news, devoting enormous energy to selecting a story of the day and providing television with the pictures to illustrate it. The classic example was when Reagan stood proudly in front of a senior citizen housing project built under a program he had tried to abolish; while reporters duly noted the contradiction, the White House was happy with the pictures on the evening news. Speakes had chilly relations with reporters and sometimes declared an offending correspondent "out of business," refusing to have any more dealings with him. And Speakes was not above twisting the truth. After Reagan's 1985 summit meeting with Mikhail Gorbachev in Geneva, Speakes quoted the president's private remarks to the Soviet leader—which he later admitted he had simply made up. Marlin Fitzwater, a career bureaucrat who succeeded Speakes and stayed on as George Bush's spokesman, restored amicable relations with the press. But it was a mark of Bush's frustration with the fourth estate that his favorite 1992 bumper sticker read "Annoy the Media—Re-Elect Bush."

Clinton's first press secretary, Dee Dee Myers, the first woman to hold the job, was a popular figure with reporters, but she was widely viewed as ineffective and out of the policy loop. One Saturday in 1993, Myers infuriated the press corps by announcing a "lid"—meaning no more news was to be made that day and the captive reporters were free to leave—hours before Clinton launched a missile attack on Iraq. Much of the Washington bureau of *The New York Times* headed off on an outing to Baltimore to attend a Yankees-Orioles game, and they were not pleased about having to rush home to cover the story. Myers sheepishly admitted afterward that she had known the attack was imminent but didn't want to "tip anything off" by delaying the Saturday news lid. Her credibility was never quite the same.

By the time Mike McCurry inherited the podium, the press operation had become increasingly crucial to the success or failure of any administration. On one level the growing bureaucracy was needed to deal with an expanding media universe, from all-news cable networks to online magazines to weekend chat shows to more than 1,200 talk-radio stations, all clamoring for interviews and attention. But it was also a natural outgrowth of television's need to dramatize stories, to focus the camera's eye on a single leader doing battle against the forces of politics and nature. Congress, with its 535 wrangling lawmakers and endless speechifying and molasses-like deliberations, made for terrible television. Executive departments, from HUD to Agriculture, were too widely dispersed to cover efficiently. It was so much easier to have your star reporter standing on the White House lawn, the North Portico over one shoulder, framing each government controversy as a victory or setback for the newsmaker-in-chief. There was a natural story line: president under fire, president traveling abroad, president at war, president on vacation. The constant tensions of the Cold War had injected an undercurrent of drama, for Kennedy or Nixon or Reagan might at any moment have to stand up to the Soviets or one of their allies, prompting the networks to go live. Superpower summits became an exercise in spin control. The White House press corps swelled to 2,000 accredited correspondents, all of whom had to be serviced by the press staff, and the most important among them had to be personally massaged by the press secretary, who, as much as any underling, personified the administration.

By the 1990s all manner of partisan magazines and radio talk shows and television shoutfests and Internet chat groups were filling the air with raw opinion and sheer attitude, making it harder for the president to connect with the public. The irony was unmistakable: Bill Clinton had all the accoutrements of high office, but he no longer commanded the public stage. McCurry and his colleagues spent endless hours honing the Clinton message, trying to hype each modest proposal into another news cycle, as if the president were some freshman congressman desperate for a flicker of recognition from the media machine. The competition was intense, for Bill Clinton dwelt in the same murky precincts of celebrity as Dennis Rodman, Courtney Love, and David Letterman. In a hundred-channel world the president had become just another piece of programming to be marketed, and high ratings were hardly guaranteed.

From a distance, in the headlines and on the evening news, most Americans saw Bill Clinton as a singular figure, holding forth, posing with foreign leaders, making newsworthy pronouncements. But much of what they saw was stagecraft orchestrated by the likes of McCurry,

Davis, Emanuel, Podesta, Baer, and Lewis, a small collection of loyalists who worked relentlessly at presenting the boss in a favorable light
and deflecting the scandal questions that seemed constantly to nip at
his heels. The mundane reality of White House life was that the top
players spent perhaps half their time either talking to the press, plotting press strategy, or reviewing how their latest efforts had played in
the press. They did not let Clinton have the briefest exposure to
journalists without rehearsing what he would say to this or that question, lest he serve up an unscripted sound bite that would mar the
day's story line. The modern presidency was, above all, a media presidency. Inside accounts tended to focus on who had Clinton's ear and
who was feuding with whom, but the plain truth was that everyone
was playing to the cameras, dishing "on background," trying to placate the journalists or find a way around their carping commentary.
The daily coverage was a way of keeping score, of measuring the
administration's progress in the messy and frustrating task of governing.

There was a time when a commander-in-chief was graded on the
traditional measures of his relations with Congress, his dealings with
foreign leaders, his ability to keep the economy moving and the
nation at peace. Now the increasingly opinionated mass media had
somehow become the arbiter of political success and the distiller of
conventional wisdom. A president's words were endlessly sliced and
diced by the self-appointed pundits, his every move filtered through
someone else's ideological lens.

It was Clinton's misfortune to be the nation's most visible politician
at a time when many people had tuned out the political world, disgusted with the endless machinations that seemed irrelevant to their
lives. The political conventions and presidential debates of 1996 had
drawn the smallest audiences of the television era. Most Americans
had long since grown resigned to Clinton's seemingly inevitable victory over Bob Dole, but a majority still did not trust him. And as
McCurry and his compatriots were acutely aware, a significant minority detested Clinton, viewing him as a lying, scheming, pot-
smoking crook. There was no shortage of conservative media outlets
that were all too happy to stoke these fires of resentment, publishing
a never-ending cascade of allegations about Clinton's personal life, a
litany of overlapping scandals and the work of four special prosecutors. Hillary Rodham Clinton, whose disdain for the press was even

greater than her husband's, was an equally frequent target of the right-wing hit squads.

The president bore much of the responsibility for the palpable media distrust that greeted his every utterance. He made clear in the early days of the 1992 campaign that his memory was awfully selective, from his first, less than candid explanations of how he had avoided the Vietnam draft, how he had tried marijuana but "didn't inhale," and how he had "problems" in his marriage but did not have a twelve-year affair with Gennifer Flowers. He grew to resent reporters, to vent his anger in public outbursts, and the feeling was mutual. Most reporters were convinced that Clinton had an almost congenital inability to tell the unvarnished truth.

This atmosphere of distrust extended to the reporters' relationship with the men and women who accompanied Bill Clinton into the White House. What made the yawning gap between the Clintonites and the journalists all the more remarkable was that both were products of the baby boom culture and seemed, superficially at least, to share the same values. They all believed in activist government, the politicians because it gave them popular programs to create and the reporters because it gave them juicy stories to cover, a welcome relief from George Bush's in-box presidency. A few romances had even bloomed between journalists and White House operatives, generally unconsummated until the officeholders stepped down. But the generational affinity also bred a certain degree of contempt. Like squabbling lovers, the two sides got off to an acrimonious start even before Clinton's first inauguration, the traditional honeymoon shattered by a series of broken promises and miscalculations on issues from the canceled middle-class tax cut to the abandonment of Haitian refugees. Most of Clinton's aides had worked on Capitol Hill during the Reagan and Bush years, enjoying a warm relationship with reporters who were always looking for fodder to attack the administration. Now they were the incumbents, and the coziness had dissolved into mutual recriminations. If the press had a natural bias toward the Democrats, as so many Republicans fervently believed, Bill Clinton and his loyalists saw no evidence of it. They viewed the journalists as another special interest group—the Press Party—to be stroked and cajoled.

For all the animosity, the White House spinners and their cynical chroniclers were ultimately joined at the hip in a strangely symbiotic relationship. Both thrived on the frenetic pace of life at the center of the political universe, all the while grousing about the impact on their families and fantasizing about quitting. Both reveled in the insider gossip, even as they struggled to stay in touch with the real America. McCurry and company needed the press to peddle their message to the public, and the journalists needed an action-packed presidency on which to build their reputations and name recognition. Yet fireworks were inevitable when the two sides got in each other's way.

The reporters' frustrations began to boil over in the final weeks of the 1996 campaign, when allegations first surfaced that foreign funny money had been funneled to the Clinton camp and the White House seemed unable or unwilling to provide answers. McCurry, who usually insisted on steering such questions to the White House lawyers, reluctantly assumed control of the scandal defense just days before the election. Even as Clinton and his compatriots celebrated his triumphant reelection in Little Rock, McCurry knew that they had kept the lid on a pressure cooker that was ready to blow.

As the fundraising scandal gathered steam, McCurry and his new ally, Lanny Davis, bore the brunt of the hostile media inquiries. Within the White House they battled for disclosure, for getting the bad news behind them. But there were limits to how far McCurry and Davis would go, documents they would not release, questions they would not answer. They insisted day after day that Bill Clinton and Al Gore had done nothing out of the ordinary in dialing for dollars, sipping coffee with shady Chinese operatives, or renting out the Lincoln Bedroom, even when an avalanche of embarrassing documents decimated their denials. A few mistakes, they maintained, but nothing the other side didn't do in spades.

The White House partisans were convinced that the public was tuning it all out, that most Americans viewed this as the typical Beltway follies, but the journalists were filled with moral fervor, determined that readers and viewers should care and that somehow they would make them care. The Clintonites were equally determined to rout the journalistic naysayers and prove that they could govern in this scandal-charged atmosphere. Neutralizing the media had become ground zero in the struggle for supremacy, and the spin would clearly be as important as the substance.

CHAPTER ONE

The Gaggle

THE ISSUE OF THE DAY, IMPROBABLY ENOUGH, WAS SLAVERY.

It was just after one o'clock on Tuesday, June 17, 1997, and Joe Lockhart, the deputy White House press secretary, was ticking off issues that might come up at the afternoon briefing. Lockhart, who had been Bill Clinton's campaign spokesman during the 1996 election, had just joined the staff, and his first big assignment was to work the press on Clinton's new initiative on race relations.

During one of a spate of interviews on the subject, the president had been asked on CNN about a bill that would require an official government apology for the era of slavery. Clinton wasn't expecting the question; in five months of endless meetings on race relations, the issue had never come up. He said such an apology could be "quite important" and he would consider it. House Speaker Newt Gingrich quickly denounced the idea. Now reporters were flooding Lockhart with questions about whether the White House would formally embrace the proposal. *USA Today* was working on a cover story. It was time to fish or cut bait.

"We need to bring this to closure," Lockhart said.

Lockhart's boss, Mike McCurry, agreed. They had checked with the Hill, and even the Congressional Black Caucus wasn't pushing for an apology over an abhorrent practice that had ended 130 years earlier. The idea was clearly going nowhere. But McCurry wasn't about to wing it on such a racially charged issue without asking the president.

Twice each day the press secretary and his staff went through this exercise before the "gaggle," as McCurry called the regular briefings. There was the 9:15 session each morning in his office, where television cameras were barred, and there was the more formal early-afternoon gathering in the White House Briefing Room, filmed by a bank of cameras and often replayed on C-SPAN. The staff had to sift through a dizzying array of complicated issues, any one of which might blow up into tomorrow's screaming headline. McCurry needed to know what to confirm, what to deny, when to bob and weave until another day. The nuances were crucial. Each issue, from air pollution to welfare, had a bureaucracy behind it that had painstakingly hashed out its position with its constituency groups. Anything McCurry uttered from the podium magically attained the status of official White House policy, and if he deviated later on, the administration would be accused of the dreaded sin of flip-flopping.

But there was a hidden benefit to all this thrashing around. The need for McCurry to field questions in the briefing room forced the administration to decide just what the hell its policy was. The very act of dealing with the press compelled a sluggish bureaucracy to resolve its interminable disputes. True, it was governing by sound bite, but in an administration obsessed with the media, it worked.

McCurry yawned. He had woken up in his Silver Spring, Maryland, home at 3:30 that morning, playing back in his head the answers to various questions that might arise that day. He was always worried about being caught unprepared. By Friday he was usually exhausted.

The scene in his sunny, spacious office, with its four television sets and working fireplace along one wall and the other plastered with his kids' crayon drawings, sometimes bordered on surreal. As McCurry and his aides sat there plotting media strategy, they watched a gang of reporters on the lawn staking out some official visitor ten yards beyond the floor-to-ceiling windows. Flipping a button on a squawk box, McCurry began listening in on the correspondents through a hidden intercom as they chatted among themselves. It was one way he could figure out where a story was heading.

The day's spin cycle had begun at the 7:45 senior staff meeting in the office of Erskine Bowles, the White House chief of staff. McCurry attended this meeting every day, as did Rahm Emanuel, Bruce Lindsey, Doug Sosnik, John Podesta, and Sylvia Matthews, the other deputy chief of staff. At the top of the agenda this Tuesday morning were the ongoing negotiations between the tobacco industry and a group of state attorneys general over an agreement that would limit the companies' liability in exchange for massive payments and stricter regulation. The man closely monitoring the talks was Bruce Lindsey, a lean, secretive Arkansas lawyer who had long been close to Clinton. Though Lindsey was regularly checking with both sides, the White House wanted to resist becoming a full-fledged participant.

The morning papers had strikingly different takes on the matter. *The Washington Post* quoted unnamed sources as saying the administration "refused to intervene" in the tobacco talks until both sides agreed on a final package. *The New York Times*, however, cited "a top Clinton administration official" in saying "that the White House might be willing to play a more active role if negotiators were not able to produce a completed plan." The reporters had obviously relied on different administration leakers.

Rahm Emanuel, the ever-intense presidential assistant who was assuming a larger role in dealing with the press, stuck his head in McCurry's office. "I had my headline in *The Washington Post*; Bruce had his in *The New York Times*," he said. It was a rare instance of two White House aides pushing their competing views in public, and Emanuel felt lucky that no journalist had called them on the contradiction.

The *Post* account was the one that reflected the White House consensus. In fact, the president's pollster, Mark Penn, had secretly surveyed the public on that very question. Only 33 percent of respondents said they would be more favorable to Clinton if he tried to broker the agreement, while 48 percent said they would be less favorable.

Bowles agreed that McCurry should say something on the record about the administration's refusal to be drawn into the tobacco talks. When McCurry returned to his office for the nine o'clock meeting with Lockhart and fourteen other press aides on his staff, he asked them to get Bruce Lindsey on the phone to bring him up-to-date.

"The consensus of the senior staff meeting is that I should just go ahead and confirm," McCurry told him. Lindsey agreed.

Lockhart raised some other issues that might arise at the morning gaggle. *The New York Times* was reporting that the Federal Communications Commission had put off the president's request to ban liquor ads on TV. *The Washington Times* was reporting that the administration was on the brink of ending a twenty-year ban on high-tech arms sales to Latin America. The New York *Daily News* was reporting that John Huang, the elusive Democratic fundraiser who had been implicated in so many aspects of the fundraising scandal (and who had been invoking the Fifth Amendment), might be willing to testify on the Hill. The consumer price index was up 0.1 percent. And the press wanted to know whether Gladys Knight would be singing at a White House dinner that night with or without the Pips. The final question proved impossible to resolve.

The meeting soon wound down. "Okay, bring 'em in!" McCurry shouted to his assistant, Lori Anderson. Two dozen reporters, led by Helen Thomas of United Press International, the seventy-six-year-old doyenne of the press corps, filed into the room.

The gaggle ranged across the global terrain. The Balkans. Title IX sports programs. Health insurance legislation. Trade with Africa. A flag-burning amendment. The tobacco talks. Aid to Jordan. From behind his desk McCurry smoothly delivered the answers. The mood was brisk and businesslike. They had all been through it hundreds of times.

But, as always, questions arose that McCurry couldn't anticipate. One reporter asked whether the president, as a Southern Baptist, would support a proposed Baptist boycott of the Walt Disney Company. McCurry said he would have to check. (Clinton later declined to back the boycott.)

The reporters were also buzzing about the day's historic import, the twenty-fifth anniversary of the Watergate break-in. CNN had just aired a poll showing that 20 percent of the American people thought Clinton's involvement in Whitewater was more serious than Richard Nixon's involvement in Watergate, compared to 49 percent who saw it the other way around. Helen Thomas, who well remembered the stonewalling tactics of Nixon's press secretary, Ron Ziegler, ribbed McCurry about sitting at Ziegler's old desk.

McCurry was in the process of turning the Watergate question into a pitch for campaign finance reform when another reporter tried to bait him.

"Ben Bradlee says the lesson of Watergate is for the White House to tell the truth," she declared.

"He's right. We do," McCurry replied, and he ended the briefing. "That's a wrap," he said.

Moments later McCurry gathered his papers and disappeared for forty-five minutes to his hideaway, a secluded spot elsewhere on the "campus," as staffers called the place. The location of his hideaway was his most closely guarded secret. Only two uniformed guards knew where to find him, and if his staff wanted to contact him they had to send messages by pager. McCurry needed time to get away from the phones, to clear the mental cobwebs. In the hideaway he would sit, read, make notes, focus on the upcoming briefing. This time alone was a way of maintaining his sanity. Jody Powell, who held the job under Jimmy Carter, once told McCurry that he had done the same thing.

McCurry soon faced another part of his job—ironing out disputes with other agencies. At 12:30 he held his daily conference call with the spokesmen at the State Department, the Pentagon, and the CIA. The call was an outgrowth of the Persian Gulf War, when Marlin Fitzwater, George Bush's press secretary, needed to coordinate the day's military and diplomatic news with the other agencies. McCurry had been on the receiving end of the call when he had been the State Department spokesman during Clinton's first term. Now he played referee from the West Wing.

Today the issue at hand concerned Secretary of State Madeleine Albright and Sandy Berger, the national security adviser, who had been skirmishing over who would get to unveil a new aid package for Jordan. Albright, who had spent considerable time on the $100 million development fund, wanted to make the announcement and thus reap the publicity benefit. Berger wanted a presidential announcement. McCurry didn't really care, and since Albright was playing host to the crown prince of Jordan, he told the State Department the secretary could go first. Clinton would put out a statement and undoubtedly be quoted in the stories as well, but Albright would have her headline.

Lockhart drifted back in to talk about the president's race initiative, which loomed large on the White House landscape. The president's speech the previous Saturday, calling for a "national conversation" on race and announcing the appointment of a special commission, had gotten the biggest publicity buildup of the second term. There was intense jockeying in the press over who would get the first interview with Clinton on the topic. Michael Frisby of *The Wall Street Journal* was throwing some sharp elbows in the process.

A few days earlier, on a different story, Frisby had found himself pointedly excluded. Rahm Emanuel had passed the word to *USA Today* that Clinton had decided to ask the Federal Election Commission to outlaw the use of "soft money," the large, unregulated donations that filled both parties' coffers. As other reporters picked up on the buzz, Emanuel also leaked the story to *The New York Times*, *The Washington Post*, and the *Los Angeles Times*. Even though it was not much of a story—the odds that the FEC would take such action were slim—Frisby immediately called Emanuel when he realized he had been bypassed.

"I'm going to fuck you," he declared.

Emanuel knew exactly what Frisby meant. Frisby was renowned inside the White House for tossing poison darts at uncooperative aides in the *Journal's* gossipy, anonymously sourced "Washington Wire" column, which ran on the front page every Friday. No one wanted to be the next target.

But Frisby was throwing a fit for a reason. He knew that some White House aides were promoting other newspapers for the first interview on race. Doug Sosnik, the president's counselor, argued that the exclusive should go to the *Los Angeles Times* because L.A. was a multicultural melting pot and because Clinton was about to deliver his race speech in San Diego. Frisby wanted to make sure Emanuel owed him, and the race interview was precisely the sort of payback he had in mind.

Emanuel had his own reasons to lobby for Frisby. Not only was he the only black reporter covering the White House for a national newspaper, but he had written about race and politics for years and understood the nuances of Clinton's position. A front-page piece by Frisby the day before the San Diego event would frame the speech in precisely the way the White House wanted. After much discussion Erskine Bowles gave Emanuel the green light. Frisby was on vacation in the Poconos, but he talked to Clinton by phone and wrote the story from his hotel room. His editors, though, were less convinced of the story's value, dismissing the effort and the newly named commission as horseshit. Frisby understood their skepticism—so much of what the White House did was smoke and mirrors—but as an African American he was impressed that Clinton was venturing into territory that other presidents had avoided. He carried the day, much to Emanuel's satisfaction. Frisby's piece, which led the paper, stressed Clinton's popularity among blacks. "Not since Lyndon Johnson has an American president devoted such energy to race relations," he wrote.

The *Journal* article was part of a saturation strategy. Clinton spoke to *Time*, *Newsweek*, and *U.S. News & World Report*, appeared on CNN's *Late Edition*, spent an hour with a group of black columnists. Some were unimpressed, but Courtland Milloy, a local columnist for *The Washington Post*, marveled that he was sitting in Janet Reno's chair in the Cabinet Room, staring out at the Rose Garden. "I could feel the wool being pulled over my eyes. And it felt good, too," he wrote.

On a purely tactical level, all this was a remarkable achievement. Simply by trumpeting a single speech, without an O.J.–like backdrop or even a tangible proposal, the White House got most of the media talking about race, or at least about the president's approach to race. Clinton, who as a white southerner with a lifetime of black support enjoyed special credibility on the issue, had, at least briefly, put the nation's rawest wound atop the public agenda.

But to what end? Was talking about race really enough to put Clinton in LBJ's class? Not in the eyes of the press, which largely dismissed the initiative as more presidential hot air. It was Clinton as college professor, as talk-show host, as pop-culture priest, feeling the nation's pain but shying away from concrete efforts on affirmative action or urban aid that might ease that pain. Even before he spoke, *The New Republic* ridiculed the whole thing as "therapeutic exercises" that were an "insult" to the public. *U.S. News* called it "hand holding as policy." Hours after the San Diego speech, the networks were strikingly skeptical. CBS's Bill Plante spoke of fears that Clinton's initiative "will be a whole lot of talk and not nearly enough action." ABC's John Donvan noted that "those 4,600 words contained few solutions."

This was the heart of the problem that McCurry and his colleagues constantly faced: how to push a substantive story that would resonate with the public without drawing overly cynical coverage from the press. They had a fair number of techniques at their command— uplifting presidential speeches, dry policy statements, grand photo ops, whispered leaks—but ultimately the dozens of news organizations that covered the building provided the filter through which the message had to pass. Ultimately the soaring rhetoric got bogged down in niggling questions of policy and politics, leaving McCurry and his staff to deal with the minutiae. The sausage-making process was not pretty.

Now, as McCurry sipped a cup of cream of asparagus soup at his desk, they had to deal with the slavery question. Lockhart went looking for Sylvia Mathews, the deputy chief of staff who was overseeing the race initiative. He returned a moment later. "She's in the Oval now," he said. "You want to barge in?"

"That's a good idea," McCurry said. Unlike some of his predecessors, he had the freedom to burst into a meeting and grab the boss whenever he needed an answer.

McCurry told the president he wanted to knock down the idea of an apology for slavery. "Enough of the press corps is interested in whipping this thing up today that we need to put it back in its box," he said.

"Look, when I got this the other day, that was the first I'd actually heard about it," Clinton said. He signed off on McCurry's approach.

McCurry also briefed Clinton on the tobacco talks and told him that reporters were asking about the Watergate anniversary. He suggested that if the press raised the subject, the president invoke the abuses of that era to underscore the need for campaign finance reform.

Lockhart was waiting when McCurry returned. "Up or down?" he asked, gesturing with his thumb.

"He agrees with what we're saying," McCurry said.

"We'll take a half a cycle of grief," Lockhart predicted.

They started playing with the wording. "With all the enormous work that lies ahead on the race initiative," McCurry began, "the president doesn't feel like this is the issue to start with. It might make sense to think about at some time. But the president has other tasks he wants to take on first."

Lockhart wanted something firmer. "If pushed, he's not prepared to support this resolution at this time," he suggested.

"Yeah," McCurry said.

"I don't think we'll get a lot of blow-back on that," Lockhart said. McCurry asked him to type something up and run it by Sylvia Mathews.

The phone calls were coming faster now as the scheduled 2:30 briefing approached. Bruce Lindsey called and started chewing over his strategy toward the tobacco negotiators.

"It's probably best for us to be where we are and say we can't write the deal for them: 'You gotta do the hard work and we'll take a look at it when you're done.' That probably keeps the heat on them anyhow," McCurry told him. It was not unusual for him to offer strategic advice on the issues, for he was more than just a passive spokesman.

As if McCurry's plate were not full enough, Cheryl Mills, the deputy White House counsel, walked in with a court ruling. A federal appeals court had overturned a judge who had supported the administration's attempt to withhold subpoenaed documents from the special prosecutor investigating former Agriculture Secretary Mike Espy. But the court had set a fairly high standard for prosecutors seeking such communications between a president and his senior aides. This could obviously affect the battle for documents in the Whitewater case. While Mills was explaining the ruling, her boss, Charles Ruff, the White House counsel, called to discuss his statement. McCurry had to skim the decision and make sure he properly described it as a moral victory for the White House.

Minutes later Dennis Boxx, a spokesman for the National Reconnaissance Office, was on the phone. In a top-secret operation, the FBI and the CIA had arrested Mir Aimal Kansi, a Pakistani native accused of killing two CIA employees in a 1993 shooting spree outside the agency's Langley, Virginia, headquarters. Kansi had been seized near the border between Pakistan and Afghanistan and was being returned to the United States by military aircraft. The question was when to announce the arrest.

"They ought to pop it around eight o'clock tonight," McCurry told Boxx, proposing a time that would barely enable the newspapers to cover the story for the next morning's editions. "You get everyone moving on it, and then you get a second-day tick-tock on it. You get two bites of the apple." A tick-tock was a journalistic reconstruction of how a complicated event unfolded. The suspect was still in the air and McCurry was trying to figure out how to stretch the arrest into a two-day story.

Boxx said he wasn't sure the story would hold. ABC was already sniffing around.

McCurry flipped on the TV. On the White House's closed-circuit feed, channel 32, the president and first lady were attending a flag-draped gathering of African diplomats to announce their new trade initiative toward the continent. Hillary was addressing the audience. This was her second public appearance of the day; she had also been at an event with Jackie Joyner-Kersee promoting Title IX sports programs for women.

McCurry was sure some reporters would ask about her sudden visibility. They were probably writing the story in their heads now: "In an effort to expand her role. . . . Privately, the first lady has been frustrated at the drift in the White House. . . . She is moving her advisers into the White House." The message of these Hillary-to-the-rescue stories, McCurry felt, was always the same: the white boys were fucking up.

As the press staff gathered again on chairs and couches around McCurry's desk, he stared at his looseleaf binder, underlining key phrases. He started tossing questions at Anne Luzzatto, his new deputy for foreign affairs, who was thumbing through the diplomatic "guidance"—the suggested answers to possible press queries—at a small table to his right. Was there anything new in this China policy? Clinton was meeting with President Kiro Gligorov of Macedonia; were American troops there under U.N. command? What was the U.S. policy on this land mines bill now before Congress?

McCurry frowned as he scanned the Espy ruling again. "It's awfully hard to get to the punch line here," he said. "The PR issue here is they're all gonna say, 'Hey, wait a minute, you guys lost.' "

He decided to push back the briefing by an hour. Four administration officials, led by Deputy Treasury Secretary Lawrence Summers, would brief first on the African trade initiative. The reporters would be steamed, for McCurry was always running late. But there was a hidden benefit. The droning on Africa would wear out the press corps and ease the pressure on him. It worked every time.

Just after 3:30 McCurry slipped a navy jacket over his crisp white shirt and maroon tie and headed past the guard's desk, down the carpeted ramp to the lower press office. He stood behind the sliding door that separated the warren of offices from the briefing room. He popped a couple of chocolates from an open box and walked in as the trade experts were winding up. It was time for some performance art.

The regulars were all in attendance. The network correspondents —Rita Braver of CBS, David Bloom of NBC, John Donvan of ABC —sat in their first-row seats. CNN's Wolf Blitzer was in the second row, next to Peter Baker of *The Washington Post*. Behind them were Alison Mitchell of *The New York Times* and Mara Liasson of National Public Radio. A few Japanese reporters were in the back, trying to find out if Clinton was going to meet with Prime Minister Ryutaro Hashimoto later in the week.

McCurry thanked the briefers for "warming up the audience." The session began with routine questions about Hill legislation. Donvan asked about the Espy case and the administration's "pretty concerted effort to exert executive privilege."

McCurry launched into his spiel. Looking down at his notes, he hailed the decision as "strongly reaffirming the president's constitutional right to protect confidential communications both directly with the president and among his senior advisers." The reporters, who had just gotten word of the ruling, didn't bother to challenge his upbeat assessment.

Blitzer asked why the White House was refusing to get involved in the tobacco talks. "If both sides have asked you to come in and close this deal, why not do that?"

"Because we're not a party to the negotiations," McCurry said.

Suddenly they all started firing at once. The tone was one of moral outrage at the administration's callousness. How dare the White House not solve this dispute in time for the evening news?

"They're clearly looking for some guidance from you," Bloom said.

Blitzer jumped in: "Did you say that if the benefits to the American people—namely, stopping children from smoking—are good enough, the White House would support a deal that would limit punitive damages that the tobacco industry—"

"I was very careful not to say that," McCurry said, sticking to the approach that he, Bowles, and Lindsey had agreed upon that morning.

"Can the president imagine a deal that would both meet his objectives and also boost the stock of the tobacco companies?" Liasson asked.

"Wildly hypothetical," McCurry said.

"How important is it to the president that this be an accomplishment that he brings to the country?" Braver asked.

"The White House is willing to walk away?" Bloom said. And then: "One of the attorneys general told us today that he thought the president was being unpresidential."

"If it was important enough for the president to step into the baseball strike," Blitzer asked, "why not important enough to step in and resolve this?"

"Because children don't die as a result of going to major league baseball games, Wolf."

"But that's the point."

McCurry knew exactly what was going on. The tobacco story was the only chance for these esteemed television correspondents to get on the air that night. They were trying to goad him into making some news, and he was stubbornly standing his ground.

Finally the topic was exhausted. After a few queries on affirmative action and Macedonia, Helen Thomas sounded the traditional thank-you—her privilege as the senior wire-service reporter—and the half-hour session was over.

Back in his office, McCurry shook his head. The one question they had sweated over all day—slavery—hadn't even come up. Rhetorical combat was like that sometimes. You spent hours in training, sizing up the enemy, mapping plans for battles that never took place. But the tobacco questions had been contentious, and McCurry's battle plans held up perfectly. At least no one had mentioned his own nasty habit. McCurry never smoked in public, had been trying to quit, but even some of his relatives didn't know about his weakness for tobacco. The White House spokesman was the most public of figures, but in some ways he had managed to remain anonymous.

McCurry got his chance to address the slavery question that evening when he appeared on the CNN program *Crossfire*. Cohost Pat Buchanan asked whether Clinton would apologize for slavery.

"The president said simply, look, that may be an issue for down the road," McCurry said. "There's apparently a piece of legislation on the Hill. The president at this time is not prepared to support that legislation."

"You seem to be backing away from the White House position," Buchanan said.

Buchanan had missed the point. There was no White House position—at least, not until that moment. It was a moving target, a floating crap game that McCurry had gradually mastered, distilling the blur of government deliberations into a ten-second made-for-TV answer.

CHAPTER TWO

The Master of Spin

ONE THING ABOUT MIKE McCURRY, HE KNEW HOW TO PLAY the game. He understood the ebb and flow of the fungible commodity called news. A trim, blue-eyed man with thinning blond hair, a pink complexion, and an often bemused expression, McCurry was a spinmeister extraordinaire, deflecting questions with practiced ease, sugar-coating the ugly messes into which the Clintonites seemed repeatedly to stumble. He would mislead reporters on occasion, or try to pass them off to one of the damage-control lawyers who infested the public payroll. He would yell at offending correspondents, denounce their stories as inaccurate, denigrate them to their colleagues and their bosses. He would work the clock to keep damaging stories off the evening news, with its huge national audience. Yet with his considerable charm and quick wit, McCurry somehow managed to maintain friendly relations with most of the reporters who worked the White House beat. He would go to dinner with reporters, share a beer, give them a wink and a nod as he faithfully delivered the administration's line. He was walking the tightrope, struggling to maintain credibility with both the press and the president, to serve as an honest broker between the antagonists.

Each day, it seemed, McCurry faced a moral dilemma. He stood squarely at the intersection of news and propaganda, in the white-hot glare of the media spotlight, the buffer between self-serving administration officials and a cynical pack of reporters. The three principles of his job, he believed, were telling the truth, giving people a window on the White House, and protecting the president, but the last imperative often made the first two difficult. If the corporate spokesman for Exxon or General Motors stretched the truth on occasion, well, that was seen as part of the job. McCurry himself had once been a corporate flack, trumpeting the virtues of the National Pork Producers Council. But now he worked for the head hog, and more was expected of the presidential press secretary, whose every syllable was transcribed by news agencies. He was the public face of the administration. His credibility, not just the president's, was on the line.

As the campaign fundraising scandal exploded, McCurry found himself facing the question that had dogged every presidential press secretary since the Nixon administration: whether it is possible to tell the truth, or something approximating the truth, in a highly polarized and constantly shifting political atmosphere. McCurry dearly prized his personal reputation for candor. He developed a series of rules and rationalizations to persuade himself that while he sometimes tiptoed up to the line separating flackery from falsehood, he never crossed it.

Yet McCurry was more than just the White House publicist. In a news-saturated age the press secretary was a celebrity in his own right, laying down the rhetorical law on dozens of issues, saying things the president wanted said but could not, for reasons of propriety, say himself. McCurry's predecessors had gone on to write books, join university faculties, or, like Dee Dee Myers, host their own television shows and give speeches for $15,000 a pop. But all this came at a considerable price: the gut-wrenching pressure, the seven-day weeks, the hostile questions day after day.

As Clinton embarked on his second term, McCurry wondered whether he could end the constant sniping between the president and the press, even as he was eyed suspiciously by both sides. Or would he get buried under a rumbling avalanche of scandal stories, his credibility tarnished, his reputation ruined? At forty-two, McCurry could be making three times his $125,000 salary had he stayed in corporate public relations, growing rich for setting up high-powered lunches and spending more time with his wife and three kids. Instead he was facing the klieg lights each afternoon, suffering the slings and arrows of an outraged press corps.

No one really cared who the press secretary was, McCurry felt. Reporters were interested in him for one reason, as a conduit to the president's thinking. There wasn't a whole lot of room for personality in the job. Sure, McCurry had plenty of opinions on the issues. He was a closet New Democrat, a committed member of the party's moderate wing. But in the endless rounds of staff meetings, he consciously tried not to take a position or express his views. He cast himself as a neutral observer. White House officials on one side of a debate might criticize his briefings if he were openly aligned with another faction. His ultimate client was the president, who expected him to make the case for whatever the administration decided, not to pursue some personal agenda.

Being the presidential spokesman was a job in which you could become well known—people saw McCurry on television all the time —but not famous. He had walked through airports with George Stephanopoulos, who was treated like a rock star. But McCurry was seen as a mouthpiece, not a political heavyweight. In the movies, he had noticed, the press secretary is always portrayed as a gray-looking man who speaks in a formal, stylized way.

Part of the job, McCurry soon learned, was adjusting to Clinton's rhythms. If the boss wanted to engage in some locker room banter, or aimlessly talk politics, or angrily let off steam, the press secretary tried to accommodate him. They weren't exactly friends—McCurry knew full well he wasn't one of the original loyalists—and that suited him just fine. He didn't want to be Clinton's bosom buddy, because then Clinton might tell him sensitive things that he couldn't share with the press. The only White House socializing McCurry did was bringing his family to the Easter egg roll and the president's annual Christmas reading for small children. Otherwise he'd rather be home watching dinosaur videos with the kids; his wife, Debra, had had their third child soon after he took the job.

Despite his easygoing persona, McCurry's own mood was erratic. He could be abrupt, some reporters felt, even short to the point of surliness. He once told a reporter his story idea was "sophomoric." He snapped at another reporter for being "puny-minded." He excelled at being noncommunicative when he felt like it. If he was really peeved at reporters, he would have one of his deputies, Barry Toiv, call them back.

Just before the election, when the Democratic National Committee decided to skip a scheduled financial disclosure statement, McCurry dutifully defended the move from the podium. But when ABC's Brit Hume asked him about it privately, McCurry said it was the biggest bonehead play of all time and he couldn't believe they could be so stupid. That enabled Hume to report that administration officials were privately dismayed over the incident. More important, it signaled to Hume and his colleagues that McCurry was not blindly loyal to his team. He wouldn't try to convince them that day was night. He knew how to wink.

That was the McCurry pattern. At the briefing one day Hume made a crack about Hillary Clinton, saying she had been surrounded by people at an event "to fend off the process servers." McCurry lectured him from the podium, telling Hume to "be careful." Later on, in private, McCurry told him not to worry about it. What Hume had momentarily forgotten was that the briefings were fed live to cable networks around the country, often shown on C-SPAN. The Clintons might be watching, and they would be unhappy if McCurry let some smart-ass reporter get away with demeaning the first lady.

It was a mark of McCurry's self-confidence that he was the first White House press secretary to allow the regular briefings to be televised. For years the rule had been that only the first five minutes were on camera, to give the networks some fresh video wallpaper for their voice-over reports. The official explanation for this rule was that there would be a more relaxed exchange of information if the participants weren't performing for television. The real reason was to save the spokesman from embarrassment. If he said something dumb —such as when Marlin Fitzwater impulsively called Mikhail Gorbachev a "drugstore cowboy"—the sound bite could not be endlessly replayed for days.

Stephanopoulos had tried allowing the briefings to be televised when he manned the podium in the first months of 1993 but quickly abandoned the idea when each encounter with the press turned combative. McCurry, though, didn't like the five-minute rule. It set the wrong tone for the briefing; reporters jumped on him with their harshest questions before the lights went out. This way, he had more control over the ebb and flow of the session. He would take his chances with the cameras.

.   .   .

IF MCCURRY UNDERSTOOD THE TRIBAL CUSTOMS OF JOURNALISM, it was because he once wanted to be part of the clan.

The son of a federal health officer, McCurry had been the editor of his high school paper in Redwood City, California, where he also served as the student representative on the city council and a volunteer in Robert Kennedy's short-lived presidential campaign. In 1976, during his senior year at Princeton University, McCurry was president of the Princeton Press Club. He had been stringing for *The Trenton Times* for almost three years, pocketing about $500 a month. The paper was then owned by *The Washington Post* and was viewed as a good ticket punch for up-and-coming journalists. McCurry had been promised a job after graduation. But the *Post* sold the paper and the editor went back to Washington and the anticipated job never materialized. McCurry volunteered for Jerry Brown's presidential campaign in New Jersey and celebrated a primary victory on the day he graduated. His fling with journalism was over.

Instead, McCurry joined the staff of Senator Harrison "Pete" Williams, an old-style New Jersey Democrat whose press secretary, as luck would have it, had quit days earlier after a spat with Williams's wife. A staffer brought McCurry in to meet the senator, and suddenly he was the new head flack. McCurry learned the arcane procedures of Capitol Hill at the hands of a master. But in 1980, without warning, he underwent a baptism of fire in the politics of scandal. He learned he was working for a crook.

On a Saturday afternoon that February, the twenty-five-year-old press secretary called his boss and said that *The New York Times* was preparing to report that he was among eight members of Congress caught in an FBI sting operation called Abscam.

"Ah, Mike, there may be something to that," Williams replied.

Unbeknownst to them, FBI agents were frantically trying to find the senator so they could trap him into committing perjury before he learned of the probe. They went to his house in Bedminster, New Jersey, only to learn he was in Washington. They chartered a plane, landed at Dulles instead of National Airport, and got lost. By the time they reached Williams, McCurry had unknowingly tipped him off.

The result of that conversation was that McCurry had to testify before a federal grand jury for seven hours. For the next year and a half, he was the spokesman charged with fielding hostile media inquires about the case. Williams continued to proclaim his innocence, even though the FBI had him on videotape telling a phony "sheik" that he would help him get government contracts in exchange for an 18 percent interest in a titanium mine. McCurry believed that Williams had come close to accepting a bribe but lacked criminal intent; at the same time, he felt Williams clearly had committed ethical violations that warranted his removal from the Senate. Still, he felt he should not abandon the slowly sinking ship, and he doggedly defended his boss to reporters. Tim Russert, then a top aide to Senator Daniel Patrick Moynihan, offered McCurry a job, but the young press secretary turned it down.

Pete Williams was convicted of bribery and conspiracy in May 1981—McCurry testified at the trial—but the senator still clung to his job. McCurry, worn out, joined Moynihan's staff that summer; Williams resigned the following year after the Senate ethics committee recommended his expulsion.

In 1988, after seven years at Moynihan's side, McCurry sharpened his partisan warfare skills as communications director for the Democratic National Committee. Even then there were questions about how the DNC was spending its money. McCurry once refused to tell reporters how much the DNC was pouring into commercials charging that the federal debt had doubled during the Reagan years.

McCurry's sound-bite savvy made him a favorite among the Washington press corps; he was a quote machine for reporters on deadline. It wasn't enough that the DNC was doing opposition research on candidate George Bush; McCurry dubbed the team "the Bushwhackers."

At the Democratic convention that year in Atlanta, McCurry supervised a Division of Spin Patrol Coordination to spread the party gospel about Michael Dukakis to pollsters, consultants, and the press. He even hired former CBS newsman Ike Pappas to do satellite TV interviews. McCurry told the party volunteers that their mission was "getting news and shaping news in a way that's going to be beneficial to the party. . . . You're all deputized as reporters."

By then McCurry had caught a well-known bug. Every four years he would take a leave and find a centrist Democratic horse to ride in the presidential sweepstakes, lending his talents to an unbroken string of losers. In 1984 it was John Glenn, the Ohio senator. In 1988 it was Bruce Babbitt, the former Arizona governor. With his gloomy frankness about the economy and social problems, Babbitt became a darling of the media, and McCurry played no small role in that relationship. He described Babbitt's appeal as "the pander of candor."

By 1990 McCurry had decided it was time to leave the DNC and get a "grown-up job." He became a senior vice president with Robinson, Sawyer, Lake, Lerer & Montgomery, a Washington public relations and lobbying firm. He represented MTV, a Hungarian-American foundation, a small computer startup firm called Cyrix. He defended the pork producers against animal-rights activists. He helped out with the firm's major clients, such as IBM and Texaco, and learned to skate along the surface of fifteen different issues for a half-dozen clients. The frustrating part was trying to create something out of nothing, to gin up artificial stories that might interest busy reporters. He was just another corporate flack. He missed politics.

When the 1992 campaign rolled around, McCurry cast his lot not with Bill Clinton, but with Bob Kerrey, the smart, somewhat spacey Nebraska senator and Vietnam War veteran. During the bruising primaries McCurry often found himself taking aim at the Arkansas governor, who was being damaged by the controversies over womanizing and draft evasion. "If I was on the Clinton staff," he declared, "I would say we have one problem and one problem only: people don't think we're honest enough to be president."

There were plenty of sexual rumors floating around about Clinton, including one that he had put the moves on Ron Brown's daughter. Over dinner or late-night beers with reporters, McCurry did not shy away from passing on some of this sexual gossip. In the tightly knit world of campaign operatives, this behavior was duly noted by the other side and did not endear him to the Clintonites. After Kerrey's candidacy collapsed, McCurry returned to Robinson, Sawyer. But in the fall he got a call from his old friend Fred Du Val, who had been

Babbitt's campaign manager and was now running Clinton's general election campaign in Colorado. McCurry agreed to come to Denver as a press assistant—the "lowliest of the low," as he put it—knowing that he had to pay some dues in case Clinton won and he wanted a job in the new administration.

After Clinton's victory McCurry figured his chances as a former Kerrey spokesman were slim and didn't bother applying for a job. Bruce Babbitt, slated to become secretary of the interior, asked him to be his chief of staff, but McCurry wasn't interested. He soon got a call from another old Democratic pal, Tom Donilon, the chief of staff to Warren Christopher, the incoming secretary of state. Christopher had interviewed a half-dozen candidates for department spokesman and didn't like any of them; Donilon thought McCurry could be the man. After chatting with McCurry, Christopher agreed, although it was no easy task for them to get McCurry cleared through the White House personnel office, which placed a high premium on loyalty.

McCurry's first task, he knew, was to learn how to curb his quick tongue. It was one thing to pop off as a Democratic Party spokesman, but making light of a question from the State Department podium could have international repercussions. He watched on closed-circuit TV as the outgoing spokesman, Richard Boucher, conducted a briefing and tried to come up with his own responses. He found he was saying way too much. The job of the State Department spokesman was to provide guidance and, except in rare instances, to avoid making news. McCurry, the master of the glib one-liner, gradually became tutored in diplo-speak.

Still, his sense of humor occasionally poked through. Once, when asked about the recurring rumors that Christopher would resign, McCurry quipped: "He's like the Energizer Bunny—he just keeps on going and going." Another time he dismissed a briefing paper as "bupkes," the Yiddish word for nothing. And then there was the time he infuriated the Iranian government by criticizing its beheading of 12,000 pigeons in a crackdown on illegal bird races. He called it "news most fowl, from a regime most foul."

McCurry had almost no contact with the president, but in early 1994 he heard that he was being considered for White House spokesman. Strobe Talbott, the deputy secretary of state and an old Clinton pal, told McCurry he might get the call. Press secretary Dee Dee

Myers was having a rocky tenure, and some thought that the White House needed a more mature presence at the podium. Over the summer word leaked that Leon Panetta, the new chief of staff, was dumping Myers and bringing in McCurry, creating an awkward discomfort between the two as Myers was left dangling in public for three long months. She even found McCurry's résumé on her office fax one day. McCurry called to say he wasn't trying to push her out.

After a tearful confrontation with Clinton, Myers won a reprieve and was able to stay on, with a raise and an enhanced title, through the end of the year, while McCurry remained at State. Soon after the debacle of the 1994 elections, with Newt Gingrich and the Republicans riding high, McCurry was summoned to the White House for talks about his new job.

It was a pivotal moment for the White House. Unlike many others on the president's staff, McCurry had not been with Clinton from the beginning; indeed, he had worked for the enemy. What's more, McCurry was a charter member of the Washington media establishment. There was hardly a political reporter with whom he had not shared long rides on small planes to tiny towns across the campaign landscape. There was also a web of social relationships; he had played basketball with Gerald Seib of *The Wall Street Journal* and other journalists every Saturday for years. By bringing McCurry on board, the White House would be buying entrée to that world, but in the person of a spokesman who would value his credibility with his old compadres as much as his standing with the new boss. Hiring him would be a tacit admission that the president didn't understand that world and needed an ambassador who spoke the language.

McCurry had a long session with the president and another lengthy chat with Hillary Rodham Clinton. It was the first lady who orchestrated his hiring. "Every once in a while I'm able to bring someone good in here, like McCurry," Hillary told Dick Morris, who had been advising the couple for two decades.

McCurry quickly realized that even though Hillary had her own press staff and no one was allowed even to joke about a co-presidency, he would be working for both of them. There would be days, as Whitewater and Travelgate and other administration embarrassments unfolded, that McCurry would be absorbed defending a first lady whose distrust of the press was even deeper than her husband's.

When McCurry took over in 1995, he quickly established that he knew what was going on. He attended any meeting he thought was worth his time. He got answers from the president when necessary. He was a year and a half into his job before he found himself misleading the press.

The messy situation bubbled to the surface on a campaign trip to Orlando in the summer of 1996. It was two weeks after the tabloid revelations about Dick Morris and his $200-an-hour call girl had upstaged the president on the final day of the Democratic convention. When the story broke, Morris called McCurry on the president's campaign train, which was chugging toward Chicago, and started to describe what had happened. "Stop, Dick," McCurry said. He warned Morris not to tell him the sordid details so he could plead ignorance with the press. A don't ask/don't tell policy was often the safest course for a spokesman.

Now White House officials wanted to put the banished political consultant and his sexual antics behind them. But the tabloid frenzy had not yet run its course. *The National Enquirer* and its sister publication, *The Star*, were back with new, equally bizarre allegations about Morris: he had a secret mistress in Texas and had fathered a six-year-old girl—a "love child," in the overheated parlance of the tabs. The story was a disaster for a campaign trying to run on a platform of school uniforms and family values. The question, McCurry knew, was whether the mainstream press had had its fill of Dick Morris, or whether the story would spread from the supermarket rags to the media elite. After all, this was no ordinary hired gun; Clinton had been friends with Morris since the consultant first helped him win the Arkansas governorship in 1978.

At the briefing that Friday afternoon, reporters asked McCurry if the president knew of the *Enquirer* and *Star* reports. McCurry was cagey. He said Clinton was aware of the articles but that "he has no knowledge of whether it is true or not."

That didn't satisfy CBS's Rita Braver. What, she demanded, was Clinton's reaction to the stories? "He said, 'Is it true?' And we said, 'We don't know,'" McCurry recalled. Trying to shut down this line of questioning, he used a tactic that had worked well for the Clinton camp during the '92 campaign. He chided Braver for basing her question on mere "tabloids," as if such behavior were beneath her.

When John Harris of *The Washington Post* called later and pressed him about the chronology, McCurry lectured him, too, about descending into the tabloid gutter.

The strategy was quite premeditated. "I was trying to blow the thing off and get back to the news the president was trying to make," McCurry said later.

But one reporter wouldn't let the matter drop. Matthew Cooper of *Newsweek* called McCurry the next day and got him to acknowledge that Clinton had known of Morris's out-of-wedlock daughter all along, that he had been given the news the previous year by Erskine Bowles.

How, then, could McCurry have stuck to his story of presidential ignorance? His explanation was as convoluted as Clinton's shifting stories about the draft. It was all a misunderstanding, McCurry claimed. He said the president's "Is it true?" response was not about Dick Morris's mistress or the child. Instead, he said, Clinton was questioning the *Enquirer*'s report that Morris was still dating the Texas woman, and had entertained her a month earlier in the $440-a-night Jefferson Hotel suite where he had also frolicked with prostitute Sherry Rowlands. In true spokesman fashion, McCurry said he saw no conflict between Clinton's employment of Morris and his "very strong concern about child support."

Still, the press secretary's ploy paid off. Unable to confirm that Clinton knew of the relationship and uneasy about chasing the tabloids, none of the networks reported on Morris's triple life. Nor did *The New York Times* or the *L.A. Times* or *USA Today*. *The Washington Post* mentioned the mistress in a single paragraph deep in a campaign story. Now that reporters knew the president had knowingly employed a political strategist who had fathered an illegitimate child— well, it was old news. The press had moved on. McCurry and his boss had dodged another bullet.

One of McCurry's pet projects in the wake of the election was to convince Clinton to court the media, to turn his fabled charm on the small band of men and women who chewed up and spit out his words for the American public. Clinton had little use for the fourth estate —he had not forgotten the way its members tormented him over the scandals of his first term, from Gennifer Flowers to Paula Jones to Whitewater, Travelgate, and Filegate—and he was stubbornly resisting McCurry's peacemaking initiatives. Why should he, the president of the United States, the man in charge of America's nuclear arsenal, have to romance journalists whose job was to cover him? And why did a small pack have to trail him whenever he went to a bookstore or a restaurant, even when he was out jogging? McCurry patiently explained that this was the "body watch," part of their job description; he might be shot, or just stumble and fall, or stop to answer questions.

"That's their game, not mine," Clinton replied. "They don't have to follow me when I jog. I'm not going to make news or talk about nuclear war."

It was a discussion they had had many times. Here was one of the great retail politicians of the modern age, a man who had to shake every hand in the room, who would spend ten minutes arguing with a recalcitrant voter while his staff anxiously beckoned him to the next event, and yet he had little patience for reporters with megaphones that could reach millions. They were, in his view, largely nitpickers, naysayers, political handicappers with little interest in the substance of governing. They thrived on building themselves up by knocking him down.

Dick Morris, who knew Clinton as well as anyone, concluded after the campaign that the president hated the press. "He is contemptuous of reporters," Morris said. "He feels they're a sleazy group of people who lie a lot, who pursue their own agendas, who have a pack mentality. He feels they are a necessary evil."

What really infuriated the president, and Hillary, was the way the press kept changing the parameters of scandal. First the two of them would be accused of improperly benefiting from an Arkansas land deal. When that didn't pan out, the focus would shift to another land development, or a fraudulent loan, or missing billing records, or, when all else failed, the supposed cover-up. But the press never told anyone they had been cleared of the original charges. The reporters just kept morphing the Whitewater saga into some new configuration. They seemed to have a bottomless appetite for the most trivial semblance of an allegation.

The president's aides believed that Clinton was surprisingly naive about the press. He thought that if you were nice to reporters, they would be nice to you. George Stephanopoulos had often been struck by Clinton's feeling of betrayal when some journalist whom he had been courting wrote a tough piece. The president didn't understand that it was nothing personal, just part of the game. White House staffers were surprised that he hadn't become more inured to this sort of rough-and-tumble during his twelve years as governor.

If you would spend a fraction of your persuasive skills winning them over, McCurry argued, there would be a big payoff. But Clinton, angry about various slights, his resolve buttressed by thick layers of scar tissue, would not play. These journalists were wedded to "the old notion that all politicians are hopelessly corrupt and incompetent," he said. Screw the press.

And yet on a Friday afternoon in the waning days of 1996, McCurry finally got his way as the president sat down in the small dining room off the Oval Office with three high-profile pundits: *Newsweek*'s Jonathan Alter, Gerald Seib of *The Wall Street Journal*, and Jacob Weisberg of *Slate*, Microsoft's online magazine. McCurry had selected them as a provocative group of progressive writers who would be receptive to Clinton's view of the world. "Alter bites my ass sometimes, but at least he understands what we're trying to do," Clinton once told an aide. The session was declared off-the-record, so Clinton could relax.

The president gave them The Treatment. He showed them around the Oval Office, the small adjacent study, where he had a bunch of ties laid out, and his private dining room. He told Alter that he had liked one of his recent columns. Weisberg gave him a *Slate* cap, and Clinton put it on and posed for a picture. They chatted about China policy and other issues over cider and cookies. When Alter asked about campaign finance reform, Clinton noted that Weisberg had just written "a great story" on the subject and proceeded to critique it. The atmosphere seemed far less stilted than during the four times that Alter had formally interviewed Clinton.

Perhaps it was mere coincidence, but after the off-the-record meeting, Alter hailed the president in *Newsweek* as "the salesman with the best understanding of women" and "the creator of a new kind of values politics. . . . Clinton's first important insight—confirmed by his constant reading of polls—is that Americans are not nearly as divided as we sometimes think. . . .

"We mostly missed a big story sitting right under our noses, one of the great acts of political theft in recent memory. In 1996, Bill Clinton—that's right, BILL CLINTON—grabbed family values for the Democrats, and he's not about to give them back."

Seib cast his *Wall Street Journal* column as an exercise in mind reading. "If you're President Clinton, here's how you might see things this holiday season. . . . What is to be your legacy? Perhaps it lies in being the Baby Boomer who saves entitlement programs for the Baby Boomers as they head toward retirement. . . . Maybe you try some small confidence-building measures before attempting any big fix." Readers never suspected that the columnists had gotten their information from a certain inside source.

But McCurry was interested in more than just a couple of favorable columns. He wanted Clinton to see journalists in what he called a "defanged mode,"not peppering him with prosecutorial questions. McCurry's fantasy was that POTUS, as White House aides called the president of the United States, could have sessions like this with Howell Raines, the editorial page editor of *The New York Times*, and Leonard Downie, executive editor of *The Washington Post*, who would see, in an easygoing atmosphere, that Clinton was a thoughtful guy.

The biggest complaint among White House reporters was how remote they felt from the man they were supposed to be covering. McCurry agreed that this was a problem. When the campaign was over he arranged a get-acquainted session between Clinton and seven of the new correspondents who would be covering him in the second term. They gathered in the Map Room, whose wall is adorned by the 1945 military map that hung there when FDR left the White House for the last time. Clinton, nursing a sore throat, slouched on the couch sipping tea. He told the reporters, who munched cookies on the chairs around him, that they would have to do most of the talking. Then, of course, he held forth for an hour and ten minutes.

Clinton was surprisingly candid, and the chat ranged from whether he and his wife would adopt a child—they had decided against it—to his view of Steve Stockman, the far-right Texan congressman. "He's crazy," Clinton said.

That session was also off-the-record. Soon afterward, the seven reporters got together and compared the notes they had hastily scribbled after the meeting. Karen Tumulty of *Time* magazine wanted to use an anecdote about Madeleine Albright. Peter Baker of *The*

Washington Post wanted to cite a comment Clinton had made about his old pal James Carville. McCurry finally cut a deal in which seven items could be used without attributing them to Clinton. The reporters could say "the president has told friends . . ." or "the president is known to believe . . ."

Reporters didn't like the off-the-record rule, since they had to beg for each usable crumb. But McCurry felt it was best that Clinton be able to sound off without weighing each word. He had not forgotten the infamous "funk" episode of 1995, when the president, in jeans and cowboy boots, had a forty-five minute chat with reporters aboard Air Force One about the mood of the country. The conversation was going fine until Clinton declared that he wanted to "get people out of their funk."

The pack quickly pounced. Clinton was widely ridiculed for his assessment of the national disposition, which was likened to Jimmy Carter's disastrous "malaise" speech in 1979.

"See, this is what happens," Clinton told his staff. "You try to let people understand what you are thinking and what your motivations are, and it just becomes a game of gotcha."

Senior White House officials chastised McCurry for putting the president in such a vulnerable position, and he considered it his greatest blunder as press secretary. But he didn't want to shut off all informal communication. Six months later, when Clinton was returning from a trip to Israel on Air Force One, McCurry tried again, this time decreeing that the conversation was on something called "psych background," meaning that reporters could pretend to tap into the president's brain without attributing any comments to the Big Guy. Clinton rambled for three hours about the Middle East, the Bible, the college basketball playoffs, violence on television, even the peach cobbler aboard the flight, all without saying anything inflammatory. But the exercise was so transparent that it came off as silly. John Harris of *The Washington Post* attributed the remarks to "a talkative and opinionated fellow" on the plane who was "intimately familiar with the thinking of Clinton."

Still, the president seemed to be growing more comfortable with the give-and-take. Flying back from Little Rock on the day after the election, he fell into a freewheeling conversation with print reporters on the plane. But nothing was ever simple in dealing with the press.

The television and radio correspondents quickly complained to McCurry that the session did them no good because they had no usable videotape or sound. McCurry pondered the situation for a moment.

"Come up to the front of the plane," he said. "We'll re-create the moment. You can ask the same questions." In a remarkable bit of staging, the cameramen gathered around the president while the reporters asked the same questions that had been asked moments before, eliciting the same answers. Then one reporter slipped in an extra question and McCurry got mad.

.   .   .

McCurry could give as good as he got, and when he didn't want to answer a question, he could stonewall with the best of them. Deborah Orin found this out the hard way.

The feisty *New York Post* reporter with the jet-black hair and tabloid-tough manner had known McCurry for fifteen years and liked him, most of the time. But she couldn't stand the way he dealt with her from the podium. If he didn't want to address a sensitive question, he would deflect it, duck it, dismiss it. He would needle the person who asked it. What he wouldn't do was provide a straight answer.

It was "an attempt to marginalize reporters who asked embarrassing questions," Orin said later. She took the briefings seriously. Orin was naturally combative, but it was more than that. The daily encounter was a chance to hold the White House accountable, one of the few public opportunities to challenge the official line.

Many of the veterans considered the briefings stupefyingly dull, a colossal waste of time. CBS's Rita Braver skipped them whenever possible. Brit Hume, the longtime ABC correspondent, would stand up and leave if the droning went on too long. At other times Hume would sit in his booth at the back of the pressroom and listen with one ear to the closed-circuit monitor. If he heard something that annoyed him, he would come loping up to the front and interrogate McCurry, just to show him that the reporters were still awake. But with McCurry slinging so much bull from the podium, it hardly seemed worth the bother. If he uttered any newsworthy syllables, the reporters could read the transcript on their computer screens within minutes.

Orin worked for a conservative newspaper that delighted in Clinton sex scandals, and in the summer of 1996, the scandal of the moment involved Gary Aldrich's book, *Unlimited Access*. A former FBI agent assigned to the White House, Aldrich had written a screed that depicted the Clintonites as sloppy, rude, drug-addled Deadheads. The first headlines, gleefully trumpeted by the *New York Post* (which serialized the book), had Clinton sneaking out under a blanket in the back seat of a car for late-night trysts at the downtown Marriott. It was, as it turned out, a fourth-hand rumor that no one could corroborate.

The White House assumed a full War Room footing in an effort to discredit the book. George Stephanopoulos called every reporter he knew, arguing that the book was tabloid trash, riddled with errors and beneath the dignity of any serious news organization. Stephanopoulos and Mark Fabiani, the White House lawyer in charge of scandal management, went to the ABC bureau a few blocks from the White House and urged producers there to bump Aldrich from a scheduled Sunday appearance on *This Week with David Brinkley*. Leon Panetta called Bob Murphy, ABC's vice president for news, with the same message.

McCurry, traveling with the president in Lyons, France, pulled aside Robin Sproul, ABC's Washington bureau chief, and launched into a red-faced tirade. He was really hot. There would be consequences if ABC put Aldrich on the air, he said. The network's requests to talk to the president would be dropped, including Clinton's planned interview with Barbara Walters that fall, McCurry warned. White House officials might be reluctant to appear on ABC programs. When the Brinkley show put Aldrich on anyway—along with Stephanopoulos—McCurry said that ABC had "damaged" the president. "We'll remember that," he said. Stephanopoulos even made the ludicrous claim that Bob Dole's campaign was involved, since Craig Shirley, a conservative publicist who had once done volunteer work for the Dole camp, was helping to promote the book.

Though the administration's counterattack didn't scare ABC, it did help to turn the rest of the establishment media against the Aldrich book. After the book's numerous errors and rumors were exposed by the Brinkley show, *Newsweek*, and other news organizations, *Larry King Live* and *Dateline NBC* both dropped planned interviews with

Aldrich. And while *Unlimited Access* went on to become a best-seller —ballyhooed as The Book the Clinton White House Doesn't Want You to Read—the assault had sent an important signal. The Clintonites were willing to use intimidation tactics to quash an unfavorable story. If journalists found them too heavy-handed, well, that was a price they had to pay to neutralize the book. McCurry later apologized to Robin Sproul, but he had clearly shown his willingness to use the brass knuckles.

Still, Orin believed that there was legitimate material in Aldrich's book, incidents that the ex-FBI man would be in a position to know. He had written that Craig Livingstone, a low-level White House aide who later resigned for improperly obtaining FBI files on Republicans, had once issued a memo chastising White House staffers for writing bad checks. What about that? Either there was a memo or there wasn't. Orin soon pressed McCurry at the gaggle, but he deflected the question. A few days later she tried again to ask about "some of the charges made by Gary Aldrich."

"Still trying to resurrect him, huh?" McCurry shot back.

Orin pressed on: Was there a Craig Livingstone memo on bad checks? True or not?

"I am not going to check, because most of what he writes in that book has already been proven to be without merit," McCurry said.

"If it's not true, why don't you want to check it?"

"I don't think it's worth my time to check."

A CBS producer, Mark Knoller, piped up. "But Deborah's question is legitimate, isn't it, Mike?"

The book, McCurry told Orin, was "filled with lies. And your newspaper, as I recall, reprinted large portions of it."

"And it printed your denials, Mike. But the question is a question about a memo. Did or didn't he issue such a memo?"

"I do not know."

"Will you check?"

"No."

Why not?

"Because I don't want to," McCurry said. Then he threw down the gauntlet: "Does any other news organization want to pose the question?"

It was a tense moment. McCurry was suddenly the playground

bully, challenging the rest of the gang to stand up for Deborah Orin. There was an uncomfortable silence. "Okay, hearing none, any other questions?" McCurry said. Another reporter asked about a Pentagon initiative, and the briefing moved on.

Orin felt humiliated. Her whole body was shaking. Afterward, several reporters approached her and apologized for their behavior. "They felt as if their balls had been cut off while my limb was cut off," Orin said later. "The press corps was totally emasculated."

One reporter told her, "I didn't want to use up any chits for your story." Orin was stunned. The dirty little secret of covering the White House, she felt, was there wasn't much that McCurry and his colleagues would do to help you. Oh, you might get an early leak on some budget proposal or presidential appointment, but by and large everyone, whether in favor or not, was fed the same thin gruel. And most of the reporters would not stick their necks out and risk losing what little access they had. They had become too passive. McCurry, she realized, was winning the war.

CHAPTER THREE

In the Dungeon

F EW OUTSIDERS WHO WATCHED THE WHITE HOUSE REPORTERS doing their stand-ups on television realized what they grappled with inside the famed building. For all the glamor of the job, all the perks and prestige, the working conditions were worse than in the average small-town city hall. The White House pressroom wasn't really a room at all but an enclosed corridor connecting the main building with the West Wing. In an earlier incarnation, before the White House pool was closed, it housed a sauna, two massage rooms, a flower room, and a kennel for the presidential dogs. Richard Nixon ordered the renovation in 1969 after visiting the old, cramped pressroom off the West Wing lobby, which was authorized by Theodore Roosevelt so the reporters wouldn't have to stand out in the cold. When Nixon moved in, briefings were still conducted in the press secretary's office. Nixon couldn't believe the squalid conditions. "Is this where you have to work?" he asked Helen Thomas.

The new press corridor was divided into three sections. At the front—behind a sliding door that separated it from the minions of the lower press office—was the briefing room, its podium and blue-curtain backdrop a familiar television scene. On the left wall was a photograph of Jim Brady, the fallen Reagan press secretary; along the right wall were four seats for the staffers who always seemed to loiter at official pronouncements. The raised podium looked out on eight rows of six wooden press seats, movie theater style, all of them marked with small gold nameplates—the networks and wire services in the front, the big newspapers and newsmagazines in the second and third rows, a fixed pecking order.

To get to the middle section, past the tangle of television cables and sound equipment, one passed through a hallway so narrow that a reporter had to turn sideways to let another pass. Inside was a warren of desks with phones for the big newspapers and chains, a paper-strewn workspace so cramped that even a whispered conversation could be heard by a rival on either side. Two enclosed cubicles housed the AP and UPI. A staircase descended to "the dungeon," a dark basement peopled by CNN, Fox, a tiny closet housing National Public Radio, and a few foreign news outlets.

At the back of the corridor were the private booths of CBS, NBC, and ABC, each an isolation chamber little more than the width of an overweight correspondent. The booths consisted of three seats along a countertop, like some miniature luncheonette, and four TV sets resting on a high shelf. In the rear of each enclosure was a one-person sound booth for radio reports and voice-overs. It was impossible for viewers to imagine the claustrophobic feeling of sitting in that space, day after day, making phone calls and waiting for news.

The journalists had clawed their way to the top of their profession, but now many felt trapped by the limitations of the job. They were constantly fuming over the lack of access to the man they were ostensibly covering, the limited number of aides who would tell them anything beyond the party line. Relegated to a dingy, overcrowded pressroom, herded behind ropes on long, arduous trips, they grew to resent their captors and the demands of their supposedly glamorous jobs. Most of them had a jaundiced view of Clinton, and while they liked McCurry, he was ultimately just another roadblock to finding out what was going on. The briefing room turned into a bullfighting ring, with the reporters doing their damnedest to make McCurry see red. They would badger and taunt him each afternoon, but it was mostly for exercise, to give them a chance to work out their frustrations.

The assembled journalists danced to different rhythms. The fastest-paced of the bunch were Wolf Blitzer, CNN's main man at the White House, and the wire-service scribes for the Associated Press, United Press International, and Reuters. They were voracious for news around the clock, since any presidential comment or photo op could be transformed into news. They constantly harassed McCurry for snippets of information and measured their best scoops by minutes.

In the video age Blitzer was the closest thing to a court chronicler at the White House. Whenever the administration made a minor announcement, he would be out on the North Lawn within minutes, informing the world. If McCurry put out the word that Mexico had repaid its loans from the United States a ho hum story in the papers the next day—CNN would cut into regular programming, flash its "Breaking News" logo, and go live to Wolf. Other CNN reporters shared the beat, but everyone knew Wolf, the man with the beard and the too-weird-to-be-real name.

McCurry liked to tease Blitzer; he once opened a briefing by announcing, "Mr. Blitzer, the president was just having a very good laugh at your most recent report." And some White House correspondents would snicker when Blitzer went into his this-just-in routine. They figured McCurry and company were just spoon-feeding him predigested morsels of news, the sort of routine announcements that would only reflect positively on the president when Blitzer repeated them.

Blitzer was aware of his reputation, and he didn't particularly care. He knew how hard he worked, how many phone calls he had to make to the Hill, party officials, lobbyists, to find out what was up. If there was news brewing, Blitzer would ask McCurry or another aide to step onto the lawn for a quickie interview. CNN, after all, had a bottom-less appetite for news. If that helped administration officials get their message out, so be it. His job was to cover the president.

Blitzer's constant presence gave him the status of an insider. Clinton had him over to the White House theater—for the movie *Wolf*, naturally—with the star, Jack Nicholson; the director, Mike Nichols; and his wife, Diane Sawyer. Hillary invited him twice for coffee. And CNN gave him his own show, first *Inside Politics Weekend* and, later, *Late Edition with Wolf Blitzer*.

But the White House wasn't always happy with Blitzer's reports. George Stephanopoulos used to run onto the lawn after a live shot and berate him if he broadcast something that offended administration sensibilities. It was the ultimate instant-feedback loop.

As a courtesy, Blitzer would warn McCurry before going live with an important story. He knew that McCurry would be flooded with press calls and wanted to give him one final shot. The press secretary sometimes tried to talk him out of a story on grounds that Blitzer's sources were misleading him. Wolf, you'll embarrass yourself, he would say. Wolf, you're making a big mistake. Most of the time, Blitzer felt, it was merely news that the White House didn't want to leak prematurely.

The richest and best-known reporters in the pressroom, of course, were the network correspondents—Rita Braver, Brit Hume, and Jim Miklaszewski at the end of Clinton's first administration. In television terms, the White House was the holy grail. Correspondents who had worked the beat—Dan Rather, Tom Brokaw, Lesley Stahl, Sam Donaldson, Chris Wallace, Judy Woodruff, Brian Williams—had gone on to big anchor jobs and bigger paychecks. There was no better platform, no faster ticket to the top of the nightly news. The most dramatic stories—war, recession, diplomacy, scandal—were there for the picking. The prestige of following around the commander-in-chief invariably rubbed off on the correspondents as well. The confrontations—Rather challenging Nixon during Watergate, Donaldson shouting at Reagan over the helicopter engines —were fixed in the public mind. The reporters' ninety-second segments for the evening broadcasts skated along the surface of the news, with clear story lines and compelling visuals that could be capped with a couple of pithy remarks on whether the president was sinking or swimming.

The reporters for the biggest newspapers, led by Alison Mitchell and James Bennet at *The New York Times* and John Harris and Peter Baker at *The Washington Post*, probably did the most to set the overall tone of the media coverage. A front-page exclusive would ripple through the rest of the press corps, dominate the briefing, and most likely wind up on the network news. The newsmagazine reporters were not quite as influential as in years past, but they could still change the dialogue or cement the conventional wisdom with a cover story or a behind-the-scenes report.

Two vital groups of reinforcements backed up the White House regulars, although they did not come to the briefings or wear the laminated press cards around their necks. One was the columnists and opinion-mongers—Jonathan Alter at *Newsweek*, Joe Klein at *The New Yorker*, William Safire and Maureen Dowd at *The New York Times*, E. J. Dionne and Richard Cohen at *The Washington Post*—who could quickly change the zeitgeist and were assiduously courted by McCurry and his allies. Unconstrained by the conventions of objectivity, they could sit at their desks and, with a few mocking phrases, declare Clinton a dismal failure or deeply flawed human being. The other was the dogged band of investigative reporters—Jeff Gerth at the *Times*, Bob Woodward at the *Post*, Glenn Simpson at *The Wall Street Journal*, Alan Miller at the *Los Angeles Times*—who immersed themselves in the minutiae of scandal and on any given morning could drop a bombshell on the White House. Their main point of contact on the president's staff was Lanny Davis, fifty-one, an intense, raspy-voiced corporate lawyer who worked insane hours and always seemed overwhelmed by the sheer volume of his damage control duties. Davis wrestled openly with the gap between the upbeat script he was handed and the morally ambiguous wreckage he was surveying.

McCurry, by contrast, did not bother to conceal his disdain for the prosecutorial reporters who advanced their careers mainly by tearing down public officials. A few, he thought, were downright crazy. "Investigative reporters are by definition conspiracy theorists," McCurry would say. Their mission was to interpret material, any material, in the worst possible light, mixing fact and implication and innuendo to concoct their scandalous brew. They were like overzealous cops, McCurry felt, obsessed with The Story, listening to the wild-eyed finger-pointers, determined to prove that everyone in the administration was scum.

The journalists also knew from long experience that presidents and their lieutenants play fast and loose with the truth; some of the beat reporters, in fact, had been in the White House Briefing Room, listening to the dissembling officials, during Watergate and Iran-contra. And they knew that Bill and Hillary Clinton had a particular tendency to fudge the facts. They had watched as various White House explanations were rendered inoperative, as embarrassing disclosures were pried from the administration on one damaging story after another. With their former Arkansas business partners heading for jail, their close friend Vincent Foster a mysterious suicide, and congressional investigators and a special prosecutor breathing down their necks, Bill and Hillary Clinton lived a precarious existence in what they once promised would be the most ethical administration in history. The president was a Houdini-like figure when it came to this phalanx of investigations, always slipping out of a tight noose only to land in a nearby pot of boiling oil.

The campaign finance scandal was merely the latest example. The White House had known about much of the improper fundraising, the hot checks laundered through relatives and employees, but had kept an airtight lid on the story until Clinton's reelection was in the bag. The president had gone through the entire campaign without holding a formal news conference. Nettlesome questions were referred to the Democratic National Committee—the "other campaign," Clinton called it—as if it were some independent fiefdom rather than a wholly owned subsidiary whose officials could be fired by presidential whim. Truth was an early casualty in this administration, the reporters believed, and it was their responsibility to keep pounding on the door until they, and the public, got some adequate answers. They viewed themselves as the cavalry, the last line of defense against a corrupt White House that had perfected the art of the cover-up, the one force in society that could charge through the fog and uncover the truth.

For the big newspapers the White House beat had always been the pinnacle of prestige, a reward for seasoned journalists in their forties and fifties who had covered statehouses and Capitol Hill and were finally ready for the big time. But something had changed in the last decade. Top reporters were turning down the job. They were not enamored of the long hours and arduous travel, the inverse relationship between the perceived glamor and the mundane reality. The last journalist to truly dominate the beat was Ann Devroy, a harddriving, tenacious *Washington Post* reporter whose refusal to accept the official line set the tone and the permissible boundaries for her colleagues. Long after most reporters had forgotten Clinton's 1992 campaign promise to cut the White House staff by 25 percent, Devroy had spent months harassing aides until she got the records to prove that the president was axing obscure advisory panels, bringing in part-timers, and otherwise circumventing the pledge. And it was she who first discovered the behind-the-scenes influence of Dick

Morris. After Devroy was sidelined in mid-1996 by what proved to be a fatal bout with cancer, McCurry felt that the quality of reporting dropped by a significant notch.

The new breed of White House reporters for the major papers were younger, less driven, less awed by the job. They were men like James Bennet, a rail-thin thirty-year-old with a mustache and goatee who got the assignment just five years after joining *The New York Times.*

Bennet was immediately struck by the incredibly tight controls on information, the way it almost seemed that a White House staffer was assigned to each reporter to convey the official line, as if reading from the same script. He was struck, too, by the uselessness of the daily briefing, the way it would careen back and forth across twenty or thirty topics, from China to capital gains, from partial-birth abortion to Mexican drug enforcement, from Cabinet nominations to gun control. Each topic, no matter how esoteric, was important to some reporter at the paper, so you had to be a human vacuum cleaner, even if you were simply regurgitating the "pool report" filed by the rotating group of correspondents who got to follow the president on trips at closer range. His colleagues called it the daily feeding, and the metaphor somehow seemed apt. McCurry would stand up there like a tackling dummy, taking the hits that otherwise would be delivered to other officials. He would let the reporters cuff him around to get their daily exercise, and everyone would feel that they had accomplished something, even though precious little information was imparted. It was infantilizing, in a way. You were so dependent on a small circle of aides and your colleagues' pool reports, and had so little access to the president and first lady. If you ticked off your White House handlers, they might not return your calls or give you much information, and you would be stranded.

Bennet got a glimpse of the dilemma at the very start, when he showed up for a get-acquainted session with McCurry. It was the day that a *Times* editorial had said the press secretary's reputation was in shreds over his handling of the fundraising scandal. "Why would you bother to come over here when my credibility is in tatters?" McCurry snapped. McCurry knew full well that Bennet had nothing to do with the editorial page, but it was a reminder to the new correspondent that he was now operating in an intensely political environment.

It was quickly apparent that the beat involved colossal amounts of

wasted time. One Wednesday afternoon when Bennet drew the pool
duty, he had to drive out to Andrews Air Force Base just to watch the
president tee off on the military golf course. He arrived just after a
young wire-service reporter had shouted what sounded like "Mr.
President, what do you think of dung passing?", a question so inart-
fully phrased that Clinton had to chuckle before pronouncing on the
death of Deng Xiaoping. Then Bennet had to sit in the clubhouse
until it got dark so he could watch Clinton slip back into his limousine. Such assignments gave new meaning to the term captive audience.

Still, Bennet enjoyed the wide range of subjects afforded by the
beat. One day he would write about the economy, another day about
education, another day about Clinton intervening in an airline strike.
He liked to write analytical or offbeat pieces that required a certain
insight or imagination. But the opportunities for breaking real news
seemed incredibly slight under these tightly controlled conditions.
He had no interest in the twenty-four-hour scoop, the little advances
on some presidential pronouncement that gave his colleagues a feeling of excitement, even though the news was about to come out
anyway. But the pressure not to be beaten was constant, unrelenting.
When he picked up *The Washington Post* each morning, Bennet felt a
little pang. Had the *Times* missed a major story? Would he have to
play catch-up? It was a far cry from covering the auto industry for
the financial pages.

The suffocating circumstances hit home when Hillary Clinton
held her first issue briefing in early 1997 in the Map Room, a session
on "micro-credit" loans for small-scale entrepreneurs. This was the
first time Hillary had sat for a formal session with reporters since the
famous "pink press conference" of 1994, when the first lady—clad in
a demure pink suit—had fielded questions about Whitewater for
seventy-two minutes. Journalists were told in advance that they could
ask any question. Yet one reporter after another politely stuck to
questions about micro-credit, allowing the first lady to set the agenda.

Finally Jill Dougherty of CNN said, "Mrs. Clinton, I really hate
to bring up front-burner issues, but duty calls." She asked about
Hillary's role in compiling a White House database of political supporters and whether the contents were used for political purposes by
the Democratic National Committee. The first lady easily finessed

the question and a follow-up by Ann Blackman of *Time* magazine, and the session was over.

Bennet wrote in his story the next day that a reporter had "apologetically" raised the database issue. He got an angry letter from a reader. Why the hell were reporters apologizing for raising issues that the White House didn't want to talk about? Bennet realized the reader was right. They had all fallen into that trap.

What was equally puzzling were the off-the-record sessions, like his get-acquainted meeting with the president in the Map Room or an off-the-record dinner that he and the Clintons shared during a vacation trip to the Virgin Islands. What was the point? There was no news value. If the Map Room session with Clinton had been on the record, all seven reporters would have walked out of there and written front-page stories. But that was against the rules. There was no point in asking tough questions, since it would just piss off the president and you couldn't use the stuff anyway. You were never going to be their friend. Maybe you got a sense of how the president's mind works, what was important to him, but that was about it.

Bennet's colleague at the *Times*, Alison Mitchell, had never had such a dinner with Clinton, although she had been on the beat nearly two years. In fact, the president barely knew who she was. In her first six months on the job, she had never met him, a situation she sought to rectify in early 1996, when she was among the reporters returning with Clinton from Bosnia on a military transport plane. As the president walked down the aisle, Mitchell stuck out her hand.

"Mr. President, I'm Alison Mitchell from *The New York Times*. I've been covering you for months and I've never met you and I just wanted to introduce myself."

"Thanks for all your work on this issue," Clinton said oddly, pumping her hand as if she were some traveling diplomat.

Mitchell occasionally groused to McCurry that she never got to speak to the man she was ostensibly covering. McCurry promptly formulated the Alison Mitchell Rule, decreeing that all new correspondents would have at least a brief get-acquainted session with the president. Unfortunately, it didn't apply to Alison Mitchell, whose only other contact with Clinton came during two group interviews subsequently granted to the *Times*.

In some ways it was like reporting on the CIA—you knew it was there but you couldn't quite feel it or see it. Mitchell had enjoyed more access to Mikhail Gorbachev when she was covering Moscow, and he would occasionally stop and chat with reporters outside the Congress of People's Deputies.

Like Bennet, Mitchell never particularly aspired to covering the White House. An engaging woman with a thick tangle of black hair, she had spent most of her career with *Newsday*, including a stint in Washington during the mid-'80s, when she would tease her friends on White House duty: "Are you sure Reagan is alive? Have you seen him?" Her husband, *Times* reporter Francis X. Clines, was a former White House correspondent himself, so she had no illusions about the place. It was quite a contrast to her previous assignment at the *Times* covering Mayor Rudolph Giuliani, who once called her at 12:45 A.M. to angrily demand that a routine story she had written be pulled from the paper. But at New York's City Hall, you could roam the corridors, buttonhole top aides, check on who was waiting to see the mayor. At the White House Mitchell was surprised at how isolated she felt. She had thought that the *Times* and *The Washington Post* were fed a steady diet of high-level leaks, but there was little of that, except for an occasional break on a couple of crappy little announcements that would wind up on page B-14. Senior aides would confirm what you already knew or steer you off a bad story, but it was very hard to pry new information from them.

Even the more senior reporters on the beat were dismayed by the culture of suspicion that permeated the White House. Rita Braver of CBS was struck by how hard White House officials worked to keep unfavorable stories off television. They would go to unbelievable lengths to prevent her from breaking a story, which was hard enough in that tightly controlled environment where no reporter could wander around unescorted. Most galling of all, they would stiff her while arranging background briefings for reporters from the major newspapers. They seemed to think bad stories came across as more sensational on television or that TV reporters were just plain stupid. At the very least they understood that the three network newscasts reached a hell of a lot more people, 30 million households, than the biggest newspapers or magazines.

Braver, a tenacious blonde who had covered the Justice Department, first noticed the pattern soon after she moved to the White

House in 1993, when Clinton nominated Bobby Ray Inman to be secretary of defense. She got a tip that Inman had failed to pay Social Security taxes for his housekeeper, the same problem that had sunk Zoe Baird's bid to become attorney general earlier that year. But she needed confirmation from the White House. To keep her from getting an exclusive, administration officials put out the story to everyone by announcing that Inman would pay the delinquent tax the next day. Just a coincidence, they told her. When Inman withdrew his nomination at a rambling news conference, he said the White House had "put out a very short press release" on his tax problem after "someone gave Rita Braver a story on what has familiarly become known as Nannygate." So much for coincidence.

The same thing happened when the White House announced that it was turning over a huge batch of Whitewater documents to the Justice Department. As a former Justice reporter, Braver knew that prosecutors didn't like to do business that way; they preferred to issue a subpoena to ensure that nothing was withheld. She made some calls, confirmed that a subpoena had indeed been issued, and wrote a script that began "CBS News has learned. . . . " The network put together a graphic for her piece. Half an hour before the evening news began, White House officials publicly announced the subpoena. No way they were going to let her break the news and look like they were hiding something, which they had been. They were determined to beat her to the punch.

Braver kept pounding away. After the DNC fundraising scandal broke, she found out that Mark Middleton, a former White House aide who was raising money for the party overseas, may have been entertaining clients in the White House dining room. This was a highly unusual privilege for a Democratic fundraiser. She kept calling McCurry's office, but as her deadline passed, officials insisted that they didn't have the facts. The next morning Braver woke up and saw the Middleton story—her story—in *The Wall Street Journal*. She was incensed. McCurry called her at 8:30 A.M. and he apologized, sort of. He said that the *Journal* had called later that night and had more detail than Braver did, so the White House felt compelled to confirm the story. Braver thought this was a crock. McCurry simply preferred to have the story come out in print rather than on the *CBS Evening News*.

Privately McCurry made no bones about his view. The tone of television news was often hyperventilated, he felt. The reports had an accusatory tone, with a closing blast by the correspondent. That was the genre these days. On negative stories the administration's explanation was usually a bit complicated and often got lost on television. You needed to be able to explain the details. McCurry would much rather take a hit in a newspaper story, where at least there would be ample space for his side, than in a TV report that flashed by in a minute-twenty. Television tended to paint things in black and white and most stories were actually rather gray.

But the personality of the correspondents also came into play. If Brit Hume was close to nailing a story and needed help, well, McCurry was confident he would be even-handed, even though Hume made no secret that his personal views were conservative. But McCurry saw Braver as more prosecutorial, more likely to slam the White House, and he wasn't about to hand her a story if he could help it.

Everyone at the White House knew that Braver was married to Robert Barnett, a Democratic Party activist, superlawyer, and old friend of the Clintons; Barnett was the attorney the president had originally hired to defend him in the Whitewater mess, and he reluctantly relinquished the job only because of the obvious conflict when his wife was assigned to the White House. Clinton thought that Braver had to bend over backward to beat the shit out of him, just to prove her independence. He even kidded her about it. "You should get a divorce so you can go a little easier on me," Clinton joked. Braver thought this was nonsense and just tried to do her job.

By the time Clinton was beginning his second term, Braver wanted out. The long hours and the travel were wearing her down. She was interested in a wide range of subjects and was tired of spending most of her time thinking about one man. Besides, covering the White House was an exercise in frustration. You had to work so hard to confirm each fact that it just sucked the energy out of you.

McCurry was awfully good at his job, Braver felt, but a little arrogant. He was particularly astute at deflecting questions about Whitewater and Travelgate and the like, calmly deferring to Mark Fabiani and, later, Lanny Davis. It wasn't just that he didn't want to answer; he didn't want the questions themselves dominating the daily briefing. The sessions were sort of a running mini-series on C-SPAN, and McCurry wanted to keep the damaging stuff off camera. In fact, he had insisted on it as a condition of taking the job. He knew that once the room became obsessed with the day's scandal story, it would wipe out any other news the White House was trying to make. By directing all scandal questions to the lawyers, McCurry could stay on the high road while Lanny Davis shoveled the shit. Davis would give on-camera interviews when it suited the White House, or he might not. It was all part of what Braver saw as their slick effort to control the agenda.

.   .   .

FOR ALL THE TENSION IN THE BRIEFING ROOM, MCCURRY STILL liked to think of himself as one of the press gang. When John Broder of the *Los Angeles Times* was leaving the beat to join *The New York Times* and a bunch of reporters took him out for dinner at Sam & Harry's, a downtown steak house, McCurry tagged along. He told the group that he was a reporter, just like them, digging out information from the bowels of the White House.

McCurry talked to everyone in the press, even the most combative conservatives. He gave regular briefings to *The Washington Times*, whose editors despised Clinton, because its reporters were excluded from the "tongs," or groups of big papers that arranged background sessions with top officials. He often whispered behind-the-scenes details to Fred Barnes, executive editor of *The Weekly Standard*, a magazine so reliably hostile it once published a "Special Clinton-Bashing Issue." When Clinton gave a long emotional response to a question about his veto of the partial-birth abortion ban, McCurry told Barnes, an ardent opponent of abortion, that White House aides were surprised by the ringing defense. Speaking under the cloak of anonymity, McCurry recalled the president saying, "Well, it's important. I did it on purpose." McCurry, who was trying to underscore that Clinton was acting on principle, wasn't expecting a favorable piece, and he wasn't disappointed. "Demagoguing Abortion," the headline said. But the Clinton spin was included.

At other times McCurry seemed to buy into a more conspiratorial view of the press. The Princeton graduate would grumble about the "bratty" attitude among "Ivy League and upper-income reporters."

He embraced Clinton's view that the Washington media establishment had never really accepted the man from Arkansas and, in some quarters, was out to destroy him.

"The top management of *The Washington Post* is fairly hostile toward Bill Clinton and has been for a long time," McCurry once declared. "They've been fairly public and unabashed about it. It's just a fact of life." The notion that Clinton might deserve whatever criticism the paper was dishing out seemed not to have crossed McCurry's mind.

And McCurry was not above a little hardball. In early 1996 Chris Vlasto, an ABC producer who specialized in scandal, was working on a story about Senator Alfonse D'Amato and his Whitewater hearings. Vlasto was accustomed to criticism from administration defenders; David Kendall, Clinton's lawyer, once told him he had "a Woodward-Bernstein complex." That morning Vlasto told Mark Fabiani he might want a White House comment for the D'Amato story. While Vlasto was at a D'Amato hearing, a messenger showed up with a White House packet labeled "D'Amato Ethics Sampler"—a collection of clips about the New York senator's own history of ethical problems. Since Vlasto hadn't asked for the material or made any agreement about its use, ABC decided to mention that the White House had volunteered it.

Soon after the report on *World News Tonight*, McCurry, at Fabiani's insistence, made an angry call to Vlasto.

"You're never gonna work in this town again," McCurry said. "You've got to learn what background and off-the-record means." When Vlasto protested that he had made no such agreement, McCurry said he should assume that all material provided by Fabiani's office was on background. McCurry didn't stop there; he also complained to Vlasto's boss, Robin Sproul.

The White House was unhappy with ABC all year. *Nightline* kept revisiting the Whitewater saga, and its reporters soon learned that the administration was keeping count. "That's your twenty-first Whitewater story this year," an official would say, or "Well, that's twenty-two." When *Nightline* asked to spend the final days of the campaign with Clinton for an upbeat "72 Hours to Victory" piece, McCurry rejected the idea. McCurry sent word to Tom Bettag, *Nightline*'s executive producer, that he was unhappy with the steady stream of Whitewater programs. No one came out and said that Ted Koppel couldn't travel with Clinton because he had spent too much time on Whitewater; no one had to. The White House parceled out guests as if they were rewards for good behavior. For the moment, *Nightline* was in the doghouse.

McCurry was equally aggressive with Carl Cannon of the Baltimore *Sun*. Cannon was the second White House correspondent in his family—his father, Lou Cannon, had covered Ronald Reagan—and he had known and liked McCurry since the John Glenn campaign. But when Cannon wrote a piece for *The Weekly Standard* listing various untruths Clinton had uttered—just basic truth-squadding work, he felt—McCurry called his bureau chief, Paul West. "You've got a conservative working on your staff," McCurry said.

Cannon went to the press secretary's office to complain. "You should have called me first," McCurry said. "You essentially called the president of the United States a liar." But McCurry continued to deal with Cannon, and despite his urging, the president continued to call on him at news conferences.

McCurry's outspoken approach occasionally backfired. After radio talk-show host Don Imus caused a stir by skewering the Clintons over sex and Whitewater at a Washington dinner, McCurry called C-SPAN and urged the network not to replay the event. By attempting to squelch the raw routine, McCurry guaranteed C-SPAN one of its biggest audiences ever.

Most of the time, though, McCurry's sense of humor was his saving grace. No other press secretary had ever opened a briefing by saying, "All right, campers, what's on tap today? What should I wax poetic about?" Or: "You all look like a bunch of caged animals that have had nothing to eat all day long." Or placed a large paper bag over his head and begun the briefing as an anonymous official. Or described his own answers from the podium as "diplo-babble." And there is no record of any other presidential spokesman jumping into a Hollywood swimming pool with his clothes on to win a hundred-dollar bet. There were different tools in his survival kit, as he saw it, and the punch line was usually more effective than the right jab.

When William Safire, the old Nixon hand turned *New York Times* columnist, assailed Hillary Clinton in 1996 as "a congenital liar" over her explanations in the Whitewater affair, McCurry resisted the urge to respond with insults. Sure, he blasted the Safire column as an "outrageous personal attack that has no basis in fact." But he also served up the sound bite of the day: "The president, if he were not the president, would have delivered a more forceful response to that on the bridge of Mr. Safire's nose." Even Safire had to admit that McCurry had a nice instinct for the jocular.

When Clinton was about to go whitewater rafting on Wyoming's Snake River, McCurry got an anxious call from Ginny Terzano, a press aide on the trip. In photo-op terms it was a terrible idea. They both knew that White House reporters would be unable to resist the parallel to the Whitewater scandal. "Don't be defensive," McCurry said, feeding Terzano a line for Clinton's use.

Inevitably, a reporter in a passing raft shouted at the president: "What do you think of Whitewater now?" Clinton flashed a thumbs-up. "It's better when you have a paddle," he said, reading from the McCurry script. The quote made the next day's *New York Times*.

But McCurry's flip attitude was just as likely to get him in trouble. When Republicans were making an issue of unnamed White House aides who were granted security clearances despite past drug use, the press secretary tried to belittle the matter. "I was a kid in the 1970s," he said. "You know, did I smoke a joint from time to time? Of course I did." McCurry's instinct was right—thousands of politicians and government officials had inhaled back then—but for a White House that was professing grave concern over rising teenage drug use, his no-big-deal tone was precisely wrong. Newt Gingrich used the occasion to smack McCurry for his cavalier attitude. It was "as though every student in America this year ought to say, 'Well, I can be like Mike McCurry,'" Gingrich said.

Still, the chummy relationship with the press paid dividends, for there were times when reporters would protect McCurry from himself. At a Connecticut fundraiser in the spring of 1996, the president made a crack about a five-hundred-year-old Inca mummy that had just been discovered at the summit of a Peruvian volcano. "You know, if I were a single man, I might ask that mummy out," Clinton said. "That's a good-looking mummy."

Afterward, McCurry told the president this had not been a wise comment for a man with his reputation for philandering. Clinton snapped at him, and McCurry felt he needed a break from the boss.

On the ensuing flight to Milwaukee that night, he abandoned Air Force One to ride on the press charter.

There was much laughter on the flight. McCurry had a drink, and he was shooting the breeze with a dozen reporters clogging the aisle. One scribe asked about Clinton's appraisal of the mummy.

"Probably she does look good compared to the mummy he's been fucking," McCurry said.

Had one of the reporters published the remark, even with the expletive deleted, McCurry's tenure at the White House probably would have been over.

CHAPTER FOUR

First Blood

O<small>N</small> N<small>OVEMBER</small> 13, 1996, <small>EIGHT DAYS AFTER THE ELECTION</small>, Bill Clinton, Al Gore, Leon Panetta, Bruce Lindsey, and Mike McCurry gathered in the Oval Office and decided to inflict a serious wound on themselves.

It was not a noble gesture. The patient was getting sicker, and spilling blood now, they hoped, was a way to speed the recovery.

The assembled officials told the president that the controversy over improper donations by foreign businessmen, which had been successfully bottled up until the final weeks of the campaign, would soon spiral out of control. There were thousands of pages of documents, questionable memos, unexplained checks, all awaiting public scrutiny. They hadn't even looked at most of the material themselves. They were faced with two alternatives. One was to hunker down and wait for the congressional investigating committees to start pawing over the stuff next February. The other was to dump it all on the press and actively get out in front of the story. The president's men were recommending the latter course.

Clinton agreed. "Let's get the facts out," he said. "My only caution is, be careful. Don't give it out piecemeal so you have to backtrack.

As we've learned time and again, getting the information and then having to backtrack is a lot more painful than getting it right the first time."

The talk turned to whether there was time to do an exhaustive analysis of the fundraising documents before going public. But that would take far too long, since the White House and the DNC had only two lawyers assigned to the task. Their resources were limited. McCurry argued that the reporters would be fairer than the Republican committee staffers. They had learned during Whitewater that the committees would leak the most damaging tidbits for maximum partisan impact. Lindsey agreed that it was better to take the hit now than wait for Congress.

That meeting set in motion the scandalous disclosures that would dominate the headlines throughout the Thanksgiving and Christmas holidays. In a conversation a few weeks later, Clinton reflected on the difficulty of dealing with the press in the frenzy surrounding a complicated scandal.

"You've got to try to answer the questions, but you can't disgorge it all in a few days," he said. "Of course, then they beat you up for not telling the whole story. You just can't shovel all that shit out the door, because you've got to be careful that you don't put out anything wrong. Then you get beat up twice as bad." Clearly the president was still skeptical about this high risk strategy of attempting to cooperate with the press. McCurry had his work cut out for him.

Perhaps no one in the Oval Office gathering grasped how damaging the disclosures would be. They tended to look at the story as a series of isolated incidents: an improper contribution here, a brief meeting with the president there, a wealthy donor here spending the night in the Lincoln Bedroom. Each episode, they felt, could be adequately explained. After all, politicians had been sucking up to wealthy donors for decades. No political party could be expected to run full-scale background investigations on everyone who wanted to contribute. There had been no grand conspiracy, they believed, just sloppiness and bad judgments.

But the picture that emerged, piece by embarrassing piece, amounted to nothing less than the selling of the presidency. Political operatives raised money around the world, and especially in the Asian American community, with promises, explicit or otherwise, of White

House access. Large donors were rewarded with social gatherings at which they could lobby the president on pet issues. Favored contributors brought their business associates to meet the commander-in-chief. Some foreign companies without U.S. operations wrote campaign checks, a clear illegality, or laundered the money through employees and relatives, which was equally illegal. There was even a sliding scale: Those raising $10,000 to $25,000 were invited to large dinners with the president. Those who ponied up $50,000 to $100,000 were blessed with more intimate dinners or coffee with Clinton in the Map Room. Those who produced more than $500,000 got to ride on Air Force One, play a round of golf with Clinton, or bunk overnight at the White House. Responsible officials looked the other way while men like the former Commerce Department official John Huang shook the money tree, and everyone shared in the illicit fruit.

As the punishing headlines mounted, the president grew frustrated that the spotlight was trained exclusively on the Democrats. Why, he wondered, didn't the press point out that the GOP was equally guilty? The Republicans, after all, had also raised money abroad. Bob Dole's finance vice chairman, Simon Fireman, had even pleaded guilty to laundering $6 million of his workers' contributions through a Hong Kong bank, and yet that was kissed off as a minor story.

"How come they don't focus on the other side?" Clinton asked.

"Because you won and they didn't," McCurry replied.

Operation Candor began with an interview granted to *New York Times* reporter David Sanger, a specialist in Asian economics who had pitched McCurry by saying it looked as though some foreign business executives were exploiting their White House connections. McCurry figured Sanger would appreciate the nuances and would give the president fair treatment. McCurry himself would dish the same information—in six hours of grueling back-to-back briefings—to scribes for *The Washington Post, The Wall Street Journal,* the *Los Angeles Times,* and the Associated Press (who would all undoubtedly be pissed that *The New York Times* was getting an exclusive).

In the interview Clinton acknowledged that he had twice talked about policies toward Indonesia and China with James Riady, the high-powered executive whose family owned Indonesia's Lippo Group, which seemed to be at the center of the burgeoning scandal.

Policy was discussed. Now, for the first time, the president had conceded that Indonesians who gave big bucks to the party got more than just grip 'n' grin sessions; they got a crack, however brief, at influencing foreign policy. Still, at least the administration seemed to be getting out in front of the story rather than being dragged kicking and screaming to fess up.

That is, until Jeff Gerth called. A soft-spoken but tireless investigator who specialized in complicated financial matters, Gerth had achieved a modicum of fame as the *Times* reporter who had broken the Whitewater story in 1992. Two years later he had also helped reveal the tawdry tale of Hillary's commodities futures trading during the 1980s, in which she had quickly turned a $1,000 investment into $100,000 in trading guided by a prominent Arkansas executive. A short, balding man with sparse blond hair who preferred to toil in anonymity, Gerth didn't think reporters should sound off on television or even have bylines. When he called McCurry on the following Saturday, he made it clear that the paper was going to whack the White House for Bruce Lindsey's having previously characterized the Riady visit as "social."

"You're out to screw us," McCurry told Gerth. "Is this the thank-you note we get for getting you the interview?" Gerth thought the jab was totally inappropriate. Was he not supposed to do his job because the president had granted a colleague an audience? He felt his story was neither a thank you note nor a fuck you note.

McCurry insisted that Lindsey had been forthright. In a second conversation he gave Gerth a statement from Lindsey, insisting he had been candid about the meeting and that he had not withheld information from Jane Sherburne, one of the White House lawyers dealing with scandal management.

Gerth and his reporting partner, Stephen Labaton, agreed to hold up the story while they checked with Sherburne. She said that she and her colleague, Mark Fabiani, had objected to the description of the Riady meeting as "social," knowing that such an account would be challenged. Gerth called McCurry back on Monday with Sherburne's version of events. It was an unpleasant conversation. Gerth pressed McCurry to explain why, if Lindsey had been so forthright, McCurry hadn't offered a fuller version of the Riady meeting before now. McCurry abruptly ended the conversation by hanging up.

Gerth's story caused a major stir. A *Times* editorial called on Lindsey to resign. Clinton saw it as part of the media's continuing obsession with Lindsey, a taciturn, Zelig-like figure who seemed to pop up wherever there was trouble. The press viewed Lindsey as the keeper of the secrets. After all, he was Clinton's closest Arkansas confidant and had been named as an unindicted co-conspirator in the Whitewater case. Perhaps Lindsey's stubborn refusal to chat up reporters, in a White House filled with operatives who blabbed on background, added to the aura of suspicion toward him in the press corps.

The president professed to be puzzled by the intense focus on the Riady conversation. "I wish we had known this was going to be an issue when we did the interview because we would have told them more about it," he told McCurry. As if it weren't obvious that journalists would be fixated on the question of whether this fat-cat foreign donor was exerting behind-the-scenes influence.

McCurry, for his part, was steamed that the paper had portrayed Lindsey as evasive when it was Lindsey who had favored disclosure at the November 13 meeting and pushed for the *Times* interview in the first place. McCurry made this point to Gerth, who replied that he had quoted McCurry to that effect in the piece.

"Yeah, in paragraph 38: Here's the bullshit defense by the hired flack," McCurry said.

McCurry started telling other White House officials, even other reporters, that Gerth was waging a vendetta against Bruce Lindsey. The guy just had a hard-on for Lindsey, McCurry insisted. He told Margaret Carlson, a *Time* magazine columnist and quick-witted panelist on CNN's *Capital Gang*, that the *New York Times* story was overblown. He even gave Carlson a killer quote about Gerth trying to resurrect an inaccurate story. "I don't know why *The New York Times* is letting him play out this psychodrama in their pages," McCurry said. Carlson decided not to use the verbal slam. It was too personal.

But Carlson did take the reporters to task, criticizing them by name. The *Times* was in "a lather," she wrote, but "Fabiani has never confirmed that account. Sources close to Sherburne say that she never felt she had been overruled or lied to by Lindsey and that the *Times* torqued up a conflict."

This was the White House playing hardball, Gerth thought after reading Carlson's column. His story never said that Sherburne felt she had been overruled or lied to, just ignored. Gerth called Carlson to complain. He started yelling and demanded a written apology.

Carlson thought he was off the wall, that he was totally overreacting. She acknowledged having talked to McCurry and said she wished she'd called Gerth for comment, although she had tried to reach his editor. Gerth had Joe Lelyveld, the *Times*'s executive editor, complain to Walter Isaacson, *Time* magazine's managing editor.

Carlson, playing defense, got some help from the administration. Jack Quinn, the White House counsel, called Fabiani late one night and asked if he would talk to Carlson and work out some acceptable wording that would help vindicate her position. Fabiani shot back that he had already told Carlson the truth and if that wasn't good enough, he couldn't help her. He did talk to Carlson again but refused to disavow the *New York Times* account, which he thought illuminated a blunder that had hurt the administration's credibility. In the end, the magazine published a letter of complaint from the *Times* and a brief clarification. Carlson was furious at how the complaint had been handled.

But Gerth wasn't through. He called Mike McCurry and chewed him out. He threatened to complain to Erskine Bowles. To say he had a vendetta against Lindsey was to say he had malice, Gerth said, and that was the worst thing you could say about a reporter. The truth was he had written only two articles about Lindsey in five years. And here's something that will blow your mind, Gerth told McCurry. One of his neighbors was an attorney who represented Lindsey in the Whitewater trial. The lawyer had asked Gerth about getting some clips to prepare Lindsey's defense, and Gerth had helped him out.

McCurry tried to de-escalate the rhetoric. He apologized for accusing Gerth of a vendetta, and the conversation ended amicably. Gerth felt he had made his point. If McCurry was going to bad-mouth reporters behind their backs, he should at least know that some reporters fought back.

. . .

WHEN THE PHONE RANG AT 3:00 A.M., LANNY DAVIS THOUGHT something had happened to his mother. Or his kids. But it was the White House deputy counsel, Cheryl Mills. There was fresh damage to control.

It was the last Saturday of 1996, and Davis, a veteran political activist and failed congressional candidate in Montgomery County,

Maryland, had been working for Bill Clinton for just nineteen days. He had taken the job reluctantly. He hadn't even had the chance to talk to his old friend Bill or to Hillary, whom he had known since Yale Law School, about just what his duties would be. But Mike McCurry was desperate to get out from under the daily barrage of scandal questions. He was doing two jobs, was clearly overwhelmed. The White House needed a sharp-tongued attorney to replace Mark Fabiani, the Los Angeles operative who had handled Travelgate and Filegate and all the other gates so smoothly that McCurry dubbed him "my garbage man."

Davis, a dark-haired, bespectacled man with a perpetual five o'clock shadow and the taut manner befitting a onetime Amway salesman, had literally talked himself into the job. On his own initiative he had put himself forward on television talk shows like *Crossfire* and *Rivera Live* to defend Clinton against whatever accusations were hurled at him, and the president had called to express his gratitude. Davis had passed the audition. But what exactly was the part?

"Where does your job end and mine begin?" Davis asked McCurry.

The press secretary didn't miss a beat. "You know the expression Shit Happens?" he asked. "Well, when shit happens, it's your job."

Davis's wife didn't want him to leave his $725,000-a-year partner's perch at Patton, Boggs & Blow, a blue-chip Washington law firm whose members had included Ron Brown, the late commerce secretary. While he was mulling over the White House offer, word was leaked to *The Washington Post*'s "In the Loop" column that Davis had accepted the special counsel's job. Davis was convinced that McCurry was the leaker; he wasn't. But the planted item had its intended effect: Davis's clients began calling in droves. Suddenly, without quite making up his mind, Lanny Davis had agreed to serve as the chief presidential flak-catcher.

The son of a Jersey City dentist, Davis had learned firsthand about media scrutiny when he was a long-haired House candidate from Maryland in 1976. *The Washington Post* reported that he had failed to disclose $8,500 in campaign loans, part from members of his law firm and their wives, part from his parents. Then the paper carried GOP charges that he had taken laundered money by accepting a half-salary from Patton, Boggs while running for office. Davis fought back in bare-knuckles style, denouncing the "wild, undocumented charges" as a "smear."

Davis got another sobering lesson after his White House appointment, when *The New York Times* recounted the story of his failed venture as the owner of three weekly newspapers, which ended in litigation and millions of dollars in losses for Davis and his partners.

Once on the job, Davis soon learned how intensely competitive the White House beat was. All the reporters lived in fear of getting scooped. As one of them told him: "When you're covering something else and you get beat, no one knows it. When you're covering the White House and you get beat, your editor calls you at home."

But what ever happened to fairness? One day a *Chicago Tribune* reporter called him at 4:30 and asked a series of questions about a Democratic donor he'd never heard of. "I'm going with the story," the reporter declared. "Can you confirm or deny?"

Nerves were getting frayed in this overheated environment. Davis's philosophy on managing the news was simple: get it out early, and if it's bad, get it out even sooner. But how could you get a handle on this sprawling, hydra-headed money scandal that stretched all the way to Taiwan and Thailand? Every day there was a new, unpronounceable name, a new White House visit by some rich donor, a new crisis to defuse.

What bothered him most were the heavy-handed questions the reporters kept throwing at him. "Aren't you troubled by . . . ?" "You think it's appropriate that . . . ?" One reporter kept demanding, with thinly veiled disgust, "How can you say that?" They wanted him to characterize the transactions, to embrace their premise, to share their outrage. They seemed so sanctimonious. Why couldn't they ask the real questions: Was there a quid pro quo? Did the president change his policies in return for a contribution? Then he could flatly deny it. Instead there was this Kabuki dance between journalist and source about the shadowy issue of appearances. Not flat-out wrongdoing, but the appearance of wrongdoing. They wanted him to help connect the dots, and he wasn't willing to concede the shape of the picture.

Not that Davis hadn't made a few missteps. One day, late in the afternoon, he was ready to disclose that the Justice Department had in recent days issued subpoenas for a bunch of documents from the White House and presidential defense fund. Somebody handed him a list with thirty reporters' names on it and he made the calls, speaking as an unnamed official. But one New York newspaper reporter had been left off the list, while his rivals were notified. The reporter who missed the story called the next day. "You almost cost me my job," he said.

Now, in the grogginess of interrupted sleep, Davis tried to focus on the phone call that had rousted him out of bed. Cheryl Mills said she had just spoken to an extremely agitated Doris Matsui, Clinton's deputy director of public liaison and the highest-ranking Asian American in the White House. Matsui felt that Lanny Davis was hanging her out to dry.

Davis knew that the reason for her distress involved *The New York Times*. The previous afternoon Davis had been escorting his wife's parents on a public tour of the White House when his beeper went off. By the time he was able to return the call, it was 6:00 P.M. Tim Weiner, a *Times* investigative reporter, told Davis that the paper had some DNC documents laying out an election-year plan to raise an unprecedented $7 million from Asian Americans and to reward big donors by inviting them to White House events with Clinton. Worse, from Davis's vantage point, one memo indicated that Doris Matsui, who was also the wife of Representative Robert Matsui of California, had helped devise the strategy. The story was competitive, since the memo was among the three thousand pages of documents from the files of John Huang, the shadowy former DNC fundraiser, that had recently been given to the press. Weiner told Davis that the *Times* was going with the story as the right-hand lead of the next day's paper, the spot reserved for wars and assassinations and landmark legislation.

"How much time do I have?" Davis asked.

"About forty-five minutes," Weiner said.

Davis tried to reach Matsui but couldn't find her. Most everyone in the White House was off on Christmas vacation. What should he do? McCurry was visiting his wife's family in New Jersey. Davis had the White House signal operator track him down.

"Should I say no comment?" Davis asked.

"If you say no comment, it will look like we know what's up and aren't saying," McCurry said. "You gotta say we haven't read the documents and we'll comment when we're ready."

Davis called the reporter back with a noncommittal response. "We will review this document and have a reaction to it, if appropriate, in the next several days," he said.

Later that evening Davis called the *Times* and asked that the documents be faxed to him. He took them home and read them several times. If Matsui had seen and approved these papers, they clearly had a problem. That would bring the Asian money scandal, thus far confined to the DNC, into the heart of the White House. But it was midnight, and Davis decided not to call Matsui so late.

It turned out that Matsui and her husband were having dinner with their son in Palo Alto, California, where it was 9:00 P.M. *The Sacramento Bee* had called her for comment about the *Times* story, which had just come across the wire. Matsui was filled with outrage. The *Times* was supposed to be the paper of record, and no one had bothered to get her side. She called Cheryl Mills and demanded to know why Davis wasn't defending her. Congressman Matsui also thought the White House was abandoning his wife; that had triggered the 3:00 A.M. phone call from Mills. Davis immediately called Doris Matsui, who assured him that she had never seen the document in question and that she had had no role in the DNC's feverish drive to raise money from Asian Americans.

Matsui was beside herself. She was the ultimate straight arrow: she had been a high school cheerleader and valedictorian, had volunteered for the symphony and the public TV station and the Junior League back in Sacramento. She had been born in a California internment camp during World War II because her parents, who were also born in this country, were of Japanese descent, but she had never thought of herself as anything but American, had never been an ethnic activist, had never played the race card in what had been, until now, an unblemished career.

Davis wasn't sure whether Matsui was leveling with him, but he took her at her word and started working the phones. He called *The Sacramento Bee*, the hometown paper that Doris Matsui cared most about, and asked that the *Times* story be faxed to him. Aha! He thought he had found a mistake. The paper said that Matsui, along with Huang, had "helped create the fundraising strategy" as a member of the DNC's Asian Pacific American Working Group. That contradicted what Matsui had told him. Davis woke up Jack Quinn, the White House counsel, to clear his course of action. He called the *Bee* back with a statement, saying it was apparent that *The New York Times* had confused Matsui's role and the DNC's role. Then he phoned the Associated Press, got hold of the duty reporter, and read the same statement. He later strengthened it by dropping the word "apparent."

Sitting in his kitchen, Davis realized there was no hope of getting back to sleep. His two dogs were trying to get out, and his five cats, thinking it was morning, were demanding to be fed. Davis drove down to the White House at 7:00 A.M. He couldn't find a *New York Times* in the office, but the West Wing guard had one. Rereading the piece, he decided to go on the offensive. He set up a noon conference call with the White House scandal reporters, who were notified by beeper. It was the most efficient way that Davis could put out the official line, especially on a Saturday.

Just before noon Davis, clad in the classic Washington uniform of navy sports jacket, starched white shirt, and red power tie, walked into the upper press office, the inner West Wing sanctum a flight up from the briefing room. He slipped into a vacant office, called the president's secretary, Betty Currie, and asked her to start the conference call. When the call was over, Davis marched to the White House lawn, where he did one stand-up interview after another, boom boom boom. CBS, NBC, ABC, CNN. The White House, he said over and over, had nothing to do with the latest fundraising memo.

It was "a completely separate effort by the DNC," Davis told CNN. "Those two are kept separate for good reason, because federal employees are not supposed to raise money. And Mrs. Matsui did not raise money for the party or for the campaign."

"There was a clear separation between those activities of outreach and fundraising activities by the Democratic National Committee," Davis told CBS.

Davis returned to his office and saw McCurry. "How's it going?" McCurry asked.

"They all think *The New York Times* fucked up," Davis said, adding that the *Times* itself agreed that it had erred. "Is this a right-hand lead, page one, of *The New York Times?*" Davis asked. "Did they have to rush to do it?"

Davis was starving, but the White House mess was closed for the holidays. He walked two blocks west along G Street to the only open joint, a Subway, and ordered what he always ordered: tuna salad sub, bag of Fritos, and a Pepsi. His beeper went off. It was a *Washington Post* researcher, asking for some documents. The pager, which picked up hourly updates from Dow Jones, later flashed the erroneous headline "White House Violates Campaign Laws." Davis went back to the office and kept trying to beat back the story.

As it turned out, Davis was deluding himself. Like a good lawyer, he had zeroed in on a narrow weak point in the opposition's case. But the gist of the *Times* story was correct, whether or not Doris Matsui was involved. The foreign donations scandal was looking less like the overzealousness of a few John Huang types and more like an orchestrated effort with the Oval Office at its center. And the people involved knew full well they were pushing the legal envelope. The DNC had even issued a memo advising those who might be caught in the web of scandal: "Don't lie" (what a concept). "Announce an internal investigation, independent investigation or 'white paper' to examine the matter." (In other words, stall.) And, when all else fails: "Impugn the source."

The *Times* more or less conceded Davis's point in a short follow-up story, saying that the White House was insisting that Doris Matsui "did not improperly raise campaign money or directly participate in fund raising." Davis felt it wasn't enough. Tim Weiner agreed that the story was not as clear as it should have been and that the paper shouldn't have published until he had gotten hold of Matsui.

Doris Matsui was devastated. She had never made a single fund-raising phone call, not even for her husband's campaigns. The *Times* may have retreated on the story, but more than forty newspapers had carried the original article without running the follow-up. CNN had shown pictures of her all day. "It took me fifty years to build my reputation," Matsui told her husband. "I guess I have another twenty to rebuild it."

The *Los Angeles Times* and *USA Today* both ran pieces on the DNC fundraising memo. It was obvious to those at the White House that a tone of outrage was creeping into such stories. "It is becoming increasingly evident as each week goes by that Clinton was a major participant in the Democratic Party's efforts—some of it in violation of federal law prohibiting foreign contributions—to raise an enormous war chest for the 1996 presidential election campaign," the *L.A. Times* said.

McCurry was reduced to telling the paper that he and his crew were no Watergate-style conspirators. "We are taking hits now that we were conniving, Nixonian stonewallers only because we were in the middle of a national campaign and we didn't have the resources to respond to this story," he said. But the press wasn't buying McCurry's line. The next day *The Washington Post* ran a screaming, six-column headline on the burgeoning scandal. "A network of Democratic fund-raisers and donors with foreign connections appears to have traded on their access to President Clinton to boost their business dealings, unchecked by a White House determined not to lose an election for lack of cash," the story said.

McCurry's defense was less than ringing. He was quoted as saying the administration was "not scrupulous or strict enough" in checking the backgrounds of guests brought to White House functions.

Slowly, almost imperceptibly, McCurry was being tarred with the muck of scandal. Though he had had no role in the financial shenanigans, he was the public face of the administration, the guy most Americans kept seeing on television, the man who had to keep explaining it all away. His genial spokesman routine, keeping an ironic, sometimes jocular distance form the daily drip of disclosures, was wearing thin.

The gravity of the situation suddenly hit home when a *New York Times* editorial whacked him upside the head. Describing the Clinton White House as unable to tell the truth simply and promptly, the paper declared that McCurry, as "the press secretary assigned to defend the stonewall," had been "left with his reliability in tatters."

McCurry moped around his office for two days after that single sentence sliced into his self-image. Now he understood how Bill and Hillary felt. This was just one hit. Imagine getting pilloried two, three, four times a week, as they routinely did, your personal and professional ethics savaged. The press seemed to lose sight of the fact that these were flawed human beings, and the attacks stung. Now McCurry knew how it felt. For the first time in twenty years in public relations, his personal credibility was being questioned, and it hurt.

.   .   .

McCurry HAD LITTLE TIME TO FEEL SORRY FOR HIMSELF. HE SOON found himself trying to manage the administration's Charlie Trie problem—one that quickly underscored the far-reaching nature of what he was up against. Jack Quinn, the White House counsel, and Evelyn Lieberman, the deputy chief of staff, visited McCurry to brief him about the trouble at the president's legal defense fund, the trust set up to raise money for Clinton's bills in the Whitewater case and the sexual harassment suit by Paula Jones. The trust, it turned out, had had its own dealings with Yah Lin "Charlie" Trie, a Taiwan-born businessman whom Clinton had gotten to know while frequenting his Fu Lin restaurant, with its garish red decor, in Little Rock. Back in March—during the heart of the presidential campaign, when the news really would have been damaging—Trie had shown up with two manila envelopes containing $640,000 for the fund. But the checks were highly suspect—some came from foreigners, some from people who seemed unable to afford the $1,000 donation, and some bearing similar handwriting. All the money had to be returned.

Did the White House know? McCurry wondered. Yes, he was told, Michael Cardozo, the fund's executive director, had briefed Hillary Clinton and Harold Ickes, the other deputy chief of staff, back in April.

The following month, in a meeting in the first lady's conference room, Evelyn Lieberman told Cardozo, Ickes, Bruce Lindsey, and others that the press would describe the donors, members of a Taiwan-based sect who drank the bathwater of Supreme Master Suma Ching Hai, as crazed cultists. She scribbled some tabloid headlines: "Buddhist Cult Contributes Half Mil to Clinton Fund!" "Followers Drink Bathwater!" The donations remained under wraps.

As McCurry listened, the details got worse. No one at the legal defense fund had bothered to tell the DNC about Trie's funny money, thereby exposing the Democratic Party to the same sort of improper fundraising. And Trie, his relatives, and his company had given the party $210,000 over the previous three years. What's more, Clinton had appointed Trie to a U.S.–Pacific trade commission less than four weeks after he delivered the improper checks to the defense fund. And to top it off, Trie had visited the White House twenty-three times.

The question, Quinn and Lieberman said, was whether to make all this public now. The defense fund didn't have to file its next disclosure report until February. Would it be better to wait?

No way, McCurry said. Far better to put out the embarrassing story now, Trie and all. NBC was already poking around on Asian American contributions to the defense fund. They had to bite the bullet. Quinn and Lieberman conveyed the advice to Cardozo, who agreed to go public the following Monday.

On the morning of December 16, 1996, Michael Cardozo briefed reporters on Trie and the $640,000. The press went wild. Why hadn't this been disclosed earlier? Why wasn't the DNC told? Who else in the White House knew?

McCurry got hammered during the afternoon gaggle. But he refused the repeated invitations to criticize Trie, who, it turned out, had been at a White House Christmas party the previous Friday.

"It appears that an old friend of the president tried to lend some assistance to a president and a first lady who have a great deal of legal debt accumulated," McCurry said. "That's the fact. The appearance is someone else's judgment to make."

The briefing grew testy as McCurry bobbed and weaved.

Why was Trie appointed to the presidential trade commission?

That was in the works before he delivered any money.

Why didn't the White House refer the case to prosecutors?

Ask Michael Cardozo.

Is the president concerned that his old friend was trying to corrupt the United States government?

No.

Why not disclose the names of the donors?

That's up to Cardozo.

How often has Trie been to the White House?

Ask Lanny Davis.

What did Clinton and Trie discuss at the party?

"The president told me earlier today that he had a very brief conversation with him that was personal in nature," McCurry said.

The next day Clinton was scheduled to appear at a photo opportunity with the Irish prime minister, John Bruton. It was time for what McCurry called the "pre-brief." On any day that Clinton would be within shouting range of journalists, McCurry and a handful of other senior aides gathered around his desk in the Oval Office and ran through a pre-brief, preparing him for possible queries. Even if the day's only public event was a fleeting photo op with a foreign dignitary, McCurry felt the boss had to be ready in case a reporter fired off a question.

Lanny Davis, then in his second week on the job, joined the morning session in the Oval Office with Gore, Panetta, and McCurry, who began asking mock questions in a reporter's voice. The press, he said, would ask about Trie's attendance at the Christmas party.

"Well, Mr. President," McCurry intoned, "don't you think you should be more careful about who you let in the White House? Who's responsible for letting Trie into that party at the White House Friday night?"

"Shit," Clinton said, "this guy comes through the line to me and Hillary, says, 'I'm sorry, Mr. President, I didn't mean to embarrass you,' and he leaves." The staffers all looked at each other, speechless. Davis said that Charlie Trie had really been hung out to dry, had been depicted in the press as a disreputable character. The question was whether Clinton should say that Trie was an innocent man—he hadn't been charged with anything—or should subtly distance himself, saying that if Trie had done anything wrong, he didn't approve.

Clinton said he preferred to say that it was important to get all the facts out, but that Trie was an old friend and no one should rush to judgment.

"If you feel that, you ought to say that," McCurry said.

Nine times out of ten, McCurry thought, Clinton had the right instinct on how to answer questions, but he had a tendency to ramble. He could imagine Clinton saying, "Oh, I used to eat at that guy's restaurant and he serves the best dim sum," and then launching into a series of unguarded comments. McCurry usually suggested that he cut his remarks by two-thirds. It was his job to help the president understand how even a casual comment would play in the press.

Clinton was terse at the picture-taking session. He said that Trie was an old friend but that he didn't know about the $640,000 in checks until his wife and Harold Ickes were told. As for returning the money, he said, "I supported the decision. . . . Even any appearance of impropriety should be removed."

The pounding continued for days. Brit Hume of ABC demanded to know why White House officials had not called in the Justice Department to investigate Trie's $640,000 donation. That was the defense fund's call, McCurry insisted. "But, Mike, you had a matter that did involve the president, to the extent that he was informed about it. . . . This is not something that happened on Mars," Hume said.

"The body that conducted the investigative work, that would have to make that judgment, is the trust. . . . We make no judgment," McCurry replied.

Privately McCurry conceded to reporters—almost always under the protective cloak of background—that these events smelled less than kosher. It was important for his credibility that they knew that he knew what was going on, that he was not just mindlessly parroting the company line. From the podium, however, McCurry tried not to characterize even the slimiest of events. He didn't want to look unconcerned or overly concerned. His own spin, he felt, mattered little. What the gaggle wanted was for him to dismiss the day's hot story with some flip remark that would become part of the permanent lore. Sort of like when Ron Ziegler brushed off the Watergate break-in as a "third-rate burglary." Clinton had taken the bait a few months earlier when it turned out that two White House operatives were collecting FBI files on prominent Republicans. "A completely honest bureaucratic snafu," the president had declared, a phrase that was invoked again and again as the plot thickened. Reporters loved to get you on record with something dumb and pillory you later as they pursued their grand conspiracy theories.

But more than semantics was at stake. When McCurry ducked questions by directing reporters to Lanny Davis or Michael Cardozo or the Justice Department, he wasn't simply passing the buck. He was not a journalist out to learn whatever he could. He needed protection. There were answers he did not want to know.

If a reporter asked him, for example, whether Clinton had knocked on the door of the Lincoln Bedroom after midnight and taken a $50,000 donation from a guest, McCurry wouldn't just walk into the Oval and ask whether it was true. For all he knew, Clinton might say, "Sure, I tucked it into the pocket of my bathrobe." Then McCurry would be a potential witness who might have to testify on the Hill or before a grand jury. He had made that mistake with Pete Williams; he would not make it again. If Clinton answered the incriminating question, McCurry would no longer be able to plead ignorance with the press. What the president needed was a lawyer to gather the facts, someone who would be covered by attorney-client privilege. Then

McCurry could cite the lawyer's findings to the press without being personally exposed. He made a practice of taking few notes, just scribbling on his phone message slips and throwing them away each day. Notes could be subpoenaed.

From the White House point of view, McCurry was the radar system, the man most likely to find out if a big story was brewing. That made him the bearer of bad news, the one who pressed for an official response. One day a rumor swept the White House that Bob Woodward was about to unload a blockbuster about Democratic donors receiving various goodies. It fell to McCurry to check with his sources at *The Washington Post*. In this case, no such piece was imminent.

But this was a war with many fronts. He got a call from another *Post* investigative reporter, Michael Weisskopf, with whom he had been fencing for weeks. When Weisskopf asked for a list of guests who had stayed in the Lincoln Bedroom, McCurry promised to check. He called back and rejected the request, saying, "This is President Clinton's private home, and what he does in his private home is not public business." When Weisskopf asked for a list of friends and associates who had flown with Clinton on Air Force One, the press secretary refused to provide it. McCurry said he was swamped with requests from the *Post* and other papers, but that no one else could help because he was the only official authorized to deal with these inquiries. The much-touted policy of full disclosure, it seemed, went only so far. But this approach didn't always work. Weisskopf and a colleague got three weeks' worth of White House ushers' logs from a congressional committee and wrote a story about high rollers moving through the Lincoln Bedroom like some hot-sheets motel.

Now Weisskopf had learned that Trie had once brought an international arms dealer to the White House. The Chinese weapons merchant, Wang Jun, had met Clinton at a White House coffee the previous February.

McCurry's initial reaction was dismissive. "There are Chinese here every day in the White House," he said. "The Chinese defense minister, Chi Haotian, is here right now. What's the big deal?"

When Weisskopf made clear that he would not be dissuaded by flip remarks, McCurry checked and came back with a serious reply. "The president had no idea who Wang was," he said. "If anyone had any clue, we would have strongly advised against him being invited."

Four days after the Cardozo briefing, the *Post* weighed in with a front-page story: "DNC Fundraiser Gained White House Access for Chinese Arms Dealer." The White House was on the defensive again.

Clinton confirmed the obvious when he spoke to reporters after introducing several Cabinet nominees. He said his meeting with the Chinese weapons official had been "clearly inappropriate," but that he remembered "literally nothing" about it. McCurry, meanwhile, cast his boss as merely a gracious host extending his warm wishes to holiday revelers. "All of us, you know, enjoy entertaining friends and family and relatives and others in our home," he told the gaggle.

But why was it that big-time financial supporters kept showing up at the White House? "Is he supposed to invite his enemies?" McCurry asked.

In the seclusion of his office, McCurry knew there were only two possible explanations for Charlie Trie slipping Wang Jun into that meeting: He brought his friends in because he was doing big deals with them and wanted to impress them with how much stroke he had with the president of the United States. Or, more charitably, he had been Clinton's buddy for a long time and wanted his friends to meet him. But he couldn't say that in public.

From McCurry's standpoint, the story had turned into a feeding frenzy, pure and simple. No, it was more than that; it was advocacy journalism. The media, in their wisdom, had collectively decided that what happened in 1996 showed that the campaign finance system was broken and needed to be fixed. That's why a dozen investigative reporters were poring over every check and looking under every rock, to make the case that the system had collapsed. Every story therefore added to the pressure for campaign finance reform. Every column and editorial had to denounce the cash-crazed nature of the Clinton fundraising effort.

In the face of this organized outrage, McCurry was following a rope-a-dope strategy. He was taking the punches without swinging back, letting the reporters vent their frustrations by beating up on him. This, after all, was what they had embarked upon at the November 13th meeting: take the hits now, let the journalists draw a little blood, and all this would be considered old news by the time Congress weighed in after the inauguration.

CHAPTER FIVE

The Seeds of Paranoia

IF BILL CLINTON HAD AN ACHILLES HEEL, HIS STAFF FELT, IT was his tendency to go off half-cocked about the press. They had all seen it happen. The problem, Mike McCurry told people, was that Clinton thought the press was engaged in a "global conspiracy" to ruin his life. The president invariably got himself into trouble when he slipped into self-pitying mode. During a post-election visit to Australia, as the campaign finance scandal was beginning to heat up, the president even compared himself to Richard Jewell, the man falsely accused in the bombing at the Summer Olympics in Atlanta, as if Clinton were some innocent overweight security guard being hounded by breathless reporters. Mike McCurry winced when Clinton mentioned Jewell's name, knowing that the reporters would pounce on the ludicrous comparison and that the rest of the day's message would be utterly lost.

Blaming the press for his setbacks was a deeply ingrained Clinton trait. In the fall of 1980, when the voters of Arkansas made him the youngest ex-governor in America, journalists were quick to feel his wrath.

On New Year's Day 1981, Clinton called Bill Simmons, the AP

bureau chief in Little Rock and a renowned straight shooter. The governor sounded as though he had been drinking. Clinton screamed that Simmons had cost him the election. That was absurd, Simmons said, but Clinton wouldn't quit. Invoking a fellow Democratic politician, Jim Guy Tucker, Clinton said: "Tucker warned me to watch out for you. He said you gotta watch out for Simmons, he'll fuck you." Then Clinton hung up.

The governor even chided David Broder when the venerable *Washington Post* columnist stopped by for breakfast at the mansion toward the end of Clinton's lame-duck tenure. Broder had named the governor in *Parade* magazine as the up-and-coming politician most likely to become president one day, and opponents had seized upon this as evidence that he viewed Little Rock as a mere stepping stone. "You really caused me a lot of problems with that goddamn *Parade* piece," Clinton said.

If Clinton had little use for many Arkansas journalists, the feeling in some quarters was mutual. "We beat him," crowed John Robert Starr, the curmudgeonly managing editor of the *Arkansas Democrat*, after the 1980 election. "He was an arrogant, no-good son of a bitch. . . . A dirty, rotten scoundrel."

. Paul Greenberg, editor of the *Pine Bluff Commercial*, assailed Clinton so relentlessly that his favorite nickname—"Slick Willie"—stuck like flypaper.

Meredith Oakley, a *Democrat* columnist, once began a piece by writing: "His word is mud." Clinton called Oakley after a particularly harsh column and "proceeded to spew this invective and blasphemy," she recalls. "He accused me of coming after him with raw malice. I promised him that henceforth I would cook it well done."

John Brummett, a columnist for the now-defunct *Arkansas Gazette*, was Clinton's best friend in the press, sort of his Boswell. But they, too, had a falling out as Brummett grew fed up "with his double talk, trying to please everyone."

After he regained the governor's office in 1982, Clinton came to view the press as a necessary evil. He made himself extraordinarily accessible to the state capitol reporters, whose first-floor pressroom overlooked his spot in the parking lot. They would grab him in the hallway to talk about this or that bill, and on Friday afternoons he would stick his head in the pressroom door and ask, "You guys need anything else?" Often they just wanted him to keep quiet so they could finish their stories and go home. Clinton even began to brief John Robert Starr about upcoming initiatives in an effort to neutralize him.

But the good feelings didn't last. Clinton would often become testy when challenged at news conferences. On a slow day the reporters might pursue an aggressive line of questioning, figuring that the governor would blow up and they'd have themselves a story.

During the 1992 presidential campaign, Clinton once again came to feel that he was being brutalized by the press. At first many political reporters swooned over the young governor, anointing him as the front-runner. But they soon savaged him when Gennifer Flowers, a former Arkansas state employee, accused him of a twelve-year extramarital affair in a story she sold to the *Star* supermarket tabloid. The reporters also pounced on Clinton's shifting stories about whether he had dodged the draft during the Vietnam War and his belated admission that he had in fact once tried marijuana. These stories, along with the first reports on Whitewater, the convoluted Arkansas land deal that Clinton and his wife had trouble explaining, drove some columnists into outright opposition. "I think he deserves to be knocked out of the race," declared Mike McAlary of the *New York Post*. "Everyone seems to agree this guy is a fraud." Both the candidate and Hillary felt badly burned by this searing coverage, and the scars never quite healed.

Clinton was particularly furious over a Jeff Gerth story that appeared just three weeks after the *New York Times* reporter had broken the news about the Whitewater deal. The front-page story, published in the midst of the New York primary campaign, said that Clinton had weakened a 1988 Arkansas ethics law to exempt himself and his wife from having to disclose conflicts of interest. John King, a burly AP political reporter, was summoned to the governor's Manhattan hotel room so the campaign could explain that the *Times* had totally misinterpreted the law. George Stephanopoulos and Paul Begala, another top campaign strategist, were there, but King was stunned to see Clinton raging out of control. "Look at this piece of shit," Clinton roared, throwing down a copy of the *Times*. "This story is a fucking piece of shit!"

"Governor, do you want a minute to calm down?" King asked.

"You want me to step outside?" Finally Hillary appeared, pulled her husband out of the room, and settled him down. Clinton eventually persuaded King he had done all he could do with the ethics law.

The candidate remained convinced that the press would not give him a break. One night a few weeks later, King and CNN's Gene Randall listened helplessly on the campaign plane for forty-five minutes as Clinton rambled on about policy minutiae. They were tired, and he was driving them crazy with his endless monologue. Finally Randall tried to wind things down by asking Clinton what books he had been reading. A few other reporters wandered by as Clinton answered.

The New York Times later reported that "there is a weariness to Mr. Clinton these days," an effort with reporters "to direct the talk to safe subjects, like 'The Prince of Tides' and 'One Hundred Years of Solitude,' two of his favorite books."

That morning Clinton walked by John King's seat on the plane, held the *Times* article about nose high, paused for effect, and dropped it in his lap.

"See what I mean?" he said.

Despite his misgivings, Clinton had been carefully cultivating a small group of younger, New Democrat–style reporters and columnists, such as Joe Klein of *New York* magazine, E. J. Dionne of *The Washington Post*, and Ron Brownstein of the *Los Angeles Times*, who helped shape elite opinion. He was particularly taken with the centrist argument of Dionne's book, *Why Americans Hate Politics*, which he often cited on the campaign trail. Such writers had a way of shaping the national debate because their columns and books were influential with other reporters and television producers.

Joe Klein was a particular object of flattery. In one of their first conversations, Clinton told the bearded columnist he agreed with his view that teachers' unions were ruining efforts to save public education. He said he had sent one of Klein's columns to dozens of his friends and had even mentioned Klein's work in one of his speeches. When Klein was riding in Clinton's car after a campaign event in Harlem and got into a shouting match with Harold Ickes, who was running the New York campaign, Clinton made a point of telling him: "I want you to know I always respect your opinion."

Some of these favored reporters naturally came to feel that they would have access to Clinton in the White House, perhaps be invited over to kick around ideas. After he won the presidency, however, Clinton no longer bothered with his formerly favorite journalists, and he neglected the centrist themes that had won their admiration. They felt cut off from the administration and had little sense of Clinton's thinking. A decade earlier Ronald Reagan had been buoyed by a cheerleading squad of conservative columnists, but Clinton shut out those who were naturally sympathetic to him. "All of them came to the conclusion that the schmoozing was fake and they had all been pawns in his campaign," a Clinton friend said. Klein seemed to turn on Clinton with a vengeance. He wrote a cover story for *Newsweek*, his new employer, accusing the president of practicing "the politics of promiscuity," tying Clinton's alleged philandering to his perpetual fudging on issues.

One exception was Sidney Blumenthal of *The New Yorker*. Both the president and Hillary stayed in touch with Blumenthal, an unabashed Clinton booster who was only too happy to offer private advice. Blumenthal disdained so-called "objective" reporters and fancied himself a political prognosticator of the old school, an elite columnist in the mode of Walter Lippmann and James Reston who would inform his readers through his access to the powerful. He made no bones about his pro-Clinton views. He dismissed the Whitewater affair as insignificant and refused to write about it; Tina Brown, the magazine's editor, had to assign the scandal to another reporter. But the warm relationship did the Clintons little good. Blumenthal was widely ridiculed among journalists, dismissed as being "in the tank" for Clinton. In the newsroom culture of the 1990s, being sympathetic to a politician was cause for disdain. Blumenthal fell out of favor with Tina Brown, who eventually dumped him as Washington correspondent, replacing him with Michael Kelly of *The New York Times*, one of Clinton's harshest critics.

The president, for his part, could not control his temper when reporters antagonized him, when they dared pose questions that he found unfair. He lashed out time and again in public settings. He castigated ABC's Brit Hume for daring to suggest that politics had played a role in the selection of Supreme Court Justice Ruth Bader Ginsburg. He ripped off his microphone and abruptly ended an interview in Prague with NBC's Jim Miklaszewski after the reporter asked two questions about Whitewater instead of about Clinton's European trip. "I don't know why we talk to reporters if they're not interested in what we're doing," he told Dee Dee Myers. "Why do they bother to come? Why don't they just stay home if this is all they care about?"

Clinton was increasingly frustrated by the media's insistence on pursuing its own agenda rather than the issues he was trying to stress. In a 1993 interview with Jann Wenner and William Greider of *Rolling Stone*, he fumed about not getting "one damn bit of credit" from "the knee-jerk liberal press." This was an odd complaint from a Democratic president, but it underscored his view that the press was part of an insular, ideologically rigid establishment that found it easy to dismiss an Arkansan with an unorthodox approach to politics.

It was a vicious cycle: Clinton kept whining in public about his treatment by the press, which prompted more stories about his struggling presidency. In an odd sort of way, Clinton had more respect for his political enemies than for the men and women who wrote about him; at least the pols had conviction. He particularly admired Mary Matalin, who had savaged him when she worked for President Bush and continued to denounce him on her CBS radio show. "She's the only one who was loyal to George Bush," Clinton said a few days after greeting Matalin at a reception. "She was kicking the shit out of me every day when some of those Bush people were bailing out and dumping on the campaign. I've been in those ditches where it's cold and lonely." Even pit-bull Republicans understood loyalty, Clinton felt, while journalists were interested only in the next big story, no matter who got hurt.

Eventually, however, Clinton felt compelled to seek a rapprochement. By the middle of 1994, with his presidency in deep trouble and flailing for direction, he turned to his antagonists for advice. Top correspondents were invited in small groups for iced tea and cookies on the White House patio. There was a two-and-a-half-hour bagel breakfast with Brit Hume, Rita Braver, Andrea Mitchell, and Wolf Blitzer. In each gathering Clinton said he had made mistakes and was searching for ways to get his message out. If he believed everything that was written and broadcast about him, he wouldn't support himself either. He asked some of the journalists what they would do in a similar predicament. A few offered words of advice. But the advice was less important than the symbolism of Clinton reaching out to some of his strongest critics, searching for some middle ground.

For all his sensitivity to his media image, Clinton was in some ways curiously disconnected. Unlike many Americans, he didn't watch the evening news. Clinton occasionally called a longtime friend from his gubernatorial days, Rick Kaplan, executive producer of ABC's *World News Tonight*, a few minutes after the 6:30 program began, just wanting to chat. He seemed slightly surprised when Kaplan told him he was running a live newscast and would have to call him back.

After the Republicans won both houses of Congress in 1994, the president had little choice but to reconnect with the press, for he could no longer play the inside game of working quietly with Democratic leaders to get things done. The only way he could influence public debate was through exhortation, and he couldn't simply give speeches again and again. He needed the bank shot of friendly media coverage to give his words resonance. He needed the very journalists he had disdained. He began granting interviews to reporters like Ron Brownstein and E. J. Dionne, once calling Dionne at home to ask for advice on a speech; the columnist said that he didn't feel comfortable advising a president, but the two chatted amiably about Clinton's ideas.

Still there were flashes of the old temper, as when Clinton lashed out at Bill Plante of CBS and Paul Bedard of *The Washington Times* for pressing him about the scandal involving the firing of the White House travel office staff. Clinton later apologized, but at times like this his disdain for journalists was palpable.

"The press runs the government," Clinton told Dick Morris. "They like to destroy people. That's how they get their rocks off." But he would also scream at a staffer he suspected of leaking, accusing the person of trying to "blow his own horn to look oh so smart and oh so good to some journalist."

Morris encouraged Clinton in his jaundiced view of the press. After all, Morris, who had to quit the 1996 campaign after the supermarket tabloids revealed his relationship with a high-priced prostitute, had suffered his own humiliation in the media. After being dropped from the Democratic payroll, however, Morris continued to advise his old friend regularly by telephone. A short man with an untamed shock of graying hair and a high-pitched voice, he often gave the impression of being dazzled by his own brilliance. His sweeping analysis of press behavior contained an ample dose of paranoia, or at least the conviction that journalists were as ideological and agenda-driven as he was.

Clinton particularly despised *The New York Times* for the intensity of its Whitewater coverage. He hadn't given the paper an interview in a long time, and its reporters felt under great pressure to secure one.

Early in the campaign Morris met secretly with Joseph Lelyveld, the paper's executive editor; Andrew Rosenthal, the Washington editor; and Alison Mitchell at the Jefferson Hotel. Clinton had finally agreed to an interview with reporter Todd Purdum for a *Times Magazine* profile; Lelyveld was pushing for a second interview for an upcoming series evaluating the president's record. Lelyveld mentioned in passing that the public was tired of the endless excavation of ancient Arkansas events. Lelyveld often observed that the arcane Whitewater scandal might not amount to much in the end. That didn't mean the paper should lay off the story, he believed, for dropping it would itself be a political judgment.

Still, Morris was certain that Lelyveld was sending an important signal, that all good liberals had to end their quarreling and unite behind Clinton. Morris and Clinton convinced themselves, virtually without evidence, that *The New York Times* had called a cease-fire to ensure that the president would be reelected. This was a spectacularly uninformed reading of the way reporters functioned, as if Jeff Gerth or Alison Mitchell would somehow agree to be defanged to help a presidential candidate. But it was perfectly in sync with the consultant's Machiavellian view of journalistic conduct. And so Morris relayed Lelyveld's comment to Clinton, who softened his view and, at Morris's urging, gave the *Times* the second interview.

Shortly before the Oval Office session, Todd Purdum went to see Morris.

"What should I ask him?" Purdum said.

"Do me a favor," Morris said. "Ask him what the theme of his presidency is, because he needs it to focus his own defense of his record." Morris later rushed to tell the president what he and Purdum had discussed. He thought it was a great coup when the reporter asked those very questions and Clinton knocked them out of the park. Purdum, for his part, was pleased that Morris had been so indiscreet as to suggest that the boss lacked a political compass.

In the end Morris viewed the press as akin to the old *Pravda*, publishing the party line—that of the Press Party—and thinking they were conning the electorate. The journalists saw everything through a certain prism—congressional, diplomatic, military, or regulatory—and had little feel for real life. But the public lived outside this artificial box. Readers and viewers, he felt, had learned how to decode the propaganda. When Clinton made what was typically dismissed as a "small-bore" proposal—say, cutting closing costs on federally insured mortgages—it might get ten seconds on one network, a couple of short articles in the major papers, slightly better play in the regional press. But Morris's pollsters would find that perhaps half of those surveyed had heard of the initiative. People would rummage through the garbage and find what was meaningful to them. The snotty tone of the journalists didn't matter. Clinton didn't need to co-opt reporters like Kennedy, deceive them like Johnson, or intimidate them like Nixon. He had found a way to triumph politically, get legislation passed, communicate with the country, and win a place in history, all without the aid of the press. Devoting endless hours to shaping coverage of this or that story might be necessary in the short term, but it was largely irrelevant over the long haul. As he and the president had proved during the campaign, bad press didn't matter because most people believed Clinton was on their side and simply didn't trust the journalists.

And so, as Inauguration Day approached, Clinton grew increasingly detached from his press coverage. Morris would mention a front-page *Washington Post* story, and more often than not, Clinton hadn't seen it. "I make the news; why do I need to read the news?" he asked Morris.

The president was learning that if he allowed himself to bathe in the negative headlines, the experience would distort his judgment and get him in trouble. He made no distinction between John Harris or Peter Baker or Alison Mitchell or James Bennet; he knew only that *The Washington Post* and *The New York Times* were basically hostile toward him. If McCurry wanted him to hold off-the-record meetings with small groups of reporters, he would do it as part of the job, but he was growing bored with the process. He didn't need them.

.   .   .

IF THE PRESIDENT WAS FED UP WITH THE PRESS AND ITS PREDILECTION for scandal and gossip, his feelings were constantly reinforced by his wife. Hillary Rodham Clinton was perhaps the most influential first lady in modern history, but she was also the most controversial and relentlessly publicized, a status that quickly created a tense relationship with the journalists who analyzed her every move and change in hairstyle. Hillary was famously wary of giving interviews. In fact, when she traveled in the United States, she wouldn't allow reporters to fly on her plane. The plane was her sanctuary; she liked to unwind in the front cabin and didn't want to feel any pressure to chat with journalists in the back. The reporters could make their own reservations and try to keep up with her. This aloof stance drove Hillary's aides crazy. They begged her to change her mind. They knew their boss as a warm and funny woman who was revered around the globe, who could charm the pants off reporters if only she would let down her steely guard. Of course, these same aides recognized that Hillary's prickly attitude toward the media was at the heart of her image problem, the reason she had the highest negative poll ratings of any first lady in modern history. Her narrow, lawyerlike answers on the mounting Whitewater and Travelgate inquiries clearly made it look as if she had something to hide. She tried to put certain areas off-limits during her rare interviews, shying away from unscripted encounters where her self-deprecating sense of humor might shine through. She often seemed cold and defensive. She had been through five years of searing press scrutiny and she hated the loss of privacy. The bruises were showing.

But in the final days of November 1996, with the long reelection campaign behind them, things were looking up. Hillary Clinton was in a good mood as she embarked on a twelve-day swing around the world. Two reporters, Ann Blackman of *Time* and Martha Brant of *Newsweek*, were the only journalists to accompany the first lady on the entire trip, having been promised extensive access to Hillary and an on-the-record interview. On the first leg of the trip, in Sydney, Australia, the first lady got a rousing reception at a speech to professional women. In response to a question, she joked that the only way a president's wife could escape from politics was "to totally withdraw and perhaps put a bag over your head, or somehow make it clear that you have no opinions and no ideas about anything—and never express them, publicly or privately." As the audience cheered, Clinton continued: "There is something about the position itself which raises in Americans' minds concerns about hidden power, about influence behind the scenes, about unaccountability. . . . I think the answer is to just be who you are." The press would play it as a self-pitying declaration of independence, but Hillary's staff thought it was a home run, that her candor had charmed the hell out of the audience.

A few hours after the speech, as the two reporters stood on the Sydney airport runway waiting for the plane that would take them to Thailand, Marsha Berry, Hillary's communications director, walked over to them. "Mrs. Clinton wants to see you in her car," she announced.

"This isn't it, is it?" Blackman asked.

"You take it when you can get it," Berry replied.

Clearly Hillary was trying to keep the reporters off balance by springing the interview when they weren't prepared. Blackman grabbed her tape recorder, and she and Brant slipped into the back seat of the limousine with the first lady. Marsha Berry and Melanne Verveer, Hillary's deputy chief of staff, also squeezed into the back. The reporters sat on the jump seats.

Almost anything Hillary said was likely to make news. Reporters had been buzzing about just what she would do in the second term. Would she be the policy activist of her husband's first two years, when she headed up the disastrous effort to reform health care, or the more reserved, traditionalist figure of 1995 and 1996, when she went to great lengths to downplay her political influence? Would she continue to lie low because of the Whitewater mess? Or would she feel liberated by her husband's victory?

Brant popped the first question: What will your role be in the next four years?

Hillary Clinton started talking about welfare reform. She went on and on, delving into incredible detail. She wanted to tour the country, research the issue, bring problems to the attention of decision makers. "I want to travel around and talk to people about what is happening on the ground," Hillary said. "I intend to speak out about it and write about it." She added: "If there's a formal role, this is how I see it."

Brant asked a follow-up question; the first lady kept holding forth on welfare. Blackman, who used two pens for every interview, kept switching to her red pen, marking the important sections. There was no doubt in her mind that Hillary wanted a formal role in welfare policy, that she had thought about it, and that she was giving them the story.

When the fifteen-minute session ended, the reporters went over that part of the tape a half-dozen times. Blackman stayed up all night transcribing the tape and writing a draft of her story. Her colleague, Eric Pooley, rewrote the piece the next day. The entourage spent the next day flying to northern Thailand, where the first lady was to examine the issue of child prostitution. The reporters had an enjoyable, off-the-record dinner with Hillary. Blackman felt great. Everything was going smoothly. *Newsweek* decided not to run a story on the interview, but *Time*'s piece was going to press.

At seven the next morning, while Ann Blackman was sipping her coffee in the hotel restaurant, Marsha Berry walked up and started scolding her. "She never said those words!" Berry declared. Berry had just gotten a call from the White House press office, alerting her to the *Time* story, which was titled "Reinventing Hillary" and was causing a minor firestorm. What the first lady apparently had failed to realize was that those two words—"formal role"—were a kind of secret code signaling a return to behind-the-scenes power, which conjured up visions of the health care debacle. The White House was going haywire over the story.

Suddenly Blackman felt under siege. In twenty-five years as a journalist, she had never been treated like this, never been accused of making something up. She had covered Rosalynn Carter, Nancy Reagan, never had a problem. But it wasn't just Berry who was accusing her; even the soft-spoken Melanne Verveer told her she didn't believe that Hillary had used the words "formal role." Blackman had to produce the tape. But, tired of lugging around all her equipment, she had left her tape recorder on the plane. A long, excruciating day went by as Hillary's aides continued to trash the story.

Finally they returned to the airport. Blackman felt like a wreck. Her knees were shaking. Maybe she hadn't heard it right, she thought. Maybe she had screwed up. She turned on the tape and, yes, there it was, "formal role." She played the tape for her colleagues on the plane, who broke into a cheer. Blackman handed out copies of the transcript and sent one up to Hillary in the front cabin. She was vindicated.

It didn't seem to matter. Berry came back to Blackman's seat and continued the tirade. "Weak!" she said. "Weak!" Blackman was stunned. They had falsely accused her of lying, and now they didn't even have the decency to apologize.

By the time Mike McCurry, traveling with the president, arrived in Manila to brief the White House press, the reporters were all buzzing about the first lady's new "formal" role. "If you'll recall," McCurry reminded them, "she said much the same—or the president said much the same in a conversation that was on ABC television back in October. . . . I'm not aware the president plans to ask her to take a 'formal role' in any area. He does expect her and other experts on child welfare to help him and help the administration successfully implement welfare reform."

"So why is she saying she wants a formal role if there are no plans for her to have a formal role?" a reporter asked.

"People who remember the interview don't recollect that being a significant part of the interview," McCurry said, implicitly criticizing Blackman's account.

"With all due respect, could you explain what's really going on here? . . . It seems like you're backtracking."

"The policy has been made already. . . . People are stretching here to try to create something that's not there," McCurry said.

"Mike, why the sensitivity over the word 'role'?"

"Well, because you all will make it into something that it's not."

"Would you call it an assignment?"

"No."

In his zeal to defuse the story, McCurry may have spun a little too hard, for word began to filter back that the president was miffed at him for seeming to undercut his wife. Although McCurry's strategy made sense—it would head off another round of stories about a Hillary power grab—on that day it looked like the White House was backing away from her. Despite McCurry's best efforts, however, the story continued to ricochet around the globe. "Hillary Rodham Clinton and her operation clearly remain skittish about reopening what they call Hillary Land to the full glare of the domestic spotlight," Claire Shipman reported on CNN. She conceded that "the day-long tempest seems something of an overreaction, since her husband and others have already made plain she intends to put welfare reform on her agenda."

McCurry wasn't surprised. He knew that anytime Hillary said anything she was buying herself a front-page story about her supposed role. "She's the goddamn first lady!" he would say. "She shouldn't worry about her role."

But Hillary's aides were exasperated. Some of the reporters who wrote about the "bag over your head" remarks hadn't even been in Australia, hadn't heard how funny and confident she sounded, hadn't seen a transcript. They just used selected phrases to fit their preconceived notions. Their boss was always depicted as either beleaguered by Whitewater, acting like a bitch, pretending to be a homemaker, or the secret power behind the throne. She couldn't catch a break.

The day after the staff's blowup with Ann Blackman, Hillary Clinton was working the crowd at the Grand Palace in Bangkok. Blackman saw her coming over and braced for an unpleasant moment. The first lady put her hand on Blackman's shoulder.

"Are you okay?" she asked. "Don't worry. These things get blown out of proportion. Your story's fine."

.   .   .

FROM HER FIRST DAYS IN WASHINGTON, HILLARY RODHAM CLINton seemed to view the media as the enemy. Soon after the inauguration, she hatched a plan to move the White House press corps out of its West Wing quarters and into the bureaucratic Siberia of the Old Executive Office Building, the sprawling Victorian structure across the street. The plan was never formally proposed, but it underscored her disdain.

Hillary and her staff couldn't believe the tone of suspicion in the early wave of stories about her. There were pieces about her decision to be known as Hillary Rodham Clinton, as if using her full name were some kind of change. There were pieces about her boldness in claiming a small West Wing office; first ladies traditionally stuck to the East Wing. One cartoon had her erecting a ten-story annex to the White House. The clear message was that this was one power-grabbing broad.

Lisa Caputo, the first lady's press secretary, was given no regular allotment of press interview time, and while she lobbied for reporters to accompany Hillary on domestic trips, she was overruled by Maggie Williams, Hillary's chief of staff. Estrangement was the official policy, and a feeling of defensiveness set in. The press office tried to manipulate the coverage simply by controlling access to the first lady. All political figures played some version of this game, but never before had a president's wife been so blatant about it, certainly not a wife who intended to play a significant policy role in the administration.

Hillary granted her first newspaper interview to Marian Burros, a *New York Times* food writer, on condition that she be asked only about her hostess duties. Burros produced a front-page story about Hillary's plan to ban smoking at White House social events.

Others were not so lucky. The first lady gave interviews to *Time* and *U.S. News* but pointedly refused to talk to *Newsweek*. Aides passed the word that Hillary was still angry with *Newsweek* for printing an unsubstantiated gossip item about her having supposedly thrown a lamp at her husband. Evan Thomas, the magazine's Washington bureau chief, called the punishment "a little petty."

For a time, early in the administration, the media were in full swoon. Hillary's face on the cover seemed to sell as many magazines as Princess Di's. *Time* called her "the icon of American womanhood." *Vanity Fair* gushed that she was "arguably the most important woman in the world." *The Washington Post* declared that she was "replacing Madonna as our leading cult figure." Dotson Rader, a family friend who had once spent the weekend with the Clintons in Little Rock, helped produce a special *Parade* issue devoted to Hillary as "one of the most influential Americans of our time." *People, Mirabella, TV Guide, Good Housekeeping, Redbook, Family Circle, Vogue* all went along for the ride. She was Saint Hillary, media superstar.

But there was one Saint Hillary piece that turned the image on its head. Michael Kelly, in a *New York Times Magazine* cover story, cast her as a sort of supermoralist, lecturing lesser mortals on ethical and religious values. He described her as fiercely ambitious and heaped scorn on what became known as the politics of meaning. "The meaning of the politics of meaning is hard to discern under the gauzy and gushy wrappings of New Age jargon that blanket it," Kelly wrote.

Perhaps Hillary had asked for it, prattling on about a "spiritual vacuum" and "the underlying principles of Methodism." But her aides all knew that she was in a reflective mood because of the recent death of her father. She was in mourning, trying to talk about human values, and Kelly had treated her as if she were a navel-gazing college sophomore.

Although Hillary was being ridiculed on the spiritual front, she was casting a long shadow over the domestic policy battlefield. She began to champion a massive health reform scheme, one so complicated that even its defenders had a hard time explaining it. As the months wore on, the first lady grew increasingly defensive with the press. She turned down interview requests by health care writers for *The Wall Street Journal* and *USA Today*. When *The Washington Post*'s health care reporter asked for an interview, she had to submit her questions in advance, a galling concession for any journalist. But Hillary was quick to volunteer an interview to a writer for the *Post*'s Style section, who was preparing an essay on her spiritual beliefs.

Hillary's staff felt there was a logical reason for her reticence on policy matters. Her task force was still drawing up its health care blueprint, and the president had not yet made the key decisions about the shape of the plan. Hillary couldn't very well be talking to reporters about the specifics when the plan hadn't been finalized or sent to the Hill. But her retreat added to the aura of secrecy, the picture of an unelected woman wielding power behind closed doors.

When Whitewater began heating up in 1994, Hillary's fierce resistance to public disclosure became a major political liability. "The bunker mentality at the White House is a reflection of Hillary Clinton," Al Hunt wrote in *The Wall Street Journal*. "On issue after issue she has shown startlingly bad judgment," Michael Barone wrote in *U.S. News*.

Such attacks ripped apart the already frayed relations between Hillary and the press. She became even more wary of granting interviews. She told aides she felt she was in a "twilight zone." Reporters, it seemed, only wanted to talk about the burgeoning scandal. Whitewater had turned her into read meat, her top aides believed. Maggie Williams felt the first lady was "paralyzed" by Whitewater. Dick Morris thought her stoic exterior masked "enormous pain" as Saint Hillary was suddenly transformed by the press into the devil incarnate.

The cultural divide was striking. To many journalists the first lady was a stonewaller, a slippery pol. To Hillary's staff, however, she was being hounded about ancient events, held to an impossible standard, presumed guilty at every turn.

Hillary's view of reporters hardened like ready-mix cement. "Why should I talk to people who have no interest in getting the story straight and who only want to see the negative?" she asked one staffer.

Hillary also complained to Dick Morris. The press, she said, took a sadistic joy in destroying people's lives. The baby boomer reporters were envious of her and Bill, in a way they hadn't been of the Reagans and the Bushes, because they were so close in age. They simply weren't used to powerful political women, she believed, and held them to a different standard. "When I was in Little Rock, I thought when I got to Washington I'd deal with a press corps that was not sexist and narrow-minded the way some of the reporters in Arkansas are," Hillary told Morris. "I was shocked when I got here and they were even worse." Morris felt her disdain for the media bordered on paranoia. Indeed, Hillary insisted on attributing criticism of her health care plan to sexists who found her "threatening." "If somebody has a female boss for the first time, and they've never experienced that—well, maybe they can't take out their hostility against her so they turn it on me," she told *The Wall Street Journal*.

As the Whitewater rapids raged, Hillary's staff persuaded her to invite Len Downie, the executive editor of *The Washington Post*, to the White House. The off-the-record session in the Map Room was billed as a chance to talk frankly about the scandal, to show that she had nothing to hide. Downie tried to explain why the *Post* had to do this kind of reporting, that there was nothing personal or judgmental about it. If the first family's explanations were innocent, he said, all she had to do was provide the documents and they would publish the story. Hillary responded with lawyerly caution, saying that she couldn't produce the documents because the White House didn't have them all.

It was, from Hillary's viewpoint, a disaster. Downie didn't seem to believe her. He kept asking how she could prove that she and her husband really lost money on the Ozarks land investment. The meeting ended without any satisfactory answers from the first lady. That was the day she knew she was screwed with the *Post*, she told a colleague afterward. To expect her to have all the documents at her fingertips was just unreasonable. That meeting, Hillary felt, was when Downie decided the Clintons had something to hide and the paper was going to uncover it. Downie was bewildered when he heard about her reaction. He felt he was simply pressing for the kind of information that would put the questions to rest, that there was nothing personal about it.

Hillary's dogged insistence on never conceding a point sometimes drove her staff to distraction. When she was preparing to rebut the Whitewater charges at what became known as the "pink press conference," Mandy Grunwald, one of her outside advisers, argued that she needed to acknowledge some misjudgments in order to gain credibility on the larger issues she wanted to tackle. But the first lady came around to this viewpoint with great reluctance. There were people out there shooting at her every day. Why should she join the gang by admitting error? Another time she asked a colleague: What do they expect from us? We lost our shirts on Whitewater. We don't have any money. We don't own a home. We've never profited from public service. This venal picture they paint of Bill and me, I just don't understand it.

The first lady and her press staff grew downright paranoid about journalists, even turning down venues that clearly would have helped them. She refused to talk to *People*, agreeing only to a photo shoot and some written answers furnished by her staff. She agreed to a sit-down with *U.S. News*, but only on condition that it be limited to health care and children's issues and that her picture not be on the cover. She was clearly trying to lower her profile; the magazine said thanks but no thanks. Hillary was looking like a control freak, a hard-nosed lawyer with an icy personality. After the health plan crashed and burned in the summer of 1994, the press pack depicted Hillary as having been toppled from her throne.

Melanne Verveer increasingly found herself having to do damage control with the press. A former activist with the liberal advocacy group People for the American Way, she counted many reporters among her friends. Verveer and Alison Muscatine, a former *Washington Post* reporter and editor who had signed on as a speechwriter, had a hard time understanding why the Big Girl's press relations were so awful. They felt that Caputo was edgy and defensive with reporters, reinforcing Hillary's natural suspicions, but it had to be more than that.

Part of the problem, they concluded, was a fundamental dissonance between what Hillary thought was important and the values that drove daily journalism. Hillary was a reserved midwesterner who didn't enjoy talking about herself; she felt that whatever policy initiative she was trumpeting that week should be the story. She hated what she called "psychobabble" interviews, attempts to analyze and characterize her as being depressed, or in hiding, or turning into Barbara Bush. She wanted to be covered as a serious person, not a Hollywood celebrity. "It's just not worth it," Hillary complained. "It doesn't matter what I do. They're not going to write about any of that stuff." The effort to maintain steely control was taking its toll. When a *Boston Globe* reporter asked Hillary if her tenure had been a failure, the first lady offered a carefully composed response. Then after the reporter left, she burst into tears.

Whitewater remained an open wound for Hillary, and she read the Whitewater articles with eagle-eyed intensity. If Mark Fabiani, the special White House counsel dealing with the scandal, was quoted as saying something she didn't like, she would call him that morning to complain. She knew the bylines of all the Whitewater reporters. And the Whitewater reporter who most infuriated her was Susan Schmidt of *The Washington Post*. In the fall of 1993, the feisty Schmidt had reported that federal banking regulators had referred their inquiry into Madison Guaranty, the savings and loan at the heart of the case, for criminal prosecution, and she had doggedly pursued the story throughout the first term. White House officials had become convinced that Schmidt was the most consistently unfair of the Whitewater reporters, that she was personally invested in pumping up the scandal. And the *Post* was running more Whitewater stories on the front page than any other major paper.

Hillary decided it was time for a frontal assault on Sue Schmidt. She and others at the White House had heard that James Stewart, a former *Wall Street Journal* reporter, was about to publish a book on Whitewater that would be favorable to the Clintons. The buzz prompted Sid Blumenthal, who was still writing for *The New Yorker* but increasingly whispering political advice to Hillary, to call Mark Fabiani.

"You really ought to use the Stewart book to go after the *Post*," said Blumenthal, who had worked for the paper in the 1980s. "You ought to prepare a document outlining the difference between the *Post* and other papers." Under Blumenthal's scheme, Fabiani would go to the

Post and formally present the report to Len Downie. The White House would also publish it as a white paper, to show up the *Post* before the rest of the media.

Fabiani generally dismissed most of Blumenthal's suggestions as not terribly useful. But he quickly learned that Blumenthal had Hillary's ear. A week or so after he and Blumenthal had talked, she would reel off a list of ideas and, almost word for word, they would be Blumenthal's ideas. Now, Fabiani discovered, Hillary wanted the White House to prepare a report on Schmidt's coverage.

The first lady delivered the order during a strategy session in the White House residence. McCurry and Stephanopoulos were there, along with Fabiani, Jane Sherburne, and David Kendall, Clinton's private lawyer. Fabiani objected, saying the effort was sure to backfire. By singling out one reporter for criticism, they would simply ensure that the *Post* would rally behind her. And it would clearly signal that their media antagonists were getting under their skin.

Still, the staff was not inclined to buck the first lady. Let's put together a report, they said, and see what it looks like.

Hillary served up one other idea at the meeting. A law firm hired by federal regulators had recently done a report on Madison Guaranty and found no evidence that the Clintons did anything wrong or knew much about the Whitewater venture. The papers, more interested in Senator Alfonse D'Amato's Whitewater hearings, had barely covered it. Let's publish it as a book, Hillary said. Fabiani found a publisher in Chicago. He later discovered that no one else was taking the idea seriously.

In the meantime, Chris Lehane, a young White House attorney, was asked to write the Sue Schmidt report. Now the administration really was going after its journalistic enemies, just as its worst critics had imagined. But when the report emerged, Fabiani found it not very compelling. It was mostly a comparison of the headlines and play of Schmidt's stories with those in *The New York Times*, the *Los Angeles Times*, and *The Wall Street Journal*, along with a listing of her alleged errors. The idea that this would have an impact on the *Post*, or the rest of the press, was laughable.

But the effort had built up momentum. Alison Muscatine, who had been Schmidt's boss when she was the *Post*'s Maryland editor, thought the report was not particularly strong. She joined in the effort, however, reviewing a cover memo to be signed by Fabiani and McCurry. Fabiani went through the roof when he saw the memo. "You can't have this stuff floating around," he said.

The issue came to a head when McCurry and Fabiani met with Maggie Williams, Harold Ickes, and Ann Lewis, Hillary's longtime adviser, in the first lady's conference room in the Old Executive Office Building. McCurry, who had thought the project was moribund, laid down the law. "This is the dumbest idea I've ever heard in my life," he said. "I make these decisions. This is not happening." All copies of the report were carefully collected.

Hillary remained convinced that the *Post*'s pursuit of Whitewater stemmed from her disastrous meeting with Len Downie. Rather than accept that the newspaper that made its name on Watergate would naturally be chasing the latest White House scandal, she was convinced it was because Downie thought she had lied to him. When David Maraniss, a *Post* reporter and biographer of the president, began work on a lengthy analysis of the first lady's role in Whitewater, Hillary insisted that her lawyers brief him on the Downie encounter. "You have to tell Maraniss how this all started," she told Fabiani.

As she retreated further into a self-imposed isolation, the first lady was portrayed as a broomstick-riding witch in *The American Spectator*, denounced as a crook on talk-radio shows across the country. Hillary stopped reading the papers, tried to tune it all out, and was unaware that radio critics were assailing her in the crudest terms until reading about it in a book. "I had no idea they were saying these terrible things about us," she said.

After the election Verveer and Muscatine were determined to make a fresh start. They told the Big Girl that she had a narrow window of opportunity to improve relations with the press. There was new media interest in her second-term role. Her new chief spokeswoman, Marsha Berry, who had worked for Senator Robert Byrd, felt that Hillary allowed the pressure to build by staying away from reporters, forcing them to shout questions at inopportune times. They needed to lance the boil, to defuse the tensions. Hillary needed to reach out to the press, to abandon the defensiveness of the first four years. The staff pushed hard for allowing reporters to accompany them on domestic trips. They urged Hillary to hold regular press briefings on the issues she was pursuing. If both sides had more regular contact, they felt, there might be less of a tendency to pepper her with "got-cha" questions.

But the "formal role" fiasco seemed only to confirm the first lady's fears and she backed off from the new press strategy. When *The Washington Post* asked to interview her for a special inauguration issue, her ambivalence was obvious. From the tone of the paper's request, it was clear that the piece would be upbeat, and Marsha Berry kept saying for weeks that she would try to arrange the interview, even telling reporter Peter Baker to stay at his desk one afternoon because the first lady might call. Finally on the day of the deadline, Hillary's office faxed over a bland, four-paragraph statement. Baker got into a shouting match with Berry. Another opportunity had been lost.

CHAPTER SIX

The Laundromat

IN THE FIRST DAYS OF 1997, THE MERCURY HIT 74 DEGREES IN Washington, a rare January thaw that put the city in a relaxed mood. The atmosphere was equally upbeat at the White House, where Clinton's popularity rating had hit 60 percent, as high as it had been since he first took office. The DNC fundraising scandal had been blown off the front pages by Newt Gingrich's admission that he had misled the House ethics committee over his handling of a tax-exempt college course. The next several weeks, leading up to the second inauguration and the State of the Union address, looked like a quiet, uneventful period.

But the White House image makers were hard at work. They saw the coming weeks as a precious opportunity to position the president above the partisan fray, to stress his bipartisan approach, to cement his claim to the family values issues that had worked so well during the campaign. Critics had ridiculed Clinton's focus on such seeming minutiae as school uniforms and family leave and violence on television, but it had worked. Now they planned a series of minor events that they hoped would capture the headlines during a slow news month.

In an age of all news all the time, it was no longer enough simply to stage a presidential ceremony at the White House. Once Clinton made an announcement, McCurry felt, it was only a matter of minutes before Rush Limbaugh, cable commentators, online news services, snippy White House correspondents, and anyone else with an opinion got to tear it apart. The only way to break through the static was through repetition, which politicians loved and reporters hated. To keep a story alive through several news cycles, McCurry often resorted to the art of the leak.

It was a trick he had perfected during the campaign: give one news organization a break on an upcoming development and it was certain to get big play, leaving the other reporters to play catch-up. Few journalists could resist the urge to breathlessly trumpet that "the president will announce tomorrow. . . ." They looked like well-wired insiders, and the White House got a two-day bounce.

When Clinton was ready to announce a $5 billion plan to build and renovate schools, *USA Today* got the front-page exclusive. When Clinton was to urge a crackdown on school truants, *USA Today* again put the leak on page one. When Clinton was to unveil a computer program to track illegal gun sales to young people—even though this was similar to an initiative two years earlier—*The New York Times* got the front-page scoop. ABC's Peter Jennings read an item about Clinton's upcoming radio address, although it was merely a restatement of his view that cigarettes are addictive. Marginal stories that would barely rate a mention on television were pumped up by virtue of being exclusive. McCurry enjoyed parceling out these juicy tidbits, even though competing news organizations often got mad at him for doing so.

McCurry had other ways of shaping the agenda. He knew that Clinton was being hammered for ignoring the District of Columbia, which was sinking into insolvency despite the president's appointment of a financial control board. Clinton didn't yet have a plan for the District, but McCurry thought that he needed to demonstrate concern. Driving to work on the morning of a presidential news conference, McCurry was tuned to WTOP, the city's all-news radio station. He heard veteran reporter Dave McConnell say that if he got a chance he was going to ask the president about the city's failing finances. At the news conference the staff positioned McConnell in a noticeable spot and whispered the location to Clinton. The president called on McConnell, made sympathetic noises about the District's plight, and got the headline that McCurry wanted.

While McCurry slogged it out in the trenches, Don Baer, the communications director, took the longer view. A tall, balding man with an intellectual air, Baer thought in increments of weeks and months, plotting out the president's schedule on a calendar he kept on the desk of his spacious basement office. He had no talent for crisis management, couldn't stand doing it. He was a big-picture man. Baer was perhaps the most conservative of Clinton's top aides, one who believed it was important for the president to rise above the day-to-day strife and embrace the kind of values that would resonate with the middle class. Baer tried to ensure that every cog in the White House machine, from scheduling to speechwriting, operated toward that goal.

After the election Baer and his closest colleague, Rahm Emanuel, spent considerable time thinking about the month of January. They knew that there would be a news vacuum in the weeks before the inauguration and the arrival of the 105th Congress, and they wanted to position Clinton during this period as the national healer, the repairer of the breach. They needed to stage some events that would convey this image to the press.

Baer and Emanuel gave Clinton a strategy memo on the subject. They talked up the idea at every opportunity. The incoming chief of staff, Erskine Bowles, arranged for them to accompany Clinton on a pre-Christmas trip to Camp Lejeune, North Carolina, so they could get some face time with the boss. Clinton nodded in agreement at their suggestions, but he was obviously distracted. They couldn't quite get him to focus. He was preoccupied with picking Cabinet members. Baer and Emanuel decided to proceed on their own.

They began with a well-timed leak. Baer gave a background briefing to John Harris, a voluble, easygoing reporter who covered the White House for *The Washington Post*, laying out the broad outline of the coming events. Harris's piece ran the next Sunday, above the fold. "Clinton Prepares To Push Role as National Unifier," the headline said. Baer was thrilled. It had worked. Several other newspapers and television programs would follow the *Post*'s lead.

The kickoff event the next morning had been a tough sell. Baer and Emanuel had noticed that evangelical and other Christian leaders were scheduled to come to the White House for a prayer breakfast, and they pushed to open the session to reporters so Clinton could turn it into a high-profile event. The president wasn't pleased. He had made a point of keeping such events closed to the press so he could gain credibility with an audience that was already suspicious of him. Clinton was always sensitive that an audience not think he was using them as props in his morality play. But Baer and Emanuel talked him into it. They briefed the church leaders in advance. Everyone was on board.

The careful planning paid off. Clinton hosted the ecumenical breakfast in the State Dining Room and made the front page of *The New York Times*. "Clinton Seeks Help for the Nation's 'Spirit,' " the piece said. Details of other planned events—meeting with thirteen chief executives to talk about hiring welfare recipients, taking credit for a decline in college loan defaults—were sprinkled into the media pot.

But journalists were growing tired of this high-fiber diet. They weren't comfortable being part of the White House publicity machine and were hungry for some raw meat. When *Newsweek* put Paula Jones on the cover in early January—in a professionally posed photo for which the magazine arranged makeup and hairstyling—it was like ringing a dinner bell. The piece, based on an earlier article in *The American Lawyer*, said that Jones's charge that Clinton had exposed himself to her in a Little Rock hotel room in 1991 was far stronger than previously believed and that too many media elitists (including —in a rare mea culpa—the article's author, Evan Thomas) had unfairly dismissed Jones as trailer-park trash. The Supreme Court was about to hear oral arguments on Clinton's effort to delay her lawsuit until after he left office, giving the pack an ideal peg to follow *Newsweek*'s lead. Constitutional issues—and oral sex—were at stake. The president had successfully stalled the case until after the election. Now, like other buried ghosts of the first term, it was coming back to haunt him.

McCurry was furious that no one at *Newsweek* had warned him that the story would be on the cover. Thomas, the magazine's Washington bureau chief, had called the previous Friday to tell him that they were working on a big Paula Jones piece, but the cover decision hadn't been made yet. There was another possible cover, involving Newt Gingrich, leaving *Newsweek* with what it called an "A book" and a "B book." Thomas had been talking on background to Robert Bennett, the president's lawyer, who joked that maybe Newt would save him and needled Thomas about his change of heart on Paula Jones. But the vaunted White House spin machine was temporarily out of commission. Bennett had called Leon Panetta and given him his marching orders: "Nobody is to comment." Bennett didn't want to tick off the Supreme Court justices by having aides mouth off while they were weighing his request that the case be deferred. Panetta passed the word to McCurry, who agreed to lie low.

When *Newsweek* made the cover decision on Saturday, Thomas gave Bennett the word. "Newt didn't save you," he said. Thomas even made sure the piece was faxed to Bennett on Sunday morning before the talk shows. But he neglected to get back to McCurry.

The newsmagazines no longer occupied the influential plane they had enjoyed during the heyday of Henry Luce—news moved so fast in the '90s that dozens of outlets now dished the kind of behind-the-scenes detail that was once their franchise—but they could still propel a modest story into a front-page frenzy. A *Newsweek* cover story on Paula Jones would be a cultural event, generating plenty of copycat pieces. When McCurry told Clinton that *Newsweek* was considering the Paula cover, the president was annoyed but resigned. He saw it as part of the Washington Post Company's continuing crusade against him, even though the magazine operated quite independently from its newspaper sibling.

Temperatures began rising as soon as *Newsweek* hit the streets. John Harris wrote in the *Post* that the president was "furious" about the magazine cover, viewing it as yet another example of the media's determination to tarnish him. After the first edition went to press, McCurry admonished Harris.

"Do not write that, John," he insisted. "It's not true, it's not true. When Clinton's furious, trust me, I know." McCurry described Clinton more as feeling resigned to a spate of negative publicity over the Jones case.

For later editions Harris deleted the word "furious" and said the president saw the Paula Jones cover as confirming his "suspicion" that journalists were using the case "as an occasion for airing anew her more sensational charges, according to people familiar with his thinking."

But more than Clinton's temper was in play. Karen Breslau, *News-*

week's new White House correspondent, was approaching Clinton on Air Force One, about to hand him a copy of the magazine's book on the 1996 campaign, when McCurry starting haranguing her from behind about the cover story. Breslau, who had been on the job only a couple of days, tried not to show that she was flustered. It was McCurry's way of sending a message to her masters: he did not like to be blindsided. McCurry also refused to engage the Jones story in public. When reporters asked him about the case, he merely referred questions to Bennett, who, of course, wasn't commenting.

·   ·   ·

MCCURRY HAD BEEN THROUGH THE EXERCISE DOZENS OF TIMES. A rumor would pop up in some gossip column or tabloid or British newspaper and quickly make its way up the media food chain. Stamping out such rumors before they reached critical mass had become a major distraction, another sign of the increasingly tabloid nature of the press.

The endless allegations about Bill Clinton's infidelities, and even Hillary's, seemed to have a life of their own. The president, of course, was widely seen as the First Playboy, dogged by charges about Gennifer Flowers, Paula Jones, Arkansas troopers procuring women, supposed late-night trysts at the Washington Marriott. Nor was Hillary spared this sort of malicious gossip. In the wake of Vincent Foster's suicide in 1993, there were whispers that she had been having an affair with the late White House aide, her former partner at Little Rock's Rose Law Firm. The rumor cropped up from time to time; Barbara Walters had even asked Hillary about it during a campaign interview.

A couple of weeks before, the rumor had come back to life in *The American Spectator*, the fervently conservative monthly that had published a steady stream of Clinton scandal stories. The source was David Watkins, a former White House aide who had been fired after being photographed using a marine helicopter to check out golf courses near Camp David for presidential use. Watkins had also written a damaging memo blaming Hillary Clinton for the 1993 firings at the White House travel office.

Watkins had planned to write a book about the White House but dropped the idea after failing to secure a sufficient advance. The woman hired as his coauthor, Rebecca Borders, was using the interview material for the *Spectator* piece. She quoted Watkins as saying that Hillary had had an affair with Vince Foster. The piece also had Watkins saying that his wife, Ileene, had been told by Marsha Scott, an Arkansan named to a $95,000-a-year White House post, that she was having an affair with Bill.

McCurry wondered how to contain the story. A *Washington Times* reporter had given him an advance copy of the *Spectator* piece, and he figured it would be put through the British "laundromat." He had seen the routine many times: American reporters would shy away from some sex story involving Clinton, but the London tabloids would happily run with it. Then the most aggressively conservative American news outlets—*The Washington Times* or Rupert Murdoch's *New York Post* or *The Wall Street Journal* editorial page—would attribute the latest sleaze to the British papers, and from there it would hit the talk shows and the rest of the mainstream press.

McCurry knew that if he addressed the Watkins story in any way —even if he flatly denied it—he would give reporters the "hook" they needed to write about a salacious article that would otherwise be untouchable. His reaction would legitimize the story. He could imagine the lead: "Controversy arose today at the White House as . . ." McCurry remembered when President Bush had denounced CNN's Mary Tillotson for her "sleazy" question in asking about a book that quoted a dead ambassador as saying that Bush had once had a fling with a member of his staff. That angry denial had launched the story into the media stratosphere. McCurry didn't want to make the same mistake. After the 7:30 A.M. senior staff meeting, McCurry told Maggie Williams, the first lady's chief of staff, that he planned to no-comment the article. When reporters called to discuss the piece off-the-record, McCurry told them there wasn't much new and that the sex stuff was all attributed to "a very bitter source," Watkins's wife.

Within days, as McCurry had feared, the transatlantic conveyor belt cranked into action. Ambrose Evans-Prichard, Washington correspondent for London's *Sunday Telegraph*, wrote a story about the *Spectator* article. Evans-Prichard's political sympathies were clear; he had openly derided Clinton as a "phony" and had called the official account of Vince Foster's death "a tissue of lies." Now the Watkins charges were "news," sort of. *The Washington Times* wasted little time reprinting the Evans-Prichard piece on its front page. "Watkins talks candidly of White House infidelities," the headline said. The gossip page of the *New York Post* quickly followed suit.

While Watkins's account was "no doubt self-serving," the British reporter wrote, it provided "a fascinating glimpse into the Bohemian underworld of the Clinton coterie." He cited Hillary Clinton's supposed romance with Foster. Watkins, he said "reveals that president Clinton was having an affair with Marsha Scott, the White House director of presidential correspondence. Miss Scott is an eccentric flower child from a well-connected family in Arkansas who attended school with Mr. Clinton. . . . She is said to have slept with Mr. Clinton to comfort him on the night of Mr. Foster's death."

McCurry knew what was coming next. At that day's briefing he was asked about the *Spectator* piece.

"I don't have any comment on that article," he replied.

"Mike," a reporter said, "what's the reason you won't comment about the Watkins article and the allegations made by a former senior high—"

McCurry cut him off. "Because I want to put news organizations in the position of having to exercise careful editorial judgment. I'm not going to help them out."

The Watkins story quickly faded, but the process by which such stories were laundered into the mainstream press was soon in the spotlight again. On the morning of January 9, as the capital was pelted with snow and sleet, the atmosphere in the briefing room turned to one of chilly disdain. It seemed that the Clinton White House, which so loved to complain about its press coverage, had ratcheted up the rhetoric by compiling a report alleging an actual right-wing "conspiracy" to discredit the president by dragging him through the media mud. Once the report came to light, McCurry had a new fire to douse.

It had all started with Chris Lehane, the young Harvard Law School graduate on Mark Fabiani's staff who had helped write the report on Susan Schmidt. It was part of Lehane's job to keep and catalog the small mountain of clips on the never-ending stream of accusations against the president: Gennifer Flowers. Paula Jones. Sally Perdue. Other women no one had ever heard of. Vince Foster

handwriting analyses. Unexplained deaths in Little Rock. The mysterious airport at Mena, Arkansas. Clinton as secret CIA agent. Clinton
snorting cocaine as governor.

There was, as scandal aficionados well knew, a clear pattern to
much of this muck. Some of it was so way out that it never moved
beyond fringe publications and Internet chat groups. But some of
the accusations were laundered through the British papers, as had
happened with the David Watkins charges. None of this was exactly
new, nor was it a smoke-filled-room conspiracy. It was more like a
chain reaction, triggered under fixed laws of media thermodynamics.
The phenomenon had begun back in 1992 with Gennifer Flowers,
whose allegations of infidelity had nearly sunk Clinton's candidacy.
Flowers sold her story to *The Star*, the Florida-based supermarket
tabloid, and within days the tale spread to the *New York Post* and New
York *Daily News*, to other big papers, and to CNN, which provided
live coverage of the news conference that *The Star* staged for Flowers.

The pattern took shape. Sally Perdue, a former beauty queen who
claimed that unnamed Clinton associates had tried to frighten her
into silence over their affair, couldn't even convince *The National
Enquirer* to publish her story. But Ambrose Evans-Prichard put her
on the front page of the *Sunday Telegraph*, which was enough to
warrant coverage by *The Washington Times*.

In another case Evans-Prichard reported that an Arkansas state
trooper claimed that Chelsea Clinton's nanny, Helen Dickey, had
called the trooper about Vince Foster's death hours before his suicide
was supposed to have been known—and said he had shot himself in
the White House parking lot, not in the rural Virginia park where
his body was found. The Western Journalism Center, a far-right
conspiracy outfit funded by conservative financier Richard Mellon
Scaife, reprinted the *Sunday Telegraph* story in a full-page ad in *The
Washington Times*. *New York Post* columnist John Crudele picked up
the tale under the heading "Did Foster kill himself in White House
parking lot?" He urged Al D'Amato, head of the Senate Whitewater
Committee, to call Dickey as a witness. When D'Amato said he
would investigate Foster's death, McCurry whacked him, lumping
him in with "those that continue to try to spin conspiracy theories."
The fuss died down when the White House released a deposition
from Dickey, who said that she had called the trooper about ninety

minutes after White House aides said they had learned of Foster's death.

The way these tabloid-type stories bubbled up from the ooze was no secret. George Stephanopoulos and James Carville, who had masterminded the '92 campaign, groused about it with reporters every other week. In the spring of 1994, Carville formally peddled the conspiratorial view at a press breakfast, and David Broder wrote a story about Carville's assault. *The Washington Post* even reprinted a chart detailing the supposed conspiracy.

So it was hardly hot news in 1995 when Chris Lehane compiled three hundred pages of such articles and wrote a two-and-a-half-page cover memo titled, somewhat tongue in cheek, "The Communication Stream of Conspiracy Commerce." Lehane didn't really think there was a media conspiracy—in fact, he had great respect for most of the reporters he worked with—but he was disturbed by all the bizarre Vince Foster stuff floating around out there. He described the phenomenon as "the mode of communication employed by the right wing to convey their fringe stories into legitimate subjects of coverage by the mainstream media. . . . After Congress looks into the story, the story now has the legitimacy to be covered by the remainder of the American mainstream press as a 'real' story."

Fabiani sent the package to dozens of news organizations and delivered his spiel. No one bit. Plenty of journalists had made the same observations themselves. A year and a half passed, and no one gave the memo a second thought.

But old stories in Washington have a way of roaring back to life. Micah Morrison, a *Wall Street Journal* editorial writer, mentioned the Lehane report in a January 6 column that accused the White House of trying to intimidate the press. Three days later, *The Washington Times* splashed the story on its front page, complete with the White House chart diagramming the deep, dark conspiracy. Conservative publications loved the report, for it showed that they mattered, that they had gotten under the administration's collective skin.

By this time Chris Lehane had been gone for months and now worked at the Department of Housing and Urban Development. Lanny Davis was left behind to clean up the mess. He couldn't believe a White House lawyer had been dumb enough to put the word "conspiracy" on an official document. He would never have used that word. It violated his cardinal rule, which was to put out the facts without characterizing them. Now the press was going wild. Davis got seventy-five media calls about the report. McCurry knew it would dominate the day's briefing.

Warren Strobel of *The Washington Times* teed off first. "You folks have always denied that there's a bunker mentality here, paranoia regarding Whitewater and these other issues," he said. "Isn't that exactly what this looks like? 'Here are our enemies, they're out to get us.' "

"This doesn't say enemies," McCurry responded. "It describes pretty accurately how things were. . . . Admittedly, your news organization plays a role."

Deborah Orin of the *New York Post* was next. She cited a comment by Stephen Hess of the Brookings Institution that the report "shows the extent of paranoia, if not dementia, at the White House."

McCurry tried to dismiss the report as the product of "a younger guy in the legal counsel's office," but he didn't back away completely. "Look, everyone in here knows there's a fair amount of nut case material that floats around with respect to Whitewater," he told the gaggle. "And that stuff gets peddled . . . [to] a lot of news organizations that frankly should have known better. So we'd say, wait a minute, you guys are, you know, chasing a story that had very, very suspicious roots. . . . These are the guys who are the conspiracy nuts who have been peddling this stuff for years and years now."

Strobel tried again: Why wasn't the report a waste of taxpayers' money?

"We're trying to protect people from getting a bunch of bad stories in their papers. . . . It is certainly true that the White House was aggressive in responding to false, fallacious, damaging, and politically motivated attacks on the president," McCurry said.

The game plan was history. Whatever news the White House wanted to make was washed away by talk of media conspiracies. Whether the press had been irresponsible in printing some of these salacious stories was no longer important; White House gumshoes, in Nixonian fashion, had discovered a conspiracy. Chris Lehane's little research project had backfired. It didn't take a genius to figure out that the president would have to respond.

The next morning, during a photo op with the group of corporate executives invited to discuss welfare, Helen Thomas popped the question: "Do you think there is a right-wing cabal in the press against you?"

"No," Clinton said.

It was as terse as the president had ever been. On this subject, at least, he had concluded it was time to shut up.

·   ·   ·

THE PRESIDENT'S STAFF, MEANWHILE, WAS HARD AT WORK REFASH-ioning Clinton in Theodore Roosevelt's image.

Had Clinton simply come out and said he wanted to model his second term on TR's big-stick approach, the result likely would have been a collective snicker. There goes Bill, who couldn't even get 50 percent of the vote, posing for Mount Rushmore. But by leaking selective bits from Clinton's supposedly confidential conversations, McCurry and company were able to shape the inevitable speculation about Clinton's legacy in a decidedly Rooseveltian direction. Their dedication to spin was so complete that they dared not wait until the boss was out of office before trying to influence the first rough draft of history.

The first inkling appeared in early January. "In recent conversations with aides," John Harris wrote in *The Washington Post*, Clinton had spoken of three categories of presidents: men like Lincoln and FDR, who excelled in time of crisis; caretakers like Calvin Coolidge; and a middle tier of those like, yes, Teddy Roosevelt, who helped steer the country through times of transition. Clinton, it was said, aspired to be in the TR category.

Whenever they got the chance, White House aides invoked the Roosevelt motif. No longer would Clinton be a flabby, blabby baby boomer; he was destined for history. Soon Clinton himself was telling reporters that the Rough Rider had helped guide the country at a time when "we changed the way we worked" and "we changed the way we lived."

Within two weeks *The New York Times* was running a series of photos "morphing" Clinton into Roosevelt. "A lot of his work goes to the use of the bully pulpit," McCurry told the *Times*.

"He's got to use the bully pulpit," Panetta told *The Wall Street Journal*. The company line was clear. Bully!

All this unfolded against a backdrop of syrupy bipartisanship.

Acutely aware of polls showing that Americans were sick of Beltway infighting, the White House spin team was determined to place Clinton firmly on the high road. With much of the Washington news apparatus focused on Speaker Newt Gingrich's reprimand by the House ethics committee, Clinton, no stranger to scandal stories, chose to lay on the empathy. Asked during a public appearance if he had any comment on the speaker's travails, Clinton said: "I just want it to be over. . . . In my brief time here the last four years, way too much time and energy and effort is spent on all these things, leaving too little time and emotional energy for the work of the people."

Of course, as McCurry was forced to confirm, Clinton wasn't doing a thing to discourage Democrats in the House from continuing to beat the hell out of Newt. That would mean giving up a powerful partisan issue, since they had just spent a year running against Gingrich with nasty TV ads depicting him as a extremist bogeyman. No, it was far easier to prattle on about bipartisanship and reap the publicity benefits.

And in a brilliant bit of political stagecraft, Clinton decided to award Bob Dole the Presidential Medal of Freedom, knowing that the press would play up the image of Bill Clinton embracing the man he had just defeated in a bitter campaign.

The ultimate exercise in McCurry's theory of media management —keeping a good story alive through several news cycles—came in the days before Clinton took the oath of office for the second time. Here was an event that was guaranteed to draw world attention, hours of free network airtime, saturation coverage by the papers. Yet McCurry still felt the need for a publicity buildup. He told any reporter who would listen that the theme of the speech would be national reconciliation. He granted interview requests from selected news organizations so the president could talk about the address he was about to give. It was straight from the old public relations playbook: tell 'em what you're gonna tell 'em, then tell 'em, then tell 'em what you told 'em.

In the pre-inaugural interviews, the president told *The Washington Post* he would use the address to "help flush the poison from the atmosphere." He told *U.S. News* that there was no "long-term advantage to either party" in a "bloodbath" over ethics. He told NBC that "the American people . . . want us to lay down our partisan sniping."

Twenty-three minutes before Clinton raised his right hand, Wolf

Blitzer told viewers: "We will hear, according to his aides, several references to the toxic atmosphere in Washington. . . . The president will speak about reconciliation."

Then, as directed by the Constitution, Clinton finally took the oath, and his speech would bring one spin cycle to a close as another one was about to begin.

CHAPTER SEVEN

Breaking Through the Static

DON BAER BELIEVED THAT THE WHITE HOUSE SPENT WAY too much time worrying about the next day's headlines. In the end, he was convinced, it didn't matter all that much what the Washington reporters said.

Much of the motivation was ego, he thought. Some of his colleagues got off on picking up the phone and schmoozing with reporters and nudging the day's story in this or that direction. It made them feel important.

But after a year and a half as communications director, Baer had learned an important corollary to the old Michael Deaver rule. Deaver, who had choreographed much of Ronald Reagan's presidency, was legendary for his steadfast belief that television pictures mattered far more than what the correspondents said. The entire Reagan administration was a made-for-TV enterprise, a daily staging of visuals for the networks; all activity came to a halt when the 6:30 newscasts came on. But Baer came to believe that what the president said cut through what was said about him. He was having his own conversation with America, one that, if all went well, sailed over the heads of the journalists, who were nothing but theater critics and did little to shape public opinion. They might slam a Clinton speech, but subsequent polling would show that most voters liked it.

Baer saw the phenomenon time and again. When Clinton unveiled his plan for HOPE scholarships, which would give parents of college students up to $1,500 a year in tax credits, the media verdict was swift: cynical political ploy to pander to middle-class voters. But what the public heard was that Clinton was concerned about the difficulty of sending kids to college and was willing to help them with tax credits. Voters got it. They liked constructive proposals and hated partisan sniping.

Baer, forty-two, was one of the few journalists in the White House. He had started out as a lawyer, then became a writer and editor for *U.S. News* for seven years before signing on as Clinton's chief speechwriter in 1993. But now, from his spacious office in the White House basement, his view of the press had changed. Despite his magazine background, Baer was in some ways naive about the brutal nature of White House coverage. He was flabbergasted at some of the shoddy journalistic techniques he saw. He had a rude awakening early in his tenure as a speechwriter, when he found himself a target of *The Wall Street Journal*'s Michael Frisby, who was known for using the "Washington Wire" column to reward old sources or bring new ones to the bargaining table.

Baer had been at the White House for less than four months when his name appeared in a Frisby item claiming that the communications director's job might soon become open and that Baer was "campaigning" for the post. No one had bothered to call him. Baer was convinced that the phony leak had come from someone on his staff who was friendly with Frisby and didn't like the fact that Baer was the new boss. He complained to Alan Murray, the *Journal*'s Washington bureau chief and an old college friend from the University of North Carolina, but to no avail. Baer slowly realized that you needed to cultivate allies within the White House who would defend you against this sort of media sniping.

During the 1996 campaign Frisby struck again. He called after Baer had arranged for two ABC executives, David Westin and Sherrie Rollins, to make a Roosevelt Room presentation about an antidrug advertising campaign the network was mounting. A source—the same subordinate, Baer believed—had told Frisby that Baer was seen huddling in the hallway with Rollins about a possible job opportunity. Baer explained that his conversation with Rollins was innocuous; she was an old friend from the years that both had worked at *U.S. News.* But Frisby delivered what sounded very much like an ultimatum.

"We're desperate today for 'Washington Wire' items," he said. "Give me something else or I'm going to have to use this about you." Baer insisted it was a non-story, refusing to play Frisby's game, and the item appeared with a single line about Baer and Rollins being old friends.

In a larger sense Baer was disappointed by the reporters' relentless focus on short-term, ephemeral tactics. Most of them were fixated on the old battles—left versus right, White House against Congress. He would tell them about Clinton's New Democrat philosophy—how education, for example, was a metaphor for the president's efforts to change social policy without mounting huge Great Society programs —but too often their eyes would glaze over. Baer fared best with the columnists—Joe Klein, Jonathan Alter, Jacob Weisberg, Walter Shapiro, Ron Brownstein—who could see beyond that week's vote on the Hill. These were the opinion leaders, he believed, the journalists who could gradually, glacially change conventional wisdom.

But even the smartest writers, Baer felt, were compelled by the media culture to be cynical, doubting, filled with capital-A attitude. Klein would sit in Baer's office and complain that even at *The New Yorker,* the bible of the Manhattan intelligentsia, the pressure to be cutting and ironic was intense. In covering the president, Baer believed, it was hip to be hostile. Otherwise your colleagues thought you were in the tank, the charge hurled at Klein's predecessor, Sidney Blumenthal.

Baer had been stunned at the lack of planning when he took over as communications director in the summer of 1995. There was no sense of strategy, no coherent effort to sell a message to the press. If Clinton was scheduled to address an organization, someone in the White House would ask what he should talk about, what the group wanted to hear, rather than what might help advance the president's agenda. The place seemed inert.

As Dick Morris emerged as chief strategist, however, his explosive personality made things happen, and an energized Don Baer became Morris's closest ally in the West Wing in pushing centrist policies aimed at middle-class voters. But Morris was maniacal and kept harassing Baer: Why wasn't he getting this or that plan carried out? The reason was that a dozen other officials were ganging up against it. Clinton wanted him working with Morris, but Baer and the president had never been close. He wasn't part of the inner circle. The constant bureaucratic warfare took its toll.

By the first weeks of 1997, Baer was exhausted. His wife, Nancy, had been after him to quit. She had undergone emergency surgery soon after he became communications director and then, with two young boys to look after, had quit her job with a Washington law firm. They now had to live on Baer's $125,000 salary. Baer felt negligent as a parent. His younger son had been just three weeks old when he started working for Clinton; the older one had just turned seven. He felt he was missing out on the boys' growing up, was tired of getting beeped at home. He decided during the campaign that he would leave sometime after the election. Everyone knew he was looking around for a job. The presidential calendar on Baer's desk contained events through the NATO summit that July. That was as far ahead as he could see. After that, he was out of there.

• • •

THE MAN WHO INCREASINGLY PLAYED THE ROLE OF BEHIND-THE-scenes broker with the press was a wiry, curly-haired Chicagoan with an aura of intensity. Rahm Emanuel was convinced that the press operated within paradigms, neat little belief systems that fit the contours of elite opinion. The notion of objective reporting was hogwash; Washington journalists were incredibly, if subconsciously, biased. Their preconceived take on Bill Clinton, he believed, was that he was a petulant little child with an uncontrollable appetite.

The very thought made Emanuel angry, desk-poundingly angry. These pampered little correspondents with their gourmet cuisine and their full-time housekeepers couldn't be more wrong about Clinton, a man who had risen from a fatherless childhood in Hot Springs to the pinnacle of national power. He was more in touch with what folks out there wanted than these self-appointed Beltway oracles.

It wasn't that Rahm Emanuel disliked reporters. Indeed, he spent perhaps 60 percent of his time schmoozing them, spinning them, fencing with them, yelling at them. On a particular day he might chat up columnists Paul Gigot and Mark Shields, return calls from James Bennet and Todd Purdum at *The New York Times*, check in with the networks, have lunch with Cokie Roberts. That was part of the job.

Emanuel, thirty-seven, viewed himself as an early warning system for Clinton. He would often call the network folks at 10:05 A.M., right after their morning conference call with New York, to find out what they were working on and try to shut it down if necessary. On other days he would check in earlier, trying to put out a story line before the conference calls began. He understood the rhythms of the beast.

Rahm Emanuel had been finance director of Clinton's 1992 campaign, but he had had a rocky first term. After starting out as White House political director, he was eased into a lesser job when his overzealous style antagonized people, but he had worked his way back into Bill and Hillary's good graces. Now he had the rather ordinary title of special assistant to the president, but his clout was suggested by the fact that he had just moved into George Stephanopoulos's old office. The small but strategic piece of real estate had a back door connecting to the president's den, just off the Oval Office, a tiny hideaway dominated by bookshelves and a large photo of Clinton with his arm around Chelsea. Emanuel never presumed to slip into the Oval unannounced, but proximity was power in the West Wing. He preferred to operate outside the media spotlight, even if a spate of newspaper and magazine profiles had recently dubbed him "Rahmbo," the warrior who sometimes screamed at subordinates. He didn't want too high a media profile, for he knew that officials who were puffed up in the press eventually got deflated.

Emanuel, a dedicated ballet dancer, knew the moves; sometimes he would spin so hard that reporters felt he was insulting their intelligence or simply didn't understand the news business. He was not shy about calling a reporter a fucking idiot. And if a journalist screwed him by using something that had been off-the-record, he'd elbow the guy by leaking a story to a competitor. Emanuel was not afraid to break a few bones; he viewed politics as a contact sport.

The atmosphere in that pressroom was poison, Emanuel felt. The reporters were pissed—really pissed—that Clinton was at 60 percent in the polls. That meant that they had failed, that their daily scandal stories had missed the mark. Sure, White House officials had to take some of the blame. They weren't always as forthcoming as they should be. And there was a touch of paranoia in the Oval as well. Sometimes Emanuel told Clinton he was wrong, that the press was not beating him up because of some political agenda. But Clinton's anger was understandable. No modern president had been subjected to this level of personal vilification, to this endless barrage of stories about his sex life.

Often, Emanuel felt, the prevailing media paradigms worked in the administration's favor. He had been a chief strategist in helping to pass the 1994 ban on assault weapons, and there the paradigm was clear: gun control good, opponents NRA stooges. The same dynamic had developed in the battle over the North American Free Trade Agreement the previous year. The media wisdom was global-minded free traders in support, labor goons in opposition. Journalists simply failed to appreciate how their deeply held views shaped their coverage.

But it was this same self-absorption that caused many reporters to dismiss much of Clinton's agenda as small-bore. Take the Family and Medical Leave Act. It wasn't a big deal for a hotshot journalist to take time off from work if his or her kid was sick, but for a factory worker in Illinois the new law was a godsend. Emanuel had pushed the president to campaign for school uniforms and was proud of it. Occasionally, he had to admit, the White House went too far. The campaign proposal to give cellular phones to community watch groups had been laughably small. It wasn't presidential. But other issues, from mammograms to food safety, were resonating with voters. Yet the press didn't much care, not unless the story involved some meaningless warfare with the Republican Congress. There were two conversations going on in the country—the daily chatter between reporters and political operatives over all the maneuvering and minutiae, and the president's attempt to talk to the masses about the real issues in their lives.

Like Don Baer and Dick Morris, Emanuel believed that by mastering the second conversation, Clinton could effectively neutralize the first.

                    ·   ·   ·

DOWN THE HALL IN THE PRESS OFFICE, MIKE McCURRY HAD NO time to weave intellectual theories of journalistic behavior. The scandal stories were intensifying, the responses were growing weaker, and McCurry found himself peddling misinformation. The White House was getting not a scintilla of credit for putting out the very documents that provided the road map for all the investigative reporters. Instead, McCurry felt, they looked like conniving dissemblers.

At the same time, McCurry was feeling the heat from his boss. "You wouldn't believe the pressure I'm under," he told John Harris during a late-night chat. "I push Clinton to do these things and sometimes he feels very burned." That *New York Times* interview about the James Riady visit, and the subsequent front-page exposé, had not been forgotten. "I'm still wearing scabs from that," he said.

The whole operation was in a shambles. Lanny Davis was feeling overwhelmed. He was making mistakes and had to spend hours on the phone clarifying and qualifying his statements. He needed more staff. He didn't have a secretary, and his voice mail would fill up in about ninety minutes, forcing reporters to reach him by beeper and often wait days for him to call back. His wife, Carolyn, was urging him to leave the White House, and he begged reporters not to call him at home, where she responded coldly if she answered the phone. When Davis wasn't fencing with reporters, he was fighting with top officials over what could be released. Some of his colleagues privately wondered if he was up to the job. He didn't have that aura of command, that smooth, confident style that Mark Fabiani had shown in dousing the flames of scandal. Journalists were starting to complain that Davis didn't know what he was talking about, was dealing bad stuff, acting as if he were on *Crossfire*. Too many things were falling through the cracks.

To some extent the White House was paying the price for stonewalling in the final weeks of the campaign. Fabiani had strongly argued that someone should be the chief damage control officer for the DNC scandal. He was willing to do it, though he wasn't wild about the notion. But he had to have complete authority. He had to be able to put out the documents that needed to be made public, even if they were embarrassing, even if they hurt the president's campaign. That was how you built credibility with the press. That was how he had helped defuse Whitewater, by inviting reporters over to peruse thick stacks of documents, dispatching them by messenger, shoveling material out the door. It wasn't spin. These reporters were too smart, too well versed in the subject, to be taken in by one lawyer's slick talk. You had to bring some facts to the table.

But the White House had refused to put Fabiani in charge. And Clinton remained largely walled off from reporters throughout the 1996 election. McCurry pushed to hold a news conference in the last six weeks of the campaign, but Doug Sosnik, the political director, fought him at every turn. Who needs it, Sosnik argued. We're getting our message out. Why insist on living dangerously? Sosnik prevailed, and the reporters were left to stew as the scandal mounted. Fabiani knew that they would pay a price for stiffing the press.

Now, as January turned to February, McCurry was trying to pick up the shattered pieces. He recited his mantra—full disclosure—at every opportunity. We're putting this stuff out there. The American people can decide. We're the party of reform, campaign finance reform. Never mind that Clinton had emerged from the campaign as a battered mud wrestler, his body caked with the accumulated muck of too much sleazy fundraising and too many handshakes with too many slimy donors. We want to clean things up.

The problem, as reporters quickly learned, was that despite McCurry's claims, there was much that the White House would not disclose. McCurry dug in his heels on the Lincoln Bedroom, which had been rented by the night to the high rollers and had become the preeminent symbol of the selling of the Clinton White House. Every name of an overnight guest, McCurry knew, would produce another story about that person's big-bucks donations and legislative interests and what he wanted from the president. But it was also a matter of privacy for the president's friends. McCurry felt he had to put his foot down on this one.

"Isn't there at least an appearance of an ethical lapse when major contributors are then invited to sleep in the Lincoln Bedroom?" McCurry was asked.

"Absolutely not," he said, circling back to the theme that all contributions to the president were publicly disclosed.

"We're not handed a daily list of the Lincoln Bedroom. So there's not really full disclosure," another reporter said.

"And I don't intend to do it," McCurry said. "Because the president of the United States is a human being and is entitled to have his guests at his residence."

Clinton, for his part, declared that he had reviewed the Lincoln Bedroom roster and found it composed mainly of personal friends, relatives, and guests of Chelsea. Would he disclose the list? "I'll have to look at it and consider what the precedent would be," he said in an obvious dodge, making no mention of the big-bucks donors whom he had courted over coffee.

McCurry employed an even more creative defense in explaining why he wouldn't release these names. He was merely guarding the privacy of those who had sipped the official cappuccino and decided not to open their checkbooks. "We're not going to be bludgeoned into a process here that doesn't protect those who could have every legitimate right to want to hear the president's argument and then make a decision they just don't want to support it," McCurry told the gaggle.

"Mike, couldn't you be bludgeoned into at least releasing the names of those who attend these thank-you events and also gave money?" a reporter asked.

Time to punt. That, McCurry said, was up to Lanny Davis.

Davis, for his part, was still having trouble getting the administration's story straight. On one Saturday he told *The New York Times* that the White House had never performed background checks on the hundreds of visitors to the presidential coffees, except to verify through birth dates and Social Security numbers that they were on the day's guest list. "No vetting was ever done," he declared. On Sunday night he had to admit he was wrong. Davis issued a statement reversing himself, saying that there indeed had been a Secret Service review to determine whether the guests posed a physical threat to the president, but not whether they were politically unsuitable. It was starting to resemble a Keystone Kops routine.

Day after day the White House refused to release the list of guests at the 103 coffees, who, as it turned out, had poured $27 million into Democratic coffers. Lanny Davis kept arguing with the likes of deputy chief of staff John Podesta and the counsel's office that they needed to disgorge the list, to do what they called a "document dump." These were political events, he said; no credible argument could be made about privacy. But going public was easier said than done; there was no file at the DNC labeled "Coffees." Different events were recorded in different files. Some White House officials argued that any list they put out would be incomplete and that the press would holler "gotcha" when it became clear that some name had been omitted. Davis thought this was basically an excuse. The unspoken concern—nobody actually came out and said this, of course —was that there was damaging information on the guest lists, information that would produce a new round of embarrassing stories. Nobody wanted to give up anything they didn't have to surrender. Davis felt that some of the president's top advisers stubbornly believed that if they didn't put out the coffee list it would never come out. This was patent nonsense, at least as long as Congress had subpoena power.

Finally Lanny Davis got the green light to release the guest lists, and it wasn't long before the administration got a huge black eye. The DNC, it turned out, had invited seventeen of the nation's top banking executives—the heads of Chase Manhattan and NationsBank and other institutions—to have coffee in May 1996 not only with Clinton but with the comptroller of the currency, Eugene Ludwig. The event reeked of influence peddling; after all, Democratic Party officials had invited the banking executives, men whose financial support they were soliciting, to schmooze with a top federal regulator who held sway over their sizable corporations.

Still, the White House insisted on posturing for the press. Hours after the coffee lists were made public, the White House arranged a conference call between Lanny Davis and reporters, even though Davis had had little time to study the names and had not been warned about the bankers' coffee with Eugene Ludwig. He didn't even know who Ludwig was. When reporters pressed him about the session, he tried to put the best face on it.

"We didn't think it was inappropriate, we still don't. . . . They were here to meet the president and ask his views on the issues," he said. Some of the reporters thought that Davis was spinning so hard he had lost his balance. Tim Weiner of *The New York Times* asked whether Davis would change his view if Ludwig himself felt he should not have been at the meeting. Davis said he would not. In fact, Ludwig's spokeswoman had already told Weiner's colleague Jeff Gerth that Ludwig didn't know it had been a DNC event and wouldn't have gone near the thing if he had, making it clear that Ludwig was angry about the incident.

Davis felt sandbagged. He had been sent into battle unarmed, without even the basic facts. His ass was on the line, and his colleagues hadn't bothered to brief him properly.

At the gaggle the next day, McCurry refused to suggest that the Ludwig coffee was in any way unwise, brazenly declaring that reaching out "to leaders of various ethnic and constituency groups" was "good politics and good policy and good for democracy." Davis realized how ludicrous they looked. As Clinton was rehearsing for a news conference the following day, Davis urged him to own up to the fact that the meeting was wrong. It was time to cut their losses on this thing.

Clinton didn't need convincing. "Listen, Ludwig shouldn't have been there," he said. McCurry agreed that he should make that point at the news conference.

Several White House aides, including Rahm Emanuel, had pushed hard to hold the news conference the day before, but Clinton had insisted on having the day off. The result was an awkward bit of choreography that clumsily undercut the day's message.

When Rita Braver asked the question during the afternoon session in the spacious East Room, Clinton admitted the obvious: the Ludwig coffee had been "not appropriate." He went on to utter the damning phrase that had become Beltway-speak for passing the buck: "Mistakes were made," the same words that Ronald Reagan and George Bush had used during Iran-contra to fudge the issue of just who was responsible. McCurry would never have suggested the passive-voice construction in advance, but he understood why Clinton had used it. If you tried to specify what the mistakes were and who made them, it could get very sticky. Better just to cop a linguistic plea and try to move on.

Clinton insisted to the reporters that he was all for cleaning up a lousy campaign finance system. Then, that evening, he attended a $10,000-a-plate fundraiser that would garner more than $1 million for the Democratic Party.

It was, Emanuel decided, a classic screw-up.

. . .

MCCURRY MADE A GREAT SHOW OF CAMARADERIE TOWARD THE press. But at times, when it served his purpose, he was not above attacking the messenger.

One target was Michael Kranish of *The Boston Globe*. In the small mountain of documents generated by the fundraising scandal, Kranish had discovered a tantalizing memo from John Huang, the peripatetic DNC fundraiser, lobbying Clinton on immigration policy. The February 1996 memo gave Clinton a "heads up" that the "top priority" for Asian Americans—the very people Huang was tapping for millions of dollars and bringing to the White House—was an immigration bill pending in Congress.

The issue was the so-called "sibling preference" that enabled naturalized Asian Americans to bring their brothers and sisters to the United States. The Clinton administration had wanted to suspend this preference, but Huang wrote that the Asian Americans who would attend an upcoming fundraising dinner at the Hay-Adams Hotel—and would donate $1.1 million, a record for an Asian American event—strongly supported the provision. A few weeks later the administration reversed its stance and agreed in writing to support sibling preference.

Lanny Davis told Kranish that the administration's flip-flop had nothing to do with Huang or the fundraising. It was a mere tactical retreat, he said, because many Democrats and interest groups were fighting to save the sibling preference.

This may well have been true. Whenever presidents or congressmen took positions that happened to favor folks who had given them lots of dough, they always said their decision was made "on the merits," and it was hard to prove otherwise. People donated thousands of dollars for a reason, but the explicit cause and effect was always murky. Still, Kranish's story showed that John Huang wanted more than just presidential goodwill in exchange for all those Asian American dollars. He was using his clout to lobby for specific legislation for his community. It was the first time a reporter had tied the money to the policy, the nexus that everyone suspected was at the heart of the matter.

The White House went into a frenzy over the *Globe* piece, and Rahm Emanuel, who had assumed Stephanopoulos's troubleshooting role, swept into action. He called federal immigration officials and got hold of the "SOAP," which was insider jargon for Statement of Administration Policy. He outlined a defense in writing and briefed McCurry. He called producers at the major networks—ABC was already gearing up to run a story—and went into his knockdown mode. Emanuel's favorite word—"bullshit"—got plenty of use.

Though few reporters had seen the *Globe* story, one of them—unfortunately for McCurry—was CNN's Brooks Jackson, who picked it up and broadcast a long report that White House correspondents saw in the pressroom shortly before the briefing. McCurry, knowing it would be the topic du jour, came out swinging.

He accused Kranish of "misreporting" and said that his story suggested a connection that "does not exist" and "misleads the people who read the article." In case anyone missed the point, McCurry said: *"The Boston Globe* is just wrong."

Kranish, Rita Braver, and other reporters rose to challenge McCurry. These fundraisers have tremendous access, they said. What's to keep them from manipulating the presidency?

"Full disclosure," McCurry said, invoking the mantra, which was sounding more hollow with each passing day.

Had Clinton seen the Huang memo? McCurry, wisely, hadn't asked the boss.

"There's no indication at all it was given to him," McCurry said. "I haven't asked him personally whether he recalls ever having seen it, but no one here recalls having seen it."

Kranish felt unscathed; McCurry hadn't contradicted a single fact in the piece. But McCurry and Emanuel told several reporters that the piece was outrageous, just way off base, and the big newspapers and the networks all decided to pass on the John Huang memo. Other than the CNN segment and a couple of wire-service reports, the story didn't exist. They had killed it.

That night McCurry gave Kranish a call. "I'm sorry I dumped on you," he said. It was all in a day's work.

The defensive maneuvers prompted the *Washington Post* editorial page to ratchet up its criticism, saying that McCurry in particular "gets an Oscar" for his slippery performance. "Time after time," the paper said, the White House "puts up a false front, offers a misleading version of events. . . . The dispensing of truth in reluctant dribs and drabs does indeed have the corrosive effect that the White House itself periodically deplores."

There were also backstage battles over the timing of disclosures. *The Wall Street Journal* discovered that a Miami executive named

Mark Jimenez had been granted two meetings with White House officials, urging Clinton to back Paraguay's president in the face of a possible coup. Clinton did so, and on the day the coup failed, Jimenez gave $100,000 to the DNC. When McCurry and Davis learned that the *Journal* was about to publish its findings as a front-page story, they decided to release the details of the Jimenez meetings to the rest of the press, destroying the *Journal*'s exclusive. Washington bureau chief Alan Murray, deputy bureau chief Jill Abramson, and reporter Glenn Simpson got wind of the plan, and all called the White House to complain. "This is really going to be bad for our relationship," Simpson told McCurry. At the last minute the White House backed off, deciding that open warfare with the *Journal* would not be worth undermining the story. But notice had been served. The administration would do what was necessary to defuse investigative stories.

The dribs and drabs continued. McCurry had claimed that the White House had no idea back in 1994 that Webster Hubbell, the Clinton pal and former associate attorney general who wound up in prison, had been hired by the friendly Democratic donors at Indonesia's Lippo Group after resigning in disgrace for defrauding his old law firm. But the Associated Press discovered a deposition in which Bruce Lindsey admitted that he had known of Hubbell's hiring since soon after it happened. McCurry explained away his mistake by blaming it on a miscommunication he had with Cheryl Mills, the White House deputy counsel who had debriefed Lindsey. "Apparently I made a mistaken assumption and I'm sorry for that," he said.

The reporters weren't satisfied. Why, they asked, hadn't Lindsey corrected the false news accounts that had appeared in recent weeks? McCurry couldn't say. Once again the administration appeared to be hiding something—no one knew why Hubbell had been hired, or why he was paid around $250,000, or whether this was hush money related in some way to the Whitewater probe—and Lindsey was refusing to talk to reporters. Privately Lindsey told McCurry that it would have been absurd for him to try to hide the truth when his deposition was publicly available. But it was McCurry who was left hanging out to dry.

The Washington Times played the story above the fold. "McCurry Admits Misinformation," the headline said. A *Washington Post* editorial said that McCurry should feel "a little used." Deborah Orin wrote in the *New York Post* that "it can be death for a press secretary to say anything that turns out to be false—because then reporters can't be sure they can trust anything he says." Reuters moved a story on McCurry as "the target of harsh editorial criticism in recent weeks for relaying inaccurate or misleading information to reporters."

Still, much of the rest of the press hung back. There was no drumbeat of McCurry stories because the press corps had no desire to see McCurry thrown overboard. Wolf Blitzer thought McCurry was the best press secretary he had ever seen. Mara Liasson of National Public Radio thought there was an enormous reservoir of goodwill toward McCurry. Most of the reporters saw him as the one stand-up guy on a staff full of sycophants.

It wasn't just that McCurry was smart as hell and extraordinarily helpful. There was a seductive quality to the man. He had a way of making each reporter think they had a special relationship. He would lower his voice and impart sensitive information, or chew the fat late into the evening. The networks and NPR broadcast nothing about McCurry's problems. The reporters were willing to give him a pass.

But McCurry knew he had messed up. He should have taken charge after the first news reports raised questions about the Webb Hubbell fiasco. He should have vacuumed up all the facts and put them out. But he had let it slide, and now a minor foul-up was playing out in the press as a major cover-up. No one ever allowed for the possibility that you might be trying to do the right thing.

"It really hurts like hell to be dinged in one editorial," he told Clinton. "I can't imagine how you and the first lady feel being pounded so often."

The president just shook his head. "Believe me, I know how it feels," he said. "Keep your chin up and focus on what matters. If you dwell on it, you get preoccupied and can't get your job done."

But McCurry seemed to constantly be stumbling into new disputes with the press corps. The man whose job was to help generate positive headlines for the president was instead becoming the story himself.

His latest problem was caused not by his big mouth but by his curious decision to remain silent. He stood off to the side of the podium while Barry Toiv handled the day's briefing, which was consumed by charges made by Truman Arnold, a former DNC finance chairman. The Texas oilman had been quoted as saying that party officials sometimes used a White House database to help monitor favors being dispensed to Democratic donors. The administration had long maintained that the database was nothing but an electronic Rolodex that had nothing to do with politics.

Reporters asked whether anyone at the White House had talked to Arnold about his comments to *Time* and the *Los Angeles Times*. McCurry interrupted to say that the White House legal counsel's office had been in touch with Arnold, but he neglected to add a key fact: McCurry himself had privately coached Arnold on what to say.

McCurry was worried about Toiv's feelings. He didn't want to boot Barry off the stage: Nice try, kid, now the boss will take over. He had another opportunity when he returned to the podium minutes later, but again failed to say anything.

McCurry had known Truman Arnold since helping to train him on dealing with the media back when he was with Robinson, Sawyer. When Arnold had called him about the database, McCurry thought he was confused about its purpose and advised him to issue a written statement rather than grant more interviews. In the statement that emerged, Arnold essentially retracted his earlier comments about the database. That might have been the end of it, but an Indiana congressman, David McIntosh, wrote to the White House demanding an accounting of which officials had been in contact with Arnold, and administration lawyers described McCurry's role. Five days later the briefing room grew testy when McCurry admitted that, "in retrospect," he should have fessed up during the earlier session with Toiv. Reporters were openly angry. Todd Purdum of *The New York Times* couldn't resist noting that McCurry often accused the reporters of displaying a "tiresome, prosecutorial tone."

"What this discussion today has suggested to us is, we should be even more prosecutorial in our questions, asking the perfect combination of queries," Purdum said.

The next day's headlines were bad. "McCurry Admits Misleading Press," said the front-page report in *The Washington Times*. Paul Bedard's story even invoked a phrase from the LBJ era, saying McCurry "ensnared himself in the growing White House credibility gap" over the fundraising scandal.

McCurry knew full well that the stakes were higher than a couple of critical articles and editorials. If he reached the point where he no longer had credibility with the press, McCurry felt, he would have to resign. *The Washington Post* was arguably the most important newspaper covering the White House, and he was its latest target. Clinton couldn't have a press secretary who was not credible. If things didn't improve, he would have to find other work.

. . .

INSIDE THE BUBBLE OF THE BELTWAY POLITICAL COMMUNITY, THE president's top aides figured that their main competition for the nation's attention span was the steady, corrosive drip of scandal news. In a larger sense, however, they were competing for headlines and air time with every sensational or titillating tale around the world. News of the latest hot movie star or multimillion-dollar athlete or philandering celebrity consumed much of the media oxygen, particularly as the news business was increasingly drawn toward seamy tabloid stories. Against this backdrop, Bill Clinton was just another big-name star trying to peddle a message.

There were, however, a handful of political rituals—the political conventions, the presidential debates, the inauguration—for which massive media attention was virtually guaranteed. One of these was the State of the Union, the annual presidential address to Congress that had become a major television-age moment, if only because all the networks felt compelled to cover it. Every president knew that the speech was a rare opportunity to commune with the country at length rather than in the brief bursts normally permitted by the sound-bite culture.

Bill Clinton was preparing for the first State of the Union of his second term, doing his final run-through in the White House theater, when McCurry called. Don Baer, who had supervised the drafting of the speech, answered the phone in the back of the theater.

"I don't know if you have the heart to break it to the Big Guy," McCurry said, "but there will probably be an O.J. verdict about the time he starts the speech." He had just gotten the news from CNN.

Baer and Al Gore gave Clinton the news minutes later, and he seemed to take it in stride. "Let me know how it comes out," he said.

It was nothing short of remarkable: Here was the president's big ceremonial moment, the House chamber packed with lawmakers and

Supreme Court justices and dignitaries of every stripe. Yet Rather, Jennings, and Brokaw were blathering on all evening about the imminent Simpson verdict, essentially blowing off the president.

At 8:10 McCurry called Robin Sproul, ABC's Washington bureau chief, who was coordinating the pool coverage for the networks. He sounded agitated as he pressed her on the situation. "I want to know if I'm going to see the president of the United States in a little box with O.J. filling up the screen," he said.

Next McCurry put together a conference call with Sproul and the bureau chiefs from CBS, NBC, CNN, and Fox. "We're essentially mandated to do this before the Congress and we fully intend to do it," he declared. "The president is going to deliver the State of the Union to Congress at nine o'clock. It's a responsibility we take very seriously. I hope you'll all do the right thing."

An awkward feeling hung in the air. "What exactly are you saying here?" asked NBC's Tim Russert. Was the White House presuming that it had the power to tell the networks what to do?

But McCurry would go no further. "The ball's in your court," he said. He wanted to put pressure on them to make the proper journalistic decision, O.J. or no O.J. Some truths were self-evident, he felt. It was not the time for a harangue by the press secretary. You simply didn't upstage the president of the United States during his annual address to the nation.

Still, McCurry was not oblivious to reality. When Sproul called back, he suggested a bit of wiggle room. If the verdict comes in right at nine o'clock, he said, "we can make the walk into the hall last a little longer."

Fortunately for the White House, the verdict from the civil trial in Santa Monica, California—Simpson held liable for two brutal murders—did not hit the screen until Clinton was finishing his hourlong oration. The Simpson case dominated the postgame analysis. Clinton couldn't believe it the next day when *The Washington Post* printed a huge O.J. headline above the State of the Union story, as if this tabloid trial was more important than a presidential address to the nation. The press was out to screw him again.

. . .

BILL CLINTON, AL GORE, AND ERSKINE BOWLES WERE IN THE Treaty Room, the president's private study in the residence, where he often watched CNN, on the evening of February 12. McCurry walked in around 10:30, having just dispatched an aide to the loading dock of *The Washington Post*, six blocks north, where you could buy the bulldog edition for a quarter. Even in an age when most newspapers were on the World Wide Web, this was still the fastest way to get the next day's *Post*, especially if your business was damage control.

There it was, the paper's lead story, an ominous-sounding Bob Woodward bombshell. McCurry knew it was coming because he had been on the phone with Woodward. The four men and a few aides, seated on chairs and sofas, sat reading the handful of copies that had just come of the presses.

It was the strangest goddamn piece: the Justice Department had uncovered evidence that representatives of the People's Republic of China tried to direct foreign contributions to the Democrats before the 1996 election. The Chinese embassy was used for the planning, according to electronic eavesdropping by federal agencies.

That was it. Who was involved? What contributions did they direct? How much money? When did it happen? The story didn't say. Just a couple of tantalizing details from Woodward's legendary sources. What the hell did it mean? The president and the vice president and the chief of staff didn't know anything about it. They chewed over the story, tried to decipher its meaning like some ancient hieroglyphics. It seemed like a work in progress.

Still, they knew all too well that any story with Woodward's byline had a certain cachet around town. The tireless reporter had helped drive Richard Nixon out of this very house two decades earlier, was one of the heroes of the movie *All The President's Men.* The assembled officials recalled the scene in which Jason Robards, playing Ben Bradlee, threw a half-baked story back at Woodward and Bernstein and barked, "You just don't have it." Perhaps, it was suggested, a *Post* editor should have delivered that line on this story.

McCurry received few press calls about the piece that night. It was almost as if the entire Washington press corps was still trying to divine its importance. Upon convening the 9:15 gaggle in his office for about thirty reporters the next morning, he said: "I'm having a hard time making heads or tails of the story." He added that Clinton was "puzzled" by it but "very concerned" about the allegation. That was about all he could say.

Helen Thomas was dissatisfied. "Every question is like pulling teeth," she said.

"I'm being very careful, and you know from recent experience I have good reason to be very careful," McCurry said. "You got a problem?"

"Yeah, the problem is trying to figure out what's going on."

"I'm not breezy on this subject," McCurry allowed.

"I forgive you," Thomas said.

Administration officials were worried that the flap would over-shadow the visit later that day of Israel's prime minister, Benjamin Netanyahu. At a photo session with the Israeli leader, Clinton asked the assembled reporters not to start a "feeding frenzy." He promised to take their questions later in the day.

McCurry held the two o'clock gaggle for the cameras. The briefing room, crowded with visiting Israeli journalists, was unusually noisy. On television it looked as though he had the audience's undivided attention. In the room, journalists were whispering along the wall, stepping outside for a smoke, walking in from lunch. It took all of McCurry's concentration to focus on the seven cameras mounted along a riser at the back of the room and ignore the chatter in the aisles.

McCurry began by referring questions on the possible role of the Chinese government to Deputy Attorney General Jamie Gorelick, who, as he well knew, wasn't commenting.

Wolf Blitzer, undeterred, tried a different tack: "How concerned is the president, though, that there is a story out there that there possibly could have been some improper Chinese government activity designed to influence us—"

"The story, while puzzling to the president, was of concern to him, and he fully expects that any matters like that would be properly investigated," McCurry replied.

Helen Thomas tried to get McCurry to detail the gist of the matter. "Can you explain why it is that the president is puzzled or what in particular it is that causes him puzzlement?"

"The story."

"Yes, but what about it?"

"The story, what's reported, the news in the story."

"But what about it is puzzling?"

"It just seems puzzling, the news of the story."

McCurry wasn't about to repeat the allegations for television. Let the reporters characterize it any way they wanted. He wasn't going to serve as Woodward's press agent.

Two hours later, fielding questions with Netanyahu, Clinton tried to frame the issue in general terms. "Obviously, it would be a very serious matter for the United States if any country were to attempt to funnel funds to one of our political parties for any reason whatever," he said.

The China story was all over the networks. "In Washington tonight, there's a major buzz in the highest circles over a page-one story in today's *Washington Post* about the possible role of the Chinese government in raising funds for the Democratic National Committee," Tom Brokaw said on NBC.

Over at CBS, Rita Braver reported that "White House insiders are genuinely puzzled and concerned about this report—especially the possibility it may be another indirect result of their aggressive fundraising tactics."

McCurry barely had time to catch his breath before the press found new grist for its ever-churning mill. The next morning the administration released more than one hundred pages of National Security Council documents in an effort to bolster the nomination of outgoing White House aide Anthony Lake to head the CIA. In one document an NSC official warned that a major Democratic contributor, Johnny Chung, was a "hustler" trying to exploit the Clintons; Chung was nevertheless allowed to bring six Chinese businessmen to watch the president's Saturday radio address in March 1995. Wolf Blitzer was on the lawn within an hour, standing on a rubber mat to avoid the muddy grass. "Some of these documents do contain additional political embarrassments for the White House," he said into the camera.

The White House decided to put Lanny Davis on the talk-show circuit that weekend. The shows had been clamoring for Davis for weeks, but the White House booker, Stuart Schear, kept saying he wasn't ready, wasn't sufficiently steeped in scandal minutiae. The real reason was tactical in nature. White House officials didn't like to put Davis on the weekend shows because that would trigger another round of scandal segments. Since Davis's sole mission was to clean up after the fundraising mess, his very presence set the agenda. But a critical mass of scandal stories had been building up, and the White House needed someone to respond to the charges. Schear sent word that Davis was available.

In the space of twenty-four hours, Davis spoke to Wolf Blitzer on *Inside Politics Weekend*, to Tony Snow on *Fox News Sunday*, to Tim Russert on *Meet the Press*. Davis had clearly decided to stay on defense. "I'm not here to make news," he told Fox staffers before the show. The litany of questions was remarkably similar: The alleged Chinese involvement in Democratic fundraising. The parade of thugs and favor seekers at the White House coffees. A new *Washington Post* report that the administration had changed its policy toward Guam after a visit by Hillary Clinton prompted $900,000 in contributions to the Clinton campaign and the party. Davis listened to the questions with a slightly bemused expression and then unleashed his rapid-fire answers, trying to finish each rhetorical salvo before he was interrupted.

"The president regards these allegations as very serious," he told Blitzer.

"No governmental action ever resulted from a contribution," he told Snow.

"There's no policy affected by contributions to this president," he told Russert.

Darting from studio to studio, Davis got the names confused. He called Tony Snow "Brit." He twice referred to Congressman McIntosh as McIntyre. But the only time he really stumbled was when he had to acknowledge that, for all his assurances that contributions did not change administration policy, he had never personally discussed the question with the president. Brit Hume quickly moved in, asking how often he had met with Clinton since becoming White House special counsel.

"Several times," Davis said.

"Three? Two?"

"I don't want to go into it any further than that," Davis said.

· · ·

JOE LOCKHART, MCCURRY'S DEPUTY, UNDERSTOOD THE MEDIA culture because he had grown up in its midst. His parents had both spent decades working for NBC, and his wife, Laura, worked for

ABC. Lockhart had bounced around the political game for years, but he had also found work on the journalistic side of the tracks: assignment editor at ABC, producer at CNN, London producer for NBC. He had launched his career thinking that journalism was pure—a bunch of people dedicated to serving the public by ferreting out the truth—and concluded, sadly, that it wasn't. In fact, it wasn't all that different from being a political spokesman. Both professions waxed and waned according to the news cycle, and both had their share of shortcuts and compromises. You got your hands dirty in both arenas. But Lockhart came to believe you could have more of an impact from the inside.

A stocky man whose thick brown hair was streaked with gray, Lockhart, thirty-seven, had gotten to know McCurry when both men worked for the Robinson, Sawyer firm in the early '90s, and McCurry had personally picked him to be the spokesman for Clinton's 1996 campaign. Ironically enough, Lockhart had spent much of the campaign pushing the story of campaign finance abuses—in Bob Dole's campaign. After Dole's finance guy pleaded guilty, Lockhart had a researcher do a database search and found several enticing leads about questionable donations to the Republican campaign. But he couldn't make the sale. Reporters on the plane were sick of hearing him talk about it. The few journalists who were interested told him they couldn't get the stories in the paper; Dole was clearly toast and no one cared about his finances. One reporter actually said that his news organization would take a closer look if Dole started climbing in the polls. It was a blatant double standard, Lockhart felt. But he also knew, in the campaign's final weeks, that the Clintonites would pay a price for not answering questions about their own emerging financial mess.

Now Lockhart was dealing with the aftermath from a cramped office in the West Wing. He had been on the verge of accepting a lucrative job with America Online and was planning to spend more time with his two-year-old daughter when McCurry persuaded him to sign on as deputy press secretary. Once on the job, Lockhart was stunned by the one-sided thrust of the scandal. How could it be fair, he wondered, when all these newspapers had their entire investigative teams digging into Democratic fundraising? Lockhart understood the arms-race mentality, the constant pressure not to get beaten on the biggest story in town. But what about a semblance of balance? If your investigators weren't looking at Republicans, they weren't going to find anything on Republicans.

But the pendulum eventually swung in these matters, and now there were signs of movement. *The Boston Globe* weighed in with a front-page piece on the White House spokesman defending a private presidential reception for six-figure donors and closed-door sessions with Cabinet secretaries for big contributors. But the spokesman was Marlin Fitzwater, defending President Bush in 1992 after the GOP had reaped $9 million from just one dinner. And here were ABC, NBC, and *The New York Times* reporting on a lavish three-day Republican reception in Palm Beach for members of Team 100, a group of fat-cat donors who were enjoying private meetings and dinners with Newt Gingrich, Trent Lott, and other Republican congressional leaders, simply by virtue of having ponied up enough cash. That sure sounded like selling access, the charge so frequently hurled at the White House.

Still, a foreigner reading the daily coverage would conclude that the president was bloodied, staggering backward, up against the ropes. Every day Clinton took a journalistic punch from another direction. *The Wall Street Journal* discovered two big Democratic donors who, after several coffees with the president, got a fat federal housing contract with unusual guarantees. *The Boston Globe* led the paper with comments by former Democratic chairman Donald Fowler, who said that of course the party hit guests up for money after the White House coffees.

Deborah Orin was all over McCurry at the gaggle. "But, Mike, doesn't that make these essentially fundraisers held at the White House?"

"The question is whether the president directly solicited funds during these occasions, and he did not," McCurry said. He had been reduced to the narrow, legalistic response: donors were brought in to press the presidential flesh and solicited for cash afterward, but this was not an abuse of the White House. It was the same sort of fictional pretense as McCurry maintaining that these guests were just plain old ordinary Americans sharing their views with the nation's leader, not wealthy businessmen purchasing face time with Clinton to press their special issues.

But the hothouse environment was limited to certain Washington zip codes. The same front page of *The Boston Globe* carried another story reporting, in a slightly amazed tone, "that Clinton's popularity has soared even as the media's focus on scandal intensifies." Baer, Emanuel, and other presidential aides were not surprised. The president was still riding high at 60 percent because he was talking about real issues, like tax credits for college, that were as important to voters as they were sleep-inducing for White House correspondents.

Clinton was resigned to the shrill scandal coverage. They were in the middle of a media vortex, he felt, and there wasn't much they could do about it. His staff had noticed that he wasn't allowing himself to be torn apart or angry or perplexed over every negative story. He wasn't obsessing on each nuance of the coverage, as he had during the early days of Whitewater. He told his staff he had to stay focused on the big issues.

But the president was clearly frustrated by the sporadic attention to his agenda. There were exciting opportunities to make progress on education, welfare, balancing the budget, and yet all that was taking a back seat to the seamier stuff. No matter what he said or did, the reporters were obviously more excited about the fundraising allegations.

"I'll go out and give a good speech about education and I assume it'll be back in the middle of the paper," Clinton complained. His aides had to agree.

Still, their internal polls convinced them they were somehow breaking through the media static. Education had surpassed the economy as the voters' top concern. This was in part because the economy was booming, but also because the president was out there promoting education as his top issue. Dick Morris had just done a poll in which 61 percent of those surveyed said they didn't care about the fundraising charges and more than half said they believed that both parties used the same tactics to raise money. The scandal stuff was not a major concern, at least not yet. It was the reporters who were simply out of touch.

CHAPTER EIGHT

Hezbollah

THE WHITE HOUSE WAR AGAINST KENNETH STARR WAS A CURI-
ous and covert operation. No responsible official would come out
and publicly attack the independent counsel who could bring charges
against anyone in the administration. But through whispered conversations and strategic use of surrogates, White House aides assailed
the former judge they viewed as their persecutor.

The campaign had begun in earnest in the last weeks of 1996,
when James Carville went nuclear against Starr. Carville, the Louisi-
ana-bred political consultant who masterminded the Clinton campaign in 1992, had grown increasingly obsessed with the Whitewater
prosecutor, all the while acting as if he were just some private citizen
speaking his mind. His assault started on *Meet the Press*, when Carville
announced he was forming a group that would raise money and run
ads attacking Starr and his "right-wing agenda." Carville's wife and
sparring partner, Mary Matalin, dismissed him as "a rabid dog," but
he barked his anti-Starr message across the media landscape, frothing
on every network this side of the Home Shopping Club.

It was an extraordinary assault on a sitting prosecutor, as if Richard
Nixon's friend Bebe Rebozo had launched a campaign against Archi-

bald Cox. It was Nixon's firing of Cox, of course, that had led to the independent counsel law in the first place, as a way of insulating investigators of high-level chicanery from a president's displeasure. And here was Clinton's close friend denouncing the prosecutor as a Republican hatchet man, without the president, or his spokesman, lifting a finger to dissuade him.

All of which presented a daunting challenge for the president's press secretary. Would he embrace Carville's criticism or cut him loose?

McCurry calmly told reporters that Carville's actions did "not represent the president's thinking." The leader of the free world, he insisted, "is not in a position to dissuade Mr. Carville." In fact, he maintained, Carville seemed hell-bent on pursuing his campaign "regardless of what anyone at the White House, including the president, has to say."

"Even if the president asks him to stop?" a reporter demanded. "Are you serious?"

"I am serious, yes," McCurry said.

"It's a remarkable 'Look, ma, no hands' operation here, isn't it?" asked ABC's Brit Hume.

"You can characterize it as you see fit—and I'm sure you will," McCurry shot back.

The *New York Times* editorial page wasn't buying. "President Clinton must have been embarrassed by his press secretary's statement that the president couldn't get James Carville to pipe down," the paper said. Rather than criticize such "buffoonery," the *Times* said, Clinton "assigned his press secretary, Mike McCurry, the scuzzy task of arguing . . . that Mr. Carville is beyond the reach of presidential instruction."

McCurry knew that it looked like the White House was giving tacit approval to Carville's shenanigans, but that was better than overt approval. And it was certainly better than a holier-than-thou stance that no one would believe. James was having too much fun popping off in front of the cameras. If he had chided Carville, McCurry knew, the Ragin' Cajun would have shrugged it off with a slap at "those sissy-ass people in the White House."

Privately Clinton told McCurry that he didn't think Carville's attacks were helping him. McCurry, too, believed that Carville had become a distraction and had made himself, not Ken Starr, the issue. The only marginal benefit, McCurry thought, was that people might get the impression that Whitewater was just a political game on all sides.

Still, there was a method to McCurry's aw-shucks routine. He had to be careful when he didn't have all the facts, lest he be caught in a damaging contradiction. For all he knew, Carville had discussed his anti-Starr diatribe with some White House official, maybe even with Clinton himself. McCurry hadn't asked the president so that he could honestly say he didn't know. The worst thing a press secretary could do, he knew, was make a flat, categorical statement. There was always some gray area that would turn up later. Nothing was black and white. McCurry often served up what he called "gray mush" from the podium. That was part of the job.

"That clearly would be wrong for anyone to draw any inference that the president meant not to imply," McCurry said at the gaggle, his language so tortured that the room broke into laughter.

McCurry needed more wiggle room. He knew that George Stephanopoulos, Carville's old campaign partner, had talked to the Louisianan about the Starr matter. Stephanopoulos was about to leave the White House for a perch at ABC News, but his office was still down the hall in the West Wing. "I didn't rule out the prospect that some at the White House may have talked to James about this issue," McCurry cautioned. "And I know, specifically, George probably did, but George tells me he was reflecting his private views. To my knowledge, no one has communicated anything representing the president's views to Mr. Carville."

The Carville episode was a perfect example of why journalists had come to view much of what McCurry said with extreme skepticism. To argue, with a straight face, that the president's pal was attacking the president's prosecutor and the president had no way of stopping him, and that the president's senior adviser had discussed this with the president's pal but was reflecting only his personal, nonofficial view—well, it was hard to watch a grown man twist himself into a pretzel. And for reporters to listen to this sort of drivel day after day was an a exercise in frustration.

But McCurry's job was to spin, not to confirm facts that might tarnish the president. He would no more admit that Clinton was enjoying watching Carville trash Starr than the spokesman for Coke would say something nice about Pepsi. McCurry had to stick to the approved story line, no matter how ludicrous, no matter how much it insulted the intelligence of the journalists who gathered each day in the briefing room.

"I have to send McCurry a case of wine," Carville later told Stephanopoulos. "I put him through misery."

Now, in the middle of February, Ken Starr abruptly announced that he was resigning as independent counsel to become dean of the law school at Pepperdine University. Everyone in the press leaped to the same conclusion, that Starr had no case against the president and first lady, or else he would not simply walk away from such a historic prosecution. Perhaps Whitewater, which had gone on twice as long as Watergate, was finally nearing an end.

McCurry gave strict orders to the staff: No comment, on or off the record. He didn't want the White House to appear to be gloating as its adversary limped off the battlefield. Besides, who knew what evidence Starr had up his sleeve or how high his indictments might reach? They had to be careful. McCurry said that Clinton had "no reaction" and "had no clue as to what it meant."

But McCurry's dictum was widely ignored. The reporters called their usual White House sources, who couldn't resist the urge to pontificate, on background, about Starr bailing out.

"Privately, White House officials are confident that Starr's announcement to step down . . . must mean he has no case and there will be no indictments against the president or Mrs. Clinton," Jim Miklaszewski reported on NBC.

"There's joy in Mudville," an unnamed aide told Sue Schmidt of *The Washington Post*.

McCurry was furious. They had allowed themselves to look like they were popping champagne corks when no one knew what prosecutorial traps lay ahead. And when Starr reversed himself four days later and said he would stay in the job after all, the natural conclusion was that the administration's glee had turned to misery.

McCurry found it frustrating that his colleagues didn't have the good sense to shut up when that was clearly the wisest course. It was typical of these midlevel apparatchiks, who got a thrill from being called "senior officials" in print. It was a way for them to score private points, to bank political credit in their dealings with the press. They should keep their goddamn musings to themselves. It was one of those intoxicating habits of Washington, these background conversations between reporters and anonymous White House aides. McCurry often spoke on background too, but he was the press secretary, not some munchkin trying to impress journalists with how important he was. Clinton was equally mystified by this culture of leaking. He often picked up the paper and wondered: Who are these people? Why are they saying these things? It was impossible to have a private conversation in the White House anymore. Clinton had made it a rule not to say anything sensitive in a room with more than one aide; he might as well just give it to the AP. They had all been sucked into playing the speculation game. Even the press secretary, McCurry realized, couldn't plug all the leaks in this place.

·   ·   ·

ON FRIDAY AFTERNOON, FEBRUARY 21, THE WHITE HOUSE DE-cided to hang tough on the Lincoln Bedroom documents.

For nearly four months McCurry had insisted to the press corps that those who stayed over at the White House were personal guests of the first family and that the list would remain private. It was a line in the sand, an outer limit on the strategy of disclosure. But now the line was about to be washed away. A Republican House committee chairman, Dan Burton of Indiana, was getting his hands on a big batch of documents involving the Lincoln Bedroom and other fund-raising efforts. Harold Ickes, the former deputy chief of staff, was voluntarily turning over many of his personal files. Ickes had been squeezed out of the inner circle by the new chief of staff, Erskine Bowles—he learned about his ouster from *The Wall Street Journal*—and some believed that this was his way of getting even. Burton, a fierce partisan, wasn't likely to be shy about exploiting the issue. Reality was staring the White House in the face.

Lanny Davis sat down with Bowles and John Podesta, the new deputy chief of staff, to devise some talking points on the issue. Davis had argued all along that the administration should release the list of Lincoln Bedroom guests, whatever the short-term pain. If you had "bad facts" and didn't disclose them, Davis contended, you wound up with two stories, one about the latest embarrassment and another about how you tried to cover it up. Davis was amazed at how the simple logic of disclosure escaped so many White House officials, despite the public rhetoric about coming clean. They were living in a fantasy world, pretending that a hostile Congress wouldn't get this stuff and put it out.

But Davis and McCurry were having a rough time in their campaign for disclosure. They were constantly battling what their allies called the Hezbollah wing of the White House, the hard-liners, led by Bruce Lindsey and the counsel's office and sometimes Hillary, who never wanted to surrender a document without a fight. That was how lawyers operated in private practice, where never giving an inch was a badge of professional honor. Even McCurry's allies occasionally chided him for going too far.

"Mike wants to shovel all the documents out the door," Doug Sosnik would say. "Some of us think we should read them first." Worse, when the material was released, the press gave the administration no credit for making it public, just hammered away with negative stories. The next day the officials who didn't want to release the documents would sneer at them: What did you accomplish? In a strange way, the McCurry faction was being blamed for the bad publicity.

On the other side, Charles Ruff, the new White House counsel, thought it was a myth that he was opposed to disclosure. He worried about press coverage almost as much as McCurry and Davis did, but he had to balance that against the legitimate demands of Congress, the Justice Department, and Ken Starr. Ruff made no effort to argue his case in the press, and he was often the one who ordered Lanny Davis to stay off television. A wheelchair-bound former Watergate prosecutor, Ruff was circumspect by nature and felt he got paid for day-to-day lawyering, not for popping off in public.

Cheryl Mills, the black former public defender who was deputy counsel, felt she had to live with the fact that she was seen as the don't-get-it-out person. But her real concern was rushing out with the wrong version. Mills, who talked a mile a minute, was the one who first asked all the senior White House officials whether they had used the Map Room coffees as fundraisers. They all insisted they had not. Mills was suspicious; you couldn't trust people's initial recollections in situations like this. We cannot go public with this line, she argued. But the White House did, and when documents surfaced showing that fundraising budgets had been built around the coffees, the public thought they were all lying. That was why she often wanted to slam on the brakes.

Podesta was a middle-of-a-roader, positioning himself between the McCurry-Davis faction and the Hezbollah resistance. He was the only official with the stature and gumption to stand up to Ruff in meetings, sometimes rolling his eyes when Ruff wasn't looking. Podesta also felt each set of documents had to be weighed individually, but he was far more conscious of the need to wage the public relations war. In this case the question was time. He wasn't sure they had enough time to digest the Ickes material before disgorging it. Could they answer the inevitable deluge of questions—including the third, fourth, fifth, and sixth questions? Could they work out their talking points? What was the rush?

Bowles and Podesta decided to slam on the brakes. Let Burton release the material if he insists on invading the president's privacy. They would have to take the hit. There was nothing they could do.

Davis tried again. Let's not let someone else frame the story, he said. We should get out front with our own explanation. No luck.

Davis was supposed to fly to Florida that night to visit his mother, who was not well. But the White House was scrambling to get hold of the Ickes papers, to see just what was in them. When Ickes's lawyer, Robert Bennett, who was also representing Clinton in the Paula Jones case, agreed to provide copies, Davis put off his trip until the next day.

There was a four-inch stack of papers to be scrutinized. Davis stayed up till 2:00 A.M. with Cheryl Mills and another White House lawyer, Karen Popp, poring over the material. He could see that some of the stuff was explosive. There were handwritten notes from the president. "Ready to start overnights right away," Clinton had scribbled on one memo. And "Get other names at 100,000 or more, 50,000 or more." Clinton had personally approved a Democratic Party plan to "energize" donors by rewarding them with overnight stays, coffees, golf outings, and morning jogs with the leader of the free world. After a lengthy effort to distance Clinton from the crass money-grubbing, this was the smoking memo. He had been a driving force behind the whole effort.

The other lawyers didn't see it that way. This is old stuff, they said. It won't be much of a story.

Lanny Davis headed for the airport on Saturday. While he was waiting for the flight, Podesta beeped him. The decision had been reversed. The White House would put out the Ickes papers after all. The gory details had finally convinced Podesta and Ruff that they had to seize the initiative.

Over the weekend the senior staff huddled with Bowles to plan their response to the stack of documents. McCurry looked over the Ickes papers for the first time, saw Clinton's handwritten notations. It figured. He had always assumed that the hundreds of Lincoln Bedroom visits would not have been undertaken without the president's express approval. McCurry spotted another document he thought would be big news. It was an unsigned memo to a DNC official named Martha Phipps, laying out the possible elements of a fundraising program: Air Force One trips, White House overnights, appointments to presidential commissions and boards. Whether these goodies were actually given out didn't matter; it smelled like a quid pro quo.

Davis's assistant, Adam Goldberg, called him in Florida on Sunday. The documents would be released the next day, he said. Davis moved up his reservation and returned to Washington.

Back at the office, Davis and McCurry made a wager on what the lead of the story would be. Davis said it would be the memo in which Ickes and the other former deputy, Evelyn Lieberman, described the coffees as fundraisers. Nah, McCurry said, the coffees were old news. The Lincoln Bedroom overnights and the president's handwritten notes would grab the headlines.

The release of the documents was put off for a day. At the Monday briefing a reporter complained that information about the Lincoln Bedroom was coming out "in dribs and drabs."

"You're getting information that we are, in most cases, voluntarily providing," McCurry said. "Remember that, quote unquote, dribs and drabs come about because we are working very hard to provide documentation and information to various people who are looking into these matters."

He made his standard pitch for a bipartisan scandal: "I'm waiting for some of the same information to become available on things like the Eagles program at the Republican National Committee, the Team 100 program, the Season Ticket Holder program. . . . I think then there will be probably dribs and drabs of information about their fundraising program as well."

On Tuesday morning the White House put out the Ickes documents, and the scandal immediately reached fever pitch. Whatever else the administration wanted to talk about was obliterated. From the very first news stories about questionable contributions in the final weeks of the campaign, the media drumbeat had been building toward this moment, when the layers of denial would be stripped away and the president would have to account for the whole revolting money mess, for what the press saw as the selling of the White House.

There was a deeper subtext to the media outrage. On some level the fundraising scandal had become a proxy for reporters convinced of Clinton's essential slipperiness. They had been grappling with this question since 1992—the lawyerlike answers on philandering, the draft, marijuana, Whitewater, Paula Jones. Clinton simply could not be trusted to provide an unvarnished version of the truth, many journalists felt. He had twice won the presidency in spite of this, in spite of their dogged efforts to expose his penchant for dissembling. Now they had him dead to rights, his few scribbled words looming as large as the Nixon tapes.

What's more, the Lincoln Bedroom was a piece of Americana, a colorful bit of political shorthand. Harry Truman had turned it into a shrine to the Civil War leader. Millions of Americans had seen its nineteenth-century decor when Jackie Kennedy provided a televised tour of the White House. Now Clinton "may have cheapened a symbol of American history," as Rita Braver put it. The ornate bedroom made a complicated story easy to visualize.

Clinton's first public event that day was a late-morning appearance with General Barry McCaffrey, the White House drug czar, to unveil an antidrug initiative. Reporters demanded a reaction to the latest information about selling White House perks. The assembled police officers and antidrug activists booed in unison. "The Lincoln Bedroom was never sold," Clinton snapped. "That was one more false story we have had to endure."

The president was in the self-pitying mode, much as he had been when he complained to *Rolling Stone* about the knee-jerk liberal press. He had convinced himself that the charges were bogus. After all, he told his staff, he had fond memories of the overnight visits, loved showing off the White House to his friends. He and Hillary felt like they were in a bubble. They craved conversation, some contact with real people. That some of the overnight visitors were big donors, or rich strangers whom the DNC hoped would become donors, was a minor detail in Clinton's mind.

Three hours later it was McCurry's turn. He could no longer wall off the briefing by directing unpleasant inquiries elsewhere. The story was just too big. McCurry stood at the podium with Lanny Davis and Ann Lewis, the veteran Democratic activist who had just come on board as deputy communications director. For an hour and ten minutes, they tried to defend the indefensible.

"Don't you think there is a lot of hypocrisy in always advocating reform and doing exactly the opposite?" Helen Thomas demanded.

"No," McCurry said, "because we're not doing exactly the opposite."

Rita Braver, Bill Plante, and others pressed McCurry about the odious appearance of the overnights and the coffees. He remained calm and measured, even as he retreated to increasingly Jesuitical distinctions. Again and again McCurry maintained that the coffees and sleepovers "were not fundraisers." They were "part of the effort to build financial support for the party."

Ann Lewis took the podium. "He does have thousands of friends. . . . The president and Mrs. Clinton enjoy spending time with their friends. . . . He decided he wanted to see his old friends," she said, as if they were talking about some big pajama party.

"We regard the notion of special access because a contribution is made as something that is contrary to our policies," said Lanny Davis, sounding very much like a lawyer.

This, then, was what it had come down to: McCurry and company insisting that the Map Room coffees were not fundraisers, even though White House aides referred to them in memos as fundraisers, even though some of the finance people used them to coax big contributions, even though Clinton knew this was being done, because the guests were hit up for dough before and after the coffees but not while sipping the stuff. The overnight guests, some of them high rollers unknown to the president, were simply "friends" and "supporters" and the means for a talkative president to take the public pulse. The spin had become surreal. For the first time in the scandal, McCurry was close to insisting that day was night. The only lingering mystery, he mused, was that there were no questions on the Martha Phipps memo. He discovered later that the White House had not released it under a confidentiality agreement worked out with Congress.

The press, not surprisingly, went wild over the revelations. News outlets calculated that the 958 overnight guests had contributed more than $10 million to Clinton and the Democratic Party, prompting Tom Brokaw to call the Lincoln Bedroom "the most expensive bed and breakfast in North America."

"Critics say the president blundered badly," added Wolf Blitzer.

That night Lanny Davis went on *Nightline* and got eviscerated. He stuck to the line that Clinton was merely using the Lincoln Bedroom to "thank" his "friends" who "hadn't been adequately thanked."

Ted Koppel was having none of it. "There you go again with 'friends' and 'supporters' . . . This is strictly money that we're talking about here," he scoffed.

Koppel had a way of slicing through the verbal fog. "Doesn't it look slightly unseemly," he said in a haughty tone, "for the president to be engaged in effect paying major contributors back by having them sleep in the Lincoln Bedroom, by going jogging with them, by letting them play golf with him, by coming to these coffees, doesn't it look sleazy to you?"

"Well, I don't agree that it looks sleazy for the president," Davis said gamely, "whether it's President Clinton or President Bush or Reagan, to have people who supported him in the past come and stay overnight in his home."

Davis knew it was a mediocre performance. He gave himself a B-minus. There was no good way of explaining away Clinton's handwritten notes, and Koppel wouldn't let him off the hook. But his biggest mistake had been trying to pass off the overnight guests as just "friends." That line of defense, he knew, was simply not credible. The White House, he believed, had to take responsibility for the excesses of 1996. He would argue over and over that the system was broken, that the Republicans had fundraising problems too, but that didn't excuse what the Clintonites had done.

The next morning Davis slipped into a senior staff meeting in the Oval. The whole team was there: Clinton, Gore, Erskine Bowles, Mike McCurry, Rahm Emanuel, John Podesta, Doug Sosnik, Ann Lewis, Cheryl Mills. Clinton was scheduled to hold a news conference with Chilean President Eduardo Frei. Everyone knew that Chile's bid for admission to the NAFTA alliance would not be at the top of the media's agenda. They had to prepare Clinton for the inevitable fundraising questions.

"I understand, I understand," Clinton said. "I'm fine with that. We actually have an opportunity here."

But Clinton expressed concern about his foreign guest. "You'll have to explain to the president of Chile that he'll have no idea what we're talking about here," he said.

A striking gap emerged between the staff's advice and the president's instincts. Clinton wanted to counterpunch, to defend his honor, to fight back against the beating he was taking. But several aides believed that he had sounded whiny and defensive the day before when he complained about "false" stories. Their advice was simple: Keep it low-key. Stay on script. Don't show any emotion. Don't show that you're angry and frustrated at being blamed for a system that has been rotten for a hundred years.

Clinton took the advice. Most of the questions were about the scandal, and he responded coolly as Frei looked on. "Did the people hope that the folks who came to the events would subsequently support me? Yes, they did. . . . But there was no solicitation at the White House, and the guidelines made clear that there was to be no price tag on the events."

Despite Clinton's calm denials, the media mob was in full battle regalia and charging at full speed. NBC reported that some donors were promised a day at the White House for a $250,000 contribution, complete with swimming privileges and a barbecue. *The New York Times* and *The Wall Street Journal* found a memo from Peter Knight, the campaign manager, saying he expected to collect $500,000 by having a group of Texas donors stop by for coffee with Clinton. The *Times* found the Democrats raising $1 million from bankers and bankruptcy lawyers who attended an Illinois dinner with Clinton and the man he had named to head a commission on overhauling the bankruptcy system. The *Journal* had Clinton making angry late-night calls to Democratic senators, complaining about their support for appointing a special prosecutor in the case. The AP unearthed the Martha Phipps memo on rewarding donors with Air Force One trips and presidential appointments. The DNC had to return another $1.5 million in improper contributions.

Even Hillary was taking her lumps. She had insisted weeks earlier that she knew nothing about the official White House database being used for political ends. "I certainly thought the White House needed a computer database," she said, "but the design of it, the use of it, that was for other people to figure out. I didn't know anything about that." Once again she had a selective memory. House Republicans released a 1994 White House memo to the first lady that spoke of sharing the database information with the DNC or others "for political purposes." She had jotted at the top: "This sounds promising. Please advise. HRC."

No one was defending the president, not even the normally sympathetic columnists. Jonathan Alter wrote in *Newsweek* that Clinton was "looking like a greedy fool." In *The Washington Post*, Richard Cohen wrote: "Not since Richard Nixon's 1972 campaign has so much money been raised so cynically." No other story seemed to exist. James Bennet wrote in *The New York Times* of the president's efforts that week on education, fighting drugs, and curbing teenage smoking —but only to illustrate that Clinton was working at "projecting an image that his aides believe slices through the babble about campaign finance scandals." The substantive work of the presidency had, for the moment, been reduced to a sidebar. And yet, as the scandal reached white-hot intensity, journalists openly wondered about the absence of a national uproar. Man-on-the-street interviews revealed a collective yawn, a feeling that this was all politics as usual. The latest *USA Today* poll showed Clinton's approval rating at 57 percent. "We believe that the American people care more about college costs than coffees," Rahm Emanuel insisted.

Still, the knives were clearly out by week's end. Some West Wing officials told Michael Frisby of *The Wall Street Journal* that Lanny Davis might be on his way out. Davis began scrambling for support. He asked Lorraine Voles, Gore's communications director, to call Frisby and vouch for him.

"Don't go hanging this guy when he's in an impossible situation," Voles told Frisby. "People should support him and not go trashing him behind his back."

Still, Frisby drew blood in the paper's "Washington Wire" column: "The White House moves to bring in somebody to help Clinton counsel Lanny Davis after he bombs on ABC's 'Nightline' in trying to defend fundraising," it said. "Some in and out of the White House want him removed, but he still has some support." Davis was convinced that Rahm Emanuel, with whom he had been feuding, had done the anonymous deed. It was the low point of his White House tenure.

When the *NewsHour with Jim Lehrer* wanted a spokesman to talk about the fundraising scandal, the White House sent Ann Lewis instead.

"I have the privilege of working there every day," she said. "And I truly feel it's a privilege. President and Mrs. Clinton have the privilege of living there. And they know it is a privilege. They also have the privilege of sharing that opportunity with their friends."

With her graying hair, old-fashioned glasses, string of pearls, and fixed smile, Lewis looked like everyone's favorite fifth-grade teacher. She managed to sound sweet and reasonable, no matter how disingenuous the spin she was delivering. She had honed this style during three decades as a Democratic activist, and she had proved her loyalty as communications director for the 1996 Clinton campaign. Unlike McCurry, she never gave reporters a wink or a nod or conceded that anything was less than perfect. If it was raining outside, reporters joked, she would insist the sun was shining. She was "on" all the time, always defending the president, for whom she would declare, on or off the record, her undying admiration. Many exasperated reporters had stopped calling her because she seemed to exude contempt for them and their questions. She snacked on raw carrots and was just as tough. She wouldn't play the game, wouldn't talk about backroom strategy, wouldn't accommodate their desire to cover politics like sports. It wasn't a sport, she felt; it was about important issues that affected people's lives.

If was a style of spin that caused even some of Lewis's colleagues to roll their eyes. The alternative approach, followed to some extent by McCurry and, in the first term, by David Gergen, was to privately agree with reporters that the place was screwed up, that Clinton had glaring weaknesses—and then use the credibility of these confessions to make some positive point about the president. This routine was popular with the press but made Clinton suspicious—someone, he knew, was providing reporters with those caustic background quotes. By never ceding a centimeter, Lewis drove reporters crazy but was loved and trusted by the first family. It was Lewis who solemnly declared during the campaign that the Lincoln Bedroom charges were "outrageous" and that the guests had included the president's cook, the president's pastor, and an old friend recently diagnosed with cancer. Hillary had wanted her to be communications director in the first term, but when Dick Morris pushed Don Baer for the job, Lewis joined the campaign instead. When others were weary after the campaign, Lewis, fifty-nine, was more than willing to join the White House staff, to help the Clintons in any way she could. And when Don Baer signaled that he would be leaving soon, Lewis signed on as deputy communications director and heir apparent, settling into the long conference room attached to Baer's office.

She grew up in a political family in Bayonne, New Jersey—Representative Barney Frank is her brother—and she understood the rules of engagement. One friend affectionately called her "the nicest nasty person I know." A careful listener could detect in Lewis a note of annoyance with the journalists who covered the White House. They were so holier-than-thou, she felt, about the fact that politicians had to raise money to run their campaigns.

It was Lewis's job to help decide what events Clinton should attend in the coming months. Should he speak to the Boy Scouts? The Council of Chief State School Officers? A coalition working for free air time for candidates? Deliver a series of Blue Room lectures on the presidency? Schedule was strategy. The president's time was their most valuable commodity, and Lewis was determined to use it as effectively as possible.

But it wasn't long before Lewis was sucked into the damage control operation. She did not consider it beneath her; if that was how she could best serve the president, she would do it with a smile. If the White House wanted her to pore over the roster of Lincoln Bedroom guests for Hillary and divide them into categories so the list could be made public, she would salute and get down to work.

Lewis was a seasoned television performer. As a private citizen she had gone on the talk circuit to defend Hillary in the early days of Whitewater. She realized she was a shield, a body blocker who could absorb blows meant for the first family. It was awfully hard for even the most ferocious critic to yell at her or get ugly with her. She would just smile sweetly and recite her script in a tone that made it sound like she was correcting your homework.

If Ann Lewis viewed the press as a roadblock to be circumvented, John Podesta had a distinctly medical view of the administration's suffering. Dealing with scandal news, he felt, was a question of managing the pain. The White House had only a certain tolerance for bad news at any given time. They had to bleed bad stories off the front page and the evening news. One negative disclosure might be the equivalent of a headache; they would shake it off and move on. But putting out really damaging documents—"Ready to start overnights right away"—was not unlike chemotherapy. You had to build your blood cell count back up or it could kill you. You would take your medicine eventually, but sometimes you had to wait until you felt stronger.

It was a natural comparison for Podesta, who suffered from arthritis. On bad days it was hard to use his hands. Sometimes it hurt more, sometimes less. It was something he had to live with.

A thin man with sharp features, closely cropped black hair, and a fondness for cowboy boots, Podesta, forty-seven, had an advanced degree in damage control. Part of it was his political experience as a Democratic lobbyist, as a longtime aide to Vermont Senator Patrick Leahy, and as a warrior for presidential campaigns ranging from Eugene McCarthy's in 1968 to Bill Clinton's in 1992. Back in the first Clinton term, when he was staff secretary, Podesta found himself designated the chief Whitewater flak catcher, long before Mark Fabiani arrived. He pulled together documents, fielded hundreds of calls from reporters, helped Hillary prepare for her pink press conference. He conducted an internal inquiry of the Travelgate mess. He testified before a grand jury. He even disclosed that the Clintons owed back taxes on their 1980 return. Despite his full-disclosure philosophy, Podesta was every inch the combative attorney. Once, when Richard Cohen criticized him in his *Washington Post* column, Podesta fired off a letter. "I have to publicly eat my mistakes. I hope you acknowledge yours," he said.

The constant warfare left Podesta in a permanently bad mood. Exhausted, he quit in the summer of 1995 to take a teaching post at Georgetown. He had to be persuaded to return after the election as deputy chief of staff. One thing he had learned from his Whitewater duty was not to personalize disputes with the press. There were investigative reporters out there who never wrote a decent story about the Clinton administration, never cut the president any slack. Why the hell should I help them, his colleagues would ask. But Podesta never dwelled on the journalists' motivation; he tried to deal with them as hard-working professionals. The key, he believed, was to provide information that was credible and consistent and to do so in low-key fashion. That was the way to get the bad stories relegated to page A-6.

Podesta understood why the fundraising saga was big news. It was the foreign angle, the Asian connection that made it sexy for the media. There was a certain amount of steam in that pressure cooker, and there was no way to turn down the heat. Every new official who arrived at the White House said the same thing: The strategy's not working; let's fix it. Podesta had been through the worst of the Whitewater frenzy, and it wasn't that easy. Fortunately, most Americans were sick of Washington scandal stories. That's not what their lives were about. The whole thing was like a TV show whose ratings were sinking.

Podesta's approach was crucial. His boss, Erskine Bowles, had largely delegated to him the business of scandal management, making him the most important official in the White House on the fundraising mess. Podesta usually wound up agreeing with McCurry about the need to come clean with the press, although sometimes Mike went a bit too far. The president's top aides loved and respected McCurry, but they had grown weary of his spiel: if we only give the press the morsel they're lusting after today, they'll get off our backs. Yeah, for a day or two, and then they would be panting after something else. What the White House had to do, Podesta felt, was put the scandal in the isolation ward. It kept bleeding back into McCurryland, and Mike hated that, just despised it. They had to direct all the questions to the counsel's office, as they had during Whitewater, so they could get on with the business of the administration. The two-track strategy had broken down during the campaign, when Clinton and McCurry were usually on the road, and they were still paying the price.

Podesta also believed that the reporters had gotten more irresponsible since the first term There was a constant ratcheting up of the need for edge, for engaging in pseudo-analysis, simply to distinguish themselves from what someone else said on the tube a half-hour earlier. You saw it on MSNBC, where journalists said opinionated things that wouldn't be allowed on CNN. You saw it with all the print reporters trying to imitate *The New York Times*'s Maureen Dowd and her nasty, snarky, but invariably funny column. Now even David Broder, the respected dean of the punditocracy, had caught the bug. He had a hard-on about Clinton and the character issue. Broder had become fixated on the notion that Clinton's callowness was preventing him from doing anything about soaring entitlement costs. Podesta meant to call him about it. They were getting hammered from all sides.

In his new job, rushing from one high-level meeting to the next, John Podesta had far less time to deal with reporters than before. He felt he should interact more with the press and that Bowles and Sylvia Mathews, the other deputy, should join in the effort. They were starving the reporters, and that created animosity and put unnecessary pressure on McCurry. Reporters liked to triangulate the place, to bounce one person's view off another, and if they felt they were being screwed, they started writing stories about White House stonewalling. There was no getting around the media in this hothouse environment. Podesta was a senior manager now, closer to Clinton than ever before, but he realized he had to get back in the PR game. Even if it made his blood pressure rise.

And so the Clintonites decided to reach out to some of the journalists who were kicking them in the shins. William Safire was officially a White House enemy for having assailed Hillary as a congenital liar, but Don Baer spent a fair amount of time talking to him. Rahm Emanuel affectionately called him Uncle Bill, even had Safire over for dinner. Michael Kelly, now the editor of *The New Republic*, berated Clinton each week as "a shocking liar," "occasional demagogue," and "breathtakingly cynical," but Emanuel asked him to lunch. If the fiercest critics could be persuaded to occasionally say something nice about Clinton, these officials felt, it would carry more weight than bouquets from his boosters.

Joe Klein was mystified by the White House reaction to him. Sure, he was harshly critical of Clinton at times, but he never wrote about

Whitewater, or Paula Jones, or the fundraising scandal. He was interested in substance, not sleaze, and supported Clinton when he thought he was right. But the administration never pitched him on anything, never tried to use him to deliver a message on some issue, like education, where he was sympathetic. To their credit, they never cut him off, even after the famous "Politics of Promiscuity" piece, even after his scathing novel *Primary Colors*. But a few aides put out the word that he was an asshole, some kind of spurned lover who still wanted Clinton's affection. In an era when so many columnists were obsessed with Clinton's personal life, the White House had never quite figured out that Klein cared deeply about policy.

But olive branches were extended to other naysayers, especially the most prominent Clinton-bashers at *The New York Times*, Howell Raines and Maureen Dowd. Emanuel helped arrange for Raines, the *Times*'s harshly critical editorial page editor, to be invited to a state dinner. The Birmingham-born Raines, with his courtly southern manner, felt that protocol required him to accept; Clinton introduced him to the president of Chile as representing "one of our most important newspapers." But the president's politeness masked a decidedly jaundiced view of the Timesman. The Clintons blamed Raines for pushing Jeff Gerth to pursue the Whitewater story back in 1992, when he was running the paper's Washington bureau. "Howell Raines writes bad editorials because he resents me," Clinton told Dick Morris. "He resents me because I'm a southerner who didn't have to leave to make good."

For his part Raines was stunned by the way the Clintons seemed to equate disagreement with personal animosity, and by the intensity of the bad-mouthing. His criticism wasn't personal at all; in fact, he was one of the first national reporters to tout Clinton as an up-and-coming southern governor back in 1979. Perhaps the president had grown accustomed to his predecessor on the editorial page, Jack Rosenthal, an ardent Democrat who had worked in the Kennedy administration and had run the paper's endorsement of Clinton in the 1992 New York primary. Raines, who took over in 1993, belonged to no political party and was immediately more critical of the new president. To those at the White House he seemed a remote, mythically powerful figure who harbored a fierce contempt for them.

Another harsh critic to be courted was Raines's star pupil, Maureen

Dowd, who routinely ridiculed the president as "hypocritical and sanctimonious and self-righteous" in her *Times* column. McCurry had given up on talking to Dowd, but Don Baer had known her for years and had always liked her, though they never spoke anymore. Baer decided to call her, just to stay in touch, and they wound up chatting about the Lincoln Bedroom controversy. Dowd was puzzled by the call. She wondered whether Baer had been "assigned" to her.

Dowd had gotten the red-carpet treatment once, in 1993, when the Clintons invited author John Grisham and some journalists over for a screening of *The Pelican Brief,* and the president prattled on about his prowess in cow-chip-tossing and frog-jumping contests at a place called Toad Suck. The Clintons were both charming, but then, as Dowd noted, being charming was the whole point of the exercise.

George Stephanopoulos had once accused Dowd of hating Clinton. She believed that he simply didn't get it. Her job was not to like or dislike Clinton, but to render judgment on whether he had a good week or gave a bad speech or was sinking into sanctimony. The White House was always trying to personalize these things; you were either on the team or off the team. That was the trouble with Democrats. The Republicans didn't expect fair treatment and were thrilled if you gave them an even break; the Dems secretly believed all journalists were liberals and got all sullen and whiny if you kicked them around. The White House gang seemed to long for the days when journalists were royal courtiers in JFK's Camelot. But times had changed; the culture was coarser, more confrontational. It was harder to write viciously about someone who had charmed you over popcorn, Dowd felt, which is why it wasn't wise for reporters to get too close to their subjects.

Mike McCurry also believed in the power of personal contact and kept urging Clinton to schedule more off-the-record sessions with reporters and columnists. There was a background chat with Thomas Friedman, the *New York Times* foreign affairs columnist and an occasional golfing partner, that Clinton enjoyed so much he asked for a copy of Friedman's tape. There was a get-acquainted session with new White House reporters from mid-sized news organizations, such as Jody Enda of Knight Ridder and Ann Scales of *The Boston Globe.* There was a talk with the new Washington bureau chief of *The Econo-*

mist, which was deemed important because of its sizable readership among the American elite. And there was a Friday afternoon coffee with two columnists, Gloria Borger of *U.S. News* and Thomas Oliphant of *The Boston Globe*.

As Borger listened to Clinton ramble on about the consumer price index and its relationship to cost-of-living adjustments, she had a renewed appreciation for his policy acumen. She realized she had forgotten how smart Bill Clinton was. He even had a sense of humor. When Clinton said he was having trouble getting statistics out of the bureaucracy, Borger asked if he had tried bribery.

"Maybe I should ask my Indonesian friends," the president quipped.

The intensity of the charm offensive was impressive. This was the most seductive politician in the universe, one who gave you his undivided attention. He began by telling Borger that he had liked her recent column on Bill Daley, the new commerce secretary; clearly an aide had given him a file with her writing. He talked a little Boston politics with Oliphant. He showed them around the Oval Office. Here was his collection of political buttons. Here was John Kennedy's leather writing blotter, which Jackie had given to Pamela Harriman and which Harriman had given to him before her death. Here was the famous angry letter that Harry Truman wrote to the *Washington Post* critic who had slammed his daughter's singing performance in 1950. Clearly, Clinton had a sense of history.

It was as if the three of them were having an intimate chat. Clinton took off his jacket, sipped his coffee, at one point leaned over and touched both reporters at the same time. Borger's only regret was that it was all off-the-record. Except for one small anecdote, there was nothing she could use in the magazine. Of course, if it had been a formal, on-the-record interview, with a White House stenographer sitting there, she and Oliphant would have had to ask tough-minded questions about the fundraising scandal and received carefully parsed replies. The personal nature of the hour-long schmoozefest was what made it truly interesting.

Borger walked away thinking that this was the greatest president in the world. She had to wait for the aura to wear off, to regain her bearings and remember all the shortsighted or sleazy things Clinton had done. As a veteran journalist, of course, she remained skeptical and continued to criticize Clinton in her column. But now she looked at him slightly differently. And that was just what McCurry wanted, to let each side see the appealing human qualities of the other. If he could just arrange enough of these sessions, maybe Clinton would understand the press better, and maybe the journalists would give the leader of the free world a break.

CHAPTER NINE

Mister Clean

Bob Woodward had a blunt message for Lorraine Voles. "Gore's radioactive on this issue," he told the vice president's communications director. "The idea that this will go away is not the case."

It was January 7, well before the fundraising scandal had reached peak intensity. With all the journalistic attention focused on Clinton and his Asian American donors, the *Washington Post* reporter was quietly investigating the vice president. They were hardly strangers; Gore had been a confidential source for some of his books. But that was very different from sitting down to answer detailed questions about the way he raised campaign cash, as Woodward was demanding.

"I really want to talk to him," Woodward said in his deep, flat midwestern voice. Voles said that would not be possible. Gore was turning down all interview requests on the subject. Any comment would have to come from her. Woodward, whose erect posture carried an air of rectitude, felt he was being stonewalled.

For the first time in years, Woodward was diving into a running newspaper story, one that carried at least faint echoes of Watergate, the scandal that had made him both wealthy and famous. He felt slightly guilty that he had not cracked the case in his 1996 campaign book, *The Choice.* He had gotten a piece of the scandal, the way that Clinton and Gore had used $25 million in DNC "soft money" from corporations to finance an early presidential advertising blitz, thus skirting the post-Watergate election spending limits. He had even reported that Gore had made fifty fundraising calls himself, an extraordinary task for an incumbent vice president. But he hadn't excavated any further, had missed the full dimensions of the fledgling scandal. Now he felt uniquely positioned to expose the Clinton-Gore campaign's chicanery, just as he had followed the money during the Nixon era.

Lorraine Voles was not surprised at the fierce scrutiny. She had been Gore's chief spokeswoman for three years and was popular among reporters, but everything had changed after the election. Four *Post* reporters had called, saying they would be covering the veep more closely. The newsmagazines wanted more face time with Gore. He was no longer just a loyal number two but the presumed Democratic front-runner for 2000, and that meant his every move would be judged in light of his presidential prospects.

Gore hated all the stories about 2000. They drove him crazy, just seemed wildly premature. He wanted people, especially inside the White House, to believe that he was focused on being a great vice president. He was particularly concerned about what he called his "constituency of one," the man in the Oval Office. But he and his acolytes left nothing to chance. Voles drafted a set of talking points and distributed them to Gore's friends, advising them on what they should and shouldn't say to the press. They could relate warm anecdotes about Gore but should avoid discussing any plans for 2000.

The reporters never believed Gore's demurrals, Voles found, assuming instead that his every waking second was devoted to the next election. If Gore appeared someplace with House Minority Leader Dick Gephardt, the Democrat deemed most likely to challenge him, it was invariably depicted as a showdown.

Voles sent Gore an e-mail message that *George* magazine was working on a piece contrasting him and Gephardt.

"AGGHHHHH!" Gore wrote back.

Gore was ultraconscious of his press coverage, reporters found.

The *Los Angeles Times* ran a small item on former representative Tom Downey and how he had played Jack Kemp in a mock session before the vice-presidential debate. Gore sent Downey a note saying: "Perfect!" Inside the Old Executive Office Building, Voles, an easygoing woman with short red hair, often found herself being second-guessed by the boss. Gore had begun his career as a reporter for the Nashville *Tennessean* and had once exposed a city councilman for accepting bribes in exchange for zoning measures, even testifying at his trial. Gore understood the importance of deadlines and filing time and providing access. When an investigative journalist was digging into a story, Gore would muse about what the reporter should be looking for. His relationship with the press was so relaxed that he had simply declared his '96 campaign plane off-the-record, enabling him to have casual chats with the correspondents that were never reported. Gore occasionally got angry at reporters and columnists, thought they could be terribly unfair, but he also understood how the media's own spin cycle worked—that a news analysis in Saturday's *Washington Post* could affect the Sunday talk shows and thus set the tone for the whole week.

As the highest-ranking former journalist in the White House, he didn't hesitate to overrule Voles on how to handle the fourth estate. Sitting in the green room after appearing on *Meet the Press* or *This Week*, Gore would tell Voles whether he would talk to the "stakeout" —the reporters who gathered outside the building for a few quick quotes—or avoid them because that might overshadow the news he was trying to make.

But even the media-savvy vice president could not avoid the swirling scandal. Gore's squeaky-clean reputation got a little smudged in January, when a DNC document surfaced that contradicted his insistence that he hadn't known he was attending a fundraiser when he visited a Buddhist temple outside Los Angeles. Party officials had collected about $140,000 from monks and others who lived on practically nothing. Gore's claim that it was just a "community event" had always seemed a bit far-fetched, given the tackiness of passing the Democratic collection plate in a house of worship.

Lorraine Voles decided to check out the situation for herself. She went to the DNC headquarters on Capitol Hill and began poring over the four thousand pages of John Huang files that had been released to the press. She was stunned by what she found. There was a bunch of canceled checks marked with an internal code that showed that they had been written at the Buddhist temple event. Voles immediately told her staff to stop publicly denying that the session had been a fundraiser. "If it walks like a duck," she said, then that explanation wasn't credible, and this thing quacked like a fundraiser. Sure, no money had changed hands while Gore was there, but Voles knew that most people would see that as a semantic distinction. She started telling reporters that Gore knew it was a "finance-related" event. Perhaps, she said, she should have clarified that sooner.

Voles understood all too well that Gore's blunder in attending the fundraiser at the Hsi Lai Temple had made the press wonder whether he harbored other skeletons in his financial closet. By the end of February, she was deluged with calls from reporters digging into Gore's fundraising. The *Los Angeles Times* quoted her as saying that Gore had supported a total ban on "soft money" at the DNC, and then contradicted her by citing three unnamed officials who said the veep had opposed the proposal. Voles, who was pregnant with her second child, was not accustomed to dealing with angry reporters, and she grew testy herself, snapping at journalists she had known for years.

As other reporters began to pick up the scent, Voles adopted a new philosophy: less is better. Whatever the question, she would say as little as possible, minimizing the chances that the reporter would find some scrap of information to contradict her. She would not answer any question, no matter how routine, without checking with the lawyers. This is what they asked, this is what I found, this is what I plan to say, she would tell the counsel's office. Only then would she deliver her response.

What made the job even more difficult was that Voles no longer kept her notes and memos. She had learned her lesson during her unhappy months working as a deputy White House press secretary under Dee Dee Myers in 1993. She was subpoenaed in the Travelgate investigation over a single note she took during a conversation with a reporter. She then had to testify before a grand jury and shell out thousands of dollars in legal fees. Other aides, like George Stephanopoulos and Maggie Williams and Lisa Caputo, had had similar experiences. Even the Clintons themselves had been saddled with more

than $2.5 million in Whitewater legal fees. Now Voles played it safe
—she just tossed all her notes in the wastebasket.

When one reporter asked her, on background, for a ballpark estimate on an issue, she started to answer, then stopped herself. "Not in
this climate," she said. If the estimate was off, "you'll come back and
say we weren't forthcoming." The atmosphere, she felt, had turned
absolutely poisonous.

Voles recommended that Gore not speak to Woodward. She didn't
see how it would help the veep. Who were these unnamed sources he
was citing? Did they have an agenda? How did you combat that?
But Gore had great respect for Woodward. At one point Voles was
convinced that Gore was going to call and invite him for dinner. But
he changed his mind at the last minute.

On Sunday, March 2, Gore found himself shoved onto center stage
in the scandal extravaganza. Woodward's lengthy piece dubbed Gore
the campaign's "solicitor-in-chief," saying he had directly solicited
millions of dollars for the Democrats. He had been "heavy-handed"
and had placed some of the calls from his West Wing office. One
unnamed donor called Gore's conduct "revolting"; another, who gave
the DNC $100,000, said the approach resembled a "shakedown."
The story clearly had an aggressive tone; Woodward seemed personally offended at the spectacle of the vice president dialing for dollars,
asking businessmen for $50,000 donations. How could they say no?
Gore was misusing the power of his office.

Gore's defense was relegated to Voles, who told Woodward:
"There is nothing inappropriate about the vice president calling people for money." That view was not widely shared by the press. The
story was all over the Sunday talk shows. Alison Mitchell's catch-up
piece ran on the front page of the next morning's *New York Times*,
observing that the scandal "threatens to undermine" Gore's political
future. Reporters flooded Gore's office with calls, and no one was
calling back.

Clinton and Gore appeared that morning for a photo op with
Yassir Arafat, the visiting Palestinian leader. This time it was Gore's
turn to be embarrassed by a reporter's shouted question:

"Vice President Gore, did you solicit money in the White House,
Mr. Gore, during the campaign?"

"I'll talk with you all later, not during this," Gore replied.

McCurry knew the gaggle would be loaded for bear. He twice called the vice president's office and asked the staff for information on Gore's role. "Give me what you have," he said. But they were closeted with the lawyers and hadn't decided on their defense. McCurry had no ammunition. He would have to duck.

When the briefing began, McCurry made a tactical error. He was asked about the fact that George Stephanopoulos, now ABC's newest commentator, had said on *This Week* that the White House had used two sets of phones, one for government business and another for political fundraising, McCurry was dismissive about his former colleague "gabbing" on television.

"He was speaking in his capacity as a pundit and not trying to provide any specific authoritative account," McCurry said. "Once you're in the news business, the journalism business, your standards for accuracy are much lower than ours are standing here."

The room erupted with groans.

"How can you say such a thing?" a reporter demanded.

"It is true," McCurry said with obvious annoyance. "Because we have to be a hundred, a thousand percent correct here about the information we provide. You're free to speculate based on one or two sources that may not know what they have."

McCurry had made the same argument in private dozens of times. What he said from the podium was an official pronouncement, and if he was off by a micro-fraction, he would be denounced as venal and corrupt and a liar. But newspapers could botch a major fact and simply run a tiny correction. The *L.A. Times* could run a big headline "Up to 900 Donors Stayed Overnight at White House"—and then retract the error with a little "oops" on page 3 the next day. Journalists could race onto the air after the Oklahoma City bombing and yammer about Middle East terrorists blowing up federal buildings. When it turned out they were wrong, they simply shifted gears and nobody held them to account. He didn't have that luxury.

Still, in the midst of the fundraising scandal, which had forced McCurry to revise his account several times, suggesting that journalists had lower standards sounded like a gratuitous insult. The questions about Gore grew sharper, and McCurry clearly had no answers.

"Was the president aware," Rita Braver asked, "that one of those who was doing that work was the vice president, and did he think that was appropriate?"

"Look, I'm not in a position to say specifically how much the vice president did," McCurry replied.

"Well, his staff has acknowledged that he did solicit funds."

"Well, I'm not going to try to answer that, Rita. I made that abundantly obvious to you."

Others kept hammering McCurry.

"Was the president aware ever that Vice President Gore was directly making solicitations?"

"I don't know the degree of his awareness or unawareness," McCurry said.

Gore was watching the painful exercise from his office. As McCurry lingered with reporters after the briefing, trying to explain his remarks about journalistic accuracy, Gore's staff began to debate whether he needed to go public before the evening newscast. A dozen people gathered in his office. Six of them were lawyers.

Gore argued strongly that he had to "face the music," as he put it. But Voles wanted him to pursue a safer course. She didn't think they had enough time to pull together the information and hold a full-blown news conference. She wanted to put out a written statement, maybe grant an interview to Wolf Blitzer. They had a good relationship with Wolf and CNN. They were always mindful of the four o'clock airtime of *Inside Politics*, which was important despite its small audience because other journalists watched it. Sitting down with Wolf would certainly be calmer than facing a roomful of snarling reporters.

Ron Klain, Gore's chief of staff, argued against a press conference. Doug Sosnik, who was now Clinton's counselor, agreed that it was important to answer the questions head-on but said that they shouldn't trot out Gore in the briefing room that day. A vice presidential appearance would simply pump up the story even more.

Voles asked McCurry to join the meeting. He ambled in with a cup of soup he had grabbed after the briefing. McCurry said that if Gore held a news conference he would have to explain why. He suggested that Gore say he had watched the briefing and realized there were a number of unanswered questions.

Gore spoke to the president afterward and said that he felt he should go to the briefing room. "You've got to do what you think is right," Clinton said.

The president later told McCurry that Gore had made a smart decision. "He's got the right instincts," Clinton said. "We've just got to make sure he's got the right answers."

The senior staff staged a mock press conference in Gore's office. Many of the answers were suggested by Gore's new legal counsel, Charles Burson, who had just resigned as Tennessee's attorney general and had been on the job only a couple of days. Jack Quinn, the former White House counsel, was also there.

Much of the staff saw a problem with Gore's approach. McCurry scribbled a note to Rahm Emanuel: "This is going to be a fucking disaster." Still, McCurry and the others tried to coach Gore. You can't stand up there and be a lawyer, they said. Don't give legalistic answers. Just say what you did and why you thought it was appropriate.

The advice fell on deaf ears. Gore's performance at the five o'clock news conference was robotically defensive and legalistic. After explaining that he had decided to come out after watching McCurry's briefing, he insisted seven times that there was "no controlling legal authority" that barred him from making fundraising calls in the White House. He said he was "proud" of what he had done but wouldn't do it again. He said he had made the calls using a DNC credit card. Gore had never been through this sort of hostile inquisition before, and it showed.

"I'm sure you can understand the appearance, whether or not it was technically legal, the appearance wasn't very good," Wolf Blitzer said.

"How can you say that it was okay for you to do it?" Rita Braver demanded.

The press took off the gloves. Deborah Orin wrote in the *New York Post* that "the supposedly brainy veep looked dumb and dumber." Ridicule was the order of the day. Even NBC's perky anchor Katie Couric called the vice president "a bit cheesy." It was one of those moments that alters a politician's image forever. Mr. Clean was now streaked with dirt. Even Gore realized he had blown it.

Doug Sosnik thought there was a collective sense of guilt in the press for having been too soft on Gore for too long. Gore had been certified one of the good guys, a boy scout, an upright if boring figure. Now, as if to overcompensate, the reporters were challenging Gore's capacity for candor.

Gore's reputation suffered another blow the next day when Voles discovered, to her horror, that he hadn't used a DNC credit card to make the fundraising calls, but one paid for by the Clinton-Gore campaign. Gore was livid about the screwup. Voles, at home in north-west Washington, where she was trying out a new nanny, felt the staff had failed him. Gore was supposed to be raising money for the Democratic Party, not his own reelection campaign, and they seemed unable to answer the most fundamental questions about the calls. They should never have sent him out with bad information. The question now was how to repair the damage.

Some Gore staffers argued that it was a minor detail and didn't require a public announcement. Voles thought that was crazy. She called McCurry for advice after the briefing. He said not to do it "blanket," meaning not to put out a statement to the whole press corps. Instead, he suggested one of his favorite techniques: give the story to a single wire-service reporter. Voles called Terence Hunt of the AP and spent twenty minutes briefing him on the credit card problem. She arranged for him to talk to the general counsel of the Clinton-Gore campaign. She also called Wolf Blitzer and gave him the details in time for the four o'clock edition of *Inside Politics*. The advantage of having Hunt's report on the wire was that it framed the story in the way she wanted—Gore quickly admits error—and allowed other reporters to confirm it with minimal hassle. Voles took calls from twenty reporters after the AP story moved. Tom Brokaw read an item on the news that night. They were paying the price for the sloppy work the day before.

Voles wondered whether Gore should make a high-profile media appearance in the coming days. Should he do a sitdown interview with a major network? Was the story gaining momentum or dying down? Her options were limited by the strange rituals that governed which newsmakers could appear on which talk shows. If Gore did a Sunday show, it had to be *Face the Nation* because it was CBS's turn. If they did something on CNN, it had to be *Larry King Live* because Gore had canceled several planned appearances with King last year. Or perhaps it was better to lie low, to ride out the storm.

Voles was constantly on the defensive as she tried to deal with the "incoming," the endless waves of journalistic inquiries. One newspaper reporter called and said his campaign sources were insisting there were no Clinton-Gore calling cards, that the veep could not have used such a credit card to make the calls.

"That's not true," Voles said. "I've seen the paperwork."

The reporter kept after her. Voles lost her temper. "You're coming at me with unnamed sources and I'm supposed to drop everything?" she said. The guy shouted back. She had to dig out the AT&T records and read them to him. One said "V-Pres. Gore," the other "Vice President Al Gore." Voles had known the reporter for years and he was treating her like a junior staffer. She couldn't believe she was having to go through this.

.   .   .

THE WHOLE GORE FIASCO SEEMED TO TOUCH A NERVE. THERE WAS a new round of editorials demanding appointment of a special prosecutor. The scandal, which had been gaining velocity since the election, was suddenly racing along at warp speed, blurring everyone's sense of time. A major tale of Washington corruption usually involved two or three investigative disclosures a week. Now two or three revelations were spilling out each day, a pace so frenetic that reporters didn't have time to follow up each other's scoops. McCurry joked that they could get any mediocre investigative piece on the front page, the same pieces they used to beg their editors to publish.

In the wake of Gore's admission, McCurry knew the next obvious question was whether Clinton had also made fundraising calls from the White House. Breaking his usual rule, McCurry asked the president, who said he didn't think so but couldn't be absolutely sure he hadn't asked a donor or two for help. Don't flat-out deny it, Clinton said.

"The president doesn't have any recollection of it, but doesn't rule out that he may have talked to donors from time to time," McCurry told the gaggle.

That night NBC reported that Maggie Williams, Hillary's chief of staff, had accepted a $50,000 check from Johnny Chung in the White House and had passed it on to the DNC. To act as a bagman for Chung, the businessman labeled a "hustler" by one White House aide, was more than unseemly; federal law made it a crime to solicit or receive a contribution in a government building. White House spinmeisters cobbled together another legalistic defense about why Williams's handling of campaign funds wasn't quite soliciting or receiving. But even Williams's colleagues thought it had been dumb. McCurry would go only so far in spinning bad news. He told reporters he would have handled the situation differently, that he would have simply directed Chung to the DNC. He returned a moment later to say he was not "taking a shot at Maggie," but he did not retract his comments. It fell to Ann Lewis to work the press, insisting, "There was nothing noteworthy about this." McCurry was not a big Ann Lewis fan. He thought she sometimes came off as sanctimonious. But she was a valuable ally in his campaign for full disclosure because she had long enjoyed the first family's confidence.

Lewis and other White House aides were disgusted by the media's attacks on Maggie Williams. Where was the shock and outrage, Lewis wondered, when Representative John Boehner, a member of the Republican leadership, handed out tobacco industry checks to other members on the House floor? That had been a one-day story, a twelve-hour story, even. Why was the press giving Watergate-style headlines to every minor misstep? The White House crowd seemed not to understand that most of the country had never heard of John Boehner, while this bit of stupidity had taken place in the first lady's office.

McCurry was dying for a chance to put things in perspective. Newt Gingrich had declared the other day that the fundraising scandal was worse than Watergate. McCurry couldn't wait for the question to come up at the gaggle. McCurry thought the press corps could use a reminder of the sort of high crimes and misdemeanors that Watergate entailed. He could still remember listening to the Senate Watergate hearings in the summer of 1973 after his freshman year in college, while working as a file clerk at a Palo Alto law firm. The trouble was, with the generational shift in the White House press corps, some of the reporters had been in elementary school at the time. They had no historical memory of Watergate, of the way the Nixon gang had shredded the Constitution. The reporters were, on balance, a disappointing lot. They didn't know shit. The Clinton excesses, however seamy, did not remotely resemble the Nixonian brand of brazen law-breaking. Where Nixon's reelection committee had used a secret slush fund to harass and spy on political opponents, today the press was debating whether the handling of a single check constituted soliciting or receiving. Everyone needed a reality check here. McCurry had his staff prepare a list of all the Nixon aides who had been convicted of bribery, obstruction of justice, perjury. He was ready to cite chapter and verse. Unfortunately, no one asked.

McCurry joined Clinton on a trip to Lansing, Michigan, where the president addressed the state legislature on the need for national education standards. Clinton was in a good mood on the trip. He hugged a stewardess on Air Force One in full view of a reporter, saying: "You want scandal? Send for an independent counsel!" Journalists kept asking McCurry—on background, of course—whether Clinton was angry, furious, beside himself over the burgeoning scandal. They seemed disappointed when he said the president seemed resigned to taking his lumps. In private McCurry kept reminding Clinton of the importance of keeping his cool. "Remember—repairer of the breach," he would say.

The advice was important, for Clinton was scheduled to hold a news conference the next day. It was the worst possible time to face the press, with the scandal spinning out of control, but McCurry had promised that the president would meet with reporters every six weeks. McCurry felt it was important that they not retreat, that Clinton not hide from his media antagonists. Whatever else could be said about them, they were willing to take their medicine.

The rehearsal, as usual, lasted more than three hours. McCurry warned Clinton that 99 percent of the news conference would be about fundraising but that he should avoid personalizing his responses to tough questions. "You're not in an argument with the press corps here," McCurry said. Clinton said he understood, that he was ready. McCurry wasn't far off. Fifteen of the first seventeen questions were about the scandal. "You, sir, promised to have the most ethical administration in history," Terry Hunt began, setting the tone for the session.

Unlike Gore, Clinton seemed relaxed, smooth, in command. When he didn't like the premise of a question, he simply said, "I disagree with that" or "The American people will have to decide." While some of his defenses were highly technical—Gore hadn't acted improperly because "the law is clearly that the solicitation is consummated, if you will, when the person is solicited and where the person is solicited"—he confidently defended a system in which politicians, after all, must ask people for financial support. Rita Braver asked a long, detailed question about Johnny Chung, but Clinton just pleaded ignorance. The press barely nicked the president. McCurry felt he had survived again under hostile fire.

McCurry's staff worried that he was working too hard. He would snap at people in meetings or sit there scowling. There was talk that he was drinking at night. He was coming in on too many Saturdays, seemed to be in the office all the time. One Saturday night, when other officials were home with their families, McCurry even joined in the punditry on CNN's *Capital Gang*. On rare occasions he let his frustration show. The president was working hard on the budget, education, health care, and welfare, he told the gaggle. "The fact that you choose not to report on·that is your business, and I can't do anything about that."

McCurry was also getting his share of personal abuse. *The New York Times* editorial page was after him again. The latest salvo was called "The Truth Is Inoperative," aimed at "Mike McCurry, the man who interprets the Clinton fundraising philosophy to an astonished nation." Castigating McCurry for his "audacious" remark that journalistic standards were lower than the administration's, the editorial proclaimed: "Our breath is taken. . . . We'd like to see Mr. McCurry's whopper win a place in history." He knew he was becoming an object of ridicule. Columnist Charles Krauthammer called him a "presidential parrot." His former boss, Tim Russert, made fun of him on the Don Imus show. McCurry was painfully aware of the jokes. He felt he had become the Ron Ziegler of the Clinton administration.

The accusatory, hostile questions at the gaggle were part of an effort to badger him, to see what his breaking point was. McCurry felt that the reporters had to uncork their hardest fastballs because they assumed that government spokesmen routinely dissemble and lie. His job was to keep his cool and avoid being drawn into a shouting match on ethics. Anyone watching on C-SPAN, he believed, could see that the thing had degenerated into a witch hunt.

McCurry looked worn down. The reporters had never seen him so miserable. He had been a golden boy since high school, glib and successful, and now he was stuck in the mud with the rest of the administration. There was chatter in the pressroom about whether someone else, perhaps his deputy, Joe Lockhart, might succeed him. Al Gore called McCurry in for a pep talk. They had a good relationship, and the veep could tell he was down in the dumps. "Don't for a minute worry about this," he said. "Don't think the president and I worry about this. You're doing a very good job under the circumstances."

McCurry toyed with the idea of bailing out, of cashing in like some of his former colleagues. But he felt it would look like he was abandoning Clinton because of the scandal. He hadn't done that with Pete Williams seventeen years earlier, and he wasn't about to do it now. Instead, he forced himself to remain upbeat. He still had a mission, to mend relations between Clinton and the press. He urged the president to separate his overall view of the press corps from that of individual reporters. Clinton still felt the media were trying to destroy him, that they viewed him as a rube from Arkansas who didn't deserve to be in the White House. The columnists and editorial writers might be kicking the shit out of him, McCurry told Clinton, but most of the reporters are trying to be fair. Some of them don't like being consumed by this scandal any more than you do. Each day Clinton would try to change the subject, to resume his dialogue with the country on the issues that he thought really mattered. He spoke tirelessly about education standards, about child safety locks on guns, about hiring welfare recipients, about outlawing new cop-killer bullets, about a federal ban on human cloning. Some of this was covered by the press, some of it summarily kissed off. But Clinton kept hammering away.

In his own daily duel with reporters, McCurry established two rules to protect his personal integrity. He followed a path of willful ignorance, repeating only information that the counsel's office had assembled and not quizzing Clinton directly if he could help it. And he would not characterize the facts he regurgitated. That was the media's job; he would not go out on a limb by defending the fundraising abuses that he himself found embarrassing. This was a story he could not spin, and that approach, in the end, was the best spin of all.

CHAPTER TEN

Dribs and Drabs

FOR ALL THEIR CAREFUL PLANNING, THEIR STRATEGY SESSIONS, their systematic stroking of the press, White House aides sometimes tended to lose sight of the human factor. Even in the highest councils of government, people got tired or had problems at home or fell ill. Governing was an art, not a science, and months of detail work could be wiped out by a freak accident.

When Clinton went to Florida in mid-March, mainly for golfing purposes, McCurry blew off the trip, preferring to stay home with his family. A day later, at 4:45 A.M., McCurry was out for his morning jog on the darkened streets of Silver Spring when he heard some startling news on his Walkman.

"President Clinton has been hospitalized in Florida," a Monitor Radio announcer said in his ear.

Three and a half hours earlier, Clinton had stumbled on a staircase at golfer Greg Norman's house and torn a tendon in his right leg. When McCurry got home, he was paged by one of his deputies, Mary Ellen Glynn, who was on the trip. She had been trying to get him all night, but the paging system had melted down and she couldn't raise a White House operator. Now McCurry learned for the first time that Clinton was flying back to have surgery at Bethesda Naval Hospital.

When he arrived at Bethesda, McCurry was struck by the palpable anxiety in the press corps. The briefing room had the feel of a crisis, almost like the time in 1981 when Ronald Reagan had been shot. The president was going into surgery, facing two months on crutches, the upcoming summit with Boris Yeltsin in jeopardy. At moments like these, it fell to McCurry to address the world on the commander-in-chief's behalf. He felt he needed to lighten things up. Clinton had blown out his knee—big deal. It was hardly a life-threatening situation. McCurry huddled with the doctors and asked the head of clinical operations to help at the briefing, which was carried live by three cable networks. McCurry tried to project a calm, unruffled image, relating jokes that Clinton had been telling. He briefed twice more during the surgery because the demand for updates—when did it begin? what time would it end?—was so great. He arranged for Clinton to say a few words by speakerphone, knowing that the sound of his voice would reassure the country. In the age of twenty-four-hour news, any presidential injury was a huge story.

At a later briefing Marlene de Maio, a member of the orthopedic surgery team, said Clinton was being discharged because, among other things, he was able to go to the bathroom on his own. Geez, McCurry thought, we're at the White House podium talking about the president of the United States taking a whiz. The line between informing the public and protecting the man's privacy was a slim one indeed.

Even as Clinton was recuperating, the damage control team labored on. The following Saturday morning, after doing some fieldwork at his daughter's day care center, McCurry came to the West Wing for a long strategy session with Lanny Davis, Ann Lewis, and Maggie Williams, along with Cheryl Mills and other attorneys from the counsel's office. McCurry had been openly arguing with White House counsel Charles Ruff that they needed a schedule for more "document dumps," and he and Davis laid out the major items the press was still clamoring for, most of which they hoped to release. These included a list of Clinton pals and donors who had gotten rides on Air Force One, guests who had stayed at Camp David, and those who had been invited to DNC events at the White House. But piecing it together was a struggle. There was no single list of Camp David visitors, which McCurry very much wanted to get out because he was sure it contained few if any donors. The Air Force One manifests were a nightmare, filled with unfamiliar names that were difficult to identify. But McCurry and Davis wanted to cut loose as much material as possible. There was grumbling in various newsrooms that they had abandoned the policy of disclosure, and journalistic noses were always sensitive to the whiff of a cover-up.

The Hezbollah wing, the lawyers, had a competing agenda. They were trying to maintain amicable relations with the congressional investigators, particularly Senator Fred Thompson and Representative Dan Burton, and wanted to proceed cautiously. Thompson had made clear he would be displeased if the White House released the documents with a partisan spin before he convened his hearings. But McCurry argued that news organizations also had a legitimate claim to the documents and that satisfying the media was just as important as cooperating with the Hill. It had turned into a race for the spoils of scandal, with two competing factions, the press and Congress, panting after the same hidden treasure. The administration could service the reporters and score points for candor, but only at the risk of ticking off powerful lawmakers with subpoena power. It was not an easy choice.

The first pictures of Clinton in a wheelchair had knocked the scandal off the front pages, but not for long. Lanny Davis knew what was coming next. Michael Frisby of *The Wall Street Journal* was working on what looked to be the next blockbuster, involving Roger Tamraz, a Lebanese American businessman and major Democratic donor who had attended several White House functions with Clinton. Davis had been furious with Frisby over that front-page squib about his lousy *Nightline* performance, but they had buried the hatchet over lunch at the tony Oval Room a few weeks earlier. With Davis as the intermediary, Frisby confirmed that the National Security Council and the CIA had cleared Tamraz for the meetings, even though he was wanted for questioning in an embezzlement case. Frisby and his colleagues were finishing up the piece the weekend of Clinton's injury.

The *Journal* splashed the Tamraz tale on its Monday front page. At the briefing McCurry repeatedly ducked, saying he didn't have enough information. Later he told Davis there didn't seem to be that much interest in the case. "I don't think the story has much legs," McCurry said.

He was wrong. The immediate victim of the *Journal* story was Tony Lake, the departing national security adviser who had been nominated to be director of Central Intelligence. Lake knew nothing about the Tamraz episode, but he had ultimate responsibility for any NSC clearance that Tamraz may have received. He decided that day to pull the plug on his troubled nomination, which had been plagued by attacks on his foreign policy views and management skills.

Lake didn't want his withdrawal to be on the evening news that night, and so he waited until just before 7:00 P.M. to leak his resignation letter to reporters at the *Journal, The New York Times*, and *The Washington Post*, believing that they would handle the story responsibly. McCurry assured Lake that he would not confirm the story to anyone else but suggested that Lake take care of the wires, which would be chasing the story after the first-edition papers hit the streets. Lake said he would notify John Diamond, an AP reporter he liked.

Despite the secrecy, word was floating around that Lake was thinking of abandoning the fight. Wolf Blitzer called and asked McCurry if that was true.

"If there's a decision, it's between Clinton and Tony," McCurry replied. That was technically accurate. Of course, McCurry didn't mention that he was holding Lake's withdrawal letter in his hand. Just after 8:00 P.M. Blitzer told CNN's viewers that Lake "is rethinking whether he should continue to fight for Senate confirmation."

But big stories don't stay secret for long in Washington. Blitzer got confirmation elsewhere and reported Lake's withdrawal at 8:20. Lake was never able to reach Diamond, so his AP colleague Ron Fournier had to chase the story well into the evening. Fournier, who had covered Clinton in Little Rock, felt like he'd gotten his head handed to him. It was part of the culture of Washington, he believed, that major stories were often leaked to the *Times*, the *Post*, and the *Journal*. Lake had orchestrated the coverage pretty much the way he wanted, but none of that cushioned the blow of the president's CIA nominee going down for the count.

That wasn't the only fire that was raging. The White House released new memos on its in-house database; in one letter presidential aide Marsha Scott specifically asked that the taxpayer-funded com-

puter system be used to track political supporters and to reward them
with such goodies as Kennedy Center tickets and visits to the White
House mess. Administration officials were determined to keep the
database story off the evening news, and once again they succeeded.
At 6:15 P.M. the press office told Rita Braver, who had been working
the story, that she could have the memos. With about ten minutes to
airtime, Braver looked at the twenty-five densely written pages, but
there was no way to decipher them in time for the *CBS Evening News*.
Hours later aides to Representative David McIntosh, who had just
been given the same material, began faxing it to reporters for *The
New York Times*, *The Washington Post*, and other papers, foiling the
White House plan to bury the story.

.   .   .

THE PACKED AUDITORIUM AT BEIJING'S QINGHUA UNIVERSITY WAS
waiting for Al Gore. The Chinese television crews were ready for his
speech. But Gore kept them waiting. His staff summoned the American press corps to a classroom down the hall for a background
briefing with a senior administration official. The senior official was
Gore.

Usually presidents and vice presidents had senior aides do their
spinning rather than risk seeming overly defensive, or just plain ridic-
ulous, in explaining their position to the press under the cloak of
anonymity. Now the thirty-five assembled journalists were in the
bizarre position of having to quote the vice president on a controversy involving the vice president wihtout telling readers that their
source was the vice president. Gore, as always, was hypersensitive
about his press coverage. His whole trip had been overshadowed by
the fundraising controversy and questions about how he would
broach the subject with Chinese leaders. After Gore had met with
Chinese Premier Li Peng the previous day, his foreign policy adviser,
Leon Fuerth, and a U.S. embassy official told reporters—on background—that Gore had said there would be no consequences for
Sino-American relations if the charges of Chinese influence-buying
were true. That morning Gore's chief of staff in Washington, Ron
Klain, called the vice president and read him the account by the AP's
John King, and Gore decided to do some spinning.

"I read your story and it inadvertently creates a mistaken impression," Gore said, looking at King. The veep insisted he had made clear to Li there would be "very serious" repercussions if the allegations were true. The press pack dutifully reported the senior official's account, but Gore realized he could not escape the fundraising mess even by leaving the country.

Hillary, too, was seeking a respite through foreign travel. She drew generally upbeat coverage as fifteen journalists accompanied her on a two-week jaunt across Africa. She had off-the-record dinners with them but wouldn't grant any interviews, despite repeated requests from Peter Baker and others. Baker found himself in a small, sweltering room in Tanzania as the first lady studied a 1.75-million-year-old skull. "Now's your chance," said Marsha Berry, her spokeswoman. Baker shouted a question about her foreign role and got the usual bland response. He might as well have asked the ancient head.

The president also took his show on the road, jetting off to Helsinki for his meeting with Yeltsin. White House officials were not sorry to see global diplomacy nudge the scandal story aside. Clinton reaped some positive headlines after making modest progress on arms control and winning Yeltsin's grudging acceptance of the expansion of NATO into Eastern Europe. But McCurry was frustrated by the fleeting nature of the coverage. Here was the most interesting summit Clinton had ever had with the Russian leader, and the story was over in a day and a half.

. . .

AS CONGRESS PREPARED TO LEAVE TOWN FOR THE EASTER RECESS, Don Baer saw a prime opportunity for the president. Clinton would have the stage to himself, the chance to strut his stuff on the issues people cared about. McCurry didn't worry about that sort of thing— "I'm in sales, not product development," he liked to say—but Baer and some of his colleagues were brimming with ideas. An upcoming White House conference on childhood development could easily be made into a two-day story with a strong policy announcement on some family issue. The head of the California school system was set to embrace Clinton's push for national testing. A new commission on improving managed health care, proposed during the campaign, was finally ready for appointment.

But there was one overarching problem, and it wasn't lousy press coverage. The government itself was not geared for action. Reporters had no idea how much inertia there was inside the bureaucracy. There were no natural deadlines, nothing to force the policy cooks to quit stirring and serve up their stew. Left to its own devices, the administration would plod along for weeks without disgorging a single initiative. Baer found this way of doing business incredibly frustrating. He and his allies wanted to present the president as a man of action, but for that they needed a steady stream of initiatives. The second term seemed stalled, strangely adrift, just five months after Clinton had won reelection.

During the campaign they had all been in overdrive, making hundreds of announcements when soaring rhetoric was the coin of the realm. If Clinton went to North Carolina and delivered a stem-winder on education and got good coverage in the local papers, that was a success in itself. But now, without the imperatives of an electoral calendar, the lack of coverage in the scandal-hungry national press seemed more of a void. Now the same speech in North Carolina sounded empty unless it was backed by action, action that was damned hard to achieve with the Congress in opposition hands and a seemingly endless budget standoff casting a long shadow. The plain truth was that governing was considerably harder than campaigning, and the Clinton team, so brilliant at the latter, was struggling with the former.

The team wasn't doing much better at damage control. For the first time since the election, White House officials failed to give the press scandal documents before they leaked from the Hill, undermining their much-touted disclosure strategy. McCurry and Davis had been promising for weeks to make public a second batch of papers that Harold Ickes had turned over to House investigators. But for all the internal meetings and planning sessions, they could not pull the trigger. Meanwhile, the Hill was turning into a sieve. Alison Mitchell got hold of some of the documents, and her story led the Sunday *New York Times*. The papers showed that the White House had set specific fundraising targets—usually $400,000 a session—for each of the Map Room coffees with Clinton. They also revealed a 1995 plan to have the president make eighteen to twenty personal fundraising calls and Gore another ten in hopes of raising $1.2 million. Mitchell felt that the story would not have been that big a deal had the White House simply acknowledged all along that the coffees were about cash. But these documents made crystal clear that everyone knew at the time what was going on.

The next day McCurry and Davis met with John Podesta, Charles Ruff, and Cheryl Mills in Ruff's office. Should they release the rest of the Ickes documents and get it over with?

Davis argued that they had to stay on the disclosure route. He had publicly announced that the White House would release the documents soon. But as he scanned the room, he realized there was a disgust factor at work. They had put out the first Ickes documents and the press had kicked the shit out of them. Why continue to feed a bad story?

Ruff and Mills argued that it was a matter of resources. They had subpoenas up the gazoo from two House committees, not to mention from Ken Starr and from the Justice Department. That work was far more important than servicing the reporters. The young lawyers in the counsel's office were already working seven days a week. Screw the press. They simply couldn't spare the bodies it would take to go through the fifteen hundred pages and spend another four days trying to figure out what to say.

There was another problem, McCurry said. Putting out the material would guarantee another round of negative reports on the network news. They had carefully mapped out a week of presidential announcements on health care. Why mess up the script? The worst stuff had already leaked. The pressure was not all that great.

Davis felt like strangling McCurry. Mike was his mentor, his faithful ally in the campaign for disclosure, and here he was caving in.

McCurry's argument turned the tide. It was time to tackle their own agenda. The gathering agreed to hold back the Ickes papers.

As Don Baer had predicted, with Congress out of town, the president grabbed the spotlight. On Tuesday in the Roosevelt Room, Clinton announced a crackdown on Medicare fraud. On Wednesday in the East Room, he unveiled the new commission on managed health care. On Thursday in the Oval, he piggybacked on a National Cancer Institute recommendation that women in their forties receive annual mammograms by announcing Medicare and Medicaid funding for such tests. It was a long way from sweeping health care reform, but they were living in an incremental era. These were the kinds of initiatives that journalists dismissed as minor league but which captured the attention of average folks worried about breast cancer or their prepaid health coverage. McCurry felt that the strategy had worked. Eventually they would be forced to make all the scandal documents public, but they had to break through now and then with their own message.

Publicly, of course, McCurry continued to insist that sitting on the fundraising documents was merely a matter of logistics. Even when the new DNC chairman, Colorado Governor Roy Romer, called the administration "dumb" for allowing Congress to leak them first, McCurry stuck to his guns.

At the gaggle Wolf Blitzer asked: "Why not let the White House release everything they have and then get this thing over with in one fell swoop, instead of letting it drip out?"

"I would love to do that if that were possible. . . . We've got teams of lawyers that are still searching, still going through documents," McCurry said. It was not his most candid moment.

But the administration paid a price for stiff-arming the press. Having scored big in the Sunday *Times*, Dan Burton's House oversight committee continued to dribble out the Ickes papers to other news organizations. The *CBS Evening News* did the story on Monday, with Rita Braver saying the material on the lucrative coffee klatches "absolutely shatters the illusion the president has been trying to create that this was just an informal process." The New York *Daily News* weighed in on Friday, reporting that Clinton had personally reviewed the monthly memos. *The Washington Post* caught up on Saturday, noting that Ickes had asked not just the president and Gore to make fundraising calls but Hillary Clinton as well. Four days later the administration released hundreds of Ickes documents, generating a fresh round of front-page stories about Clinton's deep involvement in what was described as "servicing" donors. What would have been a one-day headline had the White House coughed up the material earlier had stretched into a ten-day story. That was the price McCurry paid for sitting on the documents.

Unfortunately for Don Baer, the six-inch stack of Ickes's papers was released on the day that the head of the California school system endorsed the president's education plan. Baer thought of challenging the timing of the latest "dump"—he hadn't been in the damage control meetings—but decided against it. *The New York Times* kissed off the education endorsement with a picture. ABC's *World News Tonight* briefly flashed the ceremony without sound and gave it one sentence, focusing instead on the latest scandal revelations. Baer's hard work had been in vain, and he wondered whether the president's substantive message was being drowned out.

. . .

LANNY DAVIS WAS ENJOYING HIS FIRST DAY OFF IN MONTHS.

It was a beautiful Sunday morning at the end of March, and Davis and a few pals were on the seventh green at the Norbeck Country Club in Olney, Maryland, when his beeper started vibrating. He drove the golf cart back to the clubhouse to return the call.

Mack McLarty, Clinton's Arkansas buddy since kindergarten and his chief of staff in the first term, wasted no time on pleasantries. "Jesus Christ, Lanny," he said. "This Webb Hubbell story is going to break, and we've got to break it ourselves."

That was the end of the golf outing. To his friends' annoyance, Davis drove downtown and spent the rest of the day at his desk in the Old Executive Office Building.

Hubbell again. It was the story that would not die. He was the missing link, the fallen loyalist, the nexus of the Whitewater investigation and the fundraising scandal. Memories always seemed fuzzy when it came to who had helped Hubbell after he was forced to leave the Justice Department in 1994 and who had known about it. From the president on down, White House officials acted strangely defensive when reporters asked about Hubbell's lucrative employment before he went to prison for eighteen months. Davis saw the Hubbell mess as a pool of quicksand that was dragging decent people into the scandalous muck. The stress, the long hours, the lack of sleep were taking their toll on Lanny Davis. For the first time in his life, he was having stomach pains. The low point had been that *Wall Street Journal* item back in February about his job being in jeopardy.

Soon afterward, the senior staff gathered in the Cabinet Room to conduct the pre-brief for Clinton before a news conference. An aide handed Davis a gift-wrapped package and suggested he open it in front of everyone. "Thought you could use this," the card said. "Hang in there. Bill." It was a tie with a Latin phrase: *"Non Illegitimati Carborundum."*

"Is this one of your Yalie ties, Mr. President?" Davis asked.

"Don't let the bastards get you down," Clinton said.

"Thanks, I'll try not to."

"No, no, on the tie." That was the literal translation of the Latin inscription. Davis was thrilled. The tie symbolized for him his admission to the inner circle, some high-level recognition for the work he was doing. Erskine Bowles called soon afterward to commiserate over what he called "that piece of shit in *The Wall Street Journal.*" And there were more concrete signs of support. The White House had finally given him a part-time staff. They had brought in another Lanny, a former law partner of Charles Ruff named Lanny Breuer, to help with the crushing workload. Even the lawyers needed lawyers in this disaster.

A strange thing had happened as Davis settled into the job. As a former chairman of the *Yale Daily News,* he had always been partial to journalists, and he grew to like, even admire, most of the reporters he dealt with. He lunched with them at the Oval Room, usually sipping a Bloody Mary, and began describing them as friends and buddies. He took a perverse satisfaction in their scoops. He even liked Paul Bedard and Warren Strobel at *The Washington Times,* which cut the administration no slack. The reporters were, for the most part, fair-minded and honest. They always gave him a chance to say his piece in the story. On rare occasions they even killed a story when he could persuasively knock it down.

There were a handful of journalists Davis would not deal with— the *New York Post*'s Deborah Orin, for one. Or Sheila Kaplan of MSNBC, an aggressive reporter who kept describing his spin as pathetic and promised to report that the White House was stonewalling if he refused to check on her allegations. He was learning to push back, to refuse to launch some fishing expedition unless the journalists spelled out what they knew.

Most of the reporters developed a certain fondness for Davis. They saw how he worked around the clock, how he did his best to pry information loose, how he lobbied for disclosure within the White House. He clearly wanted to be liked. He seemed less the slick Amway salesman than a tightly wound lawyer whose head was barely above water.

Privately Davis sometimes denigrated the spin he was forced to deliver in public. Everyone knew the White House coffees were about raising money, he whispered to reporters. He and McCurry had argued from the start that they should be described as money events. Every week he would go a little further in acknowledging that. But the lawyers would not let him toss away the script. They were concerned about running afoul of the law against raising money inside the White House. So Davis had to toe the semantic line, saying the coffees were not-quite-fundraisers.

Davis's clientele were not the usual beat reporters whom McCurry faced each day in the briefing room. He dealt mainly with the investigative specialists who kept chipping away at the administration's explanations: Jeff Gerth at *The New York Times*, Susan Schmidt at *The Washington Post*, Glenn Simpson at *The Wall Street Journal*, Alan Miller at the *Los Angeles Times*, Chris Vlasto at ABC, John Solomon at the AP. The scandal crowd never had anything nice to say about Clinton; their job was to dig up dirt. It was open warfare, and reputations were at stake. Each time these rock-throwing reporters nicked a White House official, they helped their own careers. And they were always nervous about being aced by the competition. Sometimes Davis couldn't resist telling one reporter that a rival was also chasing the same lead. McCurry scolded Davis, and he stopped mentioning competitors by name.

Generally, though, when Rita Braver and Jim Miklaszewski and other reporters called to ask "What's up?", Davis wouldn't let on that he was working on an explosive inquiry from some other news organization. It was a curious minuet. He was lying; they knew he was lying. He knew they knew he was lying. But they understood that he would not give up another reporter's exclusive and that they would be furious if he told others what they were pursuing. It was in this way that Davis began to earn the reporters' trust.

No story more dramatically illustrated the gulf between the White House and journalistic camps than the Webster Hubbell saga. To Davis and McCurry and Podesta and their colleagues, there was no public scandal in Hubbell's downfall, only the ignominy of personal disgrace. He was a big, likable bear of a man who had made the fatal error of bilking his Rose Law Firm partners out of a half-million bucks, essentially big-time expense account chiseling. A few old friends had tried to help him out after he was forced to leave the Justice Department by lining up some consulting work for him. The man had four children to support. The press kept trying to blow this up into some deep, dark conspiracy but, Davis believed, there was nothing there.

To reporters like Gerth and Schmidt and Simpson, however, everything about the Hubbell mess smelled funny, not least the administration's stubborn refusal to divulge the smallest details. Hubbell was an old friend of the Clintons, Hillary's former law partner, and he surely knew some unsavory secrets of the Whitewater scam. Suddenly he's under criminal investigation and is being paid hundreds of thousands of dollars for minimal work by companies with connections to Clinton. Like Nixon's approval of paying hush money to the five Watergate burglars, this reeked of an administration attempt to buy Hubbell's silence. What's more, the White House repeatedly refused to say who in the administration knew that the Lippo Group and others had hired their former colleague. Ever since his name first surfaced in the context of scandal, questions about Hubbell had been handled with special sensitivity and answers were hard to come by. White House officials would press the reporters on what they knew so they could calibrate how much they needed to divulge. McCurry had already been forced to backtrack by acknowledging that Bruce Lindsey had known in 1994 that Hubbell had gone on the Lippo payroll. The reporters were writing what seemed to the outside world to be incremental stories—when Hubbell got the payments, who approved them, whether they coincided with James Riady's White House visits—because it was the only way to tighten the factual noose. Who else in the administration knew of Hubbell's lucrative retainers? Deborah Orin pressed McCurry on this point day after day, at one point asking him nine straight questions. He said it was impossible to determine what every single person in the White House might have known about Webb Hubbell's employment.

"Deborah, it would be an exhausting exercise. . . . It's a little bit *ad absurdum*," McCurry said, reaching back to his high school Latin. And, he warned, "there's a point at which patience wears thin."

The Hubbell story kicked into high gear on March 6, when Jeff Gerth and Steve Labaton reported in *The New York Times* that he had been paid $400,000 by a dozen corporations in the months after he left the administration. Most of the businesses were controlled by Clinton pals and big donors. Now it was no longer just James Riady and the Lippo Group that had felt compelled to hire the disgraced Hubbell. Other businessmen had rushed to employ him, perhaps trying to curry favor with the White House or as part of some larger scheme.

Two weeks later Gerth and Labaton struck again, reporting that a

Lippo subsidiary had paid Hubbell $100,000 a few days after Riady visited Clinton and top White House aides over a five-day period in June 1994. Gerth quoted Davis on background—as "a presidential spokesman"—saying flatly that no one else in the White House had made any calls on Hubbell's behalf.

Davis called Gerth to say that his words had been taken out of context. He had said that no other calls had been made "to my knowledge." Gerth asked whether the White House really wanted the *Times* to run a clarification saying that a spokesman had said something but it was only "to his knowledge"; that would look even worse. It was obvious to Gerth that other shoes were about to drop.

The day the second *Times* piece was published, Mack McLarty went to see Davis. McLarty, who was keeping a low profile as a presidential counselor, had a confession to make. He had made a call to line up some work for Webb. He had contacted Truman Arnold, the Texas oilman and former Democratic finance chairman, asked him to help out Hubbell, and Arnold had done so.

"Jesus, Mack, why'd you wait so long to tell me this?" Davis demanded.

"I didn't think any innocent, independent conversation with Truman Arnold was worth volunteering," McLarty said.

"Come on, Mack!" Davis shouted. He couldn't believe it. At the same time, he knew exactly what was going on. No sane person wanted to throw himself into this cauldron of scandal, to expose himself to hostile questions from prosecutors and the press, over what he had considered a harmless favor.

Days later Lanny Davis got another call from Jeff Gerth, with whom he had settled into a friendly, joshing relationship. Once, when he asked about a private conversation between Clinton and his attorney, David Kendall, Gerth bet Davis that he wouldn't be able to come back with an answer. If Gerth won, he got to play golf at Davis's country club; if he lost, he would carry Lanny's clubs for eighteen holes. (Gerth won the wager but never collected.) Davis, for his part, praised Gerth for asking the right questions, saying these were the very questions he would ask if he were Dan Burton or Fred Thompson.

"Lanny, stop trying to butter me up," Gerth told him.

For all Davis's affability, Gerth learned that he could stonewall with the best of them. In recent weeks Gerth had discovered that James Riady had held another meeting with Clinton in the summer of 1996, a session that had never been disclosed. He knew some of what was discussed but needed a second source. Gerth pressed for six months, and Davis finally came back with an answer: they would not ask the president about the meeting because it had happened too long ago. Gerth suspected he was being stiffed by others, that Lanny was not to blame.

Now Gerth told Davis that the Hubbell story had broadened from Clinton's former chief of staff to his current chief of staff. Gerth had a businessman saying on-the-record that Erskine Bowles had called him to line up work for Hubbell: confirm or deny? Gerth had it cold; he had copies of Hubbell's phone records and appointment calendar, and Bowles's name was on them. Gerth had reached financier Will Dunbar, a former client of Bowles, who acknowledged the call.

Davis went to see Bowles. Yes, he had made a couple of calls, the chief of staff said. He barely knew Webb, but Mickey Kantor, the White House trade representative, had asked him to help the guy out. The notion that this was some sort of conspiracy was absurd. Had there been the slightest whiff of that, Bowles told Davis, "I would have called the cops."

Davis confirmed the story to Gerth, but the reporter decided to pass. After all, the call hadn't led to a job for Hubbell, and Gerth didn't like doing incremental stories based on a single new fact. The Bowles call, it turned out, wasn't that big a deal.

"Maybe I'm losing my fastball here," Gerth told Davis.

Later McCurry called while Davis was chatting with Gerth. Davis put Gerth on hold and told the press secretary that Gerth had shown some restraint in passing up the chance to skewer Erskine Bowles.

"You're right, we owe Gerth one," McCurry said. Davis partially repaid the debt by leaking Gerth the WAVES records—the Worker and Visitor Entry Systems—for Mark Middleton, the Clinton-aide-turned-lobbyist who was under investigation and not particularly beloved at the White House.

Still, there was no question that the administration had to go public—McLarty, Bowles, Kantor, even the president's close friend Vernon Jordan, all were involved in the effort to financially aid Webb Hubbell. Davis was worried that they would move too slowly and trigger a new round of "stonewalling" stories. Glenn Simpson of the *Journal* was closing in on the McLarty connection, even knew that McLarty had told Hillary of his intention to help Hubbell. Alan Miller of the *L.A. Times* was also hot on the trail. If one of them broke the story about McLarty or Bowles before the White House made an announcement, it would look like they were trying to cover up.

"We've got to get it all out," Davis told McLarty. "I'll put both of you out at the same time."

The clock was ticking. That Sunday Susan Schmidt reported more details of the effort to help Hubbell on the front page of *The Washington Post*, prompting McLarty's call to Davis on the golf course. "I just read Sue Schmidt's article," McLarty said. "It would have been nice if I'd been in that article along with Mickey Kantor and everyone else."

Davis spent the next week trying to pull the facts together. The White House planned to issue the statement on Friday, but Gerth was taking a three-day weekend with his wife and daughter in Charlottesville, Virginia. Davis didn't want to screw Gerth. They decided to wait until the following week.

On Monday they had to delay again. Davis was still trying to track down Mickey Kantor. He finally reached Kantor at midnight at a London hotel. Kantor said that he didn't remember talking to Bowles about Hubbell. This was a real problem. Erskine barely knew Webb; the only reason he had called was because of Kantor. Davis carefully calibrated the statement he was drafting, attributing the conversation to Bowles's recollection.

They were ready to go on Tuesday, but Davis was opposed to a "general drop" of the Hubbell story. He was sensitive to the fact that certain reporters had made a heavy proprietary investment in the investigation. In real estate terms, they had put substantial equity into the story. If he put out the facts to the whole press corps, he would destroy the two-week investment that Gerth and Simpson and Miller had made. Others in the White House might be happy to blow away a reporter's exclusive by announcing it to the world, but Davis didn't play the game that way. He had to deal with these people every day, and it was important to build a feeling of trust.

McCurry agreed. They would tip off the newspapers that were way ahead, giving them a chance to break the story, and put out a statement the next morning. There was, Davis discovered, just one problem. The White House leaked like a sieve.

At 5:15 Chris Vlasto of ABC called to say that he knew of the decision. Jim Miklaszewski called with the same news. So did Pete Yost of the AP.

"C'mon, Yost, gimme a break," Davis said. "We'll put it out at 10:30 tomorrow." But the secret was out.

"This thing's blowing," Davis told McCurry. "We can't hold it."

Davis quickly set up a 5:45 conference call with the key Hubbell reporters and the network correspondents. He decided to put Rita Braver on the call, even though she had no equity in the story. The call took place so late that Rather, Brokaw, and Jennings had time to read only a few sentences about McLarty and Bowles being drawn into the Hubbell saga.

Braver called the next day, irate. "You fucked us again," she said. "You waited until the end of the day."

Davis called each of the reporters who had worked on the Hubbell story to apologize. Gerth said he understood. He would have done the same thing in their place.

The news brought universal condemnation from the press. "The White House repeatedly fudged, dissembled and even lied about its actions," declared a *USA Today* editorial. Jim Miklaszewski spoke of "a growing perception that they've got something to hide." Even Ron Fournier, writing for the scrupulously neutral Associated Press, concluded: "When the bubble bursts, the explanations change." *The Washington Post* ran another of its "Dribs and Drabs" editorials, accusing the administration of putting out false information "until it is shot down or about to be shot down," then changing the story "without any sign of embarrassment."

The "Dribs and Drabs" pieces were driving Davis crazy, making it harder for him to win the internal debate over full disclosure. If they knew 99 percent of a story, White House lawyers would argue that the other 1 percent might come out later and the *Post* would again accuse them of dribs and drabs. By that standard they would never release anything. Davis was constantly being trumped by the argument that delay was the politically safest course.

There was no question that Clinton would have to respond to the Hubbell news. At a pre-brief before his appearance with Portuguese

Prime Minister Antonio Guterres, the president and his staff agreed that they would stress the friendship angle. McLarty and Bowles acted "just out of human compassion," Clinton told reporters. They were "genuinely concerned that there was a man who was out of work, who had four children."

Davis thought the press was breathlessly convicting these men of an imagined conspiracy. Here was Michael Kelly in *The New Republic* saying flatly that Clinton's friends and subordinates "had worked together to pay hush money to Webb Hubbell, and Hubbell had indeed hushed up." That was hogwash, Davis felt. The whole thing was a paradox: the individual reporters were fair, he was convinced, but they were part of an institutional process that was decidedly unfair. They were not paid to be fair, they were paid to report, to draw nasty implications. Innocent men like Mack McLarty and Erskine Bowles were being smeared by reporters who thought they were being fair.

Time and again Lanny Davis wondered whether he should have been more aggressive in ferreting out the facts in the Hubbell case. Perhaps he should have gone to every senior official in the White House and demanded that they come clean. But did the president's lawyer have the responsibility to conduct a full-scale investigation? That was a more difficult question than most people realized.

He didn't have subpoena power. He couldn't depose people. He might get it right or, more likely, he might miss something. If he missed something and it turned out to be bad, then he, Lanny Davis, might be indicted. Ken Starr could bring charges against him. He would be deemed part of the cover up. Indictments were often after-the-fact reconstructions of innocent acts. It all depended on how desperate Starr was for some high-level scalps. They were all in never-never land. The young lawyers in the White House were all scared that they would make a wrong move and wind up with a $100,000 bill for legal fees, and that was why they were so cautious. This was not some fictional nightmare; John Podesta had had to hire a lawyer, as had Lorraine Voles, Maggie Williams, George Stephanopoulos, Harold Ickes, and Dee Dee Myers, just for being snared in the web of suspicion. The counsel's office had even told Davis not to take notes, for notes could be subpoenaed. It was ludicrous. Davis took notes anyway. He had to do his job and not sink into paranoia about whether he might find himself in Starr's crosshairs.

CHAPTER ELEVEN

Purely Personal

MᶜCURRY WAS WATCHING *INSIDE POLITICS* ON ONE OF THE four TV sets along his office wall. He hated the show, thought it should be taken off the air. CNN had launched it to cover campaigns, but in odd-numbered years the program had to justify its existence by reducing everything, even serious policy matters, to crass politics.

Today was a perfect example. Clinton was wrapping up a visit to Grand Forks, North Dakota, a city of 50,000 that had been almost completely inundated by the torrential flooding of the Red River. Yet here was anchor Judy Woodruff suggesting that the president had gone there as a respite from Washington politics, particularly from Kenneth Starr's decision to extend his Whitewater grand jury for another six months. It was absurd. Grand Forks was an unprecedented disaster, and Clinton was there to boost morale, not to score political points. McCurry hit the mute button.

He and Clinton had been talking about the Webb Hubbell mess. The president felt it was a nonstory unless you made the judgment that there was something inherently wrong in Webb's friends talking to him and trying to help him out. The stories all had that tone of dark suspicion about obstruction of justice. McCurry knew that Clinton was tempted to defend his friend emotionally, which would only make matters worse. He was constantly offering the president the same advice: Don't expound at great length. Don't talk the story onto the networks.

McCurry increasingly felt that what the scandal press did was try to beat the prosecutors to the punch. The reporters had been on the Whitewater-slash-Travelgate-slash-fundraising trail so long they were starting to think like Ken Starr, to fraternize with his people and cozy up to them for leaks. That very morning Sue Schmidt had a piece in *The Washington Post* quoting the usual unnamed sources as saying that Mark Middleton, the former White House aide, was exploring a deal with prosecutors, which Middleton would vehemently deny. Another Starr leak. It was all so transparent.

Earlier that day McCurry had warned Clinton and Gore at the pre-brief that the press might ask about James McDougal, Clinton's old Whitewater business partner. McDougal had appeared the night before on *Larry King Live* and said that he was tired of covering up for Clinton.

"Don't worry, I won't comment on it," the president said.

You may also be asked about Starr's grand jury extension, McCurry said.

"The press will think you're a pussy if you don't get out there and denounce Ken Starr," Gore said. "You gotta get out there and call him an asshole." It was part of a running gag, the vice president always egging Clinton on about Starr.

Clinton had grown surprisingly mellow about much of the scandal coverage, but he was still furious at *The New York Times* and *The Washington Post*. He didn't have the same scorn for the *Los Angeles Times*, which was pursuing the scandal just as aggressively, sometimes running a half-dozen stories a day. But its editorials didn't have that sneering quality, he felt. McCurry had never been able to convince any politician he worked for that there was a church-and-state division between the editorial page and the newsroom, and Clinton was no exception. He was convinced that the senior editors at *The New York Times* and the *Post* were out to wreck his presidency and that they had given the reporters their marching orders around the water cooler, talking about how much they loathed Clinton, setting the tone for the troops. Clinton didn't watch the network news, just channel-surfed late at night, so the two papers loomed largest in his pantheon of journalistic enemies.

At times McCurry seemed to buy into the water-cooler view of his adversaries. He grumbled to John Harris that the *Post*'s newsroom and editorial page seemed to be operating in tandem, trying to stick it to the White House. Harris said that was one of the few naive comments he had heard McCurry make about the news business.

"If you think that doesn't happen, *you're* the naive one," McCurry shot back. At the very least, he said, the journalists who disdained Clinton socialized together, shared the same mindset. And lately they were getting their leaks from Justice Department and FBI sources who seemed hostile toward the White House. The administration decreed a new policy that officials would not talk to reporters, even on background, about the Chinese influence-peddling investigation or about other national security cases involving Israel and Russia. McCurry felt strongly about this. It was against the law to leak classified information. Press secretaries fought hard to be included in the intelligence loop, yet they were the most likely suspects after a sensitive leak, since they had the most contact with reporters. These leaks were putting people like McCurry in a horrible position. The press spokesmen would have to be totally uncooperative, even surly, on these intelligence stories. No background guidance or friendly advice. If you want to publish intelligence leaks, McCurry told more than one reporter, do it on your own hook.

Hillary Clinton remained equally dismissive of the scandal stories. She told friends that she was furious with the *Post*'s coverage and continued to argue that Len Downie had a vendetta against them. She was clearly frustrated. When Andrew Heyward, the president of CBS News, stopped by for a courtesy call, Hillary complained that in the current climate it was hard to get attention for the administration's programs and policies.

She was still turning down print interviews, where her words could be edited and paraphrased, but occasionally made live appearances on radio or CNN or the network morning shows, where she could deliver her message unfiltered. In a National Public Radio interview with her favorite talk show host, Diane Rehm, Hillary had ridiculed the Whitewater affair as a "never-ending fictional conspiracy that honest-to-goodness reminds me of some people's obsession with

UFOs and the Hale-Bopp comet some days." Her staff had loved the humorous outburst, which no speechwriter could have scripted.

McCurry had a more down-to-earth view. The scandal-mongering reporters were so invested in the story that they had to believe in its ultimate importance, he felt. There had to be an impeachable offense somewhere in this pile of shit. Even the great Bob Woodward was peddling cut-rate goods. Woodward had called the other day with an ominous-sounding tale about leaked National Security Agency phone intercepts. It seemed that a controversial Latvian businessman named Grigori Loutchansky had been invited to meet Clinton at a $25,000-a-person DNC fundraiser back in 1995. But the NSA's intelligence gathering discovered allegations that Loutchansky's firm had ties to organized crime. An NSA official told a White House National Security Council staffer, who told Doug Sosnik, who told the DNC, which got Loutchansky disinvited.

"I gotta tell you, Mike, we're looking at something really serious," Woodward said. Passing on NSA intelligence data without the proper security clearance was a crime, he said.

Cut the horseshit, McCurry thought. For months reporters had been slamming the White House for letting all kinds of shady characters into Democratic fundraisers. Now the White House had blocked some Latvian guy from getting in, and that was also wrong? The press couldn't have it both ways. Loutchansky was classified as a zero zero, meaning he was on a visa watch list of people to be refused admittance to the United States. He couldn't have gotten into the damn fundraiser anyway.

When McCurry asked Sosnik about the alleged passing on of secret intelligence, Sosnik replied: "What is the National Security Agency?" He didn't have a clue. Yet the *Post* ran the story on the front page. McCurry felt that the paper gave Woodward too wide a berth, that no editor would stand up and tell him when he didn't have it. When the history of the fundraising scandal was written, McCurry believed, it would not be Bob Woodward's finest hour.

McCurry knew that many reporters viewed him as a roadblock to the guts of the scandal. They all seemed to think he kept the truth in a treasure chest on his desk, and all he had to do was take out the key and unlock it. He hadn't known about McLarty and Bowles helping Hubbell. He'd had to ask the same questions as the reporters, to deal with people's spotty memories. Of course, if he was wrong and there was some kind of conspiracy to buy Hubbell's silence, they would all need some packing boxes, including the Big Guy down the hall.

Every so often a dramatic event erupted that dwarfed the routine flow of news and demanded an immediate White House response. When McCurry glanced up, CNN had suddenly switched to live coverage from Peru, where plumes of smoke were emanating from the Japanese embassy. Soldiers were racing around. McCurry reached for the remote. The sound of gunfire and explosives punctuated the action. It was obvious that Peruvian commandos were attacking the embassy in an effort to free the Japanese hostages who had been imprisoned for months by rebel guerrillas.

McCurry grabbed the phone and called Jim Steinberg, the deputy national security adviser.

"Are you watching CNN?" he asked. "It looks like they're storming the embassy. You may want to get someone who understands the subject to brief our *presidente*."

He paused while Steinberg flipped on the set. "The question we'll get asked is his level of knowledge beforehand," McCurry said. "Was he consulted in advance?" He knew how the media mind worked.

This was a perfect example of the much-ridiculed point McCurry had made at the podium a few weeks earlier. CNN reporters could go on the air, as they were doing at this very moment, and say that Peru was attempting to liberate the hostages and engage in all kinds of speculation. He couldn't. The United States government had no official confirmation, and McCurry had no information with which to answer follow-up questions.

Less than thirty minutes after the attack began, Terry Hunt of the AP and Larry McQuillan of Reuters barged into McCurry's office. "We're not going to have any comment on it," McCurry said. He knew the wire guys had to file some kind of story.

"So the U.S. had no advance warning?" Hunt ventured.

"I'm not going to comment on it."

"Where did we find out about it?" Hunt asked.

"CNN."

"CNN?" Hunt sounded stunned. "That's where the U.S. government found out about it?" With all the administration's worldwide resources, it sounded so—ordinary.

"Bye, boys."

"That's all?" Hunt wondered. Couldn't McCurry throw them a tidbit or two?

"It'll have to do until something better comes along," McCurry said. The shooting in Lima was still going on. He wasn't flying blind on this one.

·   ·   ·

THE CLINTONITES WERE GROWING TIRED OF CONSTANTLY PLAYING defense. McCurry decided to do what he could to orchestrate the bad news and cushion its impact. He had known that Monday, April 14, would be a red-letter day for scandal watchers. The DNC was releasing ten thousand pages of fundraising documents and John Huang memos. It was, he decided, the perfect day to put out the long-promised report on fifty-six donors and fundraisers who got free shuttle service aboard Air Force One and the one fundraiser—Vernon Jordan—who stayed overnight at Camp David. The avalanche approach worked, and the details got lost in the dust. The DNC papers included an embarrassing memo urging Clinton to consider sixty top fundraisers for federal jobs; indeed, about half had been hired. But that revelation, and the Air Force One guest list, didn't make the front page of most newspapers.

More important, after six months of fierce intensity, the fundraising story was finally slowing down. The basic outlines of the tale were by now well known, a fatigue factor had set in, and the journalists were well aware that the public was not terribly exercised about the scandal. Maybe it was nothing more than a lull, but McCurry was pleasantly surprised to find the president's agenda receiving more coverage. With the scandal story quieting down, the other conversation was growing louder. Clinton was making announcements and proposals as fast as his staff could churn them out, and McCurry was selectively leaking them right and left. The technique he had devised for the campaign had now become standard operating procedure: he would give the wires and the radio reporters material to use after midnight, saying Clinton would do X, Y, or Z that day. When the president planned to ask the Federal Communications Commission to crack down on televised liquor ads, the story was leaked to *The New York Times*. When the president moved to force states to tighten seat-belt enforcement, the story was passed to Ron Fournier at the AP. When the president was toying with asking the Federal Election Commission to abolish soft-money donations, the plan was leaked to Alison Mitchell—and, incredibly, to Michael Kelly, who, when prodded by Rahm Emanuel, wrote a halfway favorable column about it. When the president decided to require the federal bureaucracy to hire 10,000 welfare recipients, the advance word made it to *The Washington Post*'s front page. Clinton was for cracking down on foreign sweatshops, expanding family leave, wiring schools for the Internet, banning chemical weapons. Even when he hadn't decided what to do, his musings became news. James Bennet got wind of the fact that the president wanted to speak out on race relations, perhaps form a commission, perhaps host a conference, and Emanuel confirmed it. Don Baer felt this had leaked to the *Times* prematurely; it would have been nice to have some policy proposal to go with the story. But the substance would eventually catch up with the advance billing.

The White House was turning itself into C-SPAN. Plain old talk, if it was packaged properly, could pass for news, even if the administration wasn't doing anything except yammering. The networks jumped all over the White House conference on early childhood development; *Newsweek* even published a special issue on the subject, complete with a piece by Hillary. The networks also fell in love with the volunteerism summit in Philadelphia, which had the added attractions of Colin Powell, George Bush, Jimmy Carter, Gerald Ford, and for extra starpower, Oprah Winfrey. *Newsweek* and *U.S. News* gave it cover-story billing. McCurry's only concern was that the administration was doing a poor job of tying it all together. No one seemed aware that helping children was a theme of both conferences and a spate of other White House proposals. Indeed, for many journalists the flurry of modest proposals and glitzy conferences added to the sense of second-term drift. Alison Mitchell wrote that Clinton's agenda was "minimalist," filled with "small-scale announcements." Susan Page of *USA Today* said that the fundraising scandal was freezing everything from ambassadorial appointments to arms sales to Indonesia because "the counsel's office and the press office are increasingly preoccupied with damage control." The *Chicago Tribune* ran a huge front-page headline: "Scandal Paralyzing Washington." McCurry knew that the administration needed some larger theme, a story to tell, or it would all be dismissed as ephemeral and the scandal headlines would overwhelm them again. But for the time being, at least, the White House was breaking through the white noise.

.   .   .

ONE REASON THE SPIN WARS WERE SO IMPORTANT WAS THAT MOST people viewed national politics as largely irrelevant to their daily lives. The endless maneuvering that so obsessed the combatants and the press was dismissed as meaningless political gamesmanship. Voters were tired of lofty promises that never seemed to materialize. The image meisters of both parties constantly had to talk up the idea that what they did mattered precisely because most Americans had grown so skeptical of the federal government.

Every once in a while, though, the political leaders would pull off a substantive accomplishment whose importance transcended the need for spin. Such a breakthrough took place in Washington on May 2, giving Clinton some good news to announce after two and a half years of trench warfare. He and the Republicans had struck a deal to balance the federal budget by 2002. The agreement was the first major victory of the president's second term and a vindication, for the moment, of his effort to bridge partisan differences and govern from the center.

The reporters would be grumpy, McCurry figured. The press didn't like it when government was working and there was bipartisan agreement and warring factions came together to do good things. It was much more fun to cover a fight. The budget wars, after all, had provided plenty of journalistic ammunition, from the opening shots of the 1994 Republican revolution through two government shutdowns and a presidential campaign. Now there was an armistice, and that would leave the reporters without the drama and conflict they craved. What would really annoy the elite commentators, McCurry felt, was that the deal had been achieved almost painlessly, without squeezing Medicare patients or welfare recipients and still cutting taxes. With the stroke of a pen, the Congressional Budget Office had magically sealed the deal by decreeing that the booming economy would generate an additional $225 billion in tax revenue over the next five years. The opinion-mongers were convinced that no budget deal worth the name could be achieved without great suffering and gnashing of teeth. They were certain to complain that the deal was pie in the sky, a temporary fix bought with Washington funny money. McCurry could see the editorials now.

He flipped on the evening news. The networks all led with the budget deal. But here was Rita Braver, carrying on about an appeals court ruling that the White House had to turn over some disputed Whitewater papers, notes that its lawyers had taken during discussions with Hillary Clinton. The administration had made "a declaration of war against Kenneth Starr," she reported. This was utterly predictable. Braver was at heart a cop reporter. She was married to a lawyer, had plenty of law-enforcement sources, and sometimes acted like she was still covering the Justice Department. A couple of wacko Reagan judges drop a little stink bomb and she's off to the races. So what if they had just struck a historic budget agreement and unemployment had dropped to a twenty-four-year low? Some reporters would rather wallow in Whitewater.

Faced with a continuing drumbeat of scandal headlines, Clinton had grown increasingly annoyed that the Republicans were getting off scot-free. The previous Saturday, after his radio address, McCurry and Rahm Emanuel showed him a press release. *Time* was touting a forthcoming scoop by Michael Weisskopf, who had just joined the magazine from *The Washington Post*. It seemed that the Republican Party had its own Asian connection. A Hong Kong businessman named Ambrous Tung Young had funneled money to the GOP through an American firm with almost no assets. First he guaranteed a $2 million loan to the party in the final days of the 1994 elections, then he agreed to swallow $500,000 in debts at the close of the 1996 campaign.

This was explosive stuff, Clinton said. They all agreed that the press would shift into overdrive. Reporters would demand an explanation from Haley Barbour, the former Republican chairman. The story would even the playing field a bit.

But nothing happened. Most major newspapers either ignored the *Time* disclosures or ran a few paragraphs of wire copy. Clinton confronted McCurry a couple of days later.

"What happened to your theory that there's fairness and balance in the coverage?" he demanded. "Your theory has been that they would pressure the other side as aggressively as us. What happened to that?"

"Well, it's not the White House, so it's not as sexy," McCurry said. "Besides, the steam has gone out of this story. People are getting kind of bored with it."

McCurry knew his explanation was lame. The media's behavior had undercut his argument that if they released their fundraising documents, reporters would press the Republicans to do the same. Now Clinton was even more determined to stop flagellating himself by coughing up embarrassing internal papers just to satisfy the press.

"I'm not going to do damage to myself," the president said. "We don't need to feed this story day to day."

Rahm Emanuel knew as much about the fundraising scandal as any investigative reporter. He had his research team crank out one report after another, barking his requests into the phone, so he could play defense with the press. The White House staff spent untold thousands of dollars on Nexis searches, combing the journalistic databases for every scandalous tidbit they could find so Emanuel could knowledgeably engage in the art of spin.

He was fascinated by this mysterious Republican benefactor, Ambrous Tung Young, and furious that the press was not following *Time*'s lead, even after the magazine published a second piece. The White House research staff worked up a four-page report on Young, neatly divided into bite-sized chunks. "Born in Taiwan—Later Renounced U.S. Citizenship," said one heading. "Young's Loan Bought Access to GOP Leadership," said another.

Emanuel had the staff produce a page of talking points called "The Republican Foreign Money Connection." It began with big bold letters: "THIS IS A BOMBSHELL. The new revelations about the Republican National Committee and its foreign ties are a bombshell and they completely change the entire nature of the upcoming campaign finance hearings."

Just as important: "HALEY LIED ABOUT THE GOP'S FOREIGN MONEY CONNECTION." Emanuel's staff had dug up a transcript of Haley Barbour's appearance on NBC's *Meet the Press* six weeks earlier. Host Tim Russert had asked about the National Policy Forum, the spinoff group set up by the RNC: "Did any of that money come from overseas?"

"Well, none of the money came from overseas," Barbour said.

"Period?"

"Period."

Ten days after the *Time* piece, the RNC announced that it was returning $122,000 donated by Young. Finally the story became front-page news in *The New York Times*, the *Los Angeles Times*, *The Washington Times*, *The Washington Post*. CBS and ABC did stories. But *NBC Nightly News* didn't carry a word.

Emanuel picked up the phone and dialed Russert, the network's Washington bureau chief. He would generally call Russert a couple of times a week, to complain that he was picking on the Clintons, to push for a story, or somehow to nudge the coverage. It was like working the referee in a basketball game. Russert was accustomed to being lobbied, but no previous administration had called him as often as this one. Emanuel pointed out this time that Russert himself had the tape of Barbour saying none of the money had come from overseas. Any first-year film student could have put together the piece.

"You guys doing anything on this?" Emanuel asked. "This is a big story. Haley lied on your show." Russert said that he and his reporters were monitoring the developments. That was all.

The almost grudging coverage of the Republicans' Hong Kong pipeline provided a stunning contrast to the continuing frenzy over the Webb Hubbell matter. And yet Emanuel was not among those who thought the coverage of the Democratic fundraising mess was out of bounds. John Huang and company were certainly fair game. Were administration officials partially to blame with their shifting explanations? Absolutely. It was a cover-up in search of a crime. They had kept the story alive by being too cute, by shaving the truth here and there.

But the Hubbell case was different. There was not the slightest evidence of a hush-money scheme. The Clintons didn't think they had done anything wrong, Emanuel reasoned, so they would have felt no need to shut Hubbell up. Maybe he had been watching too many mob movies, but there was no scene where Hubbell had proclaimed, "If you don't take care of me, I'm going to spill my fucking guts." It was all an invention of the press: His pal William Safire, his lunch partner Michael Kelly, and the rest of the crew had simply willed a hush-money scenario into existence.

And then Jeff Gerth had weighed in again. He and Steve Labaton reported that two of Clinton's closest confidants, including his lawyer David Kendall, had known that Hubbell potentially faced criminal charges when he resigned. So, of course, had anyone who was reading the newspapers at the time. But the president had gone out on a rhetorical limb, insisting that "no one had any idea" about "the nature of the allegations" and "everybody thought this was some sort of billing dispute with his law firm." That was an engraved invitation to reporters to prove otherwise.

McCurry had known for weeks that Clinton's words would come back to haunt him. Despite the president's reputation for lawyerly responses to press questions, the truth was that he wasn't as sensitive as McCurry was to the way you could get hung by every word you uttered. He sometimes went too far in his denials. McCurry played semantic games for a reason, to avoid this sort of entrapment. But Clinton liked to answer questions more broadly by explaining how he felt. He sometimes forgot that transcripts of his remarks would be scrutinized by prosecutorial journalists determined to find discrepancies.

The press had lost sight of the human dimension in the Hubbell tragedy, McCurry felt. The president and first lady had wanted to believe their old friend when he insisted that he was involved in a mere billing dispute and not something far worse. The Clintons were naturally sympathetic to someone facing allegations in the press because they both felt they had been unfairly pilloried by false charges. Of course they would believe their Little Rock pal was being victimized by exaggerated newspaper stories. Unfortunately, Hubbell turned out to be a crook. He had lied, point-blank, to both of them. But that didn't mean the Clintons were part of some elaborate conspiracy.

McCurry responded to Gerth by splitting hairs. "The full nature and seriousness of allegations against Mr. Hubbell were not fully known to anyone at the White House until he pled guilty," he said. Well, of course not, Gerth thought. Even now nobody *fully* knew the *full* nature of the thing. McCurry's answer was so carefully hedged that *The Washington Post* chided him in another editorial, calling his response "magnificently deflective and meaningless."

Gerth was particularly proud of the story because his twelve-year-old daughter, Jessica, had brought it to school for discussion. The press had a responsibility to be fair, Jessica told her dad, but she had concluded that Clinton was lying.

After arriving at the *Times* bureau in the old Army and Navy Club building, Gerth was stunned to see an AP report saying that "the White House denied" the *Times* story. He called McCurry.

"What's going on? Are you denying the story?" Gerth asked.

"No," McCurry said. The AP had gotten it wrong. Gerth notified the wire service, which quickly put out a correction.

McCurry had one other headache that morning. Erskine Bowles had been telling reporters that he didn't plan to stick around and was looking forward to returning to North Carolina. The last thing the administration needed was a lame-duck chief of staff, McCurry felt, but Bowles always said what was on his mind. He had clearly been shaken by having to testify in the Hubbell case. McCurry used diplo-speak to tell reporters that Bowles had no immediate plans to leave, but everyone knew the guy would soon be history.

Bowles had supported McCurry's efforts to carve out more time for Clinton to meet privately with reporters, but the millionaire investment banker instinctively avoided the spotlight himself. McCurry tried to explain that Bowles couldn't be a reclusive CEO. "The way the game is played in Washington, you've gotta talk to the press," McCurry told him. Still, Bowles begged McCurry not to push him onto any more Sunday talk shows. Each appearance required him to spend four or five hours preparing on Saturday, which meant his other work got pushed back and he didn't have time to see his family. Most top White House officials craved television exposure, but Bowles had taken the job reluctantly and had a short-timer's mentality. Now McCurry had to deal with the inevitable questions about Bowles's successor.

McCurry boarded Air Force One that afternoon for Clinton's week-long swing through Latin America. As an old State Department hand, he had looked forward to the trip and spent hours poring over the briefing books on drug trafficking, immigration, and other diplomatic issues. But he quickly found that reporters were bored with the trip and didn't particularly care about the substance.

The next day, in Mexico City, McCurry was conducting the pre-brief before Clinton faced the press at Los Pinos Presidential Palace with Mexican leader Ernesto Zedillo. Toward the end of the session, Sylvia Mathews mentioned a front-page story in that morning's *Washington Times* by Jerry Seper, the paper's top Whitewater investigator.

Seper had found some previously sealed court records in which Ken Starr described Hillary as "a central figure" in the probe and said she had changed her sworn testimony over time. McCurry knew the press corps would be fishing for a scandal lead.

Clinton gave his suggested answer and started going on at great length, sounding increasingly defensive. The staff knew he was particularly sensitive to questions about his wife. One of the unspoken reasons for these pre-briefs was to give Clinton a chance to vent his anger, so he wouldn't fly off the handle when the cameras were rolling. After he got what he really felt off his chest, his aides would urge him to take the emotion out of his response, to strip it to its factual essentials.

"Don't say anything on this," McCurry cautioned Clinton. "Don't talk it onto the networks. It's hard for them to make much of this story unless you give them a lot of verbiage."

The strategy worked too well. Moments into the news conference, Terry Hunt of the AP popped the question. Did the president know of any discrepancies in his wife's account, and was Whitewater getting more troublesome for her?

For the first time in months, Clinton lost his composure in public. "No, and no," he snapped.

Could the president elaborate?

"Well, you have been watching for years. If you don't know, I can't help you," he said coldly. Clinton drifted back to the question moments later, saying he "did not mean to be flippant" and that he knew of no changes in Hillary's testimony. It was clear that the Whitewater scandal, now more than five years old, was again getting under his skin.

Clinton later told McCurry that he had returned to the question after realizing he had been rude to Hunt. "Terry's a good guy," he said. "I just felt like I was too sharp with him."

Back in Washington, Rahm Emanuel was plotting strategy for the talk shows, which were following in Jeff Gerth's footsteps. *Nightline* did a whole program on the Hubbell case, asking "what the Clintons knew and when they knew it," and Lanny Davis fared pretty well, much better than in his earlier appearance with Ted Koppel. Now, on Friday evening, Emanuel and Podesta had to decide who to put out on Sunday for ABC's *This Week*.

Emanuel thought Bowles's decision to avoid the Sunday shows was a mistake. There were four power centers in Washington—the White House, the Hill, the K Street lobbyists, and the press. An administration official had to deal with all of them. Leon Panetta had been superb at schmoozing reporters. But Panetta was long gone.

Lanny Davis volunteered to appear on *This Week*, which had already booked Dan Burton. But perhaps it would be better to send Henry Waxman, the California congressman who was the senior Democrat on Burton's investigating committee. Waxman would seem less defensive than an administration lawyer. Emanuel was mulling it over when Davis walked in with a Burton letter demanding that Charles Ruff appear before his panel to explain the White House's refusal to provide subpoenaed documents, or face a contempt of Congress citation.

"I don't know whether I'm on or not," Davis said of the show.

"My view is, let's pull ya," Emanuel said. "We've got Henry."

"Henry's good," Davis said.

Davis wound up working the next day anyway because Ken Starr had attacked the White House in a speech to a group of Arkansas newspaper editors. In an unusual offensive for a prosecutor, Starr said that White House lawyers were "duty bound" to turn over the notes of their conversations with Hillary. He also castigated Susan McDougal, Clinton's former business partner who remained jailed for contempt rather than talk to Starr's investigators, for seeking a "license to lie."

By this time McCurry was in Barbados on the final leg of the president's trip. He knew that the press corps wanted to hit the beach on Sunday afternoon. The last thing he wanted was a war of words with Ken Starr. Clinton casually brushed off Starr's remarks, and McCurry's staff passed the word that Davis should be circumspect. But McCurry couldn't reach him.

Davis, meanwhile, called Chuck Ruff at the counsel's office. Ruff was a single-minded litigator who didn't believe in trying cases in the press. McCurry and Ruff had been clashing in meetings about the need to fight the public relations battle. Time and again Ruff had refused to allow Lanny to return fire when Starr or some member of Congress was denouncing them. But perhaps this episode would be different.

"You think this is the time for us to draw the line on Ken Starr?" Davis asked.

"Yes," Ruff said. Davis drove to the office and stood over Ruff's shoulder as the counsel tapped out a tough statement hitting back at Starr. It was issued in Davis's name so that Ruff would remain seemingly above the fray. The statement assailed Starr's charges as "nonsense" and accused the prosecutor of conducting "a fishing expedition." Davis started working the phones, notifying reporters about the administration's rhetorical blast.

McCurry was mortified. Davis had done exactly what he had feared, boosting the story onto the front pages of *The Washington Post* and *The Washington Times*. It was, McCurry felt, a major lapse in political judgment.

The recent spate of upbeat headlines quickly faded. It had been only one week since the White House had announced the balanced budget agreement, and somehow that was already old news. Rahm Emanuel couldn't believe that the coverage of such a major domestic achievement had lasted all of forty-eight hours when the scandal coverage had dragged on for months. There had been plenty of political analysis, he felt, but little substantive examination of the deal itself and how it compared to what Clinton had been fighting for since the 1994 electoral debacle, when the Democrats had lost both houses of Congress. They had saved Medicare from slashing reductions, extended health insurance to millions of children, won enough education aid to make college more affordable than ever. They had kicked the Republicans' ass. But the reporters were already two chess moves ahead. Alison Mitchell called with a question that rankled Emanuel.

"Now that balanced budget is over, what's next on the president's agenda?" she asked. What she really meant, Emanuel believed, was: What are you going to fail at now? The press had digested the budget deal in a single gulp and moved on. Perhaps the Clintonites had screwed themselves, Emanuel thought, by allowing the stereotype to take hold during the campaign that they were only pursuing "small" ideas. John Harris had called that day and asked the subject of the president's Saturday radio address.

"Child safety locks on guns," Emanuel said.

"Another poll-driven, small-bore idea?" the *Post* reporter joked.

As if any other president had dared to take on the National Rifle Association.

What really drove Emanuel up the wall were the columnists who refused to give them the slightest shred of credit. Here was Maureen Dowd dismissing Clinton's second term as "shrunken," "defeated," "aimless." Here was Joe Klein complaining of a "mystifying torpor," a "weariness," an "odd lack of ambition," a "sense of physical and intellectual exhaustion" that began "in the Oval Office." They must be on drugs, he thought. Michael Kelly, a friend of Dowd's, would undoubtedly deliver a similar indictment next. They probably e-mailed each other to make sure they were on message. Emanuel liked Klein, thought he was a smart guy, but this latest attack was intellectually incoherent. It showed the utter disgust that these columnists felt toward Bill Clinton. Even if you didn't like the chemical weapons treaty or the volunteerism summit or the budget deal, even if you thought these developments were bad or dangerous or phony, you could not say that nothing was happening in the second term. First the Clintonites had been denounced for taking on huge, intractable challenges, like health care reform, instead of more realistic and achievable goals. Now that they were making modest progress, they were ridiculed as political pygmies. The reporters, these morally superior beings—who, of course, were never wrong—loved to denigrate the mere mortals in the White House, but their true motives had been exposed. The attacks were so vacuous, so vitriolic, so out of touch with reality that Emanuel had to conclude they were, in the end, purely personal.

•   •   •

ANN LEWIS HAD HER OWN THEORY ABOUT WHY THE REPORTERS were impatient and sometimes hostile. After taking over from Don Baer as communications director in May, she saw that her challenge was to generate news when things were going smoothly and Clinton wasn't fighting with anyone. The reporters had loved the endless warfare of 1995, when the battle lines were clearly drawn and Clinton was taking on the Republican revolution. Now they were suffering from a sort of post-partum depression after the campaign. The Clintonites and the Republicans were no longer wrestling with each other; they were waltzing together, an inherently dull story. But this business about second-term drift was a media fantasy. The place was bursting with ideas, Lewis felt. Some of the journalists seemed downright angry at the president. The real problem, she believed, was that things had never been better. America was in the sixth year of a robust economic expansion, the stock market was over 7000, but that didn't fit the cramped, conventional definition of news as conflict. If the economy were in a tailspin, it would be on the evening news every night and Clinton would be getting the blame. She and her colleagues needed to hammer home the point that good times were rolling because of the tough tax and spending decisions that Clinton had made back in 1993. If the reporters were hung up on writing about strategy, well, they would package it as a strategy story: Could the White House seize political credit for the healthy economy? That would give the reporters a narrative with a bit of an edge.

Lewis and her colleagues decided to stage several events—"bundling," they called it—to break into the headlines. They would haul out charts and graphs filled with upbeat statistics. One week they decided to hold a Friday news conference and devote the Saturday radio address to the surging economy. At the appointed hour Al Gore, Treasury Secretary Robert Rubin, Budget Director Franklin Raines, and other officials appeared in the briefing room to trumpet the era of strong economic growth and declining unemployment. "The good news just won't quit," Gore said.

The reporters were unmoved. James Bennet walked out of the briefing into the overcast afternoon. No way would he write a word about this sort of cheerleading. They would have to do better than that.

Even the president found himself having to retail the news. Gerald Seib of *The Wall Street Journal* called Emanuel one day and said he had put together a new "tong"—a group of like-minded columnists interested in having background conversations with administration officials. The group included E. J. Dionne, Ron Brownstein, David Shribman of *The Boston Globe*, and Susan Dentzer of *U.S. News*. Emanuel agreed to be their first lunch guest, but he quickly realized that these were exactly the kind of centrist, sympathetic writers who should have more access to Clinton. McCurry agreed, as did Bowles, Podesta, and eventually the president himself.

Emanuel quickly made the arrangements, and the five were ushered into the Oval Office. Clinton said that he liked Seib's recent column on his role as a New Democrat. The group chatted for nearly an hour, and the president put some of his remarks on the record so that the columnists would reap some tangible benefit from the session.

"He seems increasingly confident that he is synthesizing a nuanced blend of government activism and reform," Brownstein wrote.

"He sees new purpose in his presidency and seems to be looking at the months and challenges ahead eagerly," Shribman wrote.

Emanuel was pleased, but it was a tough slog. He was having to sell the White House message one column at a time.

CHAPTER TWELVE

Hardball

THE WHITE HOUSE OBSESSION WITH BREAKING THROUGH THE media static had produced a hunger for hard numbers. These were furnished by Mark Penn, a brainy but somewhat shy polling whiz who had been brought into the Clinton operation by Dick Morris during the 1996 campaign. Penn became such a valued adviser that he left his firm's Manhattan headquarters and leased a recently vacated suite of law firm offices a stone's throw from the White House. He did his polling under a DNC contract, sharing his findings at Wednesday night strategy sessions in the White House residence with Clinton and Gore and a raft of senior aides.

If the reporters who covered the administration knew just how detailed these polls were, how they measured each presidential proposal against those proffered by Republicans, how they ranked each possible iteration of public policy and tied them to the Democrats' chances of retaking Congress, the journalists would have been even more dismissive of Clinton's market-tested approach to governing. All modern presidents took polls, but in the Clinton administration they were virtually a religion.

At the Wednesday meetings advisers would cite poll numbers in arguing, for example, that Clinton should exploit his nearly three-to-one advantage over the Republicans on environmental issues. The most important priorities were reducing toxic waste (backed by 35 percent), cleaner air (23 percent), cleaner rivers and lakes (16 percent), preserving land from development (13 percent), safer drinking water (7 percent), and global warming (1 percent). More than half the public did not believe there was clear evidence of global warming but perhaps could be persuaded if the phrase were associated with climate disruption. When Clinton went before the press to argue this or that position, he was, in most cases, leading where he knew the public would follow.

Penn contended that the presidency had been redefined, that the family-friendly issues that elite journalists snickered at were precisely the ones that resonated with ordinary people. And, according to the shopping mall surveys that Penn loved to take, Clinton was reaching them. Nine percent named education as the nation's top priority the day before the State of the Union address, but that jumped to 17 percent the following day. Folks cared about food safety and safe drinking water and decent health care, issues that touched their lives. On the other hand, almost no one knew that Clinton had gone to Mexico, so it was as if the trip had never happened. And the really encouraging news was here, in another poll: 43 percent were paying little or no attention to the fundraising scandal.

Penn's pollsters would ask people whether they had heard of this or that administration initiative. Thirty percent would say they'd heard of anything, but 50 or 60 percent was a significant breakthrough, and 70 or 80 percent was a home run. Penn argued with White House officials who belittled the idea that the president should devote a radio address to Net Day, a campaign to hook up public schools to the Internet. But the polling showed that 60 percent had heard of Clinton's initiative, because local news organizations across the country were chronicling their own schools' Internet efforts.

Penn also measured media behavior. His staff tracked front-page stories not only in *The New York Times* and *The Washington Post*, which so absorbed the White House, but also in *USA Today*, which Penn saw as more important. Since it had to sell most of its nearly 2 million daily copies at newsstands and airports, *USA Today* was more populist, more likely to reflect what people were buzzing about and what was in the local papers. And that meant it was less likely to get bogged down in incremental scandal coverage, at least on its colorful front page, the only page that mattered, in Penn's view. He envisioned the typical reader as glancing at the top headlines for a minute or two before turning to the spots section. People were too busy to pore over long, complicated political treatises that jumped to an inside page. They didn't read page A-12. They didn't understand the Webb Hubbell story. If Clinton made the front page of *USA Today*, he was probably doing well in *The Miami Herald* and *Kansas City Star* and *Seattle Post-Intelligencer*.

It was no accident that the president had given Susan Page of *USA Today* three interviews in the last year and a half, including one to mark the first one hundred days of the second term. The relationship worked well in both directions. With its billboard-style format of short front-page stories, *USA Today* loved to shake loose those little scooplets about a forthcoming Clinton speech or announcement. Page would often call up on Thursday, trying to snag an exclusive for Friday's paper by reminding administration officials that *USA Today* didn't publish on weekends. Whatever they were planning would be old news by Monday but might well get a front-page ride the next day. White House aides, knowing there would be little space for niggling details, were usually happy to comply.

Clinton had just had a hell of a week in America's newspaper. "Army of Volunteers Called Up" was Monday's lead story, with Clinton, Bush, and Carter all smiles at the Philadelphia summit. "Chelsea Breaking Away" was Thursday's cover story, one the White House didn't spin at all, about the first daughter's decision to attend Stanford University. And the budget deal led the paper on Friday. While its office tower was just across the river in Arlington, Virginia, *USA Today* simply didn't share the narrow mindset of the Washington media establishment, and under Penn's tutelage the administration came to see the newspaper as a direct conduit to middle America.

The network newscasts, with their limited airtime, were also a good proxy for what was playing beyond the Beltway. Penn had his staff monitor what ABC, CBS, and NBC reported each night and where it ranked in the broadcast. He fed the results into his Trinitron computer and included them in his weekly report to the White House. And the findings were encouraging. A typical page from one of Penn's reports: On April 15 NBC had Clinton at Shea Stadium for the fiftieth anniversary of Jackie Robinson breaking baseball's color barrier, and CBS had him addressing an antismoking rally, although it also showed Erskine Bowles preparing to testify in the Hubbell case. On April 16 CBS featured Clinton's initiative on seat-belt enforcement and ABC reported on Hillary's conference on early childhood development. On April 17 all three networks did the childhood confab. The strategy was paying dividends. The message was getting through.

In the third week of May, Rahm Emanuel grew excited about Clinton's upcoming Sunday speech at Morgan State University in Baltimore. The president would issue an inspiring call for the United States to develop an AIDS vaccine within ten years. Emanuel's Israeli-born father was doing pediatric AIDS research back in Chicago, so the White House aide was emotional about the issue.

Emanuel called Alison Mitchell early in the week and offered her an advance scoop on the speech. "Fabulous," she said. She was fascinated by the issue. Emanuel knew a big story in the Sunday *Times* would be like a neon press release, assuring major network coverage.

On Friday Emanuel called again. He warned Mitchell that John Harris was poking around on the AIDS speech. He knew the fierce competitive psychology that drove these reporters. The *Times* would trumpet a presidential initiative that no one else had, but would kiss it off if the White House seemed to be peddling it around. *The Washington Post* was the same way about beating its rival. That's why a twenty-four-hour jump could inflate the value of an otherwise routine story.

"I'm trying to hold the exclusive for you," Emanuel said.

But Mitchell had cooled on the story. Once she started poking around, it seemed to evaporate. Clinton was offering no new spending for AIDS, no new researchers, just reallocating some existing funds. What was it, really, except another speech? It certainly wasn't a gigantic front-page story. Even more puzzling was why Clinton was putting a Kennedy gloss on the speech, explicitly comparing his challenge to John Kennedy's famous vow to put a man on the moon by the end of the 1960s. Why practically invite reporters to say he was no JFK? Mitchell looked up the Kennedy address and saw that it had contained all kinds of specific dollar figures. The Clinton speech, however laudable, seemed empty. So much of what the White House did these days was designed only to garner favorable headlines. They were obsessed with publicity, as if that were the only measure of reality, as if they were still campaigning for reelection.

That evening, as Emanuel was lighting his Sabbath candles at home, John Harris called. "We have a lot of gay readers," he said, explaining why it was important for him to get the details of the AIDS initiative.

"I cannot confirm anything," Emanuel said. "And I'm not going to do it tonight."

Harris found it demeaning to have to badger these officials so he could write a story about what Clinton was going to say before he said it. He was particularly annoyed at the way Emanuel would parcel out an exclusive to one paper and then the next instead of just playing it straight. But he couldn't opt out of the game. His editors would demand to know why *The New York Times* had the AIDS story and he didn't. Besides, this was a big issue. Three hundred thousand people had died from the disease. Sure, the lack of new funding had to be pointed out. But presidential rhetoric and goal-setting were part of the job. Clinton, he felt, deserved one clean shot at making his case before the press dismissed it as mere posturing.

At 11:30 the next morning, Bruce Reed, the White House domestic policy adviser, beeped Emanuel. Harris was still bugging him about the AIDS speech, Reed said, and Mitchell didn't think it was much of a story. In fact, she was folding it into a piece she had already filed about Clinton's agenda in the wake of the budget deal.

"Fuck her," Emanuel told Reed. "Let Harris have it."

Mitchell was miffed when she saw *The Washington Post* on Sunday morning. Harris's story ran at the top of the front page, a relatively straightforward account of Clinton's forthcoming speech, with the caveat that he was not planning any new AIDS funding. She felt the *Post* had clearly been used. Mitchell had kissed off the speech in three paragraphs in her page 19 story, citing it as one more example of a drifting president trying to stitch together an agenda. "Clinton Assembles a List of Kennedyesque Challenges," the headline said. He was seeking "new issues" like scientific research and race relations, she wrote, "to invigorate his second term." Mitchell brushed aside his accomplishments, saying that Clinton "has acted so quickly

on his initiatives . . . that his supporters and antagonists alike are asking how he will fill his remaining years in office."

Emanuel was aghast. This was further evidence of how reporters
wrote in paradigms. The paradigm here was that Clinton was incapa-
ble of a big idea. Developing an AIDS vaccine sounded like a big
idea, so it had to be reduced to Kennedy-like posturing and shoved
into a prepackaged story whose theme—Clinton's second term was
adrift—had already been determined. Did the reporters ask experts
whether such a vaccine was feasible over the next decade and how
much it might cost to develop one? Of course not. They simply
downsized Clinton's vision into the tired stereotype that he trafficked
in puny ideas and meaningless gestures. If Emanuel had told reporters before the inauguration that Clinton would get a balanced budget
deal, a chemical weapons treaty, and an agreement on NATO expansion in the first 125 days of the new term, they all would have agreed
that that was dramatic progress. Now they were demanding an encore
in time for the next deadline.

Well, maybe it didn't matter. The Harris front-page story had
done the trick. If *The Washington Post* thinks the story is that important, television executives figured, it must be a big deal. Both
CNN and MSNBC carried the AIDS speech live. It was all over the
network news Sunday night and got the banner headline in Monday's
USA Today. In the world according to Penn, that was the newspaper
that counted.

· · · ·

DESPITE HIS STAFF'S BEST EFFORTS, CLINTON SEEMED TRAPPED IN
a yo-yo presidency. Whenever he built up a bit of momentum,
something would happen to snap him back. On the day after Memorial Day, the president was at the Élysée Palace in Paris for his big
moment on the world stage. Boris Yeltsin and other world leaders
were there to sign the agreement for the NATO alliance to expand
into Poland, Hungary, and the Czech Republic. This hard-won ac-
commodation with Russia could set the balance of power in Europe
for the next thirty years. But soon after the signing, Mike McCurry
was paged by the White House press office. "Re: Supreme Court &
Paula Jones," his beeper said. McCurry was puzzled, having forgotten
about the case. He called Washington and was told that the high

court had held unanimously that a sitting president was not immune to lawsuits over personal behavior. Jones's suit, now three years old, could go forward. Clinton diplomacy had been trumped by Clinton sleaze.

The president was studiously low-key, as if he were still teaching constitutional law back in Arkansas. "It must be an interesting opinion if it's nine to zero," he said. "Let's find out what the reasoning is." In an instant the talk had turned from nuclear diplomacy to the politics of sexual harassment.

Rahm Emanuel called the president's lawyer, Robert Bennett. Clinton wanted him to handle all public comment about the case, Emanuel said. That was fine with Bennett. If there was one thing he didn't need, it was a bunch of White House aides who didn't know what the hell they were talking about popping off about the case. They knew nothing about his strategy and might well say something that could hurt his client, legally or politically. He told Emanuel that one spokesman was plenty on this sensitive issue.

Bennett conferred with Clinton after the Yeltsin meeting ended. They knew that the unanimous ruling was a disappointment, just as they knew that their earlier strategy—delaying the damn thing until after the election—had succeeded. Bennett would never say that publicly, but it was true. Now he needed the flexibility to reach an out-of-court settlement if that seemed the best course. He gave an interview to CNN and, after notifying Emanuel and Cheryl Mills, went on *Larry King Live* that night.

The reporters in Paris had no crack at Clinton all day. They were barred from his photo op with Yeltsin. They asked McCurry if the court ruling was distracting the White House. Everyone figured it was, but there was no way McCurry would say so.

"I believe the opinion appears to have distracted all of you, but the president continued to conduct the nation's business," he said.

The Paula Jones ruling led all the networks, bumping the NATO agreement to secondary status. Rita Braver reported that White House officials were "shocked" and were "trying to put an optimistic spin on the situation." McCurry felt that the reporters were making this stuff up. The ruling wasn't that much of a distraction, and no White House aide would tell the press they were stunned and flabbergasted and felt the trip had been ruined. Still, McCurry knew the correspondents would be clamoring for a comment from Clinton. They had to deal with the story, he told his colleagues. Perhaps Clinton could briefly talk to the pool on Air Force One on the way to his next stop, in the Netherlands. But the other senior staffers overruled McCurry.

"We're on our trip," Emanuel said. "Let's keep this away from the president personally."

The battering continued in the morning papers. "Sense of Siege Deepens," said *The New York Times*. *USA Today* ran a huge picture of Paula Jones with the headline: "Sex Trial Possible in Clinton Term." The story said that Jones's lawyers would "start subpoenaing Clinton and at least 10 women he allegedly had trysts with," including Gennifer Flowers. The NATO meeting got a small headline.

Something larger than another press frenzy was going on here. On talk radio, in Internet gossip columns, in office corridors, people were again debating whether Clinton had dropped his pants in the presence of a subordinate in Little Rock's Excelsior Hotel and suggested she kiss part of his anatomy. This was not simply another embarrassing news story, like Whitewater; it had become a national punchline, part of an ongoing soap opera. Clinton was providing America with its tabloid entertainment. The reporters, while pretending to be interested mainly in the lofty constitutional principles at stake, were relishing the chance to get down in the gutter. Maureen Dowd put into play the latest chatter about what Jones meant by Clinton's "distinguishing characteristics" with a sly reference to "those rumors about that bald eagle tattoo." Others said it was a large brown mole. Don Imus marveled that everyone was sitting around "discussing the president's dick."

The next day Clinton met with European Community officials at the Hague, trailed by a small press pool. Ron Fournier was under orders from his bosses not to ask Clinton about Paula Jones at the news conference. AP executives were nervous about having their man raise some domestic controversy at a foreign press gathering where they got the first question; perhaps they still remembered Clinton snapping at Terry Hunt in Mexico. The pool members decided that Ken Basinet of UPI should ask the question at the photo op. But he didn't, and when Fournier tried shouting it, Clinton kept walking out of the room.

At the press conference at Binnenhof Palace, the pool reporters kept waiting to ask a question. But the officious Dutch protocol chief recognized only foreign reporters, who asked about the Marshall Plan and future aid to Europe. A White House aide slipped the protocol man a note asking him to call on an American correspondent, but to no avail. Another chance had slipped away. John Harris wondered how they could face their colleagues in the filing center with no comment on the Paula Jones ruling.

"They've gotta get something on this," McCurry told Clinton afterward. "Maybe it's better if we do an impromptu outside."

In the pool van, dubbed Wire One, the reporters groused to McCurry that they had had no shot at Clinton. Fortunately for them, the president's car pulled over to the side of the road so he could shake some hands. The reporters raced out of the van and tried to get Clinton's attention from behind a metal gate.

"We didn't get a chance to talk to you, Mr. President!" Fournier shouted.

Clinton ambled over with his cane and fielded the inevitable question. He said he was concerned about the ruling's effect on "future presidents" but would not go beyond that. "I saw Mr. Bennett's comments this morning, or heard them, on CNN," he said, deferring to his counsel. "I don't have anything to add to that."

As he walked away, Clinton asked McCurry: "How'd I do?"

"Perfect!" McCurry said.

Some White House aides were unperturbed. Ann Lewis firmly believed that the Paula Jones imbroglio would not hurt Clinton's image at all. People had made a judgment about this president, she reasoned, character flaws and all, and had still reelected him, despite all the carping from the press.

Bob Bennett, meanwhile, was deluged with interview requests. *Meet the Press*, *Face the Nation*, and *This Week* had called. He agreed to do all three but made no commitments. He wanted to check with the White House first, just to be diplomatic. If the story was fading by week's end, Bennett didn't want to give it new life by going on television. On the other hand, if the Sunday shows were definitely going to feature Paula Jones's lawyers, who were milking this for every last drop of publicity, he should be there to counter them. Bennett called a couple of friends at the networks, trying to figure out whether they would do a Paula Jones segment if he refused to appear. It was a cat-and-mouse game.

The low-key approach was working fine, Bennett felt, until that lunatic Dick Morris called and announced his intention to discuss the case on television.

"I'm going out, can you give me some talking points?" Morris asked.

"Really, Dick, should you be doing this?" Bennett said, horrified.

But Morris would not be dissuaded; he couldn't stand being out of the limelight. Morris told the Fox News Channel that he had urged Bennett during the campaign to delay the Jones case until after the election. Even if Clinton won, he believed, being acquitted of sexual harassment was hardly the best way to begin the campaign. Morris knew that White House officials would be riled by his remarks, but he didn't care. He didn't work for them anymore. He was trying to launch a punditry career and had to speak his mind. Fox called Bennett for comment, but he didn't return the call. This was exactly the sort of thing he wanted to avoid.

One of the reasons Bennett charged $495 an hour was that he was known as a media-savvy attorney with Brooklyn street smarts who could defend his high-profile clients—Caspar Weinberger, Clark Clifford, Dan Rostenkowski—in the court of public opinion. Lately, however, his relations with many reporters had gotten testy. He seemed defensive about the fact that he had been paid $892,000 in the Paula Jones case, only to lose nine-zip in the Supreme Court. He knew that he didn't hold the moral high ground in arguing that the president was seemingly above the law and could not be sued while in office. But it had been necessary to combat what he saw as essentially a political assault on Clinton. He whispered to reporters that he had ample evidence of Jones's slutty background, describing it in graphic detail and vowing to use it if necessary. At other times he grew confrontational with the journalists themselves.

"I've talked to your colleagues about you," he snapped at Sue Schmidt. "They think you're unfair." He told another reporter she was incompetent and could not understand legal papers.

The White House decided that Bennett should go on both *Meet the Press* and CNN's *Late Edition*. He spoke to Clinton on Saturday night. "You tell the American people that this did not happen," the president said. Bennett told his client that he planned to float the idea of a payment to charity as a way of settling the case, and Clinton agreed.

Bennett said on the two Sunday shows that Clinton would never apologize for something he didn't do but might be willing to donate $600,000 or $700,000 to charity to settle the matter. He also delivered a not-so-veiled threat. If Paula Jones "really wants to put her reputation at issue, as we hear, we are prepared to do that," he told Tim Russert. He leaked word to *The New York Times* that his office had just flown one of Jones's former boyfriends to Washington and taken his deposition. It was a spectacular blunder. By threatening to pounce on Jones's sexual history, the president's lawyer seemed to be descending into the mud.

The next day Paula Jones again graced *Newsweek*'s cover. Karen Breslau, the magazine's White House reporter, had warned McCurry about the cover story, and he let her have it. *Newsweek* is too vested in this story for its own good, McCurry snapped. This is more about selling magazines than covering legitimate news. You've become infected by the tabloid culture. McCurry often groused about the media's tabloid tendencies and the proliferation of seamy questions that consumed endless hours of his staff's time.

Reporters were quick to ask McCurry whether Clinton might pay the $700,000 from his personal funds or from insurance. He wasn't biting. Paula Jones was one of the subjects he didn't touch. "I don't have anything to add to what Mr. Bennett had to say yesterday," he said.

Bennett found himself under fire for his talk-show performance. The *Times* accused him of "threatening on national television to ruin Ms. Jones's reputation by bringing up her sexual history." Patricia Ireland, head of the National Organization for Women, charged him with using a "nuts and sluts defense." Maureen Dowd called Bennett "the latest Clinton henchman to slime himself." Bennett felt he was being unfairly savaged. In his next life, he mused, he wanted to come back as a *New York Times* editorial writer so he could smack people around without worrying about the facts. He would just as soon keep everyone's sexual history out of the case. But Jones's lawyers were making an issue of her supposedly pristine reputation and threatening to depose a long line of women who had slept with Clinton. Was he supposed to stand by silently just because his client was the president of the United States? They were trying to humiliate Bill Clinton. He had to make Paula Jones feel she would pay some price for these hardball tactics.

There was another aspect to the case that only Clinton's closest confidants understood. Clinton insisted privately that Jones was a liar and a tool of the right-wing hate machine. He wanted vindication, to expose her fraudulent claims in court. He didn't want to settle, and Bennett was merely following his client's wishes.

But Bennett still didn't grasp how much trouble he was in, that he had come off like a break-your-kneecaps kind of guy. The normally sure-footed attorney wasn't accustomed to this sort of widespread denunciation. He was the newest White House spokesman to make himself the issue. Just as McCurry's credibility had come under fire, just as Lanny Davis had seemed to be putting out bad information, now Bob Bennett had taken an embarrassing situation and turned it into a public relations disaster. White House aides were furious, convinced that Bennett had behaved like an idiot. He was, as they put it, swinging his dick too hard.

"We're in a world of hurt on this thing," McCurry told Podesta. But McCurry avoided talking to Bennett. They had clashed during the campaign over this lawsuit and clearly didn't like each other. Bennett was prickly about controlling the presentation of the president's case. McCurry felt it best to lie low.

Bennett was flying back from a quick West Coast trip. He called Rahm Emanuel. Don't undercut me, he said. Don't get out there and pull the plug on me. I'm preparing to deal with this.

Bennett launched an extraordinary media counteroffensive, insisting that of course he had no desire to dig into Paula Jones's sexual background (notwithstanding his leak about deposing her ex-boyfriend). He spoke to *The New York Times, The Washington Post, The Washington Times,* NBC, AP, Wolf Blitzer, Charlie Rose, Ted Koppel. Bennett had kept the sexual harassment story in the news for another ten days, a story the White House desperately wanted to vanish.

Rahm Emanuel thought of a way to change the subject. Chelsea would be graduating from Sidwell Friends School at the end of the week. McCurry had already told an annoyed press corps that the graduation ceremony would remain closed, in keeping with school tradition, even though the president was speaking. But perhaps that could be changed. The pictures of a proud father, with his seventeen-year-old daughter in cap and gown, would remind people of what even Clinton's sharpest critics conceded, that he and his wife had raised a remarkable daughter.

Emanuel went to the president. "As a parent," he said, "I'm ashamed to bring this up. As a political person, if I didn't raise this, I wouldn't be doing my job."

Clinton waved him off. "We've made our decision," he said.

Emanuel tried his pitch on Hillary. She stared at him and invoked his three-month-old baby. "Rahm, as Zak gets older, you'll know we made the right decision," she said.

It was funny, Emanuel thought. The president who was always accused of being excessively political was passing up a sterling opportunity to exploit his daughter's high school graduation, and no one in the press had noticed.

But Emanuel didn't give up. He was determined to milk the subject. He helped arrange for Susan Page to interview Clinton and Hillary for a Father's Day piece on the president as first dad. Emanuel knew that *The New York Times* or *The Washington Post* would take a cynical approach to such a piece, casting it as a crass effort to divert attention from Paula Jones. But *USA Today* played it straight. Page wrote a remarkably upbeat front-page story that led off with Clinton recalling how he had hugged Chelsea after she got her diploma.

The president, however, was miffed. Three sentences in the fifty-three-paragraph story referred to allegations involving infidelity, Paula Jones, and Whitewater as a counterpoint to his success as a parent. Clinton let Emanuel know he found that unfair. He could not countenance the slightest bit of personal criticism, even in a piece filled with glowing praise.

Clinton also made one gesture during this period that was clearly out of character. At McCurry's suggestion, he called Len Downie, who was getting ready to deliver his own commencement address as his son Josh graduated from the equally prestigious Georgetown Day School. He asked whether Downie was as nervous as he was about writing his speech. They traded ideas, and Clinton decided that Downie had the better speech and went back to work on his own. For a brief moment he put aside his anger at *The Washington*

Post's apparent crusade against him. This was something different, something only fathers could understand. It couldn't hurt, McCurry reasoned, for Downie to discuss a personal matter with the president. Perhaps the conversation would help him to see the first family in a more human light.

.   .   .

DAVID KENDALL, THE PRIVATE LAWYER WHO WAS MANAGING THE Clintons' Whitewater defense, was as different from Bob Bennett in temperament and demeanor as it was possible for two lawyers to be. A reserved, upper-crust attorney who knew Bill and Hillary from Yale Law School, Kendall scrupulously avoided the limelight, preferring to work through private correspondence and terse public statements. From his downtown office at the blue-chip firm of Williams and Connolly, he spoke to reporters only on background. Kendall was so concerned about staying out of the public eye that when the *Post* was preparing a profile of him, he agreed to have his picture taken only by letting it be known he would be walking by a certain street corner in a trench coat at a preordained moment.

But in early June, when Kendall read a *New York Times Magazine* article on Kenneth Starr's Whitewater efforts—a piece for which Starr had posed for photos and, the paper said, provided "background assistance"—he had had enough. He persuaded the Clintons that the time had come to return fire. Kendall called McCurry and told him he was sending over a draft copy of a letter to Starr and would appreciate his comments. The letter accused Starr of "plain violations of grand jury secrecy" and of trying to inflict "leak-and-smear damage" on the Clintons. Kendall had made such protests privately to Starr, but never in a public missive.

"It's a hell of a good letter," McCurry said. "We're in a news vacuum this week. If you put this out, it'll probably get some attention."

To make sure the media didn't miss the letter's significance, Lanny Davis started lobbying reporters. "I've got to pitch you on this letter," he told Chris Vlasto, the ABC producer.

When Vlasto reported back that *Nightline* had decided not to do a program on Starr, Davis erupted. "God, you guys!" he exclaimed. "The one time we go on the offensive. . . . You guys always do it for the other side. Now you've gotta do it for us."

It was a tense period for Lanny Davis. Once again he seemed out of the loop when reporters pressed him for answers. He was getting into screaming matches with Lanny Breuer, the former Manhattan prosecutor who was actually his boss. Breuer, thirty-nine, favored suspenders and seemed to have a nebbishy, Woody Allen demeanor, but at times he would scold Davis over a provocative quote in the paper or veto his plans to launch a new spin cycle. Eventually they would make up, with Davis planting a kiss on Breuer's cheek. Other White House officials grew alarmed by Davis's tendency to get over-excited. They were relieved that the Other Lanny was around to calm him down.

The scandal reporters had an increasingly hard time reaching Davis. He once took three days to respond to a page from Glenn Simpson at *The Wall Street Journal.* By the time he called back, Simpson couldn't remember why he had called.

Sue Schmidt had so much trouble getting hold of Davis that when his secretary asked what her call was in reference to, she said: "His pending indictment."

Davis called back quickly. "I hope this is a joke!" he declared. "This isn't funny!"

But Davis did find time to harangue reporters who dared to write skeptically about the Webb Hubbell case. He screamed at columnist Richard Cohen over the phone. He chided Glenn Simpson for his remarks about the Hubbell case on *Nightline.* He rebuked David Maraniss for a routine *Washington Post* article on the Sunday talk-show chatter about Hubbell. He called Michael Kelly to complain about one of his *New Republic* columns.

"You're just a lawyer defending a client," Kelly told him. "All the people who work for Clinton are so defensive."

Despite his advocacy of full disclosure, Davis was caught up in the familiar cycle of putting out sensitive information only when the press was on the verge of exposing it. Soon he was again fielding inquiries about Roger Tamraz, the Lebanese American donor whose lobbying efforts had sunk Tony Lake's nomination to the CIA.

Ed Pound at *USA Today* and Michael Frisby at *The Wall Street Journal* had dug up new information about Tamraz's ties to Clinton, information the White House hadn't bothered to put out the first time around. It seemed that Tamraz had discussed his plans for a Caspian Sea pipeline with the president at a 1996 dinner for Democratic donors and that Clinton had asked Mack McLarty to follow up on the proposal. Nothing came of McLarty's inquiries to the Energy Department, but here was fresh evidence that major contributors got high-level favors for their trouble. There was a real quid pro quo this time. Tamraz had given the party $177,000 and Clinton had pulled some strings for his business venture. And, for good measure, a grand jury was investigating the matter.

Davis had been grappling with the story for the past month, but there were all sorts of problems. Some of the material involved was classified; his security clearance hadn't come through, and other officials weren't sure if the papers could be declassified. Even worse, Davis felt he couldn't just pick up the phone and call officials at the Energy Department. To do so might look as though the White House were orchestrating some sort of cover-up. That was what had happened in the early days of Whitewater, when White House officials had called the Treasury Department in a similar circumstance. He didn't want to repeat that blunder.

Once Davis and his colleagues realized that Ed Pound was close to popping the story, they decided to launch a preemptive strike. Davis set up a 6:00 P.M. conference call with the *Journal*, *USA Today*, *Time*, *The Washington Post*, and the *Los Angeles Times*, all of which had made inquiries about Tamraz. The White House would blow away the scoop and get out in front of an embarrassing story.

The maddeningly slow two-hour call provided a rare glimpse of the internal White House struggle over how much information to release. When one of the reporters asked a question, Davis would put them on hold for several minutes and confer with an attorney from the counsel's office who had the proper clearance and had read the classified documents. Then he would come back with the officially sanctioned answer.

Pound, a gruff investigator who looked like a 1930s private eye, was furious as he listened to Davis spill the details he had worked so hard to accumulate. He knew that the White House was trying not only to put its stamp on the story but to upstage Fred Thompson's investigating committee, which had already deposed witnesses in the Tamraz case. This was a highly skilled operation when it came to spin control. Pound vowed that in the future he would call the White House for comment as late as humanly possible. He liked to give people enough time to respond, but these guys would screw you in a heartbeat if given the chance.

Perhaps it no longer mattered. McCurry was soon throwing down the rhetorical gauntlet. The fundraising scandal, he declared, was "petering out." On the surface this appeared to be a highly questionable assertion as the newspapers continued to break fresh stories about the activities of John Huang, Charlie Trie, and Al Gore's Buddhist temple fundraiser. As the Senate hearings drew closer, the list of those promising to invoke the Fifth Amendment—Huang, Trie, Hubbell, and others—grew embarrassingly long. Fred Thompson grumbled about the lack of cooperation with his committee, saying the Clinton White House was doing more stonewalling than Richard Nixon.

Still, McCurry was clearly onto something. The steam had gone out of the story. Fewer reporters were following the money. The number of scandal reports on the network news had plummeted by more than two-thirds since March. Most Americans had made a judgment that the scrambling for cash and the favor-seeking were politics as usual. Clinton's approval rating was still close to 60 percent. The White House had managed to compartmentalize the scandal, McCurry felt, using a pooper scooper to whisk the stuff into a little box. Editors were finally exercising some judgment, not throwing every piece of manure on the front page. McCurry hoped that there wasn't much left to pursue.

In the middle of June, Lanny Davis told McCurry that one last batch of documents had been sent to the Hill committees. There were a few embarrassing stories in there, he said, but nothing explosive. Should they release the material to the press? The senior staff was against it. Lanny Breuer felt it would violate the confidentiality agreements he had hammered out with Congress. Even Davis, the staunchest advocate of full disclosure, felt they didn't need any more self-inflicted wounds. The strategy they had followed in fits and starts since the election, of shoveling this smelly stuff out the door, had been successful. They had taken the hits. There wasn't that much dirt left to shovel. He got Breuer to agree to a deal: If an individual reporter called with a piece of a story, Davis could selectively leak the material and close the sale. But no more full-scale document dumps.

The Senate hearings were clearly in trouble. Thompson's investigators were frustrated that the White House, with advance word from committee Democrats, was leaking every juicy piece of information they had found, taking the sting out of the July hearings. The reporters loved to feast on new meat, one Thompson staffer lamented. They had no interest in carrion. If the committee served up reheated allegations, the press would yawn.

The hardest of the hard-core investigative reporters were concluding that the story was going nowhere. Glenn Simpson was tired of spending his time chasing junk journalism, such as speculative reports that Hillary might soon be indicted. Chris Vlasto felt he had hit the wall, that he had been having the same conversations with sources about Clinton sleaze for the last five and a half years. Rita Braver kept getting pulled off the scandal beat to cover routine administration news. Besides, Braver felt, there were so many different characters and subplots that it was increasingly hard to explain on the evening news. Covering Iran-contra had been far easier; at least there were recognizable characters like Oliver North and John Poindexter. How many Americans knew who Charlie Trie was? Without some direct link to Clinton, it was lousy television.

Even Jeff Gerth, who had been unearthing financial scandals since the Carter administration, had all but abandoned the story. He had told his editors weeks earlier that the scandal had peaked. The major characters, the major plot lines were pretty well known. There were only so many times you could write on the front page that the administration was selling access to donors. People with big money got to make their case to politicians? That was how the system worked. Lanny Davis tried to leak Gerth a memo from Jane Sherburne, the former White House lawyer, about her long-ago contention that Clinton's meeting with James Riady was not a social visit. Gerth turned him down. He had already done that story. It was time to move on.

From time to time some new scandal news would bubble to the surface and soon dissipate. On June 23 the Supreme Court ruled that the administration would have to turn over to Kenneth Starr the notes of Hillary's discussions with White House lawyers about Whitewater. Lanny Davis wanted to tell reporters how inexplicable he found the decision, but his boss, Charles Ruff, ordered him to keep quiet. Ruff didn't want a pissing match in the press. He put out a bland statement instead, and Clinton, at a fundraising dinner, refused to comment.

Davis continued to argue that this was a losing strategy. He wanted to stand on the White House lawn and hand out the Hillary notes. He contended that there was nothing particularly harmful in the notes—someone had surreptitiously read them to him—and that the administration shouldn't act as if it were hiding some terrible secret.

McCurry also urged Ruff to put out the notes. "It's a little hard to go out and make the argument it wasn't the content of the notes but the principle of privilege we were defending," he told Ruff, "if you're not able to say in the end, 'Here are the notes.' "

But Ruff managed to change McCurry's mind. "We just had Kendall write a long letter to Ken Starr objecting to the release of material that's grand jury implicated," Ruff said. "These notes were requested by the grand jury. If we suddenly turn around and release this material, we've done exactly what we've accused Ken Starr of doing." And, like any good lawyer, Ruff was worried about precedent. "If we release this portion of grand jury testimony, why not other grand jury testimony that's of interest to the press?" he asked.

McCurry still wanted to dump the material, but he conceded that sometimes legal arguments had to trump the public relations imperative. Still, the White House wasn't entirely helpless. Unnamed sources soon cropped up in various news accounts, describing the notes as basically innocuous, and soon this story, too, faded away.

The following afternoon Ruff got a call from Bob Woodward, whom he knew from his days as a Watergate prosecutor. Woodward had been interviewing some of the Arkansas state troopers who had been part of Clinton's security detail and had once made sensational charges about his constant philandering. Two of the troopers had told Woodward that Starr's investigators were pressing them for details of Clinton's sexual escapades, asking about a list of twelve to fifteen women, including Gennifer Flowers, whom Clinton was said to have slept with. The investigators had even interviewed some of the women. Ruff declined to comment, but administration officials were privately overjoyed. The story was exactly what they needed, making Starr look like an overzealous fool. Sure, it reminded everyone of the tales of Clinton's frenetic sex life, but voters had long since digested those charges. Hillary had constantly complained that the press held

Starr, who among other things continued to represent the tobacco industry, to a lesser standard. Now the prosecutor was finally becoming the issue.

The story led the next day's *Washington Post*, clouding the president's announcement of tougher air pollution rules. McCurry deflected a question about Starr's tactics, saying the White House had no comment. During the pre-brief, he and Clinton disposed of the matter in the sort of shorthand that had become routine between them. "This is not something we want to get into," McCurry said, and Clinton nodded his assent. When reporters tried to question Clinton outside a conference on family values in Nashville, he pulled the Reaganesque maneuver of insisting he couldn't hear over the roar of the helicopter engines. Still, the administration lined up Bob Bennett, James Carville, and plenty of other surrogates to denounce Starr for the pillow-talk probe. But reaction to the Woodward story was sharply negative among the small band of Whitewater reporters who had spend five years following the twists and turns of the complicated scandal. There was an unbreakable bond among them. Although they were nominally rivals, they consoled each other during tough times, when their work was under attack from the White House or from within their own news organizations. Jeff Gerth had some of his earliest Whitewater stories killed by skeptical *Times* editors during the 1992 campaign. Sue Schmidt, the only woman in the gang, had been the subject of that scathing White House report and considerable bad-mouthing by McCurry and Bennett. Many people, the reporters knew, thought they were nuts. They were like a remote tribe who spoke an obscure dialect. They liked Starr and his prosecutors and tended to give them the benefit of the doubt. Outsiders didn't always understand their world, and they, in turn, were wary of journalistic interlopers.

Chris Vlasto argued vociferously that ABC should not chase the Woodward piece, and he got his way. It was, he felt, the ultimate in hypocrisy. Reporters talked to the girlfriends and mistresses of criminal suspects all the time. He himself had a list of thirteen alleged Clinton paramours and had interviewed them early on. Starr's approach might look bad, but it was standard prosecutorial practice.

Steve Labaton also thought the story was badly hyped. He had known for months that the troopers had been asked about Clinton's personal life, and he didn't view the technique as a big deal. He wrote a short, dismissive *Times* piece leading with Starr's assertion that the story was "incorrect," although the prosecutor was not contesting the facts, just their implication. Even Sue Schmidt, who had been drafted as Woodward's collaborator, had misgivings about the story. The Whitewater specialists were convinced Starr was getting a bum rap.

The next day, as the mercury hit a record-breaking 100 degrees, Lanny Davis had reason to sweat. He got a call from John Solomon, the AP investigative reporter, who had four sources describing the latest documents that the administration had turned over to Congress. On one note Gore's deputy chief of staff had written: "BC made 15 to 20 calls, raised 500K." This was one of the last missing pieces of the puzzle. Clinton, who had a conveniently foggy memory about whether he had made fundraising calls from the Oval, appeared to have raised a half-million dollars. He had done the same thing that Gore had been hammered for four months earlier. Reporters had suspected as much all along.

Davis scrambled to confirm the story and finally did so after 6:00 P.M. He put out an artfully worded statement saying Clinton "cannot recall specifically asking for contributions during these calls, though he may well have."

Now that the news was out, Lanny Davis wanted to tell the world and scoop the congressional investigators. He and his assistant, Adam Goldberg, called every reporter they could track down. *The Washington Times* confirmed the story and splashed it on the front page. But it was too late for the networks and most of the major papers. *USA Today* relegated it to one paragraph in a roundup column. *The New York Times* ran nothing. *The Washington Post* used a wire story on the bottom of page A-8. Sue Schmidt was miffed when she reached Davis the next day.

"You got what you wanted—the story was buried," Schmidt said.

"You still don't get it," Davis said. "I wanted it on your front page with a glaring headline. That way Fred Thompson's not going to get a glaring headline."

CHAPTER THIRTEEN

The Frontiers of Spin

IT WAS JULY 9, THE SECOND DAY OF THE SENATE FUNDRAISING hearings, the extravaganza that all Washington had been eagerly awaiting, the high-noon showdown with former movie star Fred Thompson that the White House had frantically been trying to defuse since Election Day. In media terms the hearings seemed a total bust—little drama, less news, almost no live television coverage. CNN, MSNBC, PBS, and C-SPAN had all blown off the proceedings. The hearings weren't even on the front page of that day's *Washington Post*. Everyone was buzzing about how the thing had fizzled.

Rahm Emanuel, sitting in his cubbyhole office, broke into a grin when *World News Tonight* came on. Peter Jennings led off with a new ABC poll that put Clinton's popularity at 64 percent, the highest of his presidency, before turning to the hearings. When Bruce Reed walked by, Emanuel exulted that a potentially horrible week had turned into one of their best.

"Another day where the Keystone Kops somehow shot their way out of the corral," he told Reed. Maybe they were finally learning how to do this, to stick to their game plan, to avoid hyperventilating, to contain the virus of scandal news so that it didn't ruin their political health.

Clinton was in Madrid, meeting with the NATO allies and beaming over the formal admission of the three new Eastern European members. It was yet another week of high-minded diplomacy abroad as a way of muffling lowly scandal back home, a balancing act at which the administration had grown exceedingly adept. But the network correspondents traveling with the president were doing their best to keep the scandal alive.

McCurry was miffed that NBC, alone among the major networks, did not air a separate story on the NATO expansion. David Bloom, the new White House correspondent, simply packaged the diplomatic news with his scandal story. Even worse, Bloom broke out of a press holding area and rushed up to a rope line to try to get Clinton to utter a sound bite on the Senate hearings. "Stay on me, I'm going in," Bloom told his camera crew. Clinton brushed him off with a cursory response, which Bloom used in his piece. McCurry couldn't tolerate such behavior. He saw Bloom as showy and aggressive, a Generation X version of Sam Donaldson. The previous month, during the flap over General Joseph Ralston, whose candidacy for chairman of the Joint Chiefs of Staff had been derailed by an extramarital affair, Bloom got angry calls from McCurry and Rahm Emanuel after reporting that Clinton had little political capital to spend on the issue of adultery. Don't be surprised if ABC starts getting all the leaks, Bloom was told. Don't be surprised if Clinton starts getting fucked by NBC, Bloom shot back. He would never do such a thing, but it was important to let them know he could not be rolled.

This time, McCurry concluded, Bloom had gone too far. He would mete out the punishment when Clinton met the press at the Madrid convention center.

"Why don't you not call on Bloom if you don't need to," McCurry told Clinton.

At the news conference Rita Braver asked the president about the testimony that he had urged the DNC to hire John Huang. Why did he feel so strongly about the Asian American fundraiser?

"I think I may have said to someone that he wanted to go to work for the DNC," Clinton said, as if it were a matter of minuscule importance. "I don't remember who I said it to. But I do believe I did say that to someone."

John Donvan of ABC asked a question about Chinese influence-peddling. David Bloom had his hand in the air, but Clinton quickly looked away from the row of network reporters. He began searching the audience: "I'll take a couple of foreign journalists." Then: "The gentleman from Ukraine." And: "One of the Spanish journalists?" McCurry told Bloom afterward there was no way Clinton was going to call on him. "Look, there's no point in us trying to create rules of the road if we don't have some enforcement," McCurry said. He figured that Bloom's bosses would notice that he had been ignored. Bloom erupted, yelling about the sheer pettiness of the way he had been dissed. His job was to ask tough questions, not politely defer to the president.

No matter; the networks had their story line. "President Clinton barely had time to savor his leading role in the expansion of NATO when he was plunged back into the Democratic fundraising controversy," Braver reported, not mentioning that it was the reporters who had done the plunging. "Mr. Clinton's memory was vague."

For all their studied indifference, administration officials were acutely aware that Thompson was occupying center stage in Washington. "What's going on at home?" Clinton asked Madeleine Albright as he and other alliance leaders walked along a flag-bedecked route. "Are we taking any licks yet?"

In the days leading up to the hearings, the White House had stepped up its defensive pressure. Lanny Davis and Lanny Breuer joined forces in a background briefing, assuring reporters that the Thompson investigation was strictly about scoring political points. Davis wanted to leak a damaging e-mail message that would undoubtedly be used at the hearings, but he had a problem. The message had not yet been turned over to Congress—it had belatedly been found in the wrong file—and the administration didn't like to anger the committees by releasing material before giving it to the Hill. The e-mail had been sent by the White House deputy political director, Karen Hancox, and seemed to confirm that Clinton himself had been eagerly dialing for dollars: "The POTUS and VP offered (ON THEIR OWN) to make f r [fundraising] calls for the DNC. Harold [Ickes] will be asking POTUS to carve an hour out of his schedule Monday and Tuesday for the call."

But at Lanny Davis's urging, Representative Henry Waxman's staff had promptly leaked the e-mail to the congressman's hometown paper, the *Los Angeles Times*, for the deadest possible day, July 4. Now Davis could confirm it to anyone who asked. He talked to Hancox, who claimed that she had no firsthand knowledge of the Clinton and Gore calls. Davis put out his standard non-denial: Clinton had "no specific knowledge of asking for financial help," but "if he did, we see nothing inappropriate about it." It was stretching credulity to believe that Clinton didn't remember making these calls, but the story disappeared into the black hole of a holiday weekend.

The White House also seized on an opportunity to renew its campaign against Sue Schmidt of *The Washington Post*. The opening came when three of Dan Burton's House investigators quit, charging that the committee's chief sleuth, David Bossie, was preventing them from following professional standards. Bossie was an old Clinton hater who had worked for a conservative group that aired TV ads in 1992 inviting viewers to call a special phone line to hear the Gennifer Flowers tapes of her conversations with Clinton. He had later been an investigator on the Senate Whitewater committee. Schmidt, Glenn Simpson, and Chris Vlasto all had great respect for Bossie. When Schmidt wrote a brief *Washington Post* story about the Burton probe that didn't lead with the staff defections, the administration went ballistic. John Podesta called the *Post* to complain. James Carville called the *Post* to complain. Richard Ben-Veniste, the Democratic counsel on the Whitewater committee, called the *Post* to complain. Schmidt was protecting her favorite source, they cried, refusing to report fairly on the Republicans' problems. Schmidt thought it was a garden-variety staff shakeup, but she quickly found herself on the defensive and was assigned to do a follow-up piece on the Bossie flap.

Once the hearings began, Lanny Davis stationed himself during each break in the corridor outside Room 216 of the Hart Senate Office Building. He stayed carefully out of range of the network cameras, which were set up at the bottom of a short carpeted ramp in front of a seven-story-high Alexander Calder sculpture. Davis was the designated spinner, dismissing whatever had just transpired as "old news" and having himself a grand old time. Nervously fingering a notebook or a handful of change, he kept switching between background and on-the-record, handing out newspaper clips to show that the panel's revelations were ancient history. In short, his best defense was to publicize the very White House sleaze he had been minimizing for months.

"I'm having fun," he told Francis Clines of *The New York Times*. "Isn't it fabulous?" he asked Chris Vlasto. The brazen presence of a White House spokesman at the hearings showed how far the spin game had evolved, how the administration was determined to persuade reporters that its interpretation was more important than the very facts they had just heard. Some of Davis's allies thought he seemed to be gloating. Joe Lockhart, McCurry's deputy, felt there was too much chest thumping. George Stephanopoulos, the old master spinner, believed Davis was taking the routine too far. *The New Republic* put Davis on the cover as a whirling dervish, the personification of Clintonian spin. But Davis reveled in the limelight. He sent McCurry an autographed copy: "To Mike, who taught me what to do when shit happens."

The Democratic senators on the panel began to grumble that Davis was hogging the media attention that otherwise would focus on them. One day John Glenn, the former astronaut who was the panel's senior Democrat, walked down the hall, unnoticed, as a clump of reporters surrounded Lanny Davis.

"Who's that?" Glenn wondered.

"That's Senator Davis," Phil Jones of CBS cracked. "Don't you know your colleague?"

"Oh, that's the guy from the White House," Glenn said. "Look at this—he's doing his own spin control here!"

Jones asked Davis for an on-camera interview. He refused. Jones grew angry; Davis was, after all, holding forth on the record. "This is bullshit!" he said. "C'mon! Come out here!"

When Davis demurred, Jones walked up to Glenn and asked: "Do you think it's appropriate for the White House to have a representative here outside the committee door, doing daily spin control?" Glenn sidestepped the question, but the senators soon asked the White House to cancel Davis's act. Now the question at the daily White House damage control meetings was whether they should send Lanny back to the hallway or keep him under house arrest.

Davis knew he had a tendency to get swept away by his own high-speed verbiage. Sometimes he would interrupt his monologue to announce rather sheepishly that he was delivering a spin. He sometimes came off, in his favorite Yiddish expression, as a "schlemiel." He used his son, Seth, a rookie reporter for *Sports Illustrated*, as a one-man focus group who wasn't shy about telling Dad when he had gone too far.

"How did I do today?" Lanny would ask.

"You were full of shit," Seth would often reply. One time Seth declared: "You don't convince me that you even believe what you're saying." When Davis couldn't sell his own son, he knew he had a problem.

These days, though, Davis felt vindicated. He wasn't celebrating, despite his casual hallway banter with reporters. He knew the dangers of seeming overconfident, of pissing off the reporters with his relentless "old news" mantra. But there was no denying that their dribbing and drabbing strategy had worked. Thompson's opening firecracker about a Chinese influence-peddling plan had already exploded in Woodward's story back in February. The testimony about Johnny Chung giving the Democrats $50,000 after bringing his associates to watch Clinton's radio address would ordinarily have been a major bombshell, but it had been in the papers in March. Davis tried to imagine having to rebut these charges now, with all the reporters running around on deadline—he would never get more than a minute of anyone's attention. There was too much noise in the air. They had taken their hits month after month in what seemed an insane exercise in self-flagellation, but now it all seemed worth it.

Doug Sosnik, traveling with Clinton in Madrid, kept calling the White House to monitor the hearings. But as the lead-off witness, former DNC finance director Richard Sullivan, droned on without producing much news, Sosnik could sense from Spain that the White House was paying less and less attention.

"What's going on?" he asked Podesta. "You watching the hearings?"

"Well, to tell you the truth, I've gone back to work," Podesta said. "The TV is on, the volume is off. But he looks good." Before long Sosnik had to call political friends outside the building to find out what was happening.

By the third day of the hearings, the administration was making all sorts of news that further overshadowed the recycled scandal. While Clinton waved to cheering multitudes in Warsaw, Gore claimed victory at the White House when RJR Nabisco announced it was killing the controversial Joe Camel ad campaign, a clear victim of the administration's anti-tobacco drive. Gore also invited family advocates to the White House to announce that the networks had agreed to modify their rating system by providing parents with more information about sex and violence in programming. Emanuel was thrilled when CBS and ABC both mentioned the Clinton role in their Joe Camel stories. People cared about teenage smoking and tawdry television. It was important to stay on offense while fending off Whitewater and Paula Jones and the other recurring scandals.

Clinton, for his part, seemed more relaxed, more confident overseas. After a triumphant rally in Bucharest, he strolled back to the press pool on Air Force One in a T-shirt, jeans, and white running shoes. "Oh shit," said one reporter who was settling in to watch the in-flight movie. Clinton, demonstrating his golf swing, talked about how his knee had healed enough for him to play nine holes. He said he hadn't yet seen the movie *Air Force One* but recalled having dinner with its stars, Harrison Ford and Glenn Close, in Jackson Hole, Wyoming. Barry Schweid, the AP's diplomatic correspondent, interrupted the light banter to ask about NATO's effort to arrest war criminals in Bosnia.

"That's it," McCurry said, moving to shoo Clinton back to the front cabin before he stepped on the day's story.

"No, no, this is legitimate," Schweid said, standing his ground. The president, looking almost grateful, launched into a long, discursive answer and remained for nearly half an hour. The wires had their new lead, and Clinton looked happy. Sometimes, it seemed, the staff was a bit too protective of the boss.

But even when he was riding high, Clinton could be amazingly thin-skinned about press coverage. Despite his newfound determination to tune out negative headlines, sometimes he just lost it. Clinton was furious when his staff handed him a fax of a front-page *Washington Post* story that, on the surface, appeared to contain good news. The economy was so strong, wrote financial reporter Clay Chandler, that the budget deficit, now officially down to $67 billion, might vanish by 1998 even if the president and Congress did nothing. But that meant that Clinton would get no credit for all the tough decisions he had made to erase the red ink.

"Why do they think the economy is so strong?" Clinton raged. "Don't they think we actually did something in '93? We made a conscious decision to reduce the deficit and not one bloody Republican would help us! That's why the economy is so strong!" McCurry said it was typical of the *Post's* Beltway mindset to turn even a financial story into a political one. Clinton said they had to "push hard" to get out the message that the deficit was melting because they had raised taxes and jump-started the economy four years ago. This sort of garbage could endanger the fragile budget deal by obliterating the notion that Congress had to act. They had to put a stop to it, Clinton said. This was serious business; Mark Penn's internal polls showed that six out of ten Americans didn't even believe the deficit was shrinking, let alone that it would disappear by itself.

Clinton made an early-morning call to the White House, and Gene Sperling, the tireless whiz kid who was now the top White House economics adviser, got the message. He was supposed to fix the problem. "This is really a terrible article," Sperling told the 7:45 senior staff meeting, which decided to have Treasury Secretary Robert Rubin appear on CNN to knock down the story.

Sperling had long felt that the press kept moving the goalposts whenever the administration carried the budgetary ball down the field. It was the prospect of a balanced budget agreement, with its substantial cuts in Medicare, he argued, that was keeping interest rates low and the economy booming. To say that the deficit would vanish by itself was just plain wrong. Sperling had tangled with Chandler before, during Clinton's first year in office, when Chandler had quoted one economist as saying that the surging economy would have bounced back even "if voters had elected Bugs Bunny." Sperling had warned Chandler that if he kept up this sort of thing, no one in the administration would talk to him. "You're in danger of not getting any inside information," Sperling said, spelling out what is usually an implied threat between a highly placed source and a reporter who crosses him.

Now Sperling called Chandler again, his voice breaking with anger. "This is so reckless!" he shouted. "This is so irresponsible! I can't believe you wrote such a thing! You didn't give us any credit! This is just indicative of the whole mindset of *The Washington Post*!

We don't get one fucking good day from *The Washington Post!* You have just destroyed your credibility."

Chandler was stunned. It was, after all, a good-news story. But nothing, it seemed, was more important to the White House than taking credit for any semblance of good news.

· · ·

AL GORE HAD BEEN THROUGH A ROUGH COUPLE OF MONTHS AFTER his disastrously defensive March news conference. He was stunned at how quickly and savagely the elite press had turned on him. It felt, on some level, like a personal betrayal.

Gore had always been more philosophical than Clinton about the inevitable ups and downs of press coverage. Clinton felt he suffered from his outsider status, but Gore was a purebred product of Washington, a senator's son who had attended the elite St. Albans School in the shadow of the Washington Cathedral. He had lived in the capital for thirty-nine of his forty-nine years, had known most of the top political reporters since he was a Tennessee congressman. They were of the same generation, had gone to the same parties, had risen through the ranks together. Now these same people—men like Al Hunt, Evan Thomas, Howard Fineman—were not just criticizing him but challenging his character, as if they had never known him. Gore was taken aback by the intensity and the virulence of the attacks. It was as if he had walked into a room and heard all his friends saying nasty things about him.

Gore didn't expect the reporters and columnists to write that he walked on water. If he gave a klutzy performance at a news performance and used the same goofy phrase seven times, he knew he would get bad reviews. The sort of coverage he had drawn at last summer's Democratic convention was so ridiculously, absurdly good that it obviously couldn't last. Gore knew from his days as a Nashville reporter that the media pendulum always swings back. In fact, he was so far ahead of any Democratic rival for 2000 that he had nowhere to go but down. The press always turned on the front-runner because that was the only way to create an interesting race. All the journalistic incentives were to take him down. His staff told him that there was a silver lining in being roughed up so early, that it would prepare him for the inevitable ass-kicking he would take during a presidential campaign. Gore used to worry about three negative paragraphs in an otherwise favorable story. Now he was far less sensitive.

"I took a punch, and I'm going to keep going," he told Lorraine Voles.

The conventional media wisdom was changing again, and this time Gore was the beneficiary. By July he was getting rave reviews. Gore took the shift in stride, now that he understood how chillingly fickle the press could be. "Good story today" was all he would say.

The spate of favorable headlines was no accident. Gore's staff was working overtime to insert him into breaking news stories, to fill the gaps left by Clinton's schedule. Ron Klain, who had worked on the Hill before becoming Gore's chief of staff, found his new situation downright weird. Gore was the only politician in America who couldn't do what any freshman city council member could do—come up with an idea at nine and call a press conference at ten. He couldn't say what he wanted or court controversy without upstaging Clinton. He had to wait for whatever leftover crumbs the presidential staff would toss him.

Fortunately for Gore, the White House was increasingly trying to position him front and center. And when Clinton left the country, as he did during the NATO trip, Gore could play domestic president. Klain and his staff worked overtime coming up with issues that the vice president could exploit in and around that week. Here he was making news on urban aid, on education, on tax cuts, on Mars exploration. McCurry was startled one day to see four cameras setting up in the Roosevelt Room for what he assumed was a presidential event, only to find that Gore was holding forth on airline safety. Gore's staff had had little luck selling such events in the first term, but now, as a potential president-in-waiting, their boss was far more marketable as a political commodity.

McCurry called Voles one day to say that Leo Rennert, Washington bureau chief of *The Sacramento Bee*, had asked to interview the president about an upcoming gathering on environmental issues at Lake Tahoe, Nevada. "We'll never do this, but you should do it," he said. "Gore could be on the front page." Voles added the interview to Gore's schedule. "All those who love Lake Tahoe are going to be very pleased with the results of this presidential forum," Rennert quoted Gore as saying in an "exclusive" front-page interview.

The opportunities kept coming. Bruce Reed called to suggest that Gore make a public statement on the administration's objections to the recent $368 billion settlement between the tobacco industry and the state attorneys general. Ann Lewis agreed that Gore could stand in for Clinton at a Girls Nation event at which women astronauts would talk about space exploration. The press apparatus was increasingly geared toward casting the vice president as a full partner, and the reporters, who were already handicapping the 2000 contest, were happy to oblige. McCurry saw Gore as a second communications channel, a way of doubling the administration's policy output.

Lorraine Voles's strategy was simple: She wanted Gore moving around, making news, but she would not put him in an uncontrolled media environment where questions about the scandal could ruin the day. No news conferences, no Sunday morning shows, no "press avails," as Voles called any brief opportunity at which reporters could fire questions at the veep.

This was an iron rule. Gore was about to meet with South Africa's deputy prime minister; Voles nixed a planned press availability after the session. She didn't know what the Thompson hearings would be focusing on that day. For the Lake Tahoe summit, Voles scheduled a roundtable with Nevada reporters, who were certain to ask about local issues. National reporters, who were still sniffing around the scandal, were barred.

Occasionally Voles took a chance. When David Broder arranged to spend a week following Gore, she approved an interview after ascertaining that he was primarily interested in Gore's effort to bolster his ties to Democratic constituencies. Broder listed "campaign finance" as one of three areas he would pursue, but Voles had known the *Washington Post* columnist for years and trusted him to be fair. Broder was disappointed in the interview, finding Gore as carefully programmed as ever. But the veep's staff loved the piece. Other than a few paragraphs in which Gore "curtly" said he would not volunteer to testify at the Senate hearings, Broder portrayed him as "cementing his position as the heir apparent."

More often, though, Voles kept a buffer zone between her boss and the press. When the *San Francisco Chronicle* wanted an interview on current events, she said no. It sounded too much like a fundraising piece. Two top reporters, Bill Turque of *Newsweek* and Bob Zelnick of ABC, were beginning work on books about Gore, obviously geared to 2000. Voles told them Gore would not cooperate.

Ron Klain, meanwhile, was working his contacts in the press. He kept calling Rick Berke, the *New York Times*'s chief political reporter, to lobby for a story on Gore's rising fortunes. "You put it on the front page of *The New York Times* when you had him dropping 20 points," Klain said. "It's incumbent upon you to come back and revisit how he's doing politically." Instead, Berke weighed in with a front-page piece declaring that "no president in at least 150 years" had done as much to promote his understudy as his successor. No Gore aide was quoted in the story, even on background. Klain didn't think Clinton would be pleased to wake up and read about the veep's staff boasting of the president's support for Gore.

Lorraine Voles still got her share of scandal questions—she kept the TV in her second-floor office tuned to the hearings on Fox News Channel—but the animosity level was way down. CBS's Bob Schieffer called one day with a hot lead about an e-mail message from Gore's scheduler that supposedly proved that he knew the Buddhist temple visit was a fundraiser. Voles checked with Charles Burson, Gore's counsel, and told Schieffer that the message had already been read at the Thompson hearings. They wound up having a pleasant conversation. Voles no longer felt like a rock was being dropped on her head every day. She wasn't getting much sleep with a three-month-old baby at home, but she was far more comfortable than in the dark days of March.

. . .

THE DAUNTING THING ABOUT McCURRY'S JOB WAS THAT THE White House was always one phone call away from disaster. McCurry had known for weeks that *Newsweek* was sniffing around on yet another story about Clinton's sex life, and this one was particularly explosive. A former White House aide, Kathleen Willey, was apparently telling the magazine that Clinton had propositioned her right there in the Oval Office, and that they had had some kind of furtive sex. This was not some ancient Arkansas allegation; this was said to have happened while Clinton was president, in the office where he received heads of state, in the very house where his wife lived.

It was no surprise to McCurry that Michael Isikoff, a hard-charging, invariably rumpled *Newsweek* reporter, was the man on the bimbo patrol. Isikoff had been the first national reporter to trumpet Paula Jones's charges back in 1994, when he worked for *The Washington Post*, and he was tight with Jones's lawyers, who were undoubtedly behind this latest sleazy charge. Isikoff and *Newsweek* had practically become publicists for Paula Jones, McCurry thought. The two had tangled before, and the press secretary had bad-mouthed Isikoff around town as an overzealous investigator. He once ordered the reporter out of his office when Isikoff had slipped in with another *Newsweek* correspondent—an old-fashioned ambush—and began pressing McCurry on whether he had been candid about the fundraising scandal.

The White House was right about one thing: Isikoff had gotten the tip from Jones's lawyer, Joseph Cammarata. Isikoff tracked down Kathleen Willey, a former campaign volunteer, who told him off-the-record that she had succumbed to Clinton's advances in 1993. There were other bizarre twists to the tale: The alleged encounter took place the same day that Willey's husband, an attorney accused of embezzling $275,000 from a client, committed suicide. Clinton had dispatched the one-time flight attendant as a delegate to international summits in Copenhagen and Jakarta, despite her obvious lack of expertise. But Isikoff couldn't persuade Willey to go on the record, and he wasn't going to level such a serious charge with an anonymous source. The story was stalled.

In the incestuous world of journalism, however, there was always another way for sleaze to bubble to the surface. The conduit this time was Matt Drudge, a thirty-year-old Walter Winchell wannabe who ran his own World Wide Web site, the *Drudge Report*, from a one-bedroom apartment in Hollywood. Drudge's gossip wasn't always solid—he used material from *The National Enquirer* and Clinton haters in Arkansas and had touted predictions that Hillary would be indicted before the '96 election—but he had become fashionable among the media elite. One of Isikoff's *Newsweek* colleagues whispered word of the inquiry to Drudge, who quickly declared that Isikoff was "hot on the trail of a woman who claims to have been sexually propositioned by the president on federal property." White House staffers were so fixated on the story that they logged onto the Drudge site more than 2,600 times.

McCurry told Clinton he planned to stiff the press. "My instinct here is to make it very difficult for reporters to report this story and not do anything to help them," he said. But McCurry did not ask his boss whether the charges were true. As always, he had to stay away from fact gathering, had to leave that to the lawyers, or he could be subpoenaed next in the Paula Jones case.

The White House needed some intelligence fast. Lanny Davis, who had known Isikoff for years, was asked to check things out. He felt awkward trying to smoke out a reporter in the guise of a social call, but he dialed Isikoff at home over the weekend. "I'm calling because we're old friends and some people here want me to find out what you're up to," Davis said.

Isikoff wouldn't bite. "You're asking me about an Internet gossip column?" he joked. "C'mon, Lanny."

The story soon spun out of Isikoff's control. Bill Plante learned that Cammarata had subpoenaed Kathleen Willey as a witness in Paula Jones's sexual harassment suit. He called Bob Bennett, who derided the Willey charge as "fucking horseshit" off-the-record but confirmed the issuance of the subpoena. Plante reported the subpoena, without naming Willey, on the *CBS Evening News* that Wednesday night.

Within minutes Wolf Blitzer was chasing the story. He called Cammarata, who refused to comment.

"Your no comment means it's basically true," Blitzer said.

"Why do you say that?"

"Because I've been a journalist for twenty years. If it was a lie, you'd say it was a lie." Bennett confirmed the subpoena soon afterward, and Blitzer matched the story for CNN's 8:00 P.M. newscast. *The Washington Times* named Willey in a front-page story the next morning. The New York tabloids also joined the fray.

Bennett thought all this was utter hypocrisy on the media's part. They were using the subpoena, and this Drudge guy, as an excuse to publish unsubstantiated charges that they could otherwise never touch. An analogy came to mind: when he lived with a bunch of guys in college, four were neat and one was a slob; by the end of the year they were all slobs. That's how it was with these seamy stories; a few irresponsible clowns were dragging everyone into the gutter.

McCurry, too, felt that the journalistic bar had been lowered yet again, that the press was feasting on rumor and innuendo, no matter how personally demeaning to the president. At the gaggle he repeatedly refused to discuss Kathleen Willey, would not even say whether she had once worked in the White House. "I'm not answering questions on this matter. . . . You're not going to use me at this podium to further stories that your news organizations have to decide on their own whether or not they want to publish," he said. It was the zipped-lip strategy he had employed when *The American Spectator* charged that Clinton had been sleeping with Marsha Scott, the White House aide from Arkansas. McCurry would not give the press a hook to reel in this piece of journalistic garbage. Maybe he could prick their consciences, somehow shame them into dropping it.

But the subpoena angle had rendered the unconfirmed allegations fit to print. *The New York Times, The Washington Post, Newsday,* and *USA Today* were all in hot pursuit. McCurry started hassling Peter Baker as soon as the *Post* reporter called.

"I can't believe you're gonna do this story," McCurry said. "I'm not gonna talk to the *Post* until a senior editor calls me and assures me you've thought through the consequences."

"Mike, you're not gonna talk me out of doing this story," Baker said. "This is a subpoena in a lawsuit we've been covering."

"I could subpoena you for cocksucking," McCurry replied, meaning that anyone could make a wild charge in a legal document. Then he hung up.

After Baker's editor called to assure McCurry that the paper was serious about the story, McCurry told him: "Look, I was rough with you. I just want to make sure you've thought through this thing."

"Can't we just say the president denies this happened?" Baker asked.

That, for some reason, riled McCurry again. "You have no basis on which to ask that question," he snapped. "You never ask questions based on other people's reporting." Perhaps McCurry had forgotten his own lecture to the gaggle on the White House conspiracy report, on the mainstream media's weakness for salacious stories that had been laundered through the British tabloids or *The American Spectator* or *The Washington Times.*

Newsweek, which had triggered this journalistic chain reaction, now had no choice but to publish what it had. Mike Isikoff called

McCurry, who launched into his spiel. "My policy on this—and this is not directed to you in particular—is that I'm not going to do anything with questions on this matter until I hear from a senior executive of your news organization who tells me you are seriously pursuing a story on this matter and consider it a matter for publication." Ann McDaniel, the new Washington bureau chief, called McCurry the next morning.

The sparring was just beginning. On Saturday Isikoff, Evan Thomas, and Ann McDaniel gathered in the magazine's twelfth-floor Pennsylvania Avenue office, one block west of the White House, and talked to McCurry on the squawk box. McDaniel assured him that *Newsweek* would do a balanced story reflecting that the Kathleen Willey situation was "murky."

"There was a time when if it was a murky situation and it involved the president of the United States, news organizations wouldn't publish the story," McCurry declared. "It's pretty sad that we've come to this point. You're basically writing a story involving a charge of inappropriate sexual behavior by the president of the United States of America, and your own story says you don't have any idea whether it's true. You tell me that would have been the case five years ago." He was just warming up. "*Newsweek* has an institutional investment in the Paula Jones story," McCurry said. "You've put her on the cover twice. You're pumping the story."

Evan Thomas began to talk about how the Washington press corps was handling the matter.

"No, *you*, Evan. You've got an investment in this story," McCurry shot back. "You have just made the judgment that she is telling the truth and Bill Clinton is not."

"That's not true," Thomas said.

Isikoff's piece that Monday further clouded the matter by quoting another former White House aide as saying that Kathleen Willey had emerged from the Oval Office that day with her lipstick off, looking disheveled and happy. Clinton's best defense, it seemed, was that he was a successful seducer, not a boorish harasser. Willey's lawyer said she had a good relationship with the president, and Bennett said that Clinton had no recollection of having seen Willey in the Oval. It was the Paula Jones case all over again, two dramatically different accounts. The story was at a dead end, and the reporters, vaguely embarrassed and lacking further ammunition, quietly let it drop. McCurry had contained the one story that threatened to reopen the whole seamy issue of the president's sexual behavior.

Later that week Clinton pulled McCurry aside for a rare word of thanks. "I think you handled that correctly, and I appreciate it," he said. "I know it's not easy."

.   .   .

THE FUNDRAISING SCANDAL WAS NOT SO EASILY FINESSED, OF course, but the technique of dismissing damaging stories as old news was devastatingly effective. McCurry brushed off a front-page *New York Times* piece, based on a leaked White House memo, saying that Clinton had personally requested a list of potential contributors to call in an effort to raise $1 million in early 1996. The story sounded ominous, yet strangely familiar.

"I don't believe the president would change the answer he's given in the past," McCurry said.

James Bennet challenged McCurry: "Just to briefly defend my newspaper. . . . Is it your impression that it had been previously reported that the president had personally requested a list of fundraisers to solicit? That he, himself, wanted to solicit?"

McCurry was ready with his best sucker punch. "Well, let's see," he said. "*The Washington Post* lead June 28th was . . . 'Newly disclosed memo suggests the president personally reviewed a list of names.' So, yes, they wrote about that several weeks ago."

"Damn, I walked right into that," Bennet said afterward.

Despite the media's focus on scandal news, in the country at large everything seemed to be breaking the administration's way. The Dow surged past 8000. The deficit was heading even lower, toward $37 billion. The Senate hearings were moving on to interrogate Haley Barbour about Ambrous Tung Young, the Hong Kong benefactor who had once interested no one in the press except *Time*. Clinton clearly had the upper hand in the debate with the Republicans over how much tax relief should go to middle-class families. And the House Republican leadership was coming apart at the seams; Speaker Newt Gingrich had just survived an aborted coup by his own top deputies. McCurry could barely restrain himself.

"I categorically deny that anyone is gleefully watching those actions," he told the gaggle. When reporters pressed again, McCurry said: "I'm biting my tongue."

On the evening of July 28, the White House and the GOP finally reached agreement on the complicated details of cutting taxes, balancing the budget, and as a sweeping new entitlement program, extending health coverage to five million uninsured children. Clinton had gotten virtually everything he wanted and had stolen much of the Republican agenda in the process. Rahm Emanuel called the president on a Las Vegas golf course, where he was playing with Michael Jordan, to tell him of the slam-dunk. It was a huge political achievement, even if it was a typically muddled Beltway compromise made painless by a strong economy that kept boosting tax revenues. Clinton seized the moment the next day, trotting out Gore, the Cabinet, and Democratic lawmakers for a massive photo op on the South Lawn, while Gingrich and Lott declared victory on the East Steps of the Capitol. Even conservative critics were admitting that Clinton was triumphant.

The self-congratulatory speeches also had the effect of overshadowing the day's damaging Senate testimony on how Charlie Trie had secretly reimbursed two unwitting Chinese women in Maryland for about $20,000 in contributions to the Democrats. This was the first solid evidence that Clinton's favorite Little Rock restaurateur, whom he had never publicly criticized, appeared to have flouted the campaign finance laws. But most of the press was absorbed with explaining who would be eligible for the new IRAs and college tax credits and capital gains reductions contained in the bipartisan deal. The next day's *Washington Post* ran the Trie story in the top left-hand column, but filled much of the other five columns with three separate stories about the budget deal. *USA Today* didn't even mention the Trie revelations on the front page. When unemployment dropped again, to 4.8 percent, a beaming Clinton announced the news in the Rose Garden. The big papers were running outraged editorials demanding campaign finance reform, but no one else seemed to care. There were still two distinctly different conversations emanating from Washington, and for the moment, most of the country was tuned in to the one that Clinton preferred.

CHAPTER FOURTEEN

Charm Offensive

As the summer of 1997 wore on, Clinton seemed to be warming up to the press, or at least to a few of its practitioners. McCurry and Emanuel had been pushing the president to tend to these particular constituents, to acknowledge the importance of the Press Party. The jounalists viewed themselves like members of Congress, Emanuel felt, even if Clinton did not, and the proper presidential attention could yield dividends. And so Clinton lit the candles in the Cabinet Room for Helen Thomas's seventy-seventh birthday. He sent Mark Knoller a signed copy of a newspaper picture that prominently featured the CBS producer at a bill signing, saying: "You're always there when history is made." He had dinner at the down-home Cashion's Eat Place with Cokie Roberts, the ABC newswoman, and her husband, Steve Roberts, of the New York *Daily News*. He called Carl Rowan to congratulate him on his last day as a panelist on the television program *Inside Washington*. He sent Wolf Blitzer a note when his mother died. He had an off-the-record chat with Dan Balz, *The Washington Post*'s chief political reporter, and Ceci Connolly, who had just joined the paper, and was unusually frank about the House Republican leaders. Clinton said that Newt Gingrich was "the only guy who can give us a run for our money on the vision thing," but that sometimes he "just checks out" and says something outrageous. He said he found Dick Armey an enigma but liked John Kasich because he had made nice comments about Hillary. Clinton was enjoying himself so much that he kept talking even after aides tried to break up the schmooze session, and he complained later that it had been cut short.

Clinton was still having trouble understanding why he kept getting bad press. He worked hard and had gotten some pretty good results for the country. McCurry hoped one of the journalists would use these sessions to explain that they weren't in the business of writing fawning pieces and, in any event, Clinton wasn't quite as great as he thought he was. But no one did. It was hard to say that to a president's face.

Lanny Davis felt that his reporters, too, should get a dose of the presidential charm. Davis had had a fabulous time watching a basketball game with Clinton and decided that would be the perfect forum to break the ice between Clinton and the investigative reporters with whom Davis increasingly enjoyed sparring. He drew up an elaborate plan to invite the likes of Jeff Gerth and Glenn Simpson to the White House residence to watch sports with Clinton.

McCurry was incredulous. "You're going to bring Sue Schmidt into the residence?" he asked. McCurry thought this was the wackiest idea he had ever heard, but he decided to humor Lanny. Let's think this through carefully, he said. Finally he told Davis that Clinton loved sports too much and that the reporters would just be a distraction. Davis suggested they could come after the game, but McCurry stood his ground. The idea died a merciful death.

Even when fielding reporters' questions, the venue in which he was most likely to lose his temper, Clinton was enjoying himself. It was amazing what a budget agreement and a 64 percent approval rating could do for your mood. As they prepared for a press conference on the South Lawn—Clinton, for once, seemed to have read the fifty-page briefing book—the staff turned to the inevitable question about the fact that he continued to raise big bucks for the Democratic Party. Clinton was growing exasperated on the subject. The reporters and editors knew damn well that he could not opt out of the soft-money chase, however flawed the system, while the Republicans were still raising barrels of cash. It was sheer hypocrisy to single out his efforts. Still, he agreed to give his standard answer about how he would not engage in "unilateral disarmament."

Alison Mitchell wanted to ask the president about his fundraising, but she didn't want the same old boilerplate answer. She decided to preempt his "unilateral disarmament" refrain by mentioning it in her question and then demanding whether he shouldn't set a higher example for the country. Mitchell had never been called on at a domestic press conference—she wasn't one to wave her arms and shout and hated watching herself on television—but this time she got the nod.

She rose and began her question: "At the same time that you've called for an end to soft money, you continue to raise it for your party."

Clinton cut her off: "I certainly do, and I'm proud of it."

"Well, let me ask you—" .

"I plead guilty to that," Clinton said, preempting her again. "I don't believe in unilateral disarmament. And I don't think—suppose I said to you, advertising is bad, your newspaper should stop advertising while everybody else does it, and trust me to tell everybody what a good newspaper you have. Just stop it. Just say no. You live in a competitive world." Now he was totally departing from the briefing-book script, personalizing things with *The New York Times*.

Mitchell smiled, looked embarrassed, kept glancing down at her notebook. She wanted to finish her question, but there was no way to interrupt a president in full rhetorical flight. Clinton was riffing now, going on and on in his full-sincerity mode: "The Republicans raise more money. . . . It would be a grave mistake for us to abandon any attempt to compete. . . . I'm trying to stay in a good humor about this . . . .There's too much money in this system. . . . I will not, at the same time, bankrupt the Democratic Party. . . . I think that would be wrong. . . . I just think we can't afford to just lay down our capacity to compete." Finally, it was over.

"I was too hot with Alison, wasn't I," Clinton asked his staff afterward. They agreed with his assessment. "But they're going to keep playing this game," he complained. "At some point you've got to call them on it."

The next day, as Clinton prepared to attend two Democratic fundraisers that would rake in $650,000—and spark the predictable press criticism—Rahm Emanuel left Alison Mitchell a phone message. "Do you have a follow-up?" he said, laughing.

Clinton was finally starting to grasp the strange habits of the media beast. A few days later he had Wolf Blitzer in for an off-the-record session, along with John King, who had just joined CNN, and Eileen O'Connor, a network veteran who was new to the White House beat.

After considerable chitchat about China and the Middle East, Blitzer asked: "What do you think of the way we do our job, and what advice do you have?"

The president launched into a long, good-natured critique of how CNN was too obsessed with political ephemera and needed to spend more time on substantive issues. He said *Inside Politics* was the only TV show he regularly watched, if only because everyone had it on as he walked around the White House. But the program insisted on reducing everything to raw politics. McCurry, he said, could often predict where a story was heading by how *Inside Politics* handled it.

"You've got this political show at four o'clock," Clinton said. "Everyone else sees it and thinks the news is already out there. By the time the six-thirty network news is on, they've got to find a way to spin it. Then *The Washington Post* and *The New York Times* have to spin it even more. It becomes all about spin and process."

As the reporters nodded, Clinton drifted toward some of his pet issues. Why didn't the press do more on his push for tougher education standards? Ignoring the fact that the initiative was stalled, he contrasted it with the heavy coverage of the battle against tobacco. That story had everything—money, politics, health issues. It connected to the lives of ordinary folks. Why not education standards? "These are people's children," he said.

Clinton grew reflective for a moment. "It's frustrating to me, too," he said. "We sit here all the time trying to figure out how to make these issues relevant. How can we do it in a way that will make you guys bite? Maybe we overdo it sometimes."

The gabfest lasted nearly two hours. When the reporters rose to leave, John King realized they hadn't been served any refreshments.

"We didn't pay enough to get coffee?" he asked.

· · ·

THE LATEST ADDITION TO THE WHITE HOUSE ROSTER OF SPINMEI-sters was Paul Begala, a profane, fast-talking, red-bearded Texan who had been James Carville's consulting partner during the 1992 campaign and had been a Clinton adviser in the first two years of the president's term. But after the Democratic debacle of 1994, he and his fellow strategists, Carville and Mandy Grunwald and pollster Stan Greenberg, were essentially fired as DNC consultants. As a fiery liberal populist, Begala was increasingly out of step with an administration determined to hug the center median of the political highway. He moved to Austin, began teaching at the University of Texas and representing corporate clients in what he thought of as the real world. Yet he kept his foot in the door, checking in with Rahm Emanuel every day, and he bashed the press in his column in *George* magazine.

Gradually Begala worked his way back into Clinton's good graces. He helped prepare the president for the 1996 debates against Bob Dole. When Clinton kept coming on too strong, Begala sat down at a computer keyboard and banged out the lead of two news stories. In the first the candidates sparred to a bloody draw. In the second he wrote: "Much to the frustration of a clawing Senator Dole, President Clinton looked every inch the comfortable incumbent with a 20-point lead . . ." Clinton got the message. Begala knew which buttons to press, how to communicate with the Big Guy. But like McCurry, he also knew how to peddle propaganda to the press without coming off as a blind loyalist. Begala had a tendency to shoot off his mouth —he had once insulted Rush Limbaugh's listeners as "twenty million people who hate Hillary"—but he was determined to be more circumspect this time around.

When Alison Mitchell and John Harris called him, looking to do profiles on his return to the Clinton fold, he wouldn't play. He didn't want to fall into the David Gergen–George Stephanopoulos trap, becoming a media star instead of a Clinton spear carrier. "I'm not gonna help you at all," he told Mitchell. "It's nothing against you; I don't want to hurt myself in my new position." Begala winced when Mitchell portrayed him in *The New York Times* as a crusading liberal recruited to nudge the president to the left. The truth was, Clinton had hired him because he liked him, felt comfortable around him. They had talked only about the personal side, the impact of moving back from Austin on his pregnant wife, Diane, and their two preschoolers. Begala was worried that he would somehow get ensnared in the scandal net and wind up with $300,000 in legal bills. Clinton couldn't offer any reassurance on that point. Diane had drawn up a list of negatives on a legal pad, and in the plus column she wrote only: "Cool job." In the end that had clinched it. Let the *Times* depict him as an ideologue. That wasn't what this was about.

Begala, thirty-six, was fluent in a variety of languages. He spoke politics, a rough-and-tumble trade he had learned at Carville's side. He spoke the congressional lexicon, having worked alongside Stephanopoulos in Dick Gephardt's office until the Missouri lawmaker passed up the '92 race and both men needed a new horse to ride. He spoke Washington, a company town not all that different from his native Sugarland, Texas, where everyone either worked for or was dependent on the local sugar company. He spoke Clintonese, a difficult dialect mastered only by spending as much time as Begala had traveling with the candidate in 1992. And he spoke press, understanding the rhythms and needs of reporters, the art of the leak, the slashing humor required for his regular appearances on the Imus show. This last talent was especially important. Clinton was bringing Begala back not to shore up a weary team, but to sell the administration's story to the media. He had to be careful that he didn't become the story.

Begala could be openly antagonistic toward the press. Back in '92, when Michael Kelly was covering the race for the *Times*, Begala got into a shouting match with him on the campaign plane over some anti-Clinton crack. He once called David Broder "an old gasbag." He knew from years of public pulse-taking that most people didn't care about Paula Jones or sexual peccadilloes. The old journalistic rules, that you didn't report that someone was drunk or gay or a skirt-chaser unless it affected his public performance, made sense. The media mavens of the '90s were far too quick to get down in the dirt.

Part of Begala's role was to explain the nature of journalism to Clinton. The elite press, he believed, was essentially a Gang of 200 who talked mostly to each other, a strange little subculture like stock car racers or dachshund owners. But their opinions mattered. Clinton simply did not view journalists as real leaders; he firmly believed that power derived from the ballot box. Clinton once gave a ride on Air

Force One to Al D'Amato, who had spent the past two years trying to prove that the president and his wife were crooks; to Clinton the senator still had legitimacy because he had been elected by the voters. The essence of the clash, Begala felt, was that journalists were steeped in a culture of negativity, while Bill and Hillary were incredibly earnest do-gooders. They were canny politicians, sure, but they truly believed in using government to help people, while the reporters were engaged in a never-ending search for ulterior motives.

Begala tried to act as a translator. He patiently explained how reporters went fishing for quotes to support their story line. He tried to ease Clinton's obsession with leaks. An unnamed "White House official" taking a potshot at some proposal wasn't necessarily a high-level person who had just been in the room with Clinton. "It's someone else who doesn't like the decision, or wants to be a big shot," he told Clinton. "The press keeps calling people until they find someone two, three, four levels down who will say what they want."

Clinton looked at Begala as if he had just discovered fire. "Do you really think they do that?" he said. "I don't believe it."

Soon after he joined the staff in mid-August, Begala threw a fit at the senior staff meeting, accusing *The New York Times* of stooping to the level of a sleazy tabloid. The Clintons were trying to relax on Martha's Vineyard, and some French paparazzi fellow, hiding in the bushes of the property next door, had taken a telephoto-lens shot of Hillary and Bill on the beach in their bathing suits. And here was the *Times* splashing the picture across three columns. Begala announced that he was going to call the newspaper and complain. Was there no such thing as privacy anymore? Begala said he felt like hiring a photographer to prowl the Long Island beaches and take pictures of Joe Lelyveld's wife in a bathing suit. How would the esteemed *Times* editor like that?

Begala's colleagues smiled and shook their heads, told him to calm down. It wasn't worth picking a fight over. Begala still had an outsider's sense of outrage, they suggested. He'd get used to such media slights soon enough.

· · ·

THE PROPOSAL-A-DAY PRESIDENCY WAS WORKING BETTER THAN ever. Rahm Emanuel had honed it to a science. The day before

Clinton became the first president to wield the line-item veto, Emanuel announced on *Face the Nation* that Clinton would do so on the balanced budget bill, but swore his colleagues to secrecy on the details. That turned the veto of two minor provisions into a big two-day story.

In one summertime stretch Emanuel and company leaked to several newspapers that Clinton would ban smoking in federal buildings, allow greater religious expression for federal employees, ask that prescription drugs be tested for effects on children, seek to bar insurance companies from discriminating on the basis of genetic information, even plot celebrations for the year 2000. "Clinton Lays Plans for Millennium Activities," said the front-page exclusive in *USA Today*. Next, reporters joked, they would be leaking presidential Post-it notes.

But the proposals were no accident. Mark Penn's private polls showed that 80 percent favored a smoking ban in federal buildings, that nearly three-quarters opposed genetic screening by insurance companies. There was even extensive polling on the millennium: 62 percent were looking forward to the next thousand years, while 29 percent were afraid. Forty-two percent favored the idea of Clinton holding an international summit on the millennium; 36 percent liked a billion-dollar charity drive; 30 percent supported a series of Washington and White House events on the country's progress; 73 percent backed the creation of a new women's museum, and so on. This was a president who left nothing to chance.

To be sure, some of Clinton's headline-grabbing initiatives were quietly petering out. The $5 billion plan to repair schools, which *USA Today* had splashed on the front page, was quietly killed as part of the budget deal. Only six states had embraced Clinton's proposed education standards. The request that the FCC outlaw televised liquor ads—57 percent of Americans supported the ban, according to White House polling—went nowhere. The FEC took no action on Clinton's demand that soft money be eliminated in campaign fundraising. The Supreme Court overturned the law against Internet smut. The volunteerism campaign had faded. The race initiative was fizzling after an aimless meeting by the presidential advisory panel. The proof was in Mark Penn's polls: 39 percent hadn't even heard of the race task force, 46 percent of Hispanics said the initiative had nothing to do with them, and 48 percent of all respondents said the effort was just political rhetoric.

The White House responded with more mini-proposals. On the day before Clinton was to appear at an NAACP convention in Pittsburgh, the press office leaked word to *The New York Times*, *The Washington Post*, *The Wall Street Journal*, the *Los Angeles Times*, *USA Today*, and the *Chicago Sun-Times* that the president would ask Congress for $70 million a year to recruit teachers to impoverished neighborhoods. This was the sort of piddling proposal that on a busy day barely would have rated a paragraph in the nation's top newspapers. But by whispering it to selected reporters, McCurry's people artificially inflated its market value. *USA Today* played the teaching grants at the top of one page, pushing Thompson's hearing about John Huang down to the bottom.

None of this happened by accident, for each message and measure had to be carefully vetted by the staff. John Podesta started holding an 8:30 communications strategy meeting in his office with McCurry, Joe Lockhart, Barry Toiv, Ann Lewis, Rahm Emanuel, Bruce Lindsey, Doug Sosnik, and Gene Sperling. The morning that Clinton was to call for greater testing of pediatric drugs, Emanuel proposed that he take a shot at the American Medical Association for its recently announced agreement to endorse commercial products. He knew that the AMA would be forced to back down, and he was still miffed that the group had endorsed a legislative ban on partial-birth abortions, a ban that the president had opposed. McCurry and Podesta strongly opposed the idea. They had a full plate, with Clinton and Labor Secretary Alexis Herman trying to settle the United Parcel Service strike, and there was no need to pick another fight. Emanuel yielded, but he liked these rhetorical drive-by shootings. Commenting on issues that had nothing to do with government was a good way for Clinton to make news.

The reason they were getting such good press on these two-bit initiatives, Emanuel felt, was that White House reporters were quietly reevaluating Clinton's performance. There was an unspoken acknowledgment, in the wake of the balanced budget deal, that perhaps they had been too quick to write off the second term. Emanuel tried to keep the emotional temperature down by urging both the president and Hillary not to make any casual cracks about the press. Now

Clinton seemed to be getting the benefit of the doubt in a way the media had never allowed before.

Doug Sosnik, too, was struck by the transformation in the way the reporters themselves talked about Clinton over lunch or dinner. They clearly viewed him with more respect—not in Mount Rushmore terms, but paying tribute to his political strengths, his legislative victories, his ability to keep skating out of trouble in a way that Al Gore could not. Sosnik saw the White House as a big high school, and the reporters, the noncomformists who sat in the back of the room, had always viewed those who were sympathetic to Clinton as uncool; now the definition of cool was changing. There was, of course, still a certain degree of insensitivity among the correspondents. At dinner with Sosnik one night, John Harris and James Bennet wondered why White House aides got so uptight over each critical article, but then again, they had no idea what it was like to be on the receiving end, to have your friends and family see you pummeled in print. Still, they were discussing Clinton with the kind of respect that would have been unimaginable six months earlier.

Others in the inner circle were more skeptical. John Podesta believed that Howell Raines and the other journalistic critics found Clinton's high approval rating maddening, that it simply caused them to redouble their efforts to vindicate their view by tarnishing the White House. The highs and lows, the sex and the scandals, were like something out of Fellini; all that was missing was a dwarf and some clowns. For all their success, Podesta felt, there was something about this president and this press corps and this era that kept the political pot at full boil.

McCurry was convinced that reporters, in their heart of hearts, wanted to write off the second term as inconsequential. There was no New Deal, no massive new federal spending programs. No one got the real story, that a progressive Democratic president was rewriting the book on the uses of government. The reporters were stuck in the old mindset that great presidents do great things.

But there was something more personal at work as well. The reporters tended to blame themselves for Clinton's resilient popularity. They had simply failed to do their job. They had been snookered by those con men at the White House. McCurry wondered whether he should have put the 103 White House coffees on the president's public schedule back in 1995 and 1996. He had instead followed a long tradition that meetings in the residence were deemed private, but if he had routinely listed them, the press would have discovered their fundraising nature during the campaign and the thing would not have looked like some secret, sinister operation. The reporters still felt guilty for not stumbling onto the finance scandal until just before the election. Clinton had somehow slipped away, outsmarted them, stayed out of range of their outraged questions. It still grated on their collective conscience.

CHAPTER FIFTEEN

Toughing It Out

STONEWALLING, IT SEEMED, WAS BACK IN STYLE.

In early August, nearly a year after they had embarked on a strategy of disclosure, administration officials were again being battered by the press for blatant foot-dragging and outright obfuscation. Documents were belatedly discovered, memories maddeningly vague. Just when the public was buying the Democratic line that everyone does it, the White House seemed to be slipping back into the cover-up mode.

That, of course, was not the view from the West Wing. The Clintonites felt they were doing the best they could under difficult circumstances. They had limited resources, were drowning in subpoenas, were struggling to piece things together, were still dedicated to campaign finance reform.

Lanny Davis could have headed off the first embarrassment. ABC correspondent Linda Douglass had been pressing him for five months for the WAVES records on Charlie Trie's business partner, a Macao real estate developer named Ng Lap Seng, who had funneled more than $900,000 to Trie. But Davis kept putting Douglass off, saying he was inundated with requests.

Lanny Breuer, who was as mild-mannered as Davis was over-wrought, had been only vaguely aware of the Ng request. But Breuer had quickly learned since leaving his Washington law firm that the press was the driving force in the suite of high-ceilinged EOB offices he shared with the other Lanny. He spent more of his time worrying about media inquiries than the eight black looseleaf binders beneath the oversized gavel on his bookshelf, which were filled with congressional subpoenas and requests. Breuer viewed the Thompson committee's demand for the Ng documents as a low priority, just another of its more than two hundred requests. And these WAVES records had to be laboriously assembled by hand.

Finally a staffer pulled together the Ng material for ABC, just as the Senate committee was about to spend the day examining Ng's relationship with Trie. The documents showed that Ng had visited the White House a dozen times, one of them with Wang Jun, the Chinese weapons dealer, and once with Trie at a dinner hosted by Clinton. Breuer soon learned that the files had been pulled.

"Oh shit," he thought. "Now we have them." It was one thing to withhold records that hadn't been retrieved; now they could be accused of obstructing the investigation. They certainly couldn't hand the stuff to ABC first without the senators going ballistic. Breuer huddled with other members of the counsel's office. They briefly considered holding onto the records until Congress adjourned for the summer, but decided that would be untenable. They would take the hit now. Late in the afternoon, hours after the committee's lead investigator had finished testifying about Ng Lap Seng, Breuer hand-delivered the records to the Senate panel.

Thompson exploded, accusing the White House of trying to "manipulate the press" by depriving him of the evidence he needed. The administration had played the committee members for fools long enough, he said. Every document they wanted would henceforth be subpoenaed. Lanny Davis argued that they should put out someone for the evening news, but Chuck Ruff issued a written statement instead, denying any attempt to suppress the documents.

Clearly Davis's fantasy would never come true. He told his colleagues that Clinton and Gore should march up to the Senate hearing room, shut the door, and announce to the assembled lawmakers that they weren't leaving until they had answered every question, after which everyone would agree to work for campaign finance reform.

Instead, the administration was still dribbling out the details. Al Gore had stuck to his story that he made fundraising calls from his White House office only "on a few occasions." Now the New York *Daily News* came up with documents showing he had made forty-six calls. Lorraine Voles gamely insisted this was not out of line with Gore's original comments.

The next fiasco was uncovered by Bob Woodward. Unlike many of the other investigative reporters who had drifted off the story, Woodward felt that news organizations, including his own, were not taking the fundraising scandal seriously enough. The '96 elections had been compromised, the post-Watergate reforms obliterated. The CEOs that Woodward talked to had bought special access to the administration. Thompson kept popping up in Woodward's stories; Democrats on the panel were grumbling that the reporter was carrying his water. Woodward had known Fred Thompson since the early 1970s, when the future senator was the Republican counsel to the Senate Watergate committee, and he considered Thompson to be a genuine reformer, trying to clean up a rotten system.

Woodward tended to view the sweep of history through the prism of Watergate, and soon got wind of what smelled like a Nixon-style cover-up. The DNC had belatedly discovered four boxes with four thousand pages of documents belonging to Richard Sullivan, the former finance director who had been Thompson's lead-off witness. Thompson confirmed this to Woodward, as did Roy Romer, the Colorado governor who was now the DNC chairman. Romer called Woodward back late in the day.

"There was something I didn't tell you that I need to tell you," Romer said. "When we found those boxes, we sent them to Sullivan's lawyer." The Democrats seemed to have deliberately stiffed the committee. Some party officials wanted to announce the belated discovery on their own, but Amy Weiss Tobe, the DNC spokeswoman, said they shouldn't burn Woodward. Besides, that would just make a bigger deal out of it.

Among the documents, Woodward learned, were twelve fundraising call sheets prepared for Hillary Clinton, asking her to hit up potential donors, such as designer Ralph Lauren, for $50,000 or $100,000. He called Marsha Berry, who recycled the tired line that the first lady didn't remember making such calls but "does not rule it out."

Woodward found the explanation pretty transparent. He knew Hillary, knew that she had a very sharp memory. The average person heard the Clintons' denials as a lawyerly way of saying they recalled the fundraising episodes but didn't want to say so. The idea that they had both forgotten making these big-money calls was a bit far-fetched.

Lanny Davis understood why the Clintons weren't fessing up. The president, for one, was convinced he had not made any fundraising calls. He was the sort of politician who hated to ask for money. The phrase around the White House was that Gore eats the spinach—he knew how to close the deal—but Clinton choked on it, asking poten-tial donors for support but never actually talking money.

The question had come up at one of the pre-briefs in the Oval. These sorts of issues were considered so sensitive that someone made the standard announcement: "This is just for the lawyers. All the non-lawyers leave." Charles Ruff, Lanny Davis, Lanny Breuer, and Cheryl Mills remained—only those whose conversations were cloaked by attorney-client privilege.

"I don't think I ever asked anybody for money," Clinton insisted. "But who knows, maybe I did."

The legal team had refused to let Clinton say he never dialed for dollars. If just one contributor somewhere remembered getting such a call from Clinton, the fallout would be devastating. The "can't remember" formulation was hardly satisfactory, but it was the best they could do.

McCurry was stunned when Woodward broke the story of the missing DNC documents. It was enough to make you cry. They had given the press only two choices: either they were guilty of monu-mental stupidity or malicious stonewalling. McCurry voted for the first option. How could they possibly have been so dumb?

· · ·

LORRAINE VOLES WAS STUNNED TO DISCOVER SHE HAD NEVER BEEN told about the one piece of information that could lead to a criminal investigation of Al Gore.

Throughout the long months of defending her boss, Voles never thought to question where the campaign money he had raised was going. Reporters never asked her about it. But now Bob Woodward was on the phone, saying that more than $100,000 of the donations solicited by Gore had been improperly diverted to the wrong bank account. Voles instantly understood that this seemingly arcane accounting question could explode into a fiery political issue, and she got Charles Burson on the phone with Woodward to explain the legalities.

It was all true. Burson and the Democratic Party's own lawyers had known for more than three months that some of the money Gore raised had not gone into the DNC's "soft-money" account, the largely unregulated pot of cash that both parties routinely exploited for political advertising. Instead, some $120,000 had been funneled into the tightly restricted "hard-money" account spent directly on campaigns, including the Clinton-Gore campaign. The distinction was legally crucial; hard money was much harder to raise because no one could give more than $20,000 to a national campaign organization. The lawyers had even notified the Thompson committee of the mistake. But no one had bothered to tell the woman who was dealing with the press day after day on the vice president's behalf. Here she was, the communications director, and she had been kept in the dark. Her deputy, Ginny Terzano, also knew nothing until Woodward called, also felt she had been left badly exposed.

In a meeting with Burson and his staff, Voles and Terzano made clear that they were upset.

"I'm sure you guys were trying to protect us, but we have to know all the facts," Voles said. "We could have been in a position where we lied if we didn't know about it."

There was a heated debate in Chuck Ruff's office that night over how to handle the forthcoming story. Should they take a strong position on why Gore's calls were legal and did not trigger the law requiring the appointment of a special prosecutor? Or would such an aggressive stance look like they were pressuring Janet Reno's Justice Department? Ruff was strongly opposed to saying anything. Lanny Davis vehemently disagreed.

"She might be under pressure from us and maybe she'll resent that," Davis said. "But where do you think the pressure is gonna come from now? All the press that wants an independent counsel is going to be reporting the wrong story."

John Podesta insisted they needed some talking points on the dispute. Lanny Breuer decided to placate Podesta by drawing up the talking points, knowing that Ruff would probably deep-six them.

At the senior staff meeting the next morning, Ruff decreed that no White House official could discuss the Gore matter with the press except off-the-record. "We don't want the White House to put Reno in an awkward position," he said.

Gore's staff had been trying for weeks to get out in front of the fundraising fiasco. In late August Charles Burson had held a background briefing in the ornate Indian Treaty Room of the Old Executive Office Building, where he did a major document dump. The staff put out all the papers they had gathered on Gore's calls to potential donors from his White House office, calls in which he asked for as much as $100,000. They were nervous about one glaring fact: about a third of the veep's calls were not on either a campaign or DNC credit card, as they had claimed. These calls had cost the taxpayers $24.20. But the press didn't seem to care. *The Washington Post* relegated their repayment of the $24 to the last paragraph of its story.

The day after Labor Day, Burson again appeared in the Indian Treaty Room, along with Lanny Davis, for a second background briefing. They reviewed the Buddhist temple fundraiser, trying to make clear that Gore knew nothing of the money-laundering that apparently transpired there. That was their line in the sand. They knew that three head-shaved nuns from the Hsi Lai Temple would be testifying before Fred Thompson's committee two days later under a grant of immunity, and that the unusual sight would be a magnet for the press. They even enlisted the services of Jack Farrell, a *Boston Globe* reporter who had been allowed to attend the temple event on an off-the-record basis. Gore's staff released Farrell from his confidentiality pledge, and he wrote a story, which they faxed to the world, buttressing Gore's account that he viewed it as a community visit and made no pitch for money. There was also an unexpected windfall: the media were so consumed by the heart-rending death of Princess Diana over the weekend that the Gore saga had been all but eclipsed.

But their luck was running out. The Woodward piece was published the next day, opening the floodgates to a new deluge of damaging publicity about Gore. Reno was stunned that Woodward seemed to know more than her own investigators. Hours after the front-page piece appeared, the attorney general announced that she was ordering a preliminary probe that could lead to the naming of an independent prosecutor. That would be an unmitigated disaster, Gore's staff felt, a messy criminal investigation that could easily engulf the president and drag on until the 2000 campaign. Ron Klain decided it had been a huge blunder not to go public earlier with the hard-money problem.

Gore's ham-handed efforts to contain the burgeoning scandal were almost comically inept. From the beginning, with his "no controlling legal authority" press conference, the veep and his team seemed to pour gasoline on the smoldering controversy with statements that had to be endlessly revised. Fundraising calls on just "a few occasions" somehow turned into forty-six calls, which turned into eighty-six calls. The Buddhist temple event evolved from "community outreach" to "finance related" to "donor maintenance." It was the mirror image of the well-oiled Clinton spin machine. Gore simply lacked the president's natural ability to finesse charges of wrongdoing. Unlike Clinton, he couldn't easily distract the press by making policy and pronouncements; he was running for president but remained in the role of understudy. He was being savaged by reporters and didn't know quite what to do about it. This was another feeding frenzy, Gore felt, a crazy period in which the press smelled blood. He was frustrated but now understood that such attacks came with the territory. He would have to ride it out.

"I'm really comfortable I didn't do anything wrong," Gore told Voles. "It's not eating at me." Besides, he said, "Don't you think it was much worse in March?"

"I can't even remember March," she replied.

Later that week, as Clinton prepared to read a statement condemning a terrorist bombing in Jerusalem, his staff told him to expect a question on Gore's fundraising. "Good," he said. "I want one. I'm not going to leave that guy standing there undefended." The president was sending a signal; he was appalled by what he saw as the lackadaisical reaction of his staff. He told Lanny Davis, Doug Sosnik, and others to roll up their sleeves and start helping Gore. Klain asked Podesta for help, and suddenly Paul Begala, Sid Blumenthal, and Sosnik swung into action. Davis was fielding fifty daily press calls about Gore. Breuer handled the legal research. McCurry began giving Voles regular advice. They got Democratic elders like Lloyd Cutler to write sympathetic op-ed pieces. The group gathered in

Podesta's office at 8:30 each morning to plan their defense, fifteen minutes after the communications strategy meeting in the same office. The damage control efforts were blurring into one continuous gabfest. "After this meeting, we'll have the 8:30 meeting and do it all over again," Podesta joked one morning.

Friends of Al—media adviser Robert Squier, former chief of staff Roy Neel, former spokeswoman Marla Romash, former White House counsel Jack Quinn—checked in during regular conference calls. It was like a campaign, Voles felt, and they needed a rapid-response team to combat the steady flow of leaks from Thompson's folks. This was pure politics, a Republican effort to fatally wound the probable Democratic presidential nominee, and they had to respond in kind.

Karen Tumulty of *Time* told Voles that Gore's plight would be the cover story in next week's issue. That would be a defining moment, as when *Newsweek* put Paula Jones on the cover. Voles gave Gore the news in an e-mail message.

Gore offered his trademark response: "AAGGHHH! This would not be great timing."

Voles realized that they had to get off the defensive. The best way to combat the flood of bad press, she decided, was by generating a counterwave of favorable press. The word went out to the West Wing.

Paul Begala started working the phones. He pressed Gore's case on background with reporters for *The Wall Street Journal* and the *Los Angeles Times*, with Tim Russert, with the newsmagazines, faxing out reams of legal defenses compiled by the DNC. Begala was a lawyer by training, so he argued the law, which with Gore's approval rating having dropped to 38 percent was a hell of an easier sell right now than the politics. In his Texas twang he mocked the hard-money/soft-money charges as absurd. Gore had no idea what had happened to the money after he made the calls. Begala knew reporters didn't really believe that boring old Al Gore was corrupt.

"Let's put him in fucking jail for having a bad press conference!" he told Karen Breslau of *Newsweek*. "Let's lock him up!" The country was trying to criminalize political differences, Begala insisted, echoing the very argument that Republicans had made during the Iran-contra affair. It was bizarre. For years, Begala thought, reporters had carped that Clinton was too slick when it came to slip-sliding out of scandal. Now they were indicting Gore for not being slick enough, for not being more like Clinton. But it was an irresistible story line for the press: poor Gore had been tainted by Clintonism and was paying the price for the president's sins.

Ann Lewis was more refined but no less relentless in briefing her Democratic friends and the former Gore aides who would spread the message to the media. Lewis felt that the charges were unadulterated crap. Ronald Reagan had also made fundraising calls from the White House, according to an AP report, but that didn't rate a squib in the papers. Still, Gore was vulnerable because the public didn't know that much about him. Voters couldn't put this stuff in the proper context. It was reminiscent of Clinton in early '92, when he first got engulfed by charges of infidelity and draft-dodging. By now, Lewis felt, the Clinton scandals were like *Jaws 5*—the same music, the same teeth as *Jaws*, but a lot less scary because the plot had grown tired. But Gore hadn't been through this kind of storm before. They all had to buck him up, to gradually change the view of Washington's chattering class.

Doug Sosnik was convinced that the press was slapping Gore around just for sport. He heard the question time and again from reporters: Could Gore take a punch? How would he cope with adversity? It was their ritual hazing for potential presidents, albeit three years early. How a candidate dealt with the pummeling of the press was their rough proxy for how he would withstand the pressures of the Oval Office. The self-appointed watchdogs were barking away. They didn't like the dog food the White House was serving up, they didn't like their kennel space, and they would keep howling until Gore's performance satisfied them.

The White House responded by stepping up its campaign. Lanny Davis buttonholed Walter Shapiro, the *USA Today* columnist, outside the Thompson hearing room. "Can I pitch you on a Gore story?" he asked. Ron Klain also worked on Shapiro. The columnist wound up chiding Gore for his "maladroit political instincts" but concluded: "The vice president's sins seem to me to be of the expired-parking-meter variety."

Sid Blumenthal called Anthony Lewis, the liberal *New York Times* columnist, whom he had known for twenty years and considered a mentor; Lewis's wife had once been his lawyer. "You should look into the law covering the Gore situation," Blumenthal said.

Lewis said he didn't know anything about it, hadn't been following the case at all.

"I'll send you some stuff," said Blumenthal, who promptly got the material from Lorraine Voles. Lewis wrote a column arguing that the law in quesion—part of an 1883 civil service reform act—did not apply to Gore's fundraising calls. Still, he said, Gore "has handled it fumblingly, coming across as less than candid. . . . What Al Gore did was unseemly, but it was not corrupt."

Gore's staff was thrilled with Blumenthal's handiwork. Having a *Times* columnist call the boss "unseemly" and "less than candid" was, in the current climate, a minor victory. The alternative view was succinctly summarized by the title of a *Weekly Standard* editorial: "Al Gore, Sleazebag."

. . .

LANNY DAVIS DUCKED INTO A BROOM CLOSET OF A ROOM IN THE Hart Building, a few steps to the left of the cavernous Thompson hearing room, where AP reporter Larry Margasak was banging away at a black laptop on a battered folding table.

"These were simply statements of federal law and not of DNC policy," Davis recited as Margasak typed. He peered over the reporter's shoulder.

"You want to say, based upon the understanding?" Davis asked.

"That's fine," Margasak said impatiently. "C'mon, Lanny."

Davis pointed to the screen and continued: "If you insert 'this is based upon' after the words 'soft money' . . ." He was injecting his verbiage directly into the wire story, the one that would set the tone for much of the day's coverage. A second AP reporter, James Rowley, looked on incredulously as his colleague took dictation from the White House spinmeister trying to save Al Gore's butt.

Moments earlier Davis had been in the vice president's small office in the adjoining Dirksen Senate Building, plotting strategy in a conference call with Chuck Ruff, John Podesta, Lanny Breuer, and Charles Burson. The Thompson committee had just drawn blood. The panel had unearthed a staff memo that Harold Ickes had sent to Clinton and Gore, explaining the difference between "hard" and "soft" donations and the "mix of money" required for campaign commercials. The left-handed Clinton had acknowledged the memo with his trademark backward checkmark, and a Gore aide had testified that such memos went straight to Gore's in-box. The clear implication was that Gore knew that some of the big bucks he was raising were improperly being diverted to the Clinton-Gore campaign.

Damn. Davis was aggravated. Both Rowley and an ABC producer had asked him for the memo days earlier, after the committee had leaked word of its existence. He wanted to put it out, but Burson had objected. We don't know which memo it is, Voles explained. Let them ask for it by the exact date. What utter stupidity. They never seemed to learn.

Davis always called John Solomon at the AP in midmorning to check on the Senate hearing story and see if there was anything he should respond to. That first dispatch was tremendously important in shaping the coverage of the rest of the journalistic world. Now Solomon told him about the memo to Gore.

"How much time do I have?" Davis asked.

"Twenty minutes," Solomon said.

Davis bolted out of the veep's second-floor office, down the stairs, through a connecting corridor to the Hart building, and up another flight to Margasak's side. He emerged into the tan-carpeted hallway only after Margasak had finished typing his comments.

Lanny Breuer, looking agitated, caught up with him moments later. What was he saying about Gore? "I'm not denying he saw the memos," Davis told him. "This is a very simple message and a very direct message."

Davis went back into the AP room, read his statement again— "That's pretty damn good!" he announced—and suggested a wording change.

"We're not going to edit your statement on the wire, Lanny," Rowley said.

"Are you saying I have the chutzpah to ask you to edit this?" Davis asked, sounding wounded.

"I'm uncomfortable with this dictation of statements."

"You're letting the White House respond to something pretty serious."

Soon Davis was back in the corridor in full spin mode, repeating his spiel for Mary Ann Akers of *The Washington Times* and Thomas Galvin of the New York *Daily News* and other reporters who happened by. "I can't tell you the specific memos that Al Gore reads or doesn't read," Davis said. "I'm willing to say that it doesn't matter."

A few minutes later Davis returned to the tiny room and told Rowley his comment was "too low" in the story. Rowley snapped that he had no business trying to rewrite the piece.

"It pisses me off," Rowley said. Davis backed off, looking sheepish, and later returned to apologize.

They had contained the damage, but all the networks beat up on Gore that night. NBC's Lisa Myers even asked the old Watergate question of "what he knew and when he knew it." Davis blamed himself for the fiasco. In an earlier incarnation, just a few months ago, he would have fought and burned bridges and knocked down walls and gotten that memo released beforehand. When they helped reporters understand a complicated story, he firmly believed, they helped themselves. But Davis had thrown up his hands. There were only so many times you could fight these factional battles inside the White House. He was feeling beaten down.

Lorraine Voles got one bit of good news at week's end. Gore had been bumped from the cover of *Time* by a story on American Online, and two of the three planned Gore pieces were being killed. But the same morning the front page of *The New York Times* breathlessly reported a 1996 memo from Ron Klain to Gore, outlining talking points for a White House pep talk on raising money. "Memo Appears to Reveal Gore In Active Role as Fund-Raiser/Statements Contradict Portrait Drawn By Aides," the headline said.

Voles was furious. Any piece of junk involving Gore was now a front-page story. The article was totally inconsistent, eventually admitting that "the idea that Mr. Gore was an aggressive or even enthusiastic fundraiser is not new. Indeed, his aides have said the vice president committed himself to help raise as much money as he could for the 1996 campaign." So what exactly was the news? Where was the contradiction? Voles called the reporter, Don Van Natta, and railed about the headline.

But her real problem was Alan Miller, the *Los Angeles Times* reporter who had unearthed the first small chunk of the fundraising scandal during the campaign and had kept digging for nearly a year.

Miller had faxed Voles a set of questions about just whom Gore had consulted before deciding it was okay to make fundraising calls from his West Wing office.

Voles checked with Charles Burson. "You can just say he assumed the calls were okay because the DNC wouldn't ask him to do anything inappropriate," he told her.

She relayed the answer to Miller. Besides, she said, Gore was advised that the calls were legal.

But which was it? "You know, Lorraine, this is too important to get wrong," Miller said.

"You're absolutely right," Voles said. She called back to say her original version was correct; Gore had merely assumed the calls were all right. This flatly contradicted Gore's assertion at the March news conference that he had been "advised" there was nothing wrong with dialing for dollars. Miller figured that Voles was getting her information straight from the vice president.

That Friday night John Harris called Voles. He said there was an *L.A. Times* story on the wire quoting her as saying that Gore had simply assumed his fundraising calls were legal. The story made it sound like a big deal. Voles called Burson to check again.

"No, no, no," Burson said. "That's only half the answer. He did check with someone; we don't release who he's checking with."

Voles had totally misread Burson, had thought he was guiding her in another direction. It was after eleven. She called Alan Miller at home.

"I'm very sorry, but I made a mistake," she said. "I messed up." Miller promptly killed the story, which had already run in the paper's first edition. In a subsequent piece he called the shifting stories a "new blow" to Gore's "credibility."

Voles was distraught over the weekend. She almost never made mistakes of this magnitude. The vice president would undoubtedly be angry. She told her husband, Dan, that she didn't want to go to work Monday. She didn't want to see the *L.A. Times* story. She didn't want people consoling her.

The next move was unclear. Should they put out the information about whom Gore had consulted? Voles didn't think so. It was just some staffer, not an attorney, so it didn't buy them much. Should they put Gore out there for a high-profile interview? They were swamped with requests from *Newsweek*, Wolf Blitzer, CBS, NBC. Some of the White House boys thought an interview was the way to go, but it was risky as hell.

Instead, Gore and his staff decided to follow the Clinton playbook: put the veep out there every day in carefully calibrated attempts to make news and say as little as possible about the scandal. As Janet Reno neared a decision on the independent counsel investigation, Gore stuck to the script. On Monday he talked about education. On Tuesday it was a plan for more detailed television ratings. On Wednesday he spoke about global warming to TV weathermen from around the country. On Friday he took aim at the tobacco industry. When he fielded a question or two on Reno's decision to extend the inquiry into his phone calls, it was in a middle school gymnasium in Tampa with five hundred kids screaming in the background. Meanwhile it fell to Voles to disclose that Gore had retained two criminal attorneys—both former Watergate prosecutors—to deal with the scandal. White House aides argued that he now needed to hire his own Lanny, an attorney-spokesman who could spin the press on the inevitable twists and turns of the scandal. But Gore was resisting the idea, still clinging to the notion that this was a short-term problem. He was not prepared to acknowledge that the state of siege would drag on for years.

Clinton's fate soon became intertwined with that of Gore. Reno couldn't very well investigate Gore's fundraising calls without also looking at those of the president. She quietly ordered her investigators to conduct a thirty-day review that could trigger the appointment of a prosecutor for Clinton. The decision was shrouded in secrecy; the White House had to learn the news from *Time*'s Michael Weisskopf.

The reporter called John Podesta and asked about a Justice Department probe of Clinton. Podesta seemed flummoxed, said he knew nothing about it. Weisskopf called Lanny Davis, even got Lanny Breuer out of a deposition; they also pleaded ignorance. Breuer quickly huddled with Chuck Ruff and Cheryl Mills. Ruff called Eric Holder, the deputy attorney general, and confirmed that the Justice Department review was indeed under way.

The next morning, a Saturday, word began to leak out. *Newsweek*'s Michael Isikoff called Lanny Davis, who confirmed the essentials. Davis told his colleagues that the White House should say nothing and let the two magazines break the story Sunday, when they usually faxed out their most newsworthy pieces. Davis drafted a statement confirming the Reno inquiry but hoped to hold it for a day. He felt he had made a commitment to Weisskopf, whose story was being considered for *Time*'s cover.

Clinton was out in California, where he and Hillary had just dropped Chelsea off at Stanford, and the president was now visiting a charter school in San Carlos. Ron Fournier picked up the buzz from back home and asked Joe Lockhart a broad question about the state of the fundraising investigation. Lockhart knew the official plan was to stay mum, but he also knew the story was close to popping. It wasn't worth ruining his relationship with the ever-polite AP reporter to save a few hours.

"Ron, you're not asking me the right question," Lockhart said. "If you come back with the right question, I'll help you."

At that moment Lanny Davis was welcoming the first of thirty old friends from Montgomery County for a White House tour he had promised. The phone rang. It was Fournier.

"Oh fuck," Davis said. He told Fournier to hold on and called Charles Ruff.

"What should we do?" Davis asked.

"You can't deny it, so go ahead and give it to them," Ruff said.

Lockhart knew Fournier's story was on the wire when, while chatting with Bruce Lindsey, he peered around a corner of the school and saw a dozen reporters charging at him. They had all just been paged by their offices. Weisskopf, for his part, was wondering whether he should have risked calling the White House for comment. *Time*'s publicists in New York scrambled to put out a press release so the magazine could grab credit for Weisskopf's short-lived scoop.

Now the administration was in a defensive crouch. Lindsey checked in with the legal team back home and passed on their advice to Clinton. The president told Lockhart that his instinct was not to address the Reno story. After midnight, on the flight back home, Lockhart dozed off after watching the film *Air Force One*, confident that no further news would be made. But Clinton, clad in blue jeans, always felt like talking after a big event, so he wandered back to the press section. He pleaded ignorance on the Justice inquiry. "I don't know anything about that," Clinton said.

Rahm Emanuel was scheduled to appear the next morning on

CNN's *Late Edition*, ostensibly to discuss the tobacco negotiations.
He huddled with McCurry and Davis to hammer out the party line.
For the first question he would simply repeat that Clinton didn't
remember whether he had made the fundraising calls. For the
follow-up question, he would say that Reno should make the decision
on an independent counsel free from political pressure. Emanuel
wanted to add that Washington was working itself into a lather over
this, that unleashing a prosecutor would be using a nuclear missile to
kill a gnat. But he held his tongue.

In a strange way, Clinton had caught a break. The special prosecutor, if there was to be one, would be summoned on the most narrow
and legalistic grounds. Calls that would be perfectly legal if Clinton
made them from one room, upstairs in the residence, were somehow
verboten if made from an office downstairs. Perhaps soft money had
been turned into hard dollars, most likely without the president's
knowledge. How many voters could get exercised by these technical
infractions? These were precisely the sort of legal ambiguities that
Clinton was so practiced at finessing. Over the long term, of course,
Clinton and Gore faced the very real possibility that an aggressive
prosecutor would widen the probe until the whole mess was within
his purview. But the heart of the scandal—selling access, demeaning
the presidency and vice presidency, putting the arm on donors who
could hardly say no to the nation's elected leaders—remained beyond
the reach of mere statutes. Those offenses could be tried only in the
court of public opinion, and the electorate had already spoken. Polls
showed that seven in ten believed that both parties engaged in sleazy
fundraising.

The view from the West Wing was more depressing. After nearly
four years of the Whitewater investigation, Clinton's aides could not
stomach the idea of another prosecutor probing the president for
years to come. Lanny Davis was especially exasperated, for they were
stuck on defense. He had been ordered to hold his fire, hadn't been
allowed to score a single point on television. The White House was
saddled with this weak, contradictory explanation on the phone calls:
I can't remember doing it, but I may have done it, but it's okay, but I
can't tell you why it was okay because the attorney general will think
we're pressuring her. Why not just declare up front that the fundraising calls were perfectly legal? That in 110 goddamn years nobody

had been prosecuted under this law? The lawyers were afraid to have the White House say anything, even as some Republicans were threatening Reno with impeachment unless she moved for a special prosecutor.

Even worse, Clinton's amnesia defense was practically an invitation to reporters to find someone he had hit up for money. That very morning *The New York Times* had unearthed a 1994 memo from Harold Ickes saying that "BC called" California businessman John Torkelson, with the notation "50,000" and "25, 25"—a reference to the two $25,000 checks that Torkelson soon sent to the DNC.

Privately, several White House aides concluded that Clinton had probably made a bunch of fundraising calls. They also realized that their strategy of restraint had bombed, that they had simply allowed the Republicans a clear field in pummeling Janet Reno. The only reason the aloof Reno had ordered the thirty-day review, they believed, was that she had finally buckled under the pressure. None of the facts in the case had changed. Now even Ruff realized they had to fight back, although he urged his staff to stick to arguing the law. Lanny Davis was turned loose to make the case. Lanny Breuer felt that Davis might not accomplish much, but that his arguments made the political staffers in the White House feel better. If the counsel's office continued to stay quiet, the political guys would just spin the press on their own.

The new strategy was quickly evident. Clinton publicly threatened to keep Congress in session until it acted on campaign finance reform. Davis told CNN and *USA Today* that there was no need for a special prosecutor. McCurry turned sharply combative at the afternoon gaggle, saying that Reno was "being badgered by editorial writers" about naming a special prosecutor. "It's hard to pick up a newspaper and not see her being badgered," he said.

But the worst was yet to come. Lanny Davis had gotten the first warning on a Sunday afternoon two weeks earlier, when he was at a Washington Redskins game. He was beeped by George Lardner, a *Washington Post* investigative reporter, and had to shout to make himself heard above the cheering crowd. Lardner was calling to ask about charges by Paula Jones, whose trial had recently been set for the spring of 1998, that she was being audited by the Internal Revenue Service and that this appeared to be political retribution by the White

House. Davis dismissed the allegation as ludicrous. But Lardner had also been working on another story. A historian studying the Reagan archives had told him back in July about the role of the White House Communications Agency in videotaping most presidential events, suggesting that there might be videotapes of Clinton's White House coffees. Lardner checked with Fred Thompson's investigators, who launched their own inquiry. They later told Lardner that the White House had denied that any such tapes existed. The reporter could not resist the opportunity to put the question to the administration's chief scandal spinner.

"So Nixon had his tapes and we have the audiovisual unit?" Davis said, immediately grasping the Watergate parallel. He later asked Lanny Breuer whether there were any such videotapes, and Breuer told him there were not.

Now, in the early days of October, Michael Weisskopf learned that the administration had belatedly discovered dozens of videotapes of the fundraising coffees, openly filmed by the White House Communications Agency. The *Time* reporter knew that the White House had just turned over forty-four of the tapes to the Thompson committee. This time he would not make the mistake of calling too early for comment and blowing his exclusive. Weisskopf called the White House on Saturday evening, just as *Time* was going to press, and on Sunday morning the nation learned of the secret tapes. There was nothing terribly incriminating on the tapes, but the brief snippets— Clinton praising John Huang, embracing Johnny Chung, Democratic chairman Don Fowler refusing five checks from a donor but promising to call him afterward—made for great television. What's more, their very existence showed that the Clinton crowd had again been slow to produce crucial evidence.

When Cheryl Mills gave him the news, the president was furious at the belated discovery. Podesta felt they had clearly screwed up. Worse, the White House had waited four long days to tell the Justice Department about the tapes—until the day after Janet Reno had decided that the investigation of Clinton and Gore would continue but need not include the coffees. They all knew how bad that looked.

Publicly, however, the spin on the story was very different. "Just an accident," Clinton said during an Oval Office photo session.

At least one White House official was convinced that Lanny Davis had leaked the news to his pal Weisskopf. Davis was kicking himself for not pushing Breuer earlier to find the tapes; he knew that no one would believe this was an honest screw-up. He also knew that the explanation—that he and Breuer, who were both Jewish, had failed to notify Justice earlier in part because they were off for the Rosh Hashanah holiday—wouldn't wash. Now all the commentators were making Jewish jokes. Davis wished he had never mentioned what came to be ridiculed as the Rosh Hashanah defense, especially when he learned—days later—that Ruff had met with Reno on the Jewish holiday and somehow failed to mention the discovery of the videotapes.

Davis was particularly stung when Maureen Dowd dismissed him as the "special assistant for obstruction" in her *New York Times* column. He called her to complain, but she wouldn't call back. Didn't Dowd have some obligation to check the facts before viciously sliming him as a stonewaller? Davis had once made a similar complaint to William Safire, who replied that he was an opinion writer who put things out there and let others make their own judgments. What sort of journalism was this?

Lanny Breuer, who had supervised the search for the videotapes, told friends that he was being made the fall guy. Even Clinton dumped on him. "I think he made a mistake," the president told reporters. That annoyed Breuer, who knew nothing of the comment until he read it in *The Washington Post.* His wife, Nancy, was really upset about the whole mess. Worse, Breuer was subpoenaed to testify before a federal grand jury over the handling of the tapes, as was Cheryl Mills. This was exactly what Breuer and the other White House lawyers had feared, that one of them would become a suspect in an obstruction-of-justice probe if there were problems in gathering the proper evidence. Jane Sherburne had warned him about this when he took her old job, had said that within eight months he'd become part of the story. That was almost exactly eight months ago.

Breuer, who had grown jealous of all the press attention the other Lanny was getting, now had his moment in the harsh spotlight, facing a pack of reporters outside the federal courthouse and being grilled on *Face the Nation*, where he had to "deeply regret" their delay in finding the videotapes. Breuer was also summoned for depositions by the Senate and House committees, which he felt were not even remotely making a pretense of searching for the truth. The press was totally ignoring the fact that there was nothing incriminating on the tapes themselves. The reporters were quick to compare the one tape that had no sound to Nixon's eighteen-and-a-half-minute tape gap, but barely mentioned it when the audio was found. This was getting ugly. Breuer began thinking about making his exit. Now he could see why no human being could survive in this job for very long.

McCurry, meanwhile, tried to find a way to prevent the tapes controversy from ruining Clinton's first trip to South America. Several reporters had told him privately that they didn't particularly enjoy embarrassing Clinton abroad by asking about domestic scandals, but it was often their only crack at him. As they flew south on Air Force One, McCurry took the unusual step of making the president available to answer reporters' questions about the investigation, although no television cameras were allowed. McCurry then announced that Clinton would take no questions on the subject at the upcoming press conference with Brazilian President Henrique Cardoso.

It didn't work. At the Garden of Alvorada Palace in Brasilia, Clinton was visibly annoyed as five of the eight questions asked by American reporters dealt with the fundraising scandal. As Cardoso looked on, ABC's John Donvan even asked whether Clinton found such questions embarrassing on foreign soil.

"I can't be embarrassed about how you decide to do your job," the president shot back. McCurry was in a surly mood, even suggesting that reporters who cared only about the scandal might want to "drop off the trip." Clinton later chided his press secretary, saying half-jokingly that McCurry had been "just a damn fool" to think his little maneuver would work.

Outside the Beltway echo chamber, however, the noise was growing faint. Senate Republicans had all but killed the campaign finance reform legislation with little public fuss. A new ABC poll found Clinton with a 59 percent approval rating, even though nearly three-quarters of Americans believed that the White House had deliberately hidden the coffee videotapes. Ted Koppel was clearly mystified as he questioned Paul Begala on *Nightline* that evening. The press, he said, was "obsessed" by the scandal, was pummeling the president day after day, there was the specter of "a cover-up," and yet Clinton was still riding high.

"Why do you think that no one seems to care very much?" Koppel wondered.

Begala was struck by Koppel's sense of outrage. The press really had an agenda here. The journalists wanted a special prosecutor, if only to validate their scandal-mongering over the past year. They needed to make an impact because that was how you won Pulitzer Prizes. They didn't like the way political money was raised in America. They were mad at the public for sticking by Bill Clinton and for stubbornly refusing to share their anger. There was no way the president's polls would remain this high for the rest of the second term, Begala knew, but for the moment, the cultural gap between the press and the rest of the country had never been wider, and not even Ted Koppel could change that.

CHAPTER SIXTEEN

Dodging the Bullet

IT WAS, IN THE END, AN ANTICLIMAX. LIKE SO MUCH ELSE ABOUT the fundraising scandal, Janet Reno's decision not to seek an independent counsel to investigate Bill Clinton and Al Gore was leaked to the press well before it was made public. Days before the December 2 announcement, Republican lawmakers were all over television assailing the attorney general for her not-yet-official failure to demand a special prosecutor.

The Clinton and Gore staffs were clearly split on how to handle the news. The Clintonites wanted to keep a low profile, to put out a terse statement, to avoid any praise that would suggest that Reno had done what they wanted. "We're not going to get any vindication out of this," McCurry warned the staff. He felt that any attempt to spin the decision as a major victory would quickly boomerang. You'd practically be inviting reporters to write six more paragraphs saying that the Justice Department was still investigating this, that, and the other thing.

But the Gore aides insisted that their man talk to the press, and the vice president agreed. The interests of Clinton, who would never face the voters again, and his number-two, who was gearing up to run for the top job, had finally diverged. Besides, it was Gore who had admitted making the fundraising calls and had taken the worst battering in the press. He wanted to get out there. The staff couldn't be high-fiving each other, Gore felt, but he wanted to underscore the point that the phone calls he had doggedly defended did not warrant a criminal investigation.

"This is a great thing for us, but we don't want to be arrogant," Gore told his staff. "We don't want to look like this was expected."

When Reno went before the cameras late on a chilly Tuesday, both sides were ready. Clinton issued a twenty-three-word statement expressing satisfaction with Reno's decision, and McCurry publicly insisted that not much had changed. Gore, traveling in Connecticut, told reporters that it was time for the fundraising calls to "be put behind us."

The journalists were clearly disappointed that the scandal that had consumed so much of their energy for fourteen months seemed to have run out of gas. Their stories focused on the narrowness of Reno's legal ruling, on her stubborn refusal to recognize that the administration could not credibly investigate itself. " 'Never been indicted' is not an appealing political slogan," James Bennet wrote in the *Times*. "RENO WIMPS OUT," sneered the *New York Post*.

For weeks McCurry had been growing increasingly testy over the endless media inquisition. When Clinton and Gore were interviewed by Justice Department investigators, he refused to say whether they were under oath or even how long the sessions lasted.

"Why can't you just go ask the president?" a reporter wondered.

"Because I'm not going to," McCurry snapped.

The fundraising scandal continued to spread its tentacles in strange and unexpected ways, reaching into the Democrats' relationship with the Teamsters union and to investigations of several Cabinet members. The Justice Department considered asking for a special prosecutor to probe Interior Secretary Bruce Babbitt and his involvement in an Indian gambling license; rejected one for former Energy Secretary Hazel O'Leary and her solicitation of a charitable donation; and began a preliminary probe of influence-peddling charges against Labor Secretary Alexis Herman. On other fronts, former Agriculture Secretary Mike Espy was indicted for accepting gifts from a poultry company, and former HUD secretary Henry Cisneros was indicted in a case involving payments to his former mistress. What's more, there was speculation in the press that prosecutors might seek indictments against John Huang, Charlie Trie, and Johnny Chung.

The Democrats gave up on trying to seize the moral high ground. The party quietly dropped the $100,000 limit on soft money donations that Clinton had trumpeted months earlier as evidence of his commitment to campaign finance reform. When a reporter asked for the umpteenth time how Clinton could keep aggressively raising soft money while he remained under investigation, McCurry had had enough.

"Wake up and see reality," he told the gaggle. He had to control the flow of hostile questions, even at the risk of seeming rude when television replayed his harshest sound bites again and again.

Throughout the fall, even the seemingly good news had contained seeds of trouble. When Fred Thompson folded his faltering Senate hearings on Halloween, there was no sense of relief among White House officials. They believed that Thompson was merely passing the baton to Dan Burton and his House committee, where, sure enough, Lanny Breuer and Cheryl Mills were summoned for a browbeating over their delays in producing evidence. The Clintonites were particularly upset at the way the Republican National Committee poured nearly $800,000 into negative ads in a special House election on Staten Island. With the Democratic Party $15 million in debt, the Republicans used the televised blitz—the same sort of thinly veiled "issue ads" that Clinton was being denounced for employing in early 1996—to help elect their candidate. Lanny Davis wondered what had happened to the media's sense of outrage over soft money. One reporter told him that the press simply held Democrats to a higher standard. Well, screw that. The Staten Island race was a psychological turning point at the White House, for the fundraising scandal, having depleted the Democratic coffers, was now having a real impact on real contests—and the 1998 midterm elections were looming on the horizon. The GOP strategy, the White House crew decided, was to tie them down with perpetual hearings and endless document demands, even if the investigations went nowhere.

At a Saturday morning meeting, Podesta told Davis and Breuer that they were shifting into a more aggressive gear. "Enough is enough," Podesta declared. Davis tried out some fresh attack lines.

His new spin, he said, was that Burton was "using tax dollars to abuse congressional investigative powers for blatantly partisan purposes." Perhaps it was simply that the usually measured Chuck Ruff was absent, but they got each other revved up. Soon Clinton himself was proclaiming that Republican investigators were trying to bankrupt his party.

Gore, meanwhile, felt that the worst of the storm had passed and that the media spotlight was no longer trained on him. Lorraine Voles concluded that they couldn't stay in the bunker forever. Major newspapers and magazines were embarking on big profiles of Gore, and the pieces would undoubtedly turn out better if he cooperated. The vice president agreed to talk to Joe Klein of *The New Yorker*, Rick Berke of *The New York Times*, David Maraniss of *The Washington Post*, David Shribman of *The Boston Globe*, Karen Tumulty of *Time*, Elizabeth Shogren of the *Los Angeles Times*, Marjorie Williams of *Vanity Fair*. It was a roll of the dice, Voles felt, but Gore didn't mind answering a couple of scandal questions if they were in the context of a broader look at his career. He wouldn't do a big television interview —that was still too risky—but Gore couldn't very well run for president while hiding from the political reporters.

Still, Gore had a remarkable ability to step on his story. He told Tumulty in a back-of-the-plane conversation, which he thought was off-the-record, that his old Harvard pal Erich Segal had used him as the model for the romantic hero in writing the novel *Love Story*. That little dab of color in *Time* led to a minor media uproar in which Segal finally denied to *The New York Times* that Gore had inspired the character, making it look like a clumsy attempt by the vice president to soften his image.

Clinton, the ever-resilient president, was still riding high in the polls. He reaped nearly as much publicity for adopting a chocolate Labrador puppy as his opponents had been able to generate all year in the campaign finance scandal. Clinton knew he was riding an extraordinary media wave, gleefully stoking speculation over what name he would give the dog. He felt betrayed when someone leaked the name Buddy to Wolf Blitzer hours before the president was to announce it at a news conference, and he lashed out as a half-dozen of his closest aides began to brief him in the Cabinet Room.

"I'd like to know what sorry piece of shit from my staff leaked this," Clinton barked, brushing aside McCurry's attempted explanations.

Nonetheless, he continued to suffer his share of setbacks and embarrassments. The tawdriness of the Paula Jones suit kept playing out in the press as the case lurched toward a scheduled trial date in the spring of 1998. Bob Bennett found himself discussing the president's penis on *Face the Nation*, declaring that Clinton was "a normal man" in terms of "size, shape, direction." An unruly media mob descended on Bennett's office near the White House when Jones showed up for the president's six-hour deposition in the case. *Newsweek*'s Michael Isikoff quickly got word that Arkansas trooper Danny Ferguson had testified that he escorted a woman to four late-night trysts at the governor's mansion even after Clinton was elected president. Isikoff also reported that Kathleen Willey, the former White House aide who would not go on the record with him over the summer, had told Jones's lawyers under oath that the president made an unwanted sexual advance in a room just off the Oval Office. The flurry of allegations provided a troubling taste of things to come in the case of *Jones v. Clinton*.

There was trouble as well on other fronts. Ken Starr came to the White House to interview Hillary in the Travelgate investigation. The Whitewater saga, which had been relegated to the back burner, bubbled up now and again in strange ways. A 1982 check for $27,600 from Madison Guaranty, made out to Clinton and alleged to be a secret loan, was mysteriously found in a car trunk in an Arkansas junkyard. Scandal was such an integral part of the Clinton presidency that this discovery hardly caused a stir.

On the policymaking front, there was a growing sense that the second Clinton administration was a spent force. In the predawn hours of November 10, the president suffered the humiliation of having to pull the House bill granting him "fast track" authority to negotiate international trade deals after failing to win over even a quarter of his own party's lawmakers. The reporters, long skeptical that Clinton's second term had any larger meaning, quickly pounced with their end-of-an-era pieces. "Clinton may now be a lame-duck president," declared *USA Today*. Alison Mitchell was only slightly more cautious, citing Capitol Hill observers as saying "that the setback was the beginning of the president's lapse into lame-duck status." George Stephanopoulos, the once-loyal lieutenant, told *The Wall Street Journal* that "the last three years are going to be largely a rhetorical presidency." And there was growing evidence that he was right. Even Michael Frisby, who had been willing to give Clinton the benefit of the doubt on racial matters, conceded that the ill-defined race initiative had "dropped off the radar screen." Clinton was unable to win Senate approval for his nominee to be the nation's civil rights chief, Bill Lann Lee, weeks after failing to secure a vote on William Weld, the former Massachusetts governor, as ambassador to Mexico. The carefully constructed facade of presidential power was starting to crack.

Still, the White House kept grabbing headlines by churning out modest proposals. Advance word of a Clinton plan to ban imports of new types of assault weapons made the front page of *The New York Times* and the *Los Angeles Times*. The leak of Clinton's plan to propose a "bill of rights" for patients in health maintenance organizations got page-one display in *USA Today* and *The Washington Post*. A one-day break on the announcement that the federal budget deficit had dropped to $22.6 billion—proving that the Clay Chandler story that so infuriated Clinton had been right on target—led *The New York Times*.

The strategy kicked into high gear over the Christmas holidays as White House aides worked out an elaborate computerized plan that laid out the budget proposals, from food safety to drug abuse to Social Security reform, that Emanuel would leak to selected newspapers. But there was one major initiative, marked "Hold for POTUS," that Clinton wanted to unveil himself: his proposal to lower the age of Medicare eligibility from sixty-five to sixty-two. The leaking apparatus sputtered out of control, however, and someone passed the Medicare story to *The Wall Street Journal*, frittering away on New Year's weekend of 1998 what should have been a dramatic presidential announcement. Erskine Bowles chewed out the staff, but it was too late. Clinton had been scooped by an anonymous aide.

McCurry's candor about the president's view of the press was still getting him into trouble. He told the *White House Bulletin*, a small-circulation newsletter, that Clinton was "just convinced there's some general global conspiracy out to ruin his life and make him miserable." No one noticed until Tim Russert, McCurry's former boss, told the press secretary that he planned to ask Clinton about the quote when the president appeared on the 50th anniversary program of *Meet the Press*. McCurry quickly warned Clinton about his conspiracy comment.

"Why did you say that?" Clinton exclaimed. "That's not how I feel."

"I was trying to make a light point," McCurry replied.

For all his private grousing about their irresponsible ways, the president didn't like to confront the journalists themselves. McCurry came up with a perfect opportunity for Clinton to vent his spleen about *The New York Times*, the newspaper that most consistently ticked him off. Michael Oreskes, the paper's new Washington bureau chief, was invited to the White House for an off-the-record chat. McCurry and Emanuel warned Oreskes that the Big Guy had a grudge against the *Times* and would be giving him an earful.

At the pre-brief, the two aides urged the president to level with Oreskes. "If you believe there's been a pattern where they haven't been fair to you, you should raise that and be honest with him," McCurry said. But Clinton seemed unusually mellow, saying the paper's White House reporters "have been pretty fair to us," except for one recent story where "Bennet was way off the mark."

When Oreskes arrived in the Oval, Clinton wimped out. After a lengthy discussion of the recent standoff with Iraq over nuclear inspections, Oreskes turned to what he called "the commercial portion of the program." Oreskes said that Clinton spent less time talking to journalists than his predecessors, and that the biggest problem the *Times* reporters faced was their inability to talk to the president. He fully expected Clinton to launch into a litany of the paper's sins, after which they might strike a tacit deal: You deal with my problems and maybe you'll get more access. That, after all, was how politicians did business.

Instead, Clinton looked Oreskes in the eye. "You know, you're right," he said. The president allowed that the *Times* correspondents were generally fair, although there was one article on trade in which reporter John Broder "didn't understand what I was thinking." The tirade never came.

"I gave him three or four shots if he wanted to do it," Oreskes told McCurry afterward. Days later, Clinton granted the *Times* reporters a lengthy interview.

Despite these occasional thaws, the culture of distrust remained as thick as ever. After a solid year of scandal stories, the administration's credibility with the press was so badly tarnished that even the most sickening charges rang true. Begala, Lockhart and Davis were furious over an allegation that the White House had been selling burial plots at Arlington National Cemetery to "dozens" of big Democratic donors and Clinton pals. McCurry thought the charge was so preposterous that no one could possibly take it seriously.

In classic fashion, just as Chris Lehane had documented in his "conspiracy" report, the fallacious story ricocheted from *Insight*, the conservative magazine that was part of the *Washington Times* empire, to Rush Limbaugh and Oliver North and G. Gordon Liddy, to Republican lawmakers on the Hill, to *The New York Times* and *The Washington Post* and the *Los Angeles Times* and CNN. No one seemed to believe the administration's outraged denials that it was auctioning off the hallowed gravesites like so many evenings in the Lincoln Bedroom. The press should be "ashamed," McCurry argued, to no avail. But the military had allowed the conspiracy theories to fester by refusing to release the list of those who had received special waivers for Arlington burial, despite a request seven months earlier from *Army Times*. When the Army finally coughed up the list of sixty-nine people, it included just one Democratic donor, former ambassador Larry Lawrence, who was said to have been wounded at sea during World War II.

Begala, Davis and Lockhart all went on the offensive, calling *Nightline* and *USA Today* and *The Washington Post* to flog the story as a morality tale of media excess. For once, the Clintonites felt, the facts were clearly on their side. But no one in the press expressed the slightest degree of remorse. Given Clinton's track record, the reporters insisted, the cemetery charges could well have been true. Plausibility, it seemed, was the new journalistic standard. After all, Maureen Dowd wrote, "it did not seem such a stretch to think that this White House . . . would even peddle eternity."

John Podesta was so furious he sat down and wrote Dowd a tart letter:

"What you need to know about *The New York Times* is that they would run the story without running it down. John Podesta. P.S. I call this the wolf defense—I ate the boy, he deserved it."

But by the time Podesta's letter reached Dowd, the once-buried story had been brought back to life by reports that Lawrence had fabricated his war injury, that he had never even served in the Merchant Marine, as he had claimed. Veterans were furious, and the critics had a field day. There was no evidence that the administration knew of Lawrence's deception, or even that the White House had pushed for his burial at Arlington, but it smelled once again like a coverup.

"For crying out loud, we didn't approve that over here," Clinton told his aides at the pre-brief. "We were just as misled as everyone else."

Dowd wrote another column slamming the White House. Podesta felt compelled to send her another, briefer note. "Uncle!" he cried.

McCurry couldn't believe their bad luck. They had finally beaten back a phony story, only to watch helplessly as critics forced the digging up of a dead ambassador with an imaginary war record, which never would have come out had it not been for the initial bogus headlines. A frustrating year of dribs and drabs was ending with more tawdry charges that echoed from beyond the grave. They were truly snakebit.

·   ·   ·

BY THE END OF BILL CLINTON'S FIFTH YEAR IN OFFICE, THE RE-lentless political combat had taken its toll both on the men and women around the president and on the reporters who chronicled their exploits.

Michael Kelly was fired as the editor of *The New Republic* after just nine months on the job. Martin Peretz, the magazine's owner and a close friend of Al Gore for thirty years, had grown tired of what he viewed as Kelly's endlessly shrill attacks on Clinton and Gore and the fundraising scandal. Kelly had been scheduled to have lunch that day with Lanny Davis, and word of his axing quickly spread through the White House. "There is a God!" Rahm Emanuel exclaimed before rushing off to tell McCurry and Bowles.

Alison Mitchell abruptly left the White House beat to cover Congress for *The New York Times*. She was relieved at no longer having to be part of the body watch. The beat was simply too constricting, not as much fun as dealing with 535 egocentric and publicity-hungry lawmakers. If Clinton was finally getting some good press, she concluded, perhaps he deserved it for his success with Congress and in the polls.

Deborah Orin stepped up her feud with McCurry, accusing him of "an all-out stonewall" when he refused to say whether Clinton had tried to examine government research on UFOs. Orin castigated the White House press corps for having "rolled over and played dead."

Rita Braver wound up in the hospital, having surgery for a ruptured disc in her back. All those years of lugging suitcases and laptops on and off the press plane had taken their toll. Hillary called to wish her well. Braver left the beat at summer's end to do feature stories for the evening news and other CBS programs. She was tired of chasing the flap of the day, policy proposals that never came together, a race initiative that had come and gone, scandals that never quite seemed to jell. She had had enough of the Clinton presidency and was happy to hand over her beat to a younger reporter, Scott Pelley.

ABC reassigned John Donvan, who had stumbled in questioning the president at press conferences, and brought back Sam Donaldson, the high-decibel White House correspondent of the Carter and Reagan years. A master showman, Donaldson began asking McCurry aggressive questions so he could show the exchanges—starting with himself—on the evening news.

Lorraine Voles quit just before Thanksgiving. Life as Gore's chief defender proved to be too much after she had had a second child. The job would have been difficult under any circumstances, but the fundraising scandal made it impossible, and Voles told Gore she could not continue, not with the demands of a presidential campaign approaching. She left for a part-time stint with a Washington PR firm.

Doug Sosnik wound up staying on. He had been offered a couple of high-paying jobs in public relations and crisis management but turned them down. His Argentine-born wife was tired of his long hours—"Thees ees shit," she told him—but his next job had to feel right. Weaning yourself from the White House was more difficult than he had imagined.

Don Baer began consulting for a new magazine called *Content* that criticized the media.

Erskine Bowles changed his mind and decided to stay on as chief of staff through 1998.

Doris Matsui, who had ended the previous year by being sucked into the scandal's vortex, spent 1997 trying to break free. The publicity would die down for a while, and then she would get hit again. *Insight* magazine wrongly described her as having attended the infamous White House coffees. The *San Francisco Examiner* described her as "enmeshed in the controversy because of her DNC fundraising role," even though she had raised no money. *The Sacramento Bee* said that she had met with John Huang twenty-six times, when in fact she barely knew the man and had merely cleared him into the White House for meetings twenty-six times. The Thompson committee decided to depose her and she had to raid the fund set aside for her son's law school tuition to hire a lawyer. Still, the White House insisted that Matsui remain quiet while her reputation was smudged. She now found that she could not read a newspaper story on any subject without wondering whether it was true.

Hillary Clinton continued to have a frosty relationship with the press. When *Time*'s Karen Tumulty asked McCurry for an interview pegged to the first lady's fiftieth birthday, he told her that Hillary "doesn't want to be laid out on a couch and psychoanalyzed." Tumulty was among the reporters tagging along when Hillary visited Panama in the fall and, at midnight, was finally granted fifteen minutes in a hotel room with an exhausted first lady. No matter what kind of softball that Tumulty tossed—Had she modified her role as first lady? What did she plan to do after the White House?—Hillary turned testy, refusing to discuss anything remotely personal. "I don't know what to make of that question," she said, or "I don't view my life that way." Worse, Tumulty had to submit the quotes in writing to Marsha Berry and allow Hillary to decide what could be used on-the-record. The charming and funny woman that Tumulty and her colleagues had seen over dinner and on the plane remained resolutely off-the-record. Hillary nonetheless got an upbeat *Time* cover story, announcing that she was "getting ready to come onstage again" by hosting a White House conference on child care. But the journalists kept shaking their heads over her prickly persona and the grating behavior of her closest aides.

Lanny Davis began making plans to leave after the Thompson hearings ended. A friend from Maryland told him that he had become both a noun and a verb—people spoke of hiring a Lanny and, if they had been spun particularly hard, of being Lanny'd. He was starting to worry about his own reputation. He had been badly stung by the White House videotapes disaster and felt that his friends in the press no longer believed what he was saying. One year in the vortex was enough. Davis gave Clinton the word at the staff Christmas party. Motioning to his wife, Carolyn, he said: "The good news is that Carolyn is pregnant. The bad news is that I'm leaving January 31st." The president, looking surprised, asked why. "I can do more for you on the outside than on the inside," Davis said. The reporters planned to give him a good-natured "roast" at the National Press Club.

Mike McCurry figured on leaving the White House sometime in 1998. He asked a couple of close friends to keep their eyes open, had a couple of job discussions with potential employers (which, under federal ethics rules, he had reported to the counsel's office). But it wasn't clear what he should do next. He didn't want to write a book. He didn't want to be a TV talking head. He'd had enough of being a press secretary. His greatest fear was that any job would be a giant letdown after flacking for the president. Yes, he wanted to spend more time with his kids, to teach his seven-year-old son to throw a curveball, to play a little golf, but he knew he would quickly grow restless if he wasn't sufficiently challenged at work. His wife, Debra, was warning him not to quit until he was ready. She knew what he was like when he was bored. For all the frustrations, it was hard to walk away from the world's most prominent podium.

. . .

IF THERE WAS ONE STRANGE RESONANCE IN CLINTON'S SECOND term, it was the echo of Watergate. The administration was peopled by folks who had grown up viewing Nixon and his henchmen as criminals brought down by righteous investigators and journalists; indeed, Hillary had been a lawyer for the House Judiciary Committee that had brought the articles of impeachment. Yet twenty-three years later it was Clinton, his wife, and their acolytes who were forced into many of the same defensive tactics by the investigative machinery that was Watergate's greatest legacy.

Like Nixon, Clinton and his top aides invoked attorney-client privilege. They dragged their feet on subpoenas. They blamed their problems on a hostile press. They refused to answer questions, or provided partial or misleading answers. They attacked the special prosecutor who was investigating them. They failed to turn over embarrassing tapes. They complained that Congress was unfairly exploiting the scandal for partisan gain. They denied accusations of hush money. They argued that everyone did what they were accused of doing. They said that most Americans didn't care about the scandal, and they used foreign trips to deflect attention from it.

Of course, they did not for a moment view themselves as devious stonewallers, but rather as honest, hard-working public servants trying to make the country better. They were not terribly reflective about their plight—they were, after all, partisan warriors doing what came naturally, and it was all too easy to dismiss the swirl of scandal as the product of other, nastier partisan combatants. They had been forced into a defensive crouch, they felt, by unfair political attacks and a relentlessly negative press corps. McCurry and Davis and Emanuel and Lewis and the rest were just doing their jobs, just playing the hand that had been dealt them. But it was now a bit easier for them to understand how a president could find himself under siege, how mistakes could be made, how the press could turn prosecutorial, how innocent acts could be twisted into conspiratorial allegations of corruption. Working in the White House was not quite the uplifting experience they had expected.

McCurry felt that he had done fairly well in building some rickety bridges between the president and the press, in orchestrating regular news conferences and off-the-record sessions with reporters. Clinton hadn't lost any ground with the media, but he hadn't gained much either. McCurry had thought he could persuade journalists to take a fresh look at the reelected president, perhaps allow him a second honeymoon, but it was not to be. The scandals had taken care of that. The press was convinced that the Clintonites were dragging their heels on releasing information, despite the grudging acknowledgment that they had released much of the damaging material themselves.

McCurry had recently found an old book on Watergate news coverage, and he had been struck by the restrained tone, more in sorrow than in anger, of the writing about Nixon's impending downfall. Few journalists of that era had indulged in the kind of personal abuse that was routinely heaped on Clinton. The media culture had changed dramatically.

Obviously, the fundraising mess was fair game. Had it happened to Ronald Reagan while McCurry was working at the DNC, he would have been denouncing the White House every day, just as the Republicans were doing. That was the nature of partisan warfare. But for all the journalistic indignation, the story had never caught fire because people out there already knew the script. They knew the system was corrupt and awash in too much money. They didn't have time to follow all the odd characters from China and Indonesia, McCurry felt, because they understood the bottom line. Once they had concluded that the two parties were going to pound each other about fundraising abuses without cleaning up the cesspool that spawned such conduct, they lost interest. And Clinton, by staying focused on what he was elected to do, was able to grab their attention on other issues.

When the niceties were stripped away, the press had taken on the president and lost, badly. It was an old-fashioned struggle that presented the country with two conflicting portraits. In the harsh light cast by the media, Clinton was a slippery, dishonest, cash-obsessed, sex-crazed opportunist who, by sheer dint of his political skills, had managed to fool the voters, co-opt the Republicans, and outrun the prosecutors. In the White House portrayal, the president was a proud, hard-working, consensus-building, unfairly pilloried figure who kept overcoming the odds on behalf of average American families. The grave scandals that darkened the first picture were a barely visible distraction in the official version.

In boxing terms, the White House had clearly won on points. McCurry and company didn't quite conquer the press, but they had clearly neutralized their media antagonists. McCurry had negotiated a shaky cease-fire, kept reporters reasonably content while protecting the boss, used carefully modulated doses of candor to build trust. Through ceaseless spin cycles, administration officials had walled off the burgeoning scandals and managed to convey Clinton's message, however muted, to a skeptical public.

The president, for his part, had learned to coexist with a hostile press corps that he went through the motions of befriending. He had defused the media's agenda, turning the national conversation away from their issues (sleazy fundraising, Whitewater, Paula Jones) and toward his own (balancing the budget, expanding NATO, raising school standards, fighting Internet smut and teenage smoking). He had delivered a strong economy, to be sure, but had failed to do anything dramatic with his second-term mandate, husbanding his political capital throughout 1997 and shying away from the bold strokes that might have been possible for a president with such lofty approval ratings. Indeed, though his staff hated to think of it this way, his major accomplishment was in downsizing the presidency, matching its once-imperial prowess to a public mood that remained deeply distrustful of government. For all the media scoffing, he had ratcheted down his rhetoric to the level of average family concerns and trumped the press in the process. Unlike his predecessors during the Cold War, the president was no longer at the center of the news —Washington itself was no longer at the center of the news—and that suited the electorate just fine. In an age of peace and prosperity, most people didn't want to be bothered with government.

Fortunately for Clinton, journalists were no longer the ink-stained heroes of an earlier era; they were seen as the heartless vultures who had driven Princess Diana to her death. The media had plummeted in public esteem, were distrusted by a majority of Americans, and that gave the White House a critical advantage. The battle between the president and the press was viewed as a clash between two morally ambiguous forces, not a shoot-out pitting the sheriff against the bad guys, and Clinton proved to have more firepower than anyone had imagined.

In the end, the Clinton presidency fit the tabloid times. The press had gorged itself on the Lincoln Bedroom tawdriness, the coffees with rich rogues and scoundrels, the seemingly endless womanizing charges, and the impenetrable Arkansas land dealings. But none of this had mortally wounded Bill Clinton. By parceling out the information and staging occasional document dumps, the senior staff had kept the bleeding under control and taken the sting out of the slashing press coverage. Clinton managed this feat because the public had become overloaded by all the scandal-mongering and had tuned out the constant flurry of allegations as just another form of politics. What's more, a parade of public figures in the 1990s—Newt Gingrich, Bob Packwood, Clarence Thomas, Michael Jackson, Woody Allen, Frank Gifford, Marv Albert, Bill Cosby—had also become the subject of scandalous headlines. Tabloid coverage now came with the territory. The president had clearly tarnished the office through his reckless and relentless fundraising, but he had been a media punching bag for so long that readers and viewers had become desensitized. The most investigated president in recent history had somehow become one of the most popular. Clinton was riding high, despite the barrage of negative headlines, precisely because the voters' expectations had sunk so low. The presidential flacks had done their job. For 1997, at least, their spin had carried the day.

CHAPTER SEVENTEEN

Monica

Lanny Davis was sipping a Scotch with his wife when John Podesta called to give him the unsettling news.

The Washington Post was hours away from publishing a story that Kenneth Starr was investigating whether Clinton had had an affair with a twenty-four-year-old former White House intern, had lied about it under oath, and had urged her to lie as well. Sue Schmidt, the hard-driving Whitewater reporter so loathed by the administration, had the goods on the supposed affair involving Monica Lewinsky. Schmidt's colleague Peter Baker was calling Podesta for comment. A new crisis was about to explode.

Although he was just ten days away from quitting his damage-control job, Davis left his house at 9:30 p.m., drove to his office and began the first of a dozen phone conversations with Baker. Davis didn't know much and mainly acted as a go-between for Bob Bennett. Baker had also paged McCurry, who clearly didn't want to get involved. McCurry called back and left a message about Clinton's meeting the next day with Prime Minister Benjamin Netanyahu. But Middle East diplomacy was about to be wiped off the media radar screen.

The city had been buzzing about the tantalizing intern story for three days. The word was out that Mike Isikoff had all the details. The combative *Newsweek* reporter had known about the alleged affair for a year. His source was Linda Tripp, a former White House aide who had befriended Monica Lewinsky when both were moved to the Pentagon. It was Tripp who had told Isikoff over the summer that Clinton had made sexual advances to Kathleen Willey in a room just off the Oval Office. Tripp had been furious when Bob Bennett responded to her account by publicly questioning her credibility, and she decided to secretly tape her conversations with Lewinsky to convince Isikoff of the presidential affair. Tripp told Isikoff about the tapes at an October meeting with her literary agent, Lucianne Goldberg, in the Washington home of Goldberg's son. Tripp offered to play the tapes, but Isikoff declined to listen because he was afraid of getting sucked into what appeared to be an illegal taping process.

Isikoff's longtime connection to Paula Jones was also paying off. Back in 1994, when he was pursuing the case for *The Washington Post*, he spent months battling his editors—even got into a shouting match that led to his suspension—before becoming the first reporter to detail her charges in a major newspaper. The dispute prompted him to leave the paper soon afterward. Now Isikoff learned that Tripp, outfitted with a body mike by Ken Starr's office, had taped further conversations in which Lewinsky accused Clinton and his friend Vernon Jordan of urging her to lie about their affair in her deposition in the Jones case. It was incredible: Starr was running an undercover sting against the president of the United States. And, with his deadline approaching, Isikoff agreed to listen to one of the incriminating tapes.

When he realized the enormity of what he had, Isikoff turned ashen, took a walk around the block. This was a story that could topple Bill Clinton. But late on Saturday afternoon, January 17, *Newsweek's* editors decided not to run the explosive piece. Starr had asked them to hold off, and they themselves had troubling questions about Lewinsky's credibility. Isikoff had lobbied hard for publication, saying it was not the magazine's role to help Starr do his job. Now, for the second time in six months, he was bedeviled by Matt Drudge. The gossip columnist learned of the Isikoff piece within hours and posted some of the salacious details on his Internet site. The journalistic engines were racing, especially as reports spread that during his own deposition, the president had flatly denied having sex with Lewinsky. At midnight the following Tuesday, Sue Schmidt's *Post* story on Monica Lewinsky hit the streets, quickly followed by reports on ABC radio and in the *Los Angeles Times*.

The White House staff was stunned. Paul Begala had known nothing about the story until he picked up the *Post* the next morning. Lanny Davis felt he couldn't do much with the press until he had more facts. When reporters jammed into the press secretary's office for the morning gaggle, McCurry, reading from his notes, said Clinton was "outraged" by the charges and had "never had any improper relationship with this woman."

But the White House instantly paid a price for the years of aggressive spinning, for the evasive answers that had angered so many journalists through so many scandals. Most of the reporters automatically assumed that Clinton was lying, that he had in fact been carrying on with Monica Lewinsky and was pathetically trying to cover it up. They had been through too many bimbo eruptions, heard too many of Clinton's carefully hedged denials. When a shaky-looking Clinton sat down for a previously scheduled interview that afternoon with PBS's Jim Lehrer, he said that "there is no sexual relationship" with Lewinsky. Suddenly Begala's phone was ringing off the hook: Why did Clinton use the present tense? Was he leaving open the possibility of a past affair? Was he deliberately fudging once again?

At the pre-brief the next day, before Clinton appeared with Palestinian leader Yassir Arafat, the staffers told the president that the press was focused on his verb tense. Clinton was amazed, saying he had simply done the best he could in a stressful situation.

It wasn't long before Begala was employing his trademark sarcasm with the press. "The president said there was no sexual relationship," he told more than one reporter. "The woman has said there was no sexual relationship. Vernon Jordan has said she told him there was no sexual relationship. I think we should impeach him—what do you think?"

The president's closest allies tried to rally around him. In an interview with E. J. Dionne, Run Brownstein and other columnists, Al Gore said that he believed his friend Bill Clinton. Hillary, reprising the role of loyal wife from the 1992 campaign, did a round of radio interviews in which she dismissed the charges as false. Even the secretary of state became part of the Clinton defense team as Madeleine Albright and three other Cabinet secretaries emerged on the White House driveway to express their faith in the president.

But nothing could stop the media stampede over allegations that combined possible obstruction of justice and furtive oral sex with a Beverly Hills twentysomething who lived, of all places, at the Watergate. Davis concluded that the narrowly tailored denials had been a failure. Isikoff and other reporters were unearthing more and more allegations that seemed to undercut those denials: Lewinsky had sent packages to Clinton through his personal secretary, Betty Currie. He had sent her gifts as well, including a book of Walt Whitman poems, and his voice was said to be on her answering machine. She said that he said that oral sex was not adultery. She was said to have had phone sex with Clinton, to have a dress stained with his semen, to have talked about becoming "assistant to the president for blow jobs." She was said to have visited the White House on many evenings. McCurry said they had no immediate plans to release the WAVES records that would show just when and how often Lewinsky had come to the West Wing.

Another stunning charge, tucked inside a *Post* story, was the report that Clinton, in his deposition with Paula Jones's lawyers, had admitted having an affair with Gennifer Flowers. This would mean that the very first thing most Americans had learned about Bill Clinton— his denial, on Super Bowl Sunday six years earlier, that he had slept with Flowers—was a lie. McCurry got hammered at the gaggle by David Bloom, Scott Pelley and Deborah Orin, ducking the question eleven times. All he would say was that Clinton had told the truth about Flowers in 1992 and had told the truth at the deposition.

The political team—Begala, Emanuel, Sosnik, Podesta, Lewis, McCurry, Davis—realized that Clinton needed to speak to the country, and fast. Responsible Republicans were openly debating the possibility of impeachment or resignation. Even such longtime loyalists as George Stephanopoulos, who was livid over the president's conduct, were saying that Clinton might have to go. Clinton, the aides said, should do an interview with a few reporters or a single journalist, perhaps Walter Isaacson, the managing editor of *Time*, whom they generally respected. But the Hezbollah wing was adamant that

Clinton say nothing until they had gathered more information. After all, they were in the midst of a criminal probe. Clinton was starting to rely solely on the lawyers—Bennett, Kendall, Ruff, and Bruce Lindsey—and they did not want him to complicate matters on which he had already given a sworn deposition. Hillary also opposed the idea, and her vote was crucial in such personal crises. They kept the president under wraps.

Slowly, the first attempts at White House spin began to take shape. Even as Lewinsky's lawyer was negotiating with Starr over whether she would testify against Clinton, there were whispers that she was flirtatious, obsessed with the president, not all that emotionally stable. Perhaps, the Clintonites said, Linda Tripp's tapes had been doctored —the same argument they had once raised about Gennifer Flowers's tapes of Clinton urging her to deny that they had had an affair. And why on earth was Ken Starr, the man appointed to investigate Arkansas vacation property, wiring one woman to entrap another woman into admitting that she had had sex with the president? Bennett emerged from his Washington home to tell reporters that "Mr. Starr seems hellbent on getting President Clinton." Bennett also took a swipe at the press: "I'm very disappointed that *The Washington Post*, one of the preeminent newspapers in the country, is becoming a tabloid paper." But the sad truth was that this had become a tabloid presidency.

The climate was so bizarre that the best Hollywood dramas seemed a pale imitation. Even as Clinton weighed a military strike against Iraq over its refusal to admit U.N. weapons inspectors, everyone was comparing his dilemma to the new movie *Wag the Dog*, in which a president caught with a young girl distracts the country by ginning up a war. And it couldn't have been much comfort to know that the movie version of *Primary Colors*, based on the Joe Klein novel about a Clintonesque candidate who impregnates a teenager, would be released within weeks.

The velocity of the story was incredible—Wolf Blitzer felt it was like covering the Persian Gulf War—and even the journalists themselves had a hard time keeping up with the onrushing waves of allegations. Four days after the scandal broke, Blitzer was reporting that some of Clinton's closest advisers had concluded that he did have sex with Lewinsky and were talking about whether he should resign. Begala and a handful of top aides were in the West Wing, watching CNN in amazement. "Bullshit," Begala declared, rushing out onto the lawn to berate Blitzer.

Soon the coverage was spinning out of control. The networks devoted more air time to the Lewinsky soap opera in a single week than they had given to all the Clinton scandals, from Gennifer Flowers to campaign fundraising abuses, combined. CNN kept replaying a videotape of Clinton hugging Lewinsky at a post-election rally like it was some kind of porn flick. David Bloom pressed McCurry at the gaggle in no uncertain terms: "Did the president mean to say to the American people that he had not had sexual intercourse?" Peter Jennings complained that he was uncomfortable discussing oral sex on the air. Journalists grumbled privately about the intense, seemingly relentless pressure to match each new allegation that appeared somewhere else, or at least to regurgitate the charge.

And there was no shortage of charges: Deborah Orin reported in the *New York Post* that Clinton had told Lewinsky he'd had sex with "hundreds" of women. ABC reported that Starr was trying to track down Secret Service agents or White House staffers who had seen "an intimate encounter" between Clinton and Lewinsky, either in the president's study or in the White House theater. *The Washington Times* reported that Lewinsky had offered to tell Starr in exchange for immunity that she had in fact had an affair with Clinton; the story appeared just hours after her lawyer had made the offer to Starr. Administration officials were furious over what they saw as a gusher of leaks from Starr's office. Minutes after the prosecutor subpoenaed some White House aide, a reporter would call up to ask about it. Leaking in a criminal investigation was against the law. But the reporters would never make an issue of Starr's conduct because they were all scrounging for the next illicit tidbit.

Begala tried, in phone call after phone call, to prod journalists into focusing on Starr's tactics. "It is illegal to divulge the contents of a grand jury investigation," he complained to one *Washington Post* reporter.

The reporter cut him off: "You will never get me to write a story decrying leaks. I live off leaks."

A handful of Clinton aides and cronies were dispatched to the talk shows to urge the country to wait for the facts. "There are a lot of opponents of the president who are fanning this," Ann Lewis said on *Fox News Sunday.* "An ongoing campaign of leaks and lies," Begala said on *This Week.* The press was trafficking in "rumor and innuendo and gossip," Rahm Emanuel said on *Face the Nation.* On *Meet the Press,* James Carville, the original anti-Starr pit bull, accused the prosecutor of pursuing a "vendetta" and a "scuzzy" investigation.

Joe Lockhart was so frustrated by the mess that he considered getting out of politics. Here was Matt Drudge, a mere gossip-monger who'd had to retract a bogus story about Sid Blumenthal beating his wife, booked as a commentator on *Meet the Press.* If Drudge was the new Walter Cronkite, Lockhart needed a new line of work. In a way, he felt, the Clintonites were the victims of their own past success with the press. Their in-your-face approach to spin had been so relentless that the reporters all assumed they were opting out of the spin game because they had nothing credible to say. In fact, it would be ludicrous to start spinning in this overheated climate until they could bring some facts to the table. They were simply waiting to fight another day.

Lanny Davis felt lucky that he had announced his resignation a few weeks earlier, for he would never be able to leave now; it would look like he was bailing out of the *Titanic.* McCurry, Emanuel, Sosnik—all of whom had talked about leaving sometime in 1998—were now stuck for the duration. With Davis departing and his successor, James Kennedy, just starting, the White House formed yet another damage-control team, with Joe Lockhart as chief spokesman. The plan was hammered out in a series of meetings involving Ruff, Mills, Lindsey, Emanuel, Begala, Podesta, and Sosnik. Ruff was taking the view that his conversations with Clinton and his private attorneys on the Lewinsky case were shielded by executive privilege. But someone had to hand out the few daily crumbs to the press, and McCurry was determined to keep the endless sex-and-lies questions from polluting his daily briefings. Lockhart, who had drawn scandal duty during the bitter battle over Alexis Herman's nomination as labor secretary, was the logical choice. He was not thrilled about the assignment, but he would be a good soldier.

Emanuel was in his office next to the Oval, giving his baby Zak a bottle and commiserating with Begala over the Fellini-like plot that was overtaking them all.

"I feel like I'm in a Greek tragedy," Emanuel said. "He's at 62 percent, one of the highest ratings of any president in this century. The economy is humming. The world is dancing to his tune. *U.S. News* just had a cover story on what Clintonism means. All that we've worked for, it's all there. And then you get a body blow and every accomplishment, policy and political, is hurt by this distraction."

The odd thing was that none of the loyalists seemed angry at Clinton for jeopardizing his presidency, for his apparent recklessness in forging a relationship with a young intern not much older than Chelsea, for refusing to settle the Paula Jones case and for putting himself in danger of perjury. They would not say whether they believed the boss—they were not blind, after all, to the incriminating circumstantial evidence—but took refuge in a passive tautology: The president says he didn't do it, and I work for the president.

The chaos in the West Wing was such that Clinton's advisers couldn't agree on whether he should show up at a White House event on child care or leave it to Hillary and Al Gore. But the argument soon became moot. The president made clear that he had had enough of staying silent. The political advisers worked out a compromise with the lawyers: Clinton would make a more forceful public denial, but he wouldn't say anything new. When the president appeared in the Roosevelt Room the next morning, he closed his remarks by repeating his denial about having had sex with Lewinsky, this time narrowing his eyes and jabbing his finger and delivering the message with an emotional punch. But he ignored a shouted question as he walked toward the exit. Talking to the press was still too dangerous.

Hillary had long served as a back channel for advisers trying to change her husband's mind about some decision, and now she shifted into what one aide called her "battle mode." Ann Lewis, who was close to Hillary, held a strategy session in the Old Executive Office Building, and the first lady decided it was time to publicly emerge as the president's chief defender. The next morning, she declared on the *Today* show that Starr was a "politically motivated prosecutor," part of a "vast right-wing conspiracy" of "malicious" and "evil-minded" people. She also took a whack at the "feeding frenzy" in the media, much of which, in her view, had become part of the conspiracy against the White House. The first lady would not answer questions about Clinton's relationship with Lewinsky, but she understood the value of shifting the spotlight to the political opposition, a tactic that had served her well during the endless Whitewater saga. Starr dismissed her charges as "nonsense," but the Clintonites were thrilled with the way she had recast the debate.

It was a measure of their desperation that White House aides had sounded out Congress about delaying the State of the Union address, but Clinton delivered it as scheduled that evening. The previous year's speech had been overshadowed by O.J.; this time it was Clinton's sex life that upstaged the proceedings. It was the dilemma that the president had faced so many times before: he wanted to talk about Medicare and child care and Social Security, but the press was obsessed with the latest scandal, in this case a scandal he had brought crashing down on himself.

The news cycle was stuck on fast-forward. At 9:30 one night, Joe Lockhart was deluged with calls about a *Dallas Morning News* report that Starr's investigators had spoken to a Secret Service agent who was ready to testify that he had seen Clinton and Lewinsky in an intimate encounter. Lockhart paged Doug Sosnik, who called back from his car. "Hold on," Sosnik said, turning up the radio. The CBS newscast was leading with the "explosive" new development. Lockhart tracked down David Kendall, who assured him that the story was false, and then called a *Morning News* reporter he knew. "You guys may be in for a big embarrassment on this," Lockhart said. The paper retracted the story after midnight, saying its source had bad information.

The journalists knew they were courting a backlash against the media, which was exactly what the White House wanted. Why, many people wondered, were reporters obsessed with learning the most graphic details of Bill Clinton's sex life?

But no one, it seemed, could stop talking about the subject. Even Dick Morris, who was continuing to offer Clinton private advice— he was, after all, an expert on sex scandals—was causing trouble again. He publicly suggested that Hillary was a lesbian, and thus her husband might feel the need to engage in phone sex or other "quasi-sexual" activity. Morris told KABC, a Los Angeles radio station, that Clinton's behavior might be understandable if one would "assume that some of the allegations about Hillary sometimes not necessarily being into regular sex with men might be true." When John Harris called McCurry to ask about the comment, the press secretary demanded to speak to a senior *Washington Post* editor to see whether the paper was serious about publishing such trash. Len Downie and his editors got into a shouting match over whether to run the remarks, and eventually decided against it. But it didn't matter; they were reprinted the next day in the *Los Angeles Times*, the *New York Post*, and Maureen Dowd's *New York Times* column. Clinton was furious at Morris, and his aides just groaned. Why, they wondered, did the president still talk to this head case? McCurry scolded reporters for their "disgusting" behavior in publicizing Morris's salacious speculation. "I can't believe any responsible news organization would use that," he declared.

For all the journalistic excess, the public reaction, at least initially, was more restrained. Fifty-seven percent of those questioned in a *Washington Post* poll said they believed that Clinton had had a sexual relationship with Lewinsky; like the journalists, they had dismissed his denials as lies. But fifty-nine percent said they wanted him to remain in office, even if he had been having sex in the White House with the young intern. A majority favored impeachment only if it turned out that Clinton had lied under oath about the affair. The issue for most people was trust, not sex. The reporters couldn't believe it. "The thing that's astounding to me is he's doing pretty well in the polls," said Claire Shipman, NBC's newest White House correspondent. Despite the round-the-clock media assault, the president's lofty approval rating, seemingly impervious during the campaign finance fiasco, was holding steady.

Whatever their reservations, people were devouring every juicy detail of the unfolding melodrama. For once, the public was in sync with the media's agenda. The Monica Lewinsky mess was a gripping train wreck of a story, racing down the tracks of real-time television, the seeming self-destruction of a president who only days earlier had been riding so high. It was almost comic, in a way. Richard Nixon had been driven from office for burglarizing and spying on his opponents; Clinton faced political annihilation for failing to keep his zipper zipped.

Even the most sympathetic columnists were appalled by Clinton's behavior; Tom Friedman of *The New York Times* said that the president had been a "reckless idiot." And the critics, from Maureen Dowd to Michael Kelly, were having a field day. "An almost pathological lapse in judgment," declared Joe Klein. There was a clear subtext to the deluge of news reports: See, we tried to tell you about this guy. Wouldn't know the truth if it smacked him in the face. Said he didn't inhale, said he didn't dodge the draft, said the coffees weren't fundraisers; now, according to the Lewinsky tapes, he doesn't believe oral sex is adultery. Clinton's semantic hair-splitting had always driven the reporters crazy, and now all of America could see that they were right. "The creep," as Lewinsky had called him on one tape, had whipped them in 1997, but it was only a matter of time before the truth finally emerged. The factual noose was tightening day by day. Linda Tripp broke her silence, saying that she had been present when Lewinsky got a late-night call from Clinton and that she had seen the gifts they exchanged. Jeff Gerth and Steve Labaton reported in *The New York Times* that Clinton had met privately with Lewinsky in the White House three days after Christmas, shortly before she denied the affair in an affidavit submitted to Paula Jones's lawyers. Lewinsky claimed that Clinton had counseled her to explain her White House visits by saying she was seeing his secretary, Betty Currie, and that he suggested she leave town to avoid the deposition, the *Times* said. Lanny Davis told Gerth and Labaton that he could not comment because the White House lawyers had given him no information.

There were more dangers yet to come: Lewinsky's potential testimony to Ken Starr, possible accounts of sexual episodes from other women, the Paula Jones trial itself. *The Washington Post*, which had played down the Kathleen Willey tale that McCurry worked so hard to contain, now gave her account page-one prominence, noting that she maintained that Clinton had "fondled her breast and put her hand on his genitals." And in a rude reminder that the campaign finance investigation was still going strong, Charlie Trie, Clinton's old pal, was indicted for illegal fundraising. Still, there was little joy in this dizzying blur of a scandal, even for the hard-bitten reporters, for Clinton's conduct was so breathtakingly tawdry and the conse-quences so sad for the country.

By now, the Clintonites had retreated to what they were calling a "hunker-down strategy." They would not answer further questions about Lewinsky, and neither would Clinton. After days of insisting that the president wanted to gather the facts and tell his story, the White House made clear that he would not, perhaps for a long time. After more than a year of talking up a policy of full disclosure, they now resorted, in Nixonian fashion, to an all-out stonewall. McCurry lamely told reporters he was "out of the loop." The press secretary no longer wanted to know. This was about survival now. The administration had made the hard political calculation that the public anger was subsiding and they could ride out the storm. If many Americans thought Clinton was lying, so be it. He was far more popular than his media adversaries, the strategists reasoned, and that was what ultimately mattered. The journalists would continue to investigate, to fill the air with sexual charges, but the president would trump them simply by insisting that he was busy with the country's work.

As Bill Clinton dug in for the long haul, one could see, at long last, the limits of spin. When it worked, the coordinated strategy of peddling a single line to the press, of browbeating some reporters and courting others, was stunningly effective. Damage could be contained, scandal minimized, bad news relegated to the fringes of the media world. But each time an administration did that, each time it beat back the negative publicity with shifting explanations and document dumps and manufactured announcements designed to change the subject, it paid a price. The journalists were more skeptical the next time around, less willing to give the Clinton spin team the benefit of the doubt. At some point, even a reelected president dogged by endless scandal can no longer defy the laws of political gravity.

As Clinton remained mum about the details of what did or did not happen with Monica Lewinsky, his aides' efforts to counter the negative publicity without knowing the facts were all too transparent. They asked Mark Penn to take a poll to assess the damage. They uncorked all the techniques that had worked so well for so long—blaming the press, denouncing their accusers, assailing right-wing enemies, blitzing the talk shows. But even the best spin cannot work if it is totally untethered from substance, and, in the absence of hard information about the president and the intern, the loyalists' spin had become surreal. The press wasn't buying it, and neither was much of the public. The journalists were caught up in a frenzy of unprecedented intensity, with all sorts of uncorroborated allegations echoing through the headlines and the newscasts. But for a president who loved to fill the public space with great torrents of words, his silence was the loudest sound of all.

As the state of siege grew deeper, it remained unclear whether this would be the scandal that forced Bill Clinton from office or whether he would manage yet again to hang on. What was all too clear was that the damage to his presidency would never be repaired. Clinton's efforts to persuade the press that he had an ambitious second-term agenda, to reach a rapprochement with his media antagonists, to rise above his slippery public image, had failed. The spinmeisters could no longer save him from himself. The president would have his place in history, but it was not the one he had imagined.

Epilogue

I<small>T WAS ANOTHER</small> S<small>ATURDAY MORNING DAMAGE-CONTROL MEETING</small> in the West Wing. Everyone knew the drill. But this time the stakes seemed dramatically higher.

Monica Lewinsky had briefly faded from the news, and the media's collective attention had turned to another woman making charges against Bill Clinton, one who had testified before Ken Starr's grand jury just four days earlier. The insiders all knew her name—Kathleen Willey—but most Americans had never heard of her. That was about to change.

McCurry had labored mightily to contain the Willey story when Mike Isikoff first publicized her allegations the previous summer, and he had largely succeeded. But now Willey had agreed to appear on *60 Minutes*, with its huge nationwide audience, the next day. The Clintonites were worried that this could be the story that turned the tide against the president. Willey was a dignified, well-coiffed, middle-aged widow, not some big-haired floozy whose reputation they could easily trash. Ed Bradley of CBS had already taped the Willey interview in a Richmond, Virginia hotel room. The question now was whether to respond.

It was March 14, 1998, and the meeting quickly grew heated. McCurry, Paul Begala, Charles Ruff, Bob Bennett and a half-dozen other strategists began shouting, even cursing at each other. Some argued that the White House had to produce a spokesman for the show. Others said that was crazy, that *60 Minutes* could not be trusted. The Clintons felt thay had been screwed during their famous 1992 interview about Gennifer Flowers, when the program promised them more than the nine minutes that actually aired and the chance to talk about other issues, not just adultery. At the moment, however, *60 Minutes* had the upper hand.

Bennett had already turned down an invitation to appear on the program. Willey had said in the interview that she felt pressured by Bennett when he suggested that she hire a criminal lawyer. Don Hewitt, the executive producer, quickly called Bennett and asked him to respond. Bennett refused. Hewitt put Ed Bradley on the line. "I'm not stupid," Bennet told him. "I'm not going on *60 Minutes*." There was no way he wanted to get into a televised pissing match over his own conduct.

Now the White House spin doctors concluded that they had to make a spokesman available. Bob Bennett was the logical candidate. Bennett reluctantly agreed, but he was still smarting over the anonymous White House attacks on his handling of the Paula Jones suit. "If anyone dumps on me, I'm coming back here wth an AK-47," he warned.

McCurry called Hewitt and told him Bennett had agreed to be interviewed, but that they would have to give him twelve minutes, live and unedited.

"C'mon, Mike," Hewitt said.

"You mean you're going to go on the air with one side of the story when there were only two people in the room?" McCurry asked.

"Of course I want the other person in the room," Hewitt replied. "I'll make you a deal right now—I'll cancel the Willey story if the president would come on and talk about it."

McCurry dismissed the offer—"Let's be in the real world here," he said—and retreated to his fallback position. Bennett would have to be interviewed "live to tape", meaning that his remarks could not be sliced and diced. "We don't want Bennett edited," he said.

"Then there's no way Bennett will be on *60 Minutes*."

Finally they agreed on a garden-variety interview that evening, at the CBS bureau on M Street in Washington. Bennett was miffed when the time was pushed back to 8:30, for he had made it clear he was tired after an out-of-town trip.

Ushered into a dark room, Bennett was told not to look into the camera but off to the side, as if he were talking to Ed Bradley, who was actually on West 57th Street in New York. The *60 Minutes* staff did not want it to look like a satellite interview. Without even a producer to look at, Bennett's gaze drifted downward, and he didn't seem to believe what he was saying when he denied that Clinton had groped Kathleen Willey. Bennett was furious that no one had told him how bad he looked and given him a chance to tackle some of the questions again. He felt they had deliberately sabotaged him. Hewitt would later claim that Bennett was really looking at his notes, which the attorney said he was merely keeping at his side.

The following evening, twenty-nine million Americans tuned in to watch Willey. She was on the air for twenty-seven minutes, appearing quite credible as she haltingly described how the president had kissed her, grabbed her breast and put her hand on his erect penis. Bennett, who had been questioned for three-quarters of an hour, appeared for just three and a half minutes.

On Monday morning, McCurry told the gaggle that Clinton would be willing to answer a question about Willey during an appearance at a Silver Spring, Maryland high school. During a pause in the proceedings, Bill Plante of CBS asked the question. The president pronounced himself "mystified and disappointed by this turn of events."

But it turned out the White House had been holding its fire. A few days earlier, Clinton had asked James Carville whether they should release nine friendly letters that Willey had written the president after the supposed groping in the Oval Office. In one of them she even called herself his "number one fan." Carville thought it was a good idea. But Clinton had decided to wait. The spin team understood that any conflicting evidence would be lost in the *60 Minutes* publicity build-up. On Monday afternoon, McCurry put out the letters. Bennett, meanwhile, learned that Willey's lawyer had been shopping a possible book deal before the *60 Minutes* appearance. Bennett hammered home the point that night on *Larry King Live*.

Some journalists, having been through such spin cycles before, were openly skeptical of the "organized counterattack," as Carl Cannon put it in the *Baltimore Sun*. "Let's see how long she withstands the Clinton smear machine," wrote *Boston Herald* columnist Margery Eagan. It was, Claire Shipman said on NBC, "a familiar strategy: Deny Kathleen Willey's story and question her credibility." Walter Shapiro of *USA Today* wondered whether Clinton had a "sex addiction."

Tempers flared at the afternoon gaggle. "If someone has committed perjury here, someone ought to be prosecuted for perjury," Sam Donaldson said.

"You're entitled to your opinion, Sam," McCurry said.

Paul Bedard of *The Washington Times* went further, asking if the president "has ever received any behavioral counsel or any medication."

"Paul, with all due respect," McCurry shot back, "you cannot drop the impartiality which a journalist has to have and make assumptions about what is true and not true . . . I don't think it's a fair question."

The reporters were particularly riled by what they saw as Ann Lewis's hypocrisy. The communications director went on *Good Morning America* to declare that Willey's charges were "contradicted by the person I met with who, in 1996, was so positive about the president." But Sam Donaldson was quick to point out that Lewis had been singing a different tune back in 1991, when Anita Hall accused Clarence Thomas of sexual harassment despite having followed him to a new job. "We know what it can be like to work for a boss who insults you, who degrades you and yet to feel you have to go on working, you have to go on being friendly," Lewis said then. Ted Koppel grilled her on *Nightline* about the apparent double standard. Ann Lewis insisted she was not personally attacking Willey, but some of the reporters seemed to be spanking her for her years of robotic spin. The sexual allegations were a polarizing event, and the nerve endings on both sides were rubbed raw.

Despite the journalistic carping, the spin quickly took hold. The administration counterattack dominated the week's headlines. "Willey's Lawyer Sought Book Deal for Her, Motivation of Clinton Accuser Appears More Complex Than in TV Interview," said a front-page *Washington Post* headline. "The portrait of Willey and what may have happened to her seems fuzzier today," Judy Woodruff said on CNN. McCurry denied that White House officials were trying to "undermine" Willey, but that of course was the undeniable effect of the media blitz. Once again, they had managed to turn the focus from Clinton's alleged misconduct to the motivation of his accuser. They had made Kathleen Willey the issue. Clinton's poll numbers remained sky-high. For the second time in a year, they had defused the Willey charges.

Somehow, some way, the media attacks were helping Bill Clinton. From the moment the Monica Lewinsky story broke, much of the public believed that the press was piling on, that the president's privacy was being invaded, that the talk of impeachment was wildly inflated. He now had an enemy to stand tall against, his own modest version of the Evil Empire. True, most voters did not believe Clinton's denials—two-thirds were telling pollsters that he had probably had sex with the young intern and lied about it—but substantial majorities were willing to give him a pass.

The press got carried away by its own spin, by the conviction that the president had gone too far and was barely clinging to his job. The journalistic frustrations that had built up during Whitewater and Travelgate and Filegate and the campaign finance probe now bubbled to the surface, turning the tone of the coverage unusually personal. Many reporters were rushing to judgment, gobbling up leaks from Ken Starr's office, breathlessly reporting each shaky new allegation, making high-profile blunders, and losing touch with voters who were nowhere near as exercised over the sordid situation.

The embarrassing errors by reputable news organizations fueled the feeling that the fourth estate was out of control, a notion that White House was only too happy to encourage. Late on the afternoon of February 4, Glenn Simpson of *The Wall Street Journal* called Joe Lockhart with a new allegation. Simpson said the paper had learned that a White House steward, Bayani Nelvis, had told a grand jury that he saw Clinton and Lewinsky alone in a study off the oval office. Did the White House have any comment? Lockhart said he would have to check. Moments later, Simpson told him that the *Journal* had already rushed the story onto its World Wide Web site.

Alan Murray, the paper's Washington bureau chief, broke the news on CNBC at the same time. Soon afterward, the *Journal* retracted the story.

"The sorriest day of journalism I've ever witnessed," McCurry said. The White House was thrilled every time a new story went down in flames. One side's credibility was going to be shredded in this fiasco, McCurry believed. If it was Clinton, he was gone. If it was the journalists, they would suffer a grievous blow to their already shaky reputation. Each time a new charge evaporated, like the one involving the semen-stained dress, the media looked increasingly reckless. Days later, reporters said the dress had been dry-cleaned before the FBI seized it for testing. For the moment the dress vanished from the news.

That didn't stop the spread of outlandish stories. Matt Drudge reported that Monica Lewinsky had boasted that while she was giving Clinton oral sex in the Oval Office, he was chatting on the phone with Dick Morris, who was likewise being serviced by his prostitute, Sherry Rowlands. Quadrophonic sex, the reporters called it. Whether it was true was a whole other question.

The subtext to the torrent of negative stories was a genuine anger among many of the journalists who once felt that Clinton had so much promise. Gloria Borger of *U.S. News* felt betrayed, even hurt, because Clinton had broken his implicit pledge not to stray while in the White House. Jacob Weisberg of *Slate* was furious on behalf of his New Democrat friends, people like Gene Sperling, Bruce Reed, and Sylvia Matthews, who had devoted their careers to this philanderer. In private conversations, reports would talk about what a disappointing lout the guy turned out to be.

Despite the White House insistence that Clinton remained focused on his job, the truth was that he was feeling bewildered and distracted by the mushrooming scandal. When he held a news conference with British Prime Minister Tony Blair on February 6, the reporters again embarrassed the president with scandal questions in the presence of a foreign leader. Michael Frisby of the *Journal* went so far as to ask: "At what point do you consider that it's just not worth it and do you consider resigning from office?'

"Never . . . I would never walk away from the people of this country and the trust they've placed in me," the president said. In less than three weeks, the Lewinsky story had reduced Bill Clinton to insisting that he would finish out his term.

After a stumbling start on the scandal, *The New York Times* made its presence felt. First Jeff Gerth and Steve Labaton reported that Monica Lewinsky had made thirty-seven visits to the West Wing after being transferred to the Pentagon, although the administration refused to release the WAVES records that would confirm this. Then the duo learned that Clinton's loyal secretary, Betty Currie, had told investigators that the boss had summoned her to the White House the day after his deposition in the Paula Jones suit, walking her through his testimony and appearing to coach her about what she might say before the grand jury. "We were never alone, right?" Clinton said of himself and Lewinsky.

The story seemed to put a prosecutor's spin on the episode; indeed, Gerth and Labaton had met privately with Ken Starr to brief him before publishing their piece. Peter Baker and Susan Schmidt, working late into the night to match the exclusive for *The Washington Post*, delivered a more benign interpretation of Clinton's chat with Currie. They appeared to rely more on White House sources, at one point citing "a source close to Clinton."

As Starr's strong-arm methods came under growing criticism, the White House strategists saw their opening. After a sputtering start, the spin machine was now hitting on all cylinders. They were determined to change the subject from what did or did not happen between Clinton and Lewinsky. They beat up on the press, assailed the accusers, complained about leaks from Starr's side while aggressively leaking themselves. And they often conducted the battle through key surrogates. Harold Ickes, the deputy chief of staff forced out after the first term, increasingly served as a conduit to reporters, taking his information directly from the president, the first lady, McCurry, Paul Begala, Rahm Emanuel and Ann Lewis.

The Clintonites devoted their heaviest artillery to the media offensive against what they saw as a gusher of leaks from the independent counsel's office. Begala appeared on all three network morning shows to decry the leaks. Even the normally reticent David Kendall went before the cameras to accuse Starr of "a deluge of illegal leaks." The following Sunday, Begala pressed Tim Russert on *Meet the Press*, demanding to know whether his network was improperly accepting grand jury leaks from Starr. An hour later, on *Late Edition*, Rahm Emanuel used the same line in turning the tables on Wolf Blitzer. They were ratcheting up the pressure on Starr and his media collaborators. What was once a quirky, one-man campaign by James Carville was now an all-out war waged at the administration's highest levels. And it seemed to be working: Starr's approval ratings dropped as low as 11 percent, down around Saddam Hussein levels.

The next hit came from Sue Schmidt. *The Washington Post* reporter interviewed a former Secret Service agent, Lewis Fox, who said he had seen Monica Lewinsky go into the Oval Office one weekend for forty minutes, and that Clinton had told him to close the door. Left unmentioned was that Fox had told his hometown paper in Pennsylvania that it would have been difficult for the two to have had sex inside because of the office's many windows.

White House officials were livid when the story was published on February 11. Joe Lockhart threw Schmidt's partner, Peter Baker, out of his office the next day. McCurry called the *Posts*'s national editor to complain. McCurry believed there was no way that Clinton could get it on in the Oval, not just because of all the windows but because people like him periodically wandered into the pantry for coffee. This was unfair journalism. Maybe, McCurry mused, he had been wrong to suppress the report that Hilary had ordered up on Sue Schmidt. What really struck him was the palpable excitement among the reporters when they thought that Clinton was going down. To stay energized, he felt, the journalists had to believe that the president was a liar, a crook, and that they were going to nail him. No wonder the White House was constantly on the defensive.

McCurry came up with dozens of ways to duck, looking downright glum at the gaggle when the questioning turned to the sexual allegations:

"I'm not going to speculate on that."

"I'll refer you to my transcript yesterday, which referred to my transcript the day before."

"I'm saying what I just said, and I will repeat it for you if you didn't get it."

McCurry's frustration over the whole Lewinsky mess soon spilled into public view. In an interview with Roger Simon of the *Chicago*

Tribune, he allowed himself to do the one thing he had always scrupulously avoided—speculate about Monica and the Big Guy. "Maybe there'll be a simple, innocent explanation," McCurry said. "I don't think so, because I think we would have offered that up already ... I think it's going to end up being a very complicated story, as most human relationships are."

The remarks touched off a furor. Many journalists believed that McCurry was floating an alternative scenario in which Clinton would admit to some sort of romantic involvement with Lewinsky. The truth was he had just screwed up. There was no trial balloon; he had simply rumbled on in a way that was grossly inappropriate. McCurry felt terrible, and proclaimed himself to be in the White House doghouse. But his colleagues rallied around him. At the moment, the White House needed McCurry more than McCurry needed the job. "I don't think anybody's ever seen anybody better at his job than Mike McCurry," Erskine Bowles told the next day's senior staff meeting.

Everyone involved in the unfolding drama—the press, the prosecutors, the partisans—was spinning so hard that the White House occasionally lapsed into overspinning. Mistakes were inevitable in this fast-paced blur of careening news cycles, and the administration made its share. They were caught up in a kind of nuclear arms race, each side scrambling to keep up with the opposition.

The press office soon spun itself into trouble. On February 22, Joe diGenova, a U.S. attorney in Washington during the Reagan administration, declared on *Meet the Press* that he and his wife, Victoria Toensing, also a former federal prosecutor, were being investigated by private detectives with ties to the Clinton camp. DiGenova offered no proof, simply said that he had been told this by a magazine reporter. Joe Lockhart had to scramble. After checking with the lawyers he put out a statement: "No one at the White House, or anyone acting on behalf of the White House, or any of President Clinton's private attorneys has hired or authorized any private investigator to look into the background of Mr. diGenova, Ms. Toensing, investigators, prosecutors or reporters." It was about as flat a denial as the administration had ever issued.

But Lockhart would soon learn that he hadn't asked the right questions. Reporters discovered that Clinton's lawyers had in fact retained the services of Terry Lenzner, a former Watergate prosecutor turned private eye. The White House denial had been rendered inoperative. Bob Bennett and David Kendall released an updated statement: "There is public information available, which, of course, it is our duty as counsel to research and gather. But we have not investigated, and are not investigating, the personal lives of Ms. Toensing, Mr. diGenova, prosecutors, investigators or members of the press." In other words, they were using detectives to investigate their opponents, but only about their professional records. No amount of spin could hide the fact that they had been caught in an outright lie.

Sue Schmidt called McCurry a couple of days later and said she had reason to believe that a senior Clinton adviser had lied to him about the use of private detectives. "Would you please do me a personal favor?" McCurry asked. "If you're getting ready to write that story, would you please call me and let me know? Because at that point there's a letter that I'm going to have to write."

Starr, meanwhile, was peppering the White House with subpoenas. Bruce Lindsey, Lanny Breuer, Betty Currie and John Podesta were all summoned before the grand jury. And the latest target was Sidney Blumenthal, the former New Yorker writer who had suggested the report on Sue Schmidt and was now the administration's chief proponent of a right-wing conspiracy out to get the Clintons. Blumenthal's colleagues had even nicknamed him G.K., for Grassy Knoll. He often circulated negative information about Starr and his prosecutors to the press. Now Starr struck back by having Blumenthal interrogated before the grand jury about his contacts with journalists. Starr seemed oblivious to the fact that it was hardly a criminal offense, even for a White House official, to criticize the prosecutor's office. Blumenthal read a defiant statement outside the federal courthouse, reveling in his new role as champion of the First Amendment.

Reporters were constantly fishing for secret testimony or sealed documents, and Peter Baker soon hauled in a big catch. The mild-mannered, bespectacled workaholic pieced together a lengthy, highly detailed account of Clinton's five-hour deposition in the Paula Jones case, complete with descriptions of the president's demeanor and tone of voice. The *Post* cited no source for the March 5 front-page story. Baker said that Clinton had denied ever having sexual relations—defied as including any contact with a person's groin, buttocks, breast or inner thigh if intended to arouse—with Kathleen Willey. Or with Shelia Lawrence, the widow of the former ambassador dug up at Arlington National Cemetery. Or with Beth Coulson, an Arkansas judge appointed by Clinton. Or with Dolly Kyle Browning, a one-time Arkansas classmate cited in a follow-up story, who was accusing the president of "sexual addiction." But Clinton acknowledged only a one-time encounter with Gennifer Flowers.

The Baker piece touched off an intense guessing game over who had leaked the goods. The president told reporters at the White House that the leak was "illegal" and that "I have nothing else to say. I'm going to do my job. I'm going to follow the law." The consensus in Washington was that the leak had to have come from the Clinton side, in an effort to cushion the impact, because the following week Paula Jones's lawyers were slated to reveal portions of the deposition in a legal motion. But no one knew for sure. Bob Bennett stopped talking to Baker because, he said, many people thought he had provided the deposition.

The Jones suit was rapidly turning into an open cesspool into which any piece of garbage could be dumped. In the middle of March, Jones's attorneys disgorged 700 pages of documents filled with lurid allegations and innuendo about all the president's women. Reporters got to feast on these sleazy charges because they were deemed "evidence" in an ongoing lawsuit against Clinton, even if some of the evidence was awfully thin. The Jones document dump led all the networks and the major papers.

The lawsuit remained strewn with land mines, and Bob Bennett soon stepped on one—the same one he had detonated on television the previous summer. Jones's lawyers leaked to Peter Baker a sealed letter that Bennett had sent to the court that very day, saying he planned to file "sensitive information of a sexual nature about Paula Jones" to rebut her claim that Clinton's conduct had caused her to suffer an aversion to sex. Baker's story—"Jones's Past Private Life Is Targeted"—led the first edition of *The Washington Post*.

But the ink was barely dry on the story when Bennett went into spin overdrive. A *New York Times* reporter, David Stout, called before midnight in an effort to match the *Post* piece, and the attorney quickly distanced himself from his own letter. "Unfortunately, *The Washington Post* jumped the gun on the story by relying on an interpretation from the plaintiff's side of a letter that should not have been leaked to the *Post*," Bennett declared. The result was a polar-opposite headline in the next morning's *Times*: "Clinton Lawyer Says He'll Avoid Issues of Paula Jones's Sex Life." Bennett had set a new indoor record, switching spin between editions.

The press had plenty to feast upon, for women were really coming out of the woodwork now. Christy Zercher, a flight attendant on Clinton's 1992 campaign plane, surfaced to sell her story to the *Star*. "Bill Clinton Assaulted Me Right Under Hillary's Nose," the headline said, with Zercher claiming that the candidate had stroked her breast for forty minutes while his wife napped nearby. Mike Isikoff had interviewed Zercher back in 1994, but, at the time, with no cash involved, she had said that Clinton did nothing offensive. The New York tabloids had a field day, but most of the press ignored the charge, and Zercher later flunked a lie-detector test. Still, journalists continued to be mystified at Clinton's seemingly impenetrable armor. 'How much more of this can Bill Clinton take?" wondered *The Wall Street Journal*.

One table that was not so easy to ignore was that of Elizabeth Ward Gracen, the former Miss America who had denied during the 1992 campaign that she'd had a sexual relationship with Clinton. Fighting a subpoena from Jones's lawyers, Gracen was troubled by reports that she had somehow been assaulted by Clinton. She told the *New York Daily News* that she had in fact had a one-night stand with Clinton while he was governor, but as a willing participant. She had lied about the episode six years earlier at the campaign's request. *The Washington Times* splashed the story on the front page, but most of the press gave it a few paragraphs. It was remarkable: a former beauty queen who had posed for Playboy admitting that she had slept with the president of the United States—and yet, since it was described as consensual, the media greeted the acknowledgement with a yawn. There had been so many women making so many charges against Bill Clinton that somehow the bar had been raised. The novelty had simply worn off. Only Monica Lewinsky still seemed to fascinate the media, a tangle of cameras following her as she went out to dinner or chatted at a party with the likes of William Safire and Larry King.

On March 28, the Jones' attorneys tossed one more salacious charge into the legal cauldron. In a court filing, they said that Clinton had met a woman at a conference when he was Arkansas attorney general in the late 1970s, invited her to a hotel room, and raped her. The woman had denied it in a sealed affidavit, and the lawyers were citing an unsworn account by an acquaintance. Despite a bit of hand-wringing, many news organizations recycled the twenty-year-old charge, one that they would never have touched outside the context of a politically explosive lawsuit. Some news outlets, like *The New York Times*, dismissed the allegation in a few paragraphs deep inside the paper. Others, like *The Washington Post*, mentioned it on the front page. Despite their general policy of not identifying alleged rape victims, *The Washington Times*, the *New York Post* and NBC all named the women said to be involved in the incident. White House officials were aghast. To them, the lawsuit had become nothing more than a vehicle to blacken the president's reputation, with the media's eager assistance.

By now Clinton was off on an eleven-day swing across Africa. He seemed to be in an ebullient mood. On Air Force One, the president and his wife came back into the press cabin to sing to Wolf Blitzer on his fiftieth birthday, and Clinton presented him with a couple of bottles of wine. Walter Isaacson, *Time*'s managing editor, was on the trip, and the White House decided to grant him an exclusive interview with the president, in part to stick it to *Newsweek* for its relentless coverage of Jones and Lewinsky. McCurry taunted Karen Breslau, *Newsweek*'s White House correspondent, within earshot of several correspondents on the plane. "You're fucked," he announced. He added a message for Breslau's bosses: "You've made your bed, now you have to lie in it."

McCurry was becoming increasingly testy on the trip. At one dinner with reporters, he began lecturing them about hypocrisy. They insisted on shielding their sources, but refused to allow that protecting the privacy of presidential conversations might be a legitimate concern. At another dinner, McCurry was particularly steamed about the network coverage of an event in Ghana, when the massive crowd had surged forward and the cameras showed a red-faced Clinton yelling, "Get back!" They had failed to make clear that Clinton was worried about those in the sweltering crowd being trampled, McCurry felt. Still, the African tour had provided some great pictures and had insulated the president from the latest charges in the Jones case. A flashy foreign trip had once again helped the Clintonites change the subject.

The news arrived like a bolt out of the blue. On the afternoon of April 1, Bob Bennett called the presidential party in Senegal and left a message with Bruce Lindsey. Clinton, who was finishing up an interview with Sam Donaldson about the school shootings by two teenage boys in Jonesboro, Arkansas, soon called back. Bennett gave him the word: Susan Weber Wright, the federal judge in Little Rock, had thrown out the Paula Jones case.

At first Clinton thought it must be an April Fool's joke. He got on the phone to Chuck Ruff. John Podesta, Paul Begala and Rahm Emanuel were in Ruff's office, listening in. This was unbelievable news, more than any of them had dared hope for. Even if Clinton had exposed himself to Jones, the judge ruled, there was no evidence that the Arkansas clerk had suffered discrimination as a result. The Little Rock trial, which more than 700 journalists had signed up to attend the following month, was now off. The circus had closed down. The White House had won.

Wolf Blitzer broke into live programming. "President Clinton and his entire entourage here in Senegal are obviously thrilled by this news," he said.

Clinton rushed to tell Hillary about the ruling. Back in his hotel suite, he chomped on a cigar, strummed a guitar and beat a bongo drum that his hosts had left on a table. At an impromptu briefing, a stone-faced McCurry was careful not to appear jubilant. "I think the president is pleased to receive the vindication he's been waiting a long time for," McCurry said. The reporters wanted more, but that was as far as he would go. There was no need to spin such a clear-cut victory.

As the magnitude of the ruling sunk in, McCurry and Begala and Emanuel found themselves angry. The case had consumed four years of their lives, had dragged the president through the mud, had been hyped by the press, all over a claim so weak it couldn't even get to trial. Nobody felt like celebrating.

That became clear when McCurry, Lockhart and Sosnik had dinner with a group of reporters that night. McCurry told the group—which included Maureen Dowd, Karen Breslau, Walter Isaacson and Karen Tumulty—that they and their colleagues had far too much invested in the Paula Jones saga and now would have to cope as it was suddenly snatched away.

But the press loved clear-cut wins and losses and, for the moment, was giving Clinton a rare boost. It was "a stunning legal victory," the *Baltimore Sun* said. "A major legal victory," said the *Los Angeles Times*. "A huge victory for the president," Tim Russert declared. "A monumental development," said Geraldo Rivera. A victory that "dramatically reshapes in Clinton's favor the political landscape," *Newsday* said. The *Philadelphia Daily News* said that Clinton had been "spared an O.J.-type carnival in Little Rock. No media mob filling airways with heavy-panting tales of oral sex."

Despite Paula Jones's tearful announcement of an appeal, the dismissal transformed the media climate, at least briefly. The *New York Times* said that impeachment proceedings would now be "politically inconceivable." The *Los Angeles Times* said that Clinton was "riding a wave of euphoria from his most dramatic comeback yet."

As reporters fanned out to take the public temperature, they learned that readers and viewers were even more relieved. John Pruitt, a Chicago shoe salesman, told *The Washington Post* "Does this mean I never, ever have to hear Paula Jones's name again? Yesss."

Not everyone in the press was so upbeat. Many reporters insisted that Ken Starr's investigative juggernaut would roll on, even though the perjury charges involved a lawsuit that had now been dismissed. Maureen Dowd, who had made the Africa trip, seemed downright grumpy. "I don't want to hear Michael McCurry bark at any more reporters, and offer defenses of things he knows nothing about," she wrote. "I can't listen to any more bluster from Rahm Emanuel and Paula Begala, who are beginning to have the glazed look of the children in *Village of the Damned*."

The sudden denouement left a black hole in the media universe, largely relegating the scandal watch to cable programs like *Rivera Live* and *Hardball* and *The Big Show* that feasted on the Lewinsky saga night after night. The legal machinery kept grinding on, but the reverberations barely moved the needle on the media's Richter scale.

For the spin team, the void presented a rare opportunity, for the first time in more than three months, to trump the scandals and turn the spotlight back on the president's agenda. The strategists laid out a week's worth of events to highlight familiar Clintonian themes. On Monday, it was crime; a White House leak of the president's plan to permanently ban imported assault weapons made the front page of *USA Today*, *The New York Times*, the *Los Angeles Times* and *The Washington Times*. On Tuesday, it was a town meeting on Social Security. On Wednesday, education standards. On Thursday, tobacco. On Friday, school safety.

But it was quickly apparent that something had been lost. The president's 1998 agenda had all but faded from the radar screen. Another public discussion on race relations went nowhere. The Social Security session served up more questions than answers. The tobacco deal all but collapsed as the cigarette industry withdrew its support. No one was talking about the Clinton proposals on education or child care. The president struggled to regain the initiative, but it was as if his strenuous scandal had consumed all the available media oxygen.

Still, the economy was on cruise control and most people were enjoying the ride. The federal budget, drenched in red ink for three decades, was running an incredible $39-billion surplus. The Dow surged past 9000. Unemployment dropped again to 4.3 percent. Many Americans may not have trusted Bill Clinton, but they were, for the moment, satisfied with his policies.

The crisis atmosphere lightened and the president's team started to relax. Paul Begala and Joe Lockhart blew off a damage-control meeting in favor of a Washington Capitals hockey game. Mike McCurry disappeared on vacation. Even Monica Lewinsky seemed to miss the limelight, posing on the beach in a black cocktail dress for a *Vanity Fair* photo shoot. Paula Jones, apparently suffering from publicity withdrawal, showed up at the White House Correspondents Dinner, where Clinton was the guest of honor. She was escorted by Paul Rodriguez, the *Insight* magazine editor who had leveled the false charges about selling Arlington gravesites.

The White House team found a few journalistic allies as well. They began praising the work of *Salon*, a left-leaning online magazine that had begun a drumbeat of criticism against Ken Starr. *Salon* reported allegations that Richard Mellon Scaife, a right-wing publisher and certified Clinton-hater, had funneled money through the *American Spectator* to David Hale, the convicted Arkansas ex-judge who was Clinton's chief accuser in the Whitewater case. The Clintonites began touting such *Salon* pieces to reporters, sometimes even before they were posted on the World Wide Web. Jonathan Broder, *Salon*'s Washington bureau chief, was an old friend of Sid Blumenthal, who invited Broder and three of his editors to a White House party. Clinton and his wife both stopped by to chat, and the president told Broder that he thought the charge of payoffs to Hale was "significant." At long last, the Clinton crowd felt that somebody was scrutinizing the other side.

Starr, for his part, was stepping up his efforts on the scandal that had been all but overshadowed by Lewinsky. "Whitewater prosecutors have written at least one draft indictment of Hillary Rodham Clinton but they remain divided over whether to charge the first lady," *The Washington Times* reported. Within days, Ken Starr was interviewing Hillary Clinton at the White House for five hours.

Clinton's aides had been debating for weeks whether he should hold his first solo news conference of 1998 rather than continue to hide from the press. In the wake of the Paula Jones victory, they saw a brief window of opportunity and scheduled a session in the East Room for April 30. They were miffed when word leaked that a federal judge had denied Monica Lewinsky's motion that Starr stick to his original offer of immunity from prosecution. That would complicate the Lewinsky case—she now faced possible indictment if she refused to cooperate—and, they feared, would make the scandal an even more central focus of the news conference.

They were right. From Helen Thomas's opening query about Lewinsky, half the questions focused on the various scandals that were buffeting the White House. And the reporters seemed to be voicing their exasperation, their sense of outrage.

Sam Donaldson asked: "Does it matter what you do in private

moments as alleged? And particularly does it matter if you have committed perjury or in other sense broken the law?"

Wolf Blitzer followed up: "I have to beat a dead horse . . ."

"No you don't," Clinton said.

"Why assert privilege if there's nothing to hide?" Blitzer asked.

Peter Maer of Mutual Radio said: "What effect do you think this whole wave of controversies has had on your moral authority?"

Scott Pelley of CBS ticked off a series of questions about Monica Lewinsky that Clinton had failed to answer: "Sir, could you now give us some better sense of what appears to be an extraordinary relationship that you had with this woman?"

James Bennet cited polls in which a majority of Americans "say that they no longer respect you as a person. I wonder if you find that distressing and how you account for it."

The president ducked and dodged as best he could. "I have answered it repeatedly and have nothing to add to my former answer." "I can't comment on those matters because they are under seal." "I do not think the right thing for me to do is to respond in kind." "I just don't have anything else to say." Indeed, the man who had once promised to provide "more rather than less, sooner rather than later" in the Lewinsky matter made clear that he was willing to live under this cloud for the rest of his term rather than simply come clean.

Within two hours. Ken Starr managed to overshadow the news conference. Starr's Washington grand jury indicted Webb Hubbell, his wife Suzanna, and two longtime associates on tax fraud charges—the sort of charges that normally would be dealt with in a civil suit and clearly were meant to pressure Hubbell into cooperating with the Whitewater probe. The *CBS Evening News* and *NBC Nightly News* led off with Hubbell, not Clinton.

Hubbell was also the latest target of Dan Burton, the Indiana congressman who had taken over the campaign finance investigation. That probe now seemed a distant memory. Still, the White House was fortunate to have the intemperate Burton, who'd once tried to reenact the death of Vince Foster by shooting at a watermelon in his backyard, as its adversary. In an interview with his hometown paper, the *Indianapolis Star*, Burton called Clinton a "scumbag" and said that was why he was "after him"—hardly the image of a dispassionate fact-gatherer.

When the Hubbell indictment was announced, Burton began releasing excerpts of the disgraced official's phone conversations that were recorded while he was in prison. Burton's chief investigator, David Bossie, had spent two weeks allowing reporters for *Nightline*, NBC, *The New York Times*, *The Washington Post* and *USA Today* to pore over the transcripts and listen to the tapes. Some of the phone conversations sounded pretty damaging to hush-money theorists— Hubbell saying he did not want to raise allegations that would "open it up to Hillary" and that he would have to "roll over one more time." But Burton had given the White House spin team an irresistible target. His staff had selectively edited the transcripts, excising more positive comments in which Hubbell had said the first lady had no knowledge of any wrongdoing and that no one was buying his silence.

The White House mounted a two-pronged attack. Rahm Emanuel, on *Late Edition* with Wolf Blitzer, declared that Burton was guilty of "altering and doctoring" the tapes. Lanny Davis, who was constantly appearing on television now that he had left the White House payroll, went on *This Week* and accused Starr of "an act of desperation" and "misconduct" for indicting Hubbell. The news organizations that had breathlessly reported the Hubbell tapes now turned on Dan Burton, who had to fire David Bossie, a longtime source for many of the investigative reporters.

But the spinners made little headway when Starr shut down his Little Rock grand jury. There were no charges against the first lady, despite all the speculation in the press. In fact, the jurors had indicted exactly one person, Susan McDougal, who had spent the previous eighteen months in prison for refusing to testify in the Whitewater case. The Clintonites couldn't believe there were so few stories about the effective end of the Arkansas investigation, which had drawn so much noisy coverage back in 1994 and 1995. James Carville began calling reporters, ranting about how Starr had come up empty after four years and $40 million. None of the media conspiracies had been proven, he barked. No one had won a Pulitzer prize for this crap. Journalists were quick to note that Starr still had a Washington grand jury that could hear evidence, related to Whitewater, although it was mainly devoted to the Lewinsky case. But Clinton and his loyalists felt that the reporters just kept moving the goalposts: When one scandal didn't bear fruit, they would brush it off and move on to the next tantalizing set of allegations.

Indeed, there were always new dribs and drabs about Monica Lewinsky. The Drudge Report charged that Lewinsky had said on the tapes recorded by Linda Tripp that when she went to see the president, Betty Currie was often used as a cover, even when Currie wasn't there. Sam Donaldson raised the issue at the gaggle.

"You should know that Drudge is reporting that she's been questioned about times when her name appears as having had Monica Lewinsky come in and in fact, she, Betty Currie, was on vacation," Donaldson said.

"Sam," McCurry shot back, "if ABC wants to rely on Matt Drudge as a source of news, that's your choice."

The reporters were frantically trying to track a backstage battle between Clinton and Starr over executive privilege. Rumors had first surfaced in March that the White House had quietly invoked executive privilege to shield the grand jury testimony of Sid Blumenthal and Bruce Lindsey. Administration officials fully understand that a public debate over the Nixon-era tactic would make them look like they were in a cover-up mode. They refused to comment in the executive privilege motion, but *The New York Times* managed to confirm it anyway. The night that the *Times* story was gone to press, Peter Baker was trying to get McCurry to help him on the story. Instead, McCurry taunted him about the *Times*.

"I guess they just have better sources," McCurry said. Baker was upset at McCurry's sneering tone and suggested they have a beer sometime to clear the air. McCurry said he had no interest in that.

Days later, when Bruce Lindsey was emerging for a grand jury appearance, Sue Schmidt rushed up to him. "We're running a story saying you invoked executive privilege," she said.

"How do you know that?" Lindsey snapped. "What's your proof?" The administration was determined to keep the privilege claim cloaked in secrecy.

Now, on May 5, the curtain was lifted. The White House had never even confirmed its filing on executive privilege, but word leaked that a federal judge had rejected the privilege claim. Fox News initially reported that Ken Starr's office had put out the news, then realized its mistake and switched to a suitably vague attribution. The administration notified reporters late in the day that David Kendall would seek contempt charges against Starr's office for leaking the decision. Starr, who had recently hired his own media adviser, a former Reagan White House aide, was becoming more sensitive to the daily public relations warfare. His deputy fired off a letter to Bob Bennett, accusing Kendall of "denying us the opportunity to defend ourselves within the evening news cycle."

Clinton's political advisers were acutely aware of the Watergate parallel, but they had been shut out of the process by the lawyers. Kendall, who was consulting with Charles Ruff, Lanny Breuer and Cheryl Mills, was calling the shots. Paul Begala was incensed that Starr's office seemed to be leaking on the executive privilege battle, which was under court seal, while the administration had to remain mum. They were playing by Marquess of Queensbury rules, he liked to say, and the other side was acting like Marquis de Sade. Begala and Emanuel and Sosnik hadn't even been allowed to see the legal papers. Lanny Davis urged the White House to defuse the controversy by not appealing the judge's ruling, but he was rebuffed.

When Clinton met the press with Italian Prime Minister Romano Prodi, Terry Hunt of the AP asked why he had invoked the very same privilege that Richard Nixon used to try to withhold the Watergate tapes. Clinton insisted the two cases were different. But the media fallout was swift. Cartoonists depicted Clinton with a five o'clock shadow, both arms raised in the V-for-Victory salute. The front page of *USA Today*, the administrator's favorite newspaper, carried a haunting headline; "Clinton: I Am Not Nixon."

Mike McCurry usually kept his feelings in check, but every so often he vented his frustrations. At a breakfast with thirty *Los Angeles Times* reporters, he ripped the press for having made up its mind about Clinton and Lewinsky. "Everybody here—be honest about it—there is not a person in this room who still has any presumption of innocence with respect to the president," McCurry said. There was "an overwhelming amount of discussion, coverage, analysis, speculation that starts with the premise that the president lied." The press, he felt, was just plain biased against his boss. What would happen, McCurry wondered, if it turned out that Clinton was telling the truth?

Whatever the journalistic mindset, the country was on another wavelength. When Johnny Chung, the Chinese "hustler" who had visited the White House forty-nine times, pleaded guilty to fraud, it had barely caused a murmur. But Jeff Gerth soon raised the stakes dramatically. On May 15, he reported in *The New York Times* that Chung had told investigators nearly $100,000 of the funds he had funneled to the Democrats came from a Chinese military officer— the first long-sought evidence linking the Beijing government to illegal campaign contributions. But the news was overshadowed by the death of Frank Sinatra. *NBC Nightly News* gave the Chung revelation two sentences after devoting most of the program to Sinatra.

Gerth kept the pressure on. He reported that the president had made a hotly contested decision to provide sensitive technology to the Chinese to launch an American satellite made by Loral Space and Communications - a company whose chairman, Bernard Schwartz, was the largest individual Democratic donor in 1996 and had given the party more than $1 million in recent years. Now the Republicans had an irresistible issue, one that seemed to link campaign finance abuses and national security. Both the House and the Senate immediately launched investigations into why Clinton had relaxed the export controls on technology. Newt Gingrich went so far as to suggest that the president may have committed treason. The media had a sizzling new scandal, one that enabled them to pursue the president without the seamy details of the Monica Lewinsky story.

The spin team made a calculated decision to offer a muted response rather than denouncing the allegations as illegitimate. McCurry dismissed the congressional criticism as "politics as usual," but the information, after all, had suffered from the Clinton Justice Department. After days of meetings, the administration's strategists came up with a detailed plan. Clinton granted an interview to *USAToday*, telling Susan Page and Bill Nichols that he was merely following the lead of Ronald Reagan and George Bush in allowing, Chinese rockets to launch American satellites. "This has been a policy that's ten years old now," Clinton said.

Hours later, the White House employed the technique that had worked so well for so long, an old-fashioned document dump. The timing was perfect—the Friday afternoon before Memorial Day weekend—for minimizing public attention, Jim Kennedy, who had assumed Lanny Davis's old job, arranged for reporters to examine 394 pages of material related to the China decision, but admitted the journalists in small groups and, at Ruff's direction, refused to allow them to make copies. Administration officials, meanwhile, briefed the press on background. The documents contained no smoking gun: The State Department had recommended the technology transfer to China, but the Justice Department had expressed concern that it could damage an ongoing criminal investigation of Loral. Lanny Davis made the television rounds, noting that Loral had contributed to the Republicans as well. After months of stonewalling on Lewinsky, the White House was again using carefully timed disclosure in an effort to defuse dangerous charges.

But nothing could disguise the fact that the president's second term was wobbling under the weight of so many accumulated controversies. As the summer of 1998 unfolded, Clinton's woes seemed to be mounting week by week. On one front, he was consumed by nuclear-weapons testing in India and Pakistan and by the rioting in Indonesia that toppled President Suharto. On another, he was embarrassed when most Democratic lawmakers joined the Republicans in barring further satellite ventures with China just weeks before the president was to visit Beijing. On still another, he was crestfallen that a judge had rejected his bid to block Starr from taking the testimony of Secret Service agents in the Lewinsky matter, and belatedly dropped his appeal on executive privilege. The independent counsel also took fingerprints and handwriting samples from Monica Lewinsky and edged closer to presenting Congress with what promised to be a scathing report on Clinton's impeachable offenses. Lewinsky dumped her loquacious lawyer, William Ginsburg, and hired two Washington veterans, Plato Cacheris and Jacob Stein, who immediately began exploring a deal with Starr.

As if to underscore the danger to the president, Peter Baker and Sue Schmidt reported on June 21 that Lewinsky's new legal team had offered to have her testify that she had had sex with Clinton in exchange for immunity from prosecution. In a hint of things to come, *U.S. News* said that its reporter had had access to the Lewinsky tapes and that the former intern had told of writing Clinton, "I want you in my life," but also told Linda Tripp that she was angry at

Clinton and wanted to "kick him in the balls." Some reporters harbored similar sentiments. Deborah Orin said that it was time for Clinton "to step forward and 'fess up that, oops, he did have sex with 'that woman' after all—and he's *soooo* sorry." By now it was clear that the president would be battling the press and the prosecutors for the rest of his tenure.

But he would have to do it without Mike McCurry. On the afternoon of July 23, 1988, Clinton walked into the briefing room to announce that his press secretary of nearly four years was quitting in the fall and that Joe Lockhart would replace him. McCurry had told the president he was ready to move on—he planned to do corporate consulting, teaching and lucrative lecturing—in a letter just after Memorial Day. After five and a half years of daily briefings, beginning at the State Department, he was tired of trying to explain complicated policies to reporters who demanded simple answers. He was sick of snarly opinion-meisters slicing up the boss. He'd had his fill of being assailed by conservative critics for being slippery with the truth. He had obviously picked a lousy time to try to repair relations between the Big Guy and the press, but at least he had kept the climate from turning even more poisonous.

McCurry felt he had done the right thing—for himself, above all, but also for the presidency and for Clinton personally—by refusing to engage the press on the Monica Lewinsky story. He didn't want to intrude on the confidential relationship between Clinton and his lawyers, and as much as reporters hated the idea, he believed the charges should be investigated in secret. He knew that the journalists had come to view him as part of the coverup, but that was a price he was willing to pay. Now that he had helped convince Clinton to appoint his old pal Joe, the press office would be in good hands. Lockhart, for his part, was slightly daunted by the challenge ahead. The one-time television producer and former campaign spokesman knew he had plenty to learn and would have to curb his partisan tongue at the podium. But Lockhart had been the designated scandal flack for six months now, and he knew what to expect. He was ready to be the public face of the spin machine.

No one on the Clinton team was under any illusion about what they were facing. The media had now turned the scandal watch into a rock-solid fixture of daily journalism. Just as Ken Starr had moved from examining an Arkansas land deal to the president's sexual behavior, reporters slid seamlessly from Whitewater to Chinese rockets, from Monica Lewinsky to Johnny Chung to whatever other allegation was bubbling up from the primordial ooze of Washington politics. Nightly cable shows used their "White House in Crisis" or "Investigating the President" logos to chase a dizzying array of charges, from sex to bribery to treason. Bill Clinton's second term became a full employment act for journalists.

And still the White House spin machine clanked on. By denouncing Starr's leaks, invoking judicial privilege, beating up on the Republicans and whining about press coverage, the Clintonites hoped to deflect public attention in a dozen directions until most people threw up their hands in boredom.

But the investigative noose was suddenly tightening. On July 24, White House aides leaked word that Clinton was negotiating to provide testimony to Starr—and it quickly emerged that the president had already been subpoenaed. Three days later, the Starr team let it be known that Monica Lewinsky had spent five hours talking to prosecutors. The following morning Lewinsky struck a deal for full immunity in exchange for her testimony—including her acknowledgment that she and Clinton had had a sexual relationship and discussed cover stories to keep it secret. The next day Clinton finally agreed to a videotaped deposition in August.

Once again the press was vacuuming up leaks. Once again the networks were running the tape of Clinton saying he had never had sex with *that woman*. Even the semen-stained dress was back; Lewinsky had hidden it at her mother's house, and the FBI quickly began testing it for signs of presidential DNA.

At the gaggle, Sam Donaldson warned McCurry that Lewinsky's testimony could "sink" the president.

"That's sheer speculation on your part, Sam," McCurry shot back. Lanny Davis declared on television that Lewinsky was contradicting her earlier sworn denial of a sexual affair, the first public hint of White House whispers that Lewinsky was young and untrustworthy. One White House adviser offered this sad assessment of public sentiment toward the boss: "We don't believe him but we don't want him impeached."

This, in the end, was the problem with the White House strategy of deflection and delay. Eventually there comes a point when even the president of the United States cannot hide behind his spokesmen. Eventually the questions of the scandal-seeking reporters have to be answered. The spin, the brilliant, lightning-quick spin, could not put off the day of reckoning forever. Bill Clinton's conduct may not have qualified as high crimes and misdemeanors, but he had brought his presidency low and, in the unseemly swirl of tabloid headlines, much of the country with it.

Sources

ALL CONVERSATIONS RECOUNTED IN THIS BOOK ARE BASED ON THE author's interviews with one or more of the participants, except where otherwise noted here. A wide range of people in the White House and the press agreed to cooperate with this effort on condition that they not be directly quoted by name. The characterizations and views described in this book are, in most cases, the author's attempt to convey the attitudes of those involved in the daily spin cycle.

1. The Gaggle

3 "refused to intervene": Peter Baker and Saundra Torry, *The Washington Post*, June 17, 1997

3 "a top Clinton administration official": Barry Meier, *The New York Times*, June 17, 1997

7 "Not since Lyndon Johnson . . .": Michael K. Frisby, *The Wall Street Journal*, June 13, 1997.

7 "I could feel the wool . . .": Courtland Milloy, *The Washington Post*, June 18, 1997

7 "therapeutic exercises": *The New Republic*, June 30, 1997

7 "hand holding as policy": Kenneth T. Walsh, *U.S.News & World Report*, June 23, 1997.

2. *The Master of Spin*

20 "getting news and shaping news . . .": Lloyd Grove, *The Washington Post*, July 19, 1988

20 "the pander of candor": Jim Naughton, *The Washington Post*, Jan. 11, 1988

26 "the salesman with the best understanding . . .": Jonathan Alter, *Newsweek*, Dec. 30, 1996

27 "If you're President Clinton . . .": Gerald F. Seib, *The Wall Street Journal* , Dec. 18, 1996

28 "See, this is what happens . . .": John Aloysius Farrell, *The Boston Globe Magazine*, Apr. 7, 1996

28 "a talkative and opinionated fellow . . .": John F. Harris, *The Washington Post*, Mar. 16, 1996

30 McCurry said ABC had "damaged": Fred Barnes, *The Weekly Standard*, July 22, 1996

3. *In the Dungeon*

33 "Is this where you have to work?": John Tebbel and Sarah Miles Watts, *The Press and The Presidency*, Oxford University Press, 1985. (Several other historical examples were drawn from this invaluable work.)

45 "Well, it's important . . .": Fred Barnes, *The Weekly Standard*, Dec. 30, 1996

46 would grumble about the "bratty" attitude: Ken Auletta, *The New Yorker*, Nov.18, 1996

48 "a congenital liar": William Safire, *The New York Times*, Jan. 8, 1996

48 "What do you think of Whitewater now?": John Aloysius Farrell, *The Boston Globe Magazine*, Apr. 7, 1996

4. First Blood

54 The *Times* was in "a lather": Margaret Carlson, *Time*, Dec. 16, 1996

57 "wild, undocumented charges": Milton Coleman, *The Washington Post*, Sept. 24, 1976

59 "We will review this document . . .": Tim Weiner and David E. Sanger, *The New York Times*, Dec.28, 1996

61 "It is becoming increasingly evident . . .": Glenn F. Bunting and Alan C. Miller, *Los Angeles Times*, Dec. 30, 1996

62 "A network of Democratic fundraisers . . .": Ruth Marcus, *The Washington Post*, Dec. 29, 1996

62 "the press secretary assigned to defend": *The New York Times*, Nov. 20, 1997

63 "Buddhist Cult Contributes Half Mil . . .": Glenn F. Bunting, *Los Angeles Times*, Sept. 2, 1997

68 "DNC Fundraiser Gained . . .": Michael Weisskof and Lena H. Sun, *The Washington Post*, Dec. 20, 1996

5. The Seeds of Paranoia

72 "There is a weariness . . .": Robin Toner, *The New York Times*, May 28, 1992

74 "I don't know why we talk to reporters. . . . Here we are half- way . . .": Kenneth Walsh, *Feeding the Beast*, Random House, 1996

74 "knee-jerk liberal press": Jann S. Wenner and William Greider, *Rolling Stone*, Dec. 9, 1993

75 "The press runs the government": Dick Morris, *Behind the Oval Office*, Random House, 1997

79 "I want to travel around . . .": Eric Pooley, *Time*, Dec. 2, 1996

83 "The meaning of the politics of meaning . . .": Michael Kelly, *The New York Times Magazine*, May 23, 1993

84 "The bunker mentality . . .": Albert Hunt, *The Wall Street Journal*, Mar. 3, 1994

84 "On issue after issue . . .": Michael Barone, *U.S. News & World Report*, Mar. 7, 1994

85 "If somebody has a female boss . . .": Hilary Stout, *The Wall Street Journal*, Sept. 30, 1994

6. The Laundromat

95 The president was "furious": John F. Harris, *The Washington Post*, Jan. 10, 1997

98 "Watkins talks candidly . . .": Ambrose Evans-Prichard, *The Washington Times*, Dec. 16, 1996

102 "In recent conversations with aides": John F. Harris, *The Washington Post*, Jan. 5, 1997

102 "A lot of his work goes. . .": Alison Mitchell, *The New York Times*, Jan.19, 1997

102 "He's got to use the bully pulpit": Gerald F. Seib and Hilary Stout, *The Wall Street Journal*, Jan.20, 1997

103 "help flush the poison . . .": John F. Harris and Peter Baker, *The Washington Post*, Jan. 19, 1997

103 no "long-term advantage to either party": *U.S. News & World Report*, Jan. 27, 1997

7. Breaking Through the Static

113 "No vetting was ever done": Stephen Labaton, *The New York Times*, Feb. 2, 1997

116 gave Clinton a "heads-up": Michael Kranish, *The Boston Globe*, Jan. 16, 1997

117 "gets an Oscar": *The Washington Post*, Jan.17, 1997

118 "Apparently I made a mistaken assumption . . .": John Solomon, Associated Press, Jan. 22, 1997

118 "a little used": *The Washington Post*, Jan. 23, 1997

119 "it can be death": Deborah Orin, *New York Post*, Jan. 30, 1997

119 'There is nothing I take more seriously . . .": Paul Bedard, *The Washington Times*, Feb. 5, 1997

119 "the target of harsh editorial criticism . . .": Reuters, Jan. 23, 1997

120 "the growing White House credibility gap": Paul Bedard, *The Washington Times*, Feb. 5, 1997

129 "that Clinton's popularity has soared": Ann Scales, *The Boston Globe*, Feb. 10, 1997

8. *Hezbollah*

133 "There's joy in Mudville": Susan Schmidt, *The Washington Post*, Feb. 18, 1997

142 "looking like a greedy fool": Jonathan Alter, *Newsweek*, Mar.10, 1997

142 "Not since Richard Nixon's . . .": Richard Cohen, *The Washington Post*, Feb. 18, 1997

142 "projecting an image that his aides believe . . .": James Bennet, *The New York Times*, Mar. 1, 1997

143 "The White House moves to bring in . . .": *The Wall Street Journal*, Feb. 28, 1997

147 "a shocking liar": Michael Kelly, *The New Republic*, Dec. 2, 1996

9. *Mister Clean*

156 dubbed Gore the campaign's "solicitor-in-chief": Bob Woodward, *The Washington Post*, Mar. 2, 1997

156 the scandal "threatens to undermine": Alison Mitchell, *The New York Times*, Mar. 3, 1997

159 "The supposedly brainy veep . . .": Deborah Orin, *New York Post*, Mar. 4, 1997

162 "There was nothing noteworthy . . .": Peter Baker and Sharon LaFraniere, *The Washington Post*, Mar. 6, 1997

164 "The Truth Is Inoperative": *The New York Times*, Mar. 7, 1997

164 "presidential parrot": Charles Krauthammer, *The Washington Post*, Mar. 7, 1997

10. *Dribs and Drabs*

182 "The White House repeatedly fudged . . .": *USA Today*, Apr. 10, 1997

182 "When the bubble bursts . . .": Ron Fournier, Associated Press, Apr. 7, 1997

182 "until it is shot down . . .": *The Washington Post*, Apr. 3, 1997

183 "had worked together to pay hush money . . .": Michael Kelly, *The New Republic*, Apr. 7, 1997

11 Purely Personal

190 "the counsel's office and . . .": Susan Page, *USA Today*, Apr. 8, 1997

195 "magnificently deflective . . .": *The Washington Post*, May 9, 1997

200 "shrunken," "defeated": Maureen Dowd, *The New York Times*, May 7, 1997

200 "mystifying torpor": Joe Klein, *The New Yorker*, May 12, 1997

202 'He seems increasingly confident . . .": Ron Brownstein, *Los Angeles Times*, May 19, 1997

202 "He sees new purpose . . .": David Shribman, *The Boston Globe*, May 18, 1997

12. Hardball

207 "Clinton Assembles a List . . .": Alison Mitchell, *The New York Times*, May 18, 1997

210 'start subpoenaing Clinton . . .": Tony Mauro and Tom Squitieri, *USA Today*, May 28, 1997

213 "threatening on national television . . .": *The New York Times*, June 3, 1997

213 'the latest Clinton henchman . . .": Maureen Dowd, *The New York Times*, June 3, 1997

219 "petering out": Judy Keen, *USA Today*, June 9, 1997

223 "incorrect": Stephen Labaton, *The New York Times*, June 26, 1997

13. The Frontiers of Spin

227 "no specific knowledge of asking . . .": Glenn F. Bunting, *Los Angeles Times*, July 4, 1997

231 "if voters had elected Bugs Bunny": Clay Chandler, *The Washington Post*, Dec. 19, 1993

233 "All those who love . . .": Leo Rennert, *The Sacramento Bee*, July 25, 1997

234 "cementing his position . . .": David Broder, *The Washington Post*, July 14, 1997

235 "no president in at least 150 years": Richard L. Berke, *The New York Times*, July 14, 1997

15. Toughing It Out

255 "does not rule it out": Bob Woodward, *The Washington Post*, Aug. 8, 1997

261 "maladroit political instincts": Walter Shapiro, *USA Today*, Sept. 17, 1997

262 "has handled it fumblingly . . .": Anthony Lewis, *The New York Times*, Sept. 15, 1997

262 "Al Gore, Sleazebag": The *Weekly Standard*, Sept. 22, 1997

264 "Memo Appears to Reveal Gore . . .": Don Van Natta, Jr., *The New York Times*, Sept. 12, 1997

265 "a new blow": David Willman and Alan Miller, *Los Angeles Times*, Sept. 15, 1997

271 "special assistant for obstruction": Maureen Dowd, *The New York Times*, Oct. 12, 1997

16. Dodging the Bullet

276 " 'Never been indicted' . . .": James Bennet, *The New York Times*, Dec. 3, 1997

278 "Clinton may now be a lame . . .": Bill Nichols and Susan Page, *USA Today*, Nov. 11, 1997

278 "that the setback was the beginning . . .": Alison Mitchell, *The New York Times*, Nov. II, 1997

278 "the last three years are going . . .": Bob Davis, Greg Hitt and Jackie Calmes, *The Wall Street Journal*, Nov. 11, 1997

279 "dropped off the radar screen": Michael K. Frisby, *The Wall Street Journal*, Dec. 3, 1997

281 "it did not seem such a stretch . . .": Maureen Dowd, *The New York Times*, Nov. 22, 1997

282 "an all-out stonewall": Deborah Orin, *New York Post*, Dec. 4, 1997

284 "getting ready to come onstage again": Karen Tumulty, *Time*, Oct. 20, 1997

17. Monica

296 had sex with "hundreds" of women: Deborah Orin, *New York Post*, Jan. 25, 1998

300 "reckless idiot": Thomas L. Friedman, *The New York Times*, Jan. 27, 1998

300 "an almost pathological lapse . . .": Joe Klein, *The New Yorker*, Feb. 2, 1998

301 "fondled her breast": Jeff Leen, *The Washington Post*, Jan. 29, 1998

301 "hunker-down strategy": John F. Harris, *The Washington Post*, Jan. 30, 1998

Epilogue

306 "let's see how long she withstands . . .": Margery Eagan, *Boston Herald*, Mar. 17, 1998

306 "sex addiction": Walter Shapiro, *USA Today*, Mar. 18, 1998

309 "We were never alone . . .": Jeff Gerth and Stephen Labaton, *The New York Times*, Feb. 6, 1998

309 "a source close to Clinton": Peter Baker and Susan Schmidt, *The Washington Post*, Feb. 6, 1998

311 "I don't think anyone's ever seen . . .": Dan Balz, *The Washington Post*, Feb. 22, 1998

313 "sensitive information of a sexual nature . . .": Peter Baker, *The Washington Post*, March 20, 1998

314 "Unfortunately *The Washington Post* jumped . . .": David Stout, *The New York Times*, March 20, 1998

317 "a stunning legal victory": Susan Baer, *Baltimore Sun*, Apirl 2, 1998

317 "a major legal victory": Richard Serrano, *Los Angeles Times*,

April 2, 1998

317 "spared an O.J.-type . . .": Sandy Grady, *Philadelphia Daily News*,
April 2, 1998

317 "politically inconceivable": John M. Broder, *The New York
Times*, April 2, 1998

317 "riding a wave of euphoria . . .": Robert Shogan, *Los Angeles
Times*, April 7, 1998

317 "Does this mean I never . . .": Jon Jeter, *The Washington Post*,
April 2, 1998

317 "I don't want to hear Michael McCurry . . .": Maureen Dowd,
The New York Times, April 8, 1998

317 "Whitewater prosecutors have written . . .": Jerry Seper, *The
Washington Times*, April 20, 1998

323 "Everybody here—be honest about it . . .": Jack Nelson, *Los
Angeles Times*, May 12, 1998

326 "to step forward and 'fess up . . .": Deborah Orin, *New York Post*,
June 4, 1998

Index